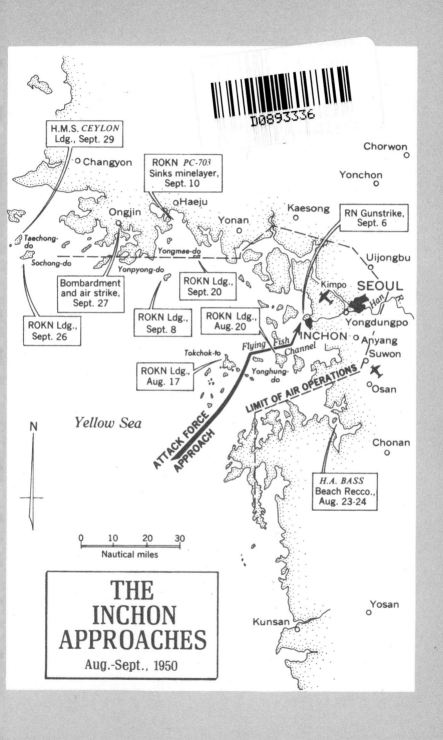

THE
INCHON
APPROACHES

Aug.-Sept., 1950

VICTORY AT HIGH TIDE

VICTORY
AT HIGH TIDE

The Inchon-Seoul Campaign

by

ROBERT DEBS HEINL

LEO COOPER · LONDON

First Published by J. B. Lippincott, New York, 1968
First Published in Great Britain, 1972, by
Leo Cooper Ltd
196 Shaftesbury Avenue, London, W C 2

ISBN 0 85052 086 X

Printed in Great Britain by
Hollen Street Press Ltd
Slough, Buckinghamshire

For Samuel Eliot Morison
Admiral and Historian of All Seas

. . . . *Illi robur et aes triplex*

PREFACE

ONE HUNDRED AND EIGHTEEN years before Communist divisions invaded the Republic of Korea, Karl von Clausewitz wrote:

> A swift and vigorous transition to attack—the flashing sword of vengeance—is the most brilliant point of the defensive.

This book is the history of one of the most dramatic such transitions from defense to attack in the annals of war. It is also a story of strategic prescience and unflinching nerve on the part of a high commander, of professional resourcefulness and expertise in the forces which were his instrument. Above all, it is the account of a triumph which could have been achieved only by maritime power, more particularly by twentieth-century American maritime power.

No mode of attack is more distinctively American than a smashing assault from the sea against the flank of an enemy. We have done this so often and so successfully (as, in the face of every conceivable impediment, we did it at Inchon) that many, including some in uniform, take this capability for granted and, like one senior participant in Operation *Chromite,* dismiss it as "merely a mechanical operation." One purpose of this book is to show in essential detail, step by step, how a great amphibious assault is planned and executed, and therefore to record for student and general reader alike the way in which Americans have learned to make this kind of war.

Besides exemplifying all that I have mentioned, the Inchon-Seoul campaign displays in silhouette the inter-Service clashes and conflicts of Washington in the early, volcanic years of unification. It presents sharply defined, often headstrong and antagonistic, personalities. Yet Inchon, 18 years later, is already too old to be clearly remembered, still almost too recent for history—an episode in that most passé and unfashionable of all events, an immediately earlier war.

To tell the story of Inchon and the reconquest of Seoul, I have consulted executive documents; Congressional proceedings; the official reports and records of all the Services which participated; the memoirs, biographies, and private papers of officers concerned; contemporary journals; and, of course, the works of other military and general historians. To capture the fleeting contemporary detail, I have read the complete files of the New York *Times,* New York *Herald-Tribune,* Washington *Post, Time,* and *Life* for the period in question. I have enjoyed free rein in the records of the Office of Naval History and of Marine Corps Headquarters. I have also had access to the records of the Army. I have corresponded extensively with individuals in all branches of the Armed Services and with civilians, all of whom participated in the campaign, and I have had the pleasure of interviewing many of those who played key roles in this magnificent operation.

To refresh my own recollections of the Korean War, I spent several weeks in the Inchon-Seoul area in 1965, reconnoitering the ground and going afloat where necessary to visualize events as seen from offshore.

So far as I know, the only sources of importance regarding this campaign which remain to be worked are the JCS records (closed save to official historians); the MacArthur Papers, in Norfolk, still not open as this work goes to the publisher; Admiral Sherman's papers, still held under seal; and the Navy's file of "Blue Flag" (personal high command) dispatches, which have never been released to the custody of the Office of Naval History. While additional information of interest will undoubtedly be found in the above sources, I doubt that much of substantive nature can be added to the story as the extensive body of available evidence now tells it.

For that matter, I feel obliged to congratulate the Army, the Navy, and the Marine Corps on their admirable official histories covering the events described in this book. Rarely has a completely unofficial historian been able to rely on such dispassionate, ably written and documented official sources.

This having been said, I must underscore that the conclusions—and surely the defects—of this history are my own. As *Navy Regulations* requires even a retired officer to avow, "The opinions or assertions contained herein are the private ones of the writer and are not to be construed as official or reflecting the views of the Navy Department or the Naval Services at large."

In conclusion, I recall with some apprehension Walt Whitman's remark "The real war will never get into the books." I hope this work may suggest that he was not entirely correct.

ROBERT DEBS HEINL, JR.
Colonel, USMC (Ret.)

Washington, D.C.

ACKNOWLEDGMENTS

No BOOK is ever written singlehanded. My debts here are widespread and heavy.

First and foremost, my gratitude goes to the Director of Naval History, Rear Admiral E. M. Eller, and to his able lieutenant, Dr. Dean Allard, keeper of the Navy's Classified Operational Archives. The hospitality, the unfailing readiness to seek answers to perplexing questions, the efficient organization of records (the uniformly savory and pungent coffee, too), all of which characterize the Office of Naval History, have made this work singularly agreeable to pursue. I must also thank Rowland Gill, Head of Archives and Library, Historical Branch, G-3, Marine Corps Headquarters. Nothing was ever too much trouble for Mr. Gill, or even enough to ruffle his unfailing courtesy and can-do attitude. Dr. Stetson Conn, Chief Historian of the Army, gave me much help and much wise counsel.

Among many who opened private files and memories, I must above all thank General O. P. Smith, whose voluminous journals and correspondence surely comprise the most important single body of primary source material on the Inchon-Seoul campaign. General L. C. Shepherd, Jr. (who first gave me access to his Korean journals during preparation of my history of the Marine Corps), has also provided primary information of utmost importance. General C. B. Cates's hitherto private "Record of Events" documents the Washington battle of Inchon and is deeply appreciated. Vice-Admiral J. H. Doyle's records of Inchon have largely been programed into his capacious and unfailing memory, without which *Victory at High Tide* could hardly have been written.

All or major portions of this work have been read in manuscript by key participants in Operation *Chromite* or by Brigadier General S. B. Griffith II, a respected friend and military scholar. For their corrections, amplifications, insights, even their dissents, I must thank the following: Colonel R. H. Barrow; Lieutenant General A. L. Bowser; Colonel C. H.

Brush; Vice-Admiral J. H. Doyle; Major General R. L. Murray; Colonel T. L. Ridge; Brigadier General E. H. Simmons; General O. P. Smith; Admiral A. D. Struble; and Major General E. K. Wright. Where I have differed from or seemed to disregard the views of such expert witnesses, I take full responsibility but am no less grateful in any case.

Besides the corps of critical readers, many others have submitted to interview, opened private papers and correspondence, checked particular portions of this work, answered my inquiries, helped me to find specific information, and generally done their best to keep me on the track of history as it seemed to them. Among these I am indebted in particular to: Lieutenant General E. M. Almond (who, despite vigorous dissent with many of my conclusions, was prompt and unfailing in lengthy correspondence over this history); Joseph W. Alsop; Major General N. J. Anderson; Major General David G. Barr; General C. B. Cates; General J. Lawton Collins; Major H. A. Commiskey; Major General R. G. Davis; Marine Gunner Arthur Farrington; Howard Handleman; Lieutenant General V. H. Krulak; Captain O. B. Lundgren; Lieutenant Colonel Park Bong-Son; Lieutenant General L. B. Puller; Admiral Arthur Radford; Colonel H. S. Roise; General L. C. Shepherd, Jr.; Brigadier General J. L. Stewart; Colonel R. D. Taplett; Colonel Robert F. Wray.

In support of my travels and research, still others (beginning with my Commandant, General Wallace M. Greene, Jr.) have rendered help in innumerable ways and far-flung places, and to all these I am more than grateful: Colonel R. B. Carney; Colonel A. J. Castagna; B. F. Cavalcante; Lieutenant R. L. Darrow; Captain A. J. Donald; Vice Admiral George C. Dyer; Barbara A. Gilmore; Colonel Ian S. Harrison; Nancy G. Heinl; Mrs. Iva Holland; Yeoman 2d Class I. L. Johnson; Lieutenant Commander P. K. Kemp; H. F. Longley; Rear Admiral F. Kent Loomis; Mrs. Mildred D. Mayeux; C. W. Mendell; B. C. Mossman; Yeoman 1st Class A. L. Poe; C. F. Romanus; Carolyn A. Tyson; Warrant Officer A. R. van Wye.

Indexing is by Nancy G. Heinl, and cartography and diagrams are by Donald T. Pitcher.

Finally, to all others in the Office of Naval History, Marine Corps Historical Division, Office of the Chief of Military History, and the reference service of the Library of Congress who have helped this work on its way, my best thanks.

R. D. H., Jr.

CONTENTS

Photographs

Following page 108
Louis Johnson and General Omar Bradley
The Joint Chiefs of Staff
Generals Smith and Shepherd studying map
General MacArthur: "Just like Lingayen."

Litter bearers
Riflemen and tank
Korean Marines herding prisoners
Hastily abandoned schoolroom
Raising the colors at capitol
"To Harry from his M.P.s"
General Cates
Liberation ceremony in the capitol

Maps and Diagrams

B

A Military, Naval, Littoral War, when wifely prepared and difcreetly conducted, is a terrible Sort of War. Happy for that People who are Sovereigns enough of the Sea to put it in Execution! For it comes like Thunder and lightning to fome unprepared Part of the World.

THOMAS MORE MOLYNEUX
Conjunct Expeditions, 1759

. . . A Twentieth-Century Cannae, ever to be studied.

DAVID REES
Korea: The Limited War, 1964

VICTORY AT HIGH TIDE

1   *OF LITTLE STRATEGIC INTEREST*

I also predict that large-scale amphibious operations . . . will never occur again.

OMAR N. BRADLEY, October 19, 1949

WHEN THE GENERAL with the steel-rimmed spectacles read the final page of his twangy, biting statement, there was no applause.

Most witnesses appearing before the House Armed Services Committee hearings on unification and strategy had their claque; in that respect, at least, it was almost like an Army and Navy game. But today, October 19, 1949, as the autumn afternoon faded, senior officers of the Navy and Marine Corps "sat in white, silent anger" while General of the Army Omar Nelson Bradley, Chairman of the Joint Chiefs of Staff, publicly flayed them as "Fancy Dans" in what the New York *Times* described next morning as "one of the most extraordinary tongue-lashings ever given to high military officers in such a forum."[1]*

Curiously, one passage in the general's bitter and sarcastic outburst seemed to have been overlooked amid the welter of angry personalities and inter-Service recrimination. In words which the Committee later noted as intentionally slighting to the Marine Corps,[2] General Bradley ventured a forecast which events proved unwise. "I also predict," he said, "that large-scale amphibious operations . . . will never occur again."

Within less than a year, the 1st Marine Division, cutting edge of X U. S. Army Corps, was fighting its way ashore over the beaches and seawalls of Inchon, a Korean west coast port which few people in Washington knew or cared about in October 1949.

*Superior figures refer to the section of Notes at the end of the text.

U. S. Defense Posture, 1949–50

At the time of General Bradley's outburst, the condition of America's defenses was less than brilliant.

Pell-mell demobilization on the heels of victory had gutted the Armed Forces. "America fought the war like a football game," mused General Albert C. Wedemeyer, "after which the winner leaves the field and celebrates." More tersely, General Marshall said, "It was no demobilization. It was a rout."[3]

What remained of the defense establishment when demobilization had blown past was wracked by strategic controversy and inter-Service rivalry.

The roots of strategic controversy twined back via Bikini and Nagasaki and Hiroshima to the early 1920s and to the ever more strident claims of Army airmen, voiced by such zealots as Brigadier General "Billy" Mitchell, to a dominant role in formulation and execution of American strategy. The atom bomb, detonating on the heels of a conflict whose iron bombs had signally failed to substantiate the dogmas of Douhet, Trenchard, and Mitchell, seemed to herald an apocalypse in which war of the most absolute and total character would indeed be waged by aerial thunderbolts. In corollary, some asserted, sea power, historically America's sword and shield, was of secondary and waning importance.

The inflamed state of relations among the Armed Services in 1949 was no accident. Steam-rollered through Congress only two years earlier, unification of the Armed Forces had, despite its avowed aims, divided the Services into suspicious and viperishly hostile factions.

Carefully planned by the War Department General Staff since 1943 (when, in November of that year, General Marshall himself had privately blocked out his goals for postwar organization not of the Army but of all the Services), the 1946–47 drive for unification had stunned the Navy and the Marine Corps. From Forrestal down, the naval establishment had been prepared for new legislation rendering permanent the successful innovations of the war, such as the Joint Chiefs of Staff, some type of central intelligence organization, formalization of the National Security Council, and an updated industrial mobilization system. But the thrust of Marshall's ideas (many untested, some obviously borrowed from the land-minded enemies which American and British maritime power had just overwhelmed) extended both in depth and direction far beyond anything the Naval Services believed necessary or were prepared to accept. To arouse controversy and suspicion on both sides, General Eisenhower's address to the graduating class at West Point in June 1946 went still further: Ike proposed that all the Services be merged outright into a single force.

Distasteful as these ideas were to the proud Marines and the austere, self-sufficient, successful Navy, they stirred outright alarm when the Army's detailed unification plans were presented to Congress by General J. Lawton Collins, soon to be named Chief of Staff of the Army. Aside from highly controversial Armed Forces high command and general staff proposals, the "Collins Plan," as it was named, obviously pointed toward absorption of naval and Marine aviation into the new Air Force and, if not to outright abolition, to reduction of the Marine Corps to military nonentity with a few ceremonial and navy-yard guard functions.

When in early 1947 the public learned through Congressional disclosures that Generals Bradley, Eisenhower and Spaatz (postwar chief of the Army Air Forces) had secretly proposed to the Joint Chiefs of Staff that the Marine Corps be stripped of its air arm, be reduced to "lightly armed battalions"—the phrase was Eisenhower's—and cede its amphibious assault role to the Army, inter-Service and public indignation culminated in a bitter Congressional fight over the entire unification legislation. To exacerbate these controversies, the unconcealed and uncritically pro-Army position taken by President Truman, himself a World War I field artilleryman and loyal National Guard officer, left the Navy and Marines in little doubt as to where they stood. "When Roosevelt was here," he said in 1946, "this place was like a damned wardroom. As long as I'm here, the admirals will never get in again."

Although the National Security Act, as finally passed by Congress in the summer of 1947, did make special provisions to prevent naval aviation's transfer to the Air Force and to guarantee continuation of the Marine Corps with the forces and missions and autonomy traditional to the Corps, it soon became clear that there would be no letup in pressures toward the full objectives of Marshall and Eisenhower. In 1949—on the basis of concept, not evaluation and performance of an organization so new that its real merits and weaknesses could not possibly be identified —major changes to the unification law were forced through Congress by President Truman with strong and effective organization of public support by the Air Force and the Army.[4]

As a backdrop to the strategic and organizational controversies which boiled among the Armed Services in 1949 were unanswered questions as to the probable nature of future war.

In the Air Force and at that time the Army view, the most likely and most dangerous contingency was "the Third World War," a nuclear holocaust which might ensue any time after Russia's atomic weapons capabilities—unveiled in October 1949—had advanced sufficiently. On the other hand, the Navy, seconded by the Marine Corps, mainly considered that limited, brush-fire wars, fought with conventional weapons, were the only practicable means of conflict as long as the United States maintained nuclear supremacy. In such wars, the Navy forecast, American maritime supremacy and her traditional maritime strategy would again be the primary instruments.

Discussions as to what kind of war we should prepare for would have been more academic but for the fact that, in the years immediately following our biggest and most expensive war, the Defense Department had only so much money to go around. Defense Secretary James Forrestal could not possibly have a 70-group Air Force (the war cry of the nuclear hawks) and still maintain a passably effective Navy and Army.

When, in late 1948, the Services made budgetary submissions for fiscal year 1950, the grand total was $30 billion. By Herculean labors which unquestionably hastened his collapse, Forrestal got this total just below $17 billion. But here came the rub: President Truman, thinking not in terms of strategic requirements but, as did so many others, of "what the economy can afford," remained adamant that the defense budget would not exceed $15 billion, not by a single penny. And when budget time actually came, the President put in for $14.2 billion.

A fiscal squeeze which would at best have been grave in its effects on the Armed Forces was seriously compounded when, on March 28, 1949, President Truman abruptly superseded the perceptive Forrestal with an insensitive political hack, Louis A. Johnson. Johnson enthusiastically set to work, in his phrase, to "trim the fat out of the Armed Forces." It soon became apparent that, with tacit White House support, the new Defense Secretary would do most of his trimming on the Navy and Marines. Putting the matter with characteristic tact to Admiral Richard L. Conolly in December 1949, Johnson said:

> Admiral, the Navy is on its way out. . . . There's no reason for having a Navy and Marine Corps. General Bradley tells me that

amphibious operations are a thing of the past. We'll never have any more amphibious operations. That does away with the Marine Corps. And the Air Force can do anything the Navy can nowadays, so that does away with the Navy.

Less than a year earlier, on April 23, Louis Johnson had abruptly halted construction of USS *United States,* the new supercarrier to which naval aviation's postwar hopes were tied. At the same time he was prevented from abolishing Marine Corps aviation only by last-minute intervention from Representative Carl Vinson, Chairman of the House Armed Services Committee. But in August 1949, anticipating the 1950 budget, he directed the Navy to prepare for a reduction of operating aircraft carriers in the Fleet from eight to four, of carrier air groups from 14 to six, and of Marine Corps squadrons from 23 to 12. He also ordered the Navy to trim current expenditures by $353 million, a cut which would practically end purchase of new aircraft.

Amphibious warfare, which General Bradley as well as many other officers in high places had decried since World War II, was, surprisingly enough, a stepchild in the Navy too (little better off than mine warfare, traditionally the Navy's orphan). The high percentage of officers passed over for promotion while serving in amphibious billets was notorious; except among a few enthusiasts, amphibious duty was shunned by the career-minded. In the Office of the Chief of Naval Operations, which included 25 admirals and 335 other captains, the amphibious warfare section (as is still true in 1968) was headed by one more captain, and no incumbent of that billet ever made admiral.

It is therefore no surprise that, although the Navy had 362 amphibious ships in commission in 1947 (from a wartime high of 610), by 1950 the total had been slashed to 91—a 40 per cent cut alone during Louis Johnson's first year as Secretary of Defense. But there was blame enough for all: in Forrestal's last year, 1948, the Navy itself had decommissioned 510 landing craft and built only one. As far as the Marine Corps was concerned, the expeditionary part of the Corps—the Fleet Marine Force—35,086 strong in 1948, would in 1950 be cut by Johnson to 23,952 officers and men. This reduction, which would pare the ground fighting strength of the Corps to six infantry battalions, would eliminate the two Marine divisions which, as events were soon to prove, comprised a substantial part of the national force in readiness.

The succession of meat-ax blows inflicted on the Navy and the

Marine Corps—as they felt, under a President and Defense Secretary without serious understanding of the maritime basis of American defense policy and strategy—stirred sentiments of desperation and revolt. These sentiments were by no means wholly emotional. The professional judgment of the Navy—a competent Service which had thoroughly mastered its own element and had just won the greatest naval war in history—was affronted by the narrow land-mindedness of the Army and the brashness of the Air Force. Moreover, both Navy and Marines dissented vigorously from the strategic views of the other Services that the next war, presumably to be waged by heavy bombers with nuclear weapons, and a few parachutists, left no room for the traditional American tools of sea power and limited war.

In the summer and fall of 1949, with encouragement from Congress, the pot boiled over. During a dramatic series of hearings on unification and strategy, conducted by the House Armed Services Committee, a parade of admirals, supported by the Marine Corps Commandant and a smaller delegation of Marines, somewhat ineptly placed the Navy's case on record both as to the false strategy being pursued and as to the damaging effects of unification on the Navy and Marine Corps. In reprisal for his summation to Congress of the Navy position, Admiral Louis E. Denfeld, Chief of Naval Operations, was scathingly attacked by General Bradley, Chairman of the JCS, and within a fortnight, on October 27—Navy Day—1949, dismissed from office. The officer appointed by President Truman to succeed Denfeld was Forrest P. Sherman, a capable though highly ambitious admiral who had supported unification consistently and who, unlike virtually all his contemporaries, felt that such a course would take him to the top.[5]

Thus by late 1949 the military posture of the United States was sadly disarrayed. The respective Services occupied separate armed camps in respect to every important question of strategy, defense organization and defense policy (being unable even to agree on common positions in support of pending pay legislation).

Amid these antagonisms—stemming, after all, not from a disposition to "bicker," but from deeply held differing professional convictions—our military force structure was sagging and unbalanced. Instead of its 70 air groups, the Air Force had but 48. With its 10 understrength divisions, the Army possessed funds and means to carry out overseas occupation duties in Europe and the Far East, but had neither resources nor organization to field a ready strategic reserve. The Navy, attempting to absorb crippling cuts in both aviation and surface capabilities, felt its back to the wall, while the Marine Corps was literally fighting for existence.

"The United States Has Little Strategic Interest . . . in Korea."

In the Far East, thanks largely to the wise proconsulship of Douglas MacArthur in Japan, the position of the United States appeared strong. True, mainland China had fallen to communism and we were waiting for the dust to settle. True also, Korea, like Germany, was divided into two parts, one Communist, one free. But both the United States and, it was said, the Russians had withdrawn their occupation forces by the end of 1948, leaving behind only the military missions required to provide indigenous sinews for the two Koreas. Reunification of Korea was now a political problem for the United Nations.

On paper, U. S. Army forces in Japan amounted to four divisions—the 7th, 24th, and 25th Infantry Divisions, and the 1st Cavalry Division which, despite its designation, was infantry, too. Like most American occupation troops of the time, these units were undermanned, undertrained, flabby and unmilitary. Their commander, whose headquarters was entitled Eighth Army, was Lieutenant General Walton H. Walker.

In early 1950, only a small fraction of the Navy's active strength was in Asiatic waters. U. S. Naval Forces Far East, assigned to General MacArthur in Japan, included in its combatant strength but one light cruiser and a four-ship destroyer division.

Vice-Admiral C. Turner Joy, MacArthur's naval commander, also had an amphibious capability. In the spring of 1950, General MacArthur had asked the Navy and the Marine Corps to provide amphibious training for U. S. Army units in Japan. Virtually alone among the Army's senior commanders, MacArthur had held undeviatingly to the view, as he later expressed it, that "the amphibious landing is the most powerful tool we have."[6]

In response to the General's request, a Marine Corps training team, 67 officers and men headed by Colonel Edward H. Forney, USMC, had been sent to Japan in April 1950. In the following month, a tiny amphibious force—an attack transport, an attack cargo ship, an LST, a fleet tug and a headquarters ship—followed the Marines from San Diego, bringing with them a tactical air control squadron and detachments of air and naval gunfire liaison teams needed to control fire support in landing operations. Flying his flag as Commander Amphibious Group 1 in USS *Mount McKinley,* the command ship, was one of the few officers in the Navy with genuine enthusiasm for and unrivaled professional grasp of amphibious operations. This rear admiral, keen, incisive, white-haired, a veteran of wartime service under Kelly Turner, the Navy's great amphibious commander in the Central Pacific, was James H. Doyle.

Soon after Doyle came to the Far East, Secretary Johnson and General Bradley visited Tokyo. "Bradley asked me what I was doing there," Doyle recounted.[7]

> . . . My response: "I'm here to give amphibious training to units of the Eighth Army at General MacArthur's request . . ." Bradley simply looked scornful. No reply. Shortly after, during a visit with Turner Joy in General MacArthur's office, I mentioned the incident in connection with Bradley's prediction. It was then MacArthur's turn to be scornful. He said: "Bradley is a farmer."

A flag officer of somewhat different outlook from Doyle's, though also with considerable amphibious experience (Normandy and MacArthur's Southwest Pacific), Vice-Admiral Arthur D. Struble, held the most powerful naval command in the Far East. This force, the Seventh Fleet, based in the Philippines, was not assigned to General MacArthur, but came directly under Admiral Arthur Radford, the diamond-hard aviator who commanded the Pacific theater and fleet. Struble, previously deputy to Admiral Sherman, Chief of Naval Operations since his predecessor's dismissal in 1949, was articulate, canny, and "unified" in his thinking to a degree unusual among naval officers of the 1940s.

But the Seventh Fleet of May 1950 was not the armada we think of today. It had a "carrier group"—with just one aircraft carrier. Its "striking force" was one cruiser, USS *Rochester,* Admiral Struble's flagship. Its only other combatant ships were a squadron of destroyers and a division of submarines. The Seventh Fleet had no amphibious shipping and no embarked battalions of Marines. Aside from ships' detachments and security forces at the two Marine barracks in Japan, the only Marines in the Far East were those in Colonel Forney's mobile training team.

So much for America's forces in the Far East. What of the American commander?

Douglas MacArthur in 1950 was senior soldier in the United States Army ("Senior," said one junior officer, "to everyone but God"). He

had been a regular officer 12 years before the incumbent Chairman of
the JCS, Bradley, was commissioned. He had been graduated from West
Point 14 years ahead of General J. Lawton Collins, Chief of Staff of the
Army (a post MacArthur had held in 1930). General Hoyt Vandenberg,
the Air Chief of Staff in 1950, had been a West Point cadet when Mac-
Arthur was Superintendent.

Besides being epochally senior to all nominal military superiors in the
Army and on the Joint Chiefs of Staff, MacArthur was a strategist without
peer—and no theoretician either, but a proven, fighting practitioner of
war at all levels of command. To find a parallel to MacArthur—in
seniority, in professional virtuosity, and in autocracy, egotism and personal style, too—would take us back a century to Winfield Scott. No
later American general could stand the comparison.

Harry Truman later recalled that, when he discussed Korean policy
with his advisers in 1948, all agreed that Korea was one of the places
where the Communists might attack. But, the President went on, the
same could be said for every point of contact between East and West,
from Norway through Berlin and Trieste to Greece, Turkey, and Iran;
from the North Pacific Kuriles to Indochina and Malaya.[8]

In weighing his chances of war and peace along the frontiers of freedom, the President could have been pardoned if he accorded less concern
to Korea than to many other trouble spots on his list. As early as September 25, 1947, the Joint Chiefs of Staff had sent a memorandum about
Korea to Secretary of State Dean Acheson. Acheson showed the paper
to Mr. Truman, who read:

> The Joint Chiefs of Staff consider that, from the standpoint of mili-
> tary security, the United States has little strategic interest in maintaining
> the present troops and bases in Korea. . . .

Speaking at a luncheon on January 12, 1950, at Washington's National Press Club, a favorite sounding board for administration policies,
Secretary Acheson publicized and appeared to support this view.

Considering that Korea and its surrounding waters have historically
been a cockpit of Far Eastern war—the battleground of China and
Japan, of Japan and Russia, of China and Russia—the fact that the
newest great power in the Orient could discover "little strategic interest"
in this three-way bridge between empires seems surprising. Nevertheless—

at least in the view of United States military and political planners—
Korea was considered a military backwater.

The 500-man U. S. Korean Military Advisory Group (KMAG)
trained the South Korean Army, little more than a constabulary and so
conceived. The weapons we gave this army were commensurate with
such a role: used American small arms (except for some formations
equipped with ancient Japanese Model 99 Mausers); short-barreled,
short-range, M3 105mm howitzers, and not many of these; vintage
2.36-inch bazookas; no mortars heavier than 81mm; no recoilless rifles;
no tanks; no medium artillery; no combat aircraft. This was the army which,
in a moment of euphoria, the homeward-bound KMAG Chief, Brigadier
General William L. Roberts, USA, described to a *Time* magazine
reporter in June 1950 as "The best damn army outside the United
States."

General Roberts to the contrary notwithstanding, at least one army
outside the United States would soon prove itself demonstrably better
than that of the Republic of Korea. The *In Min Gun,* or North Korean
Peoples Army (NKPA), was in 1950 a well-armed, strenuously trained
force of 14 divisions, including one mechanized.

Before the end of 1945, foreseeing the course of events, the Russian
masters of North Korea had commenced to build an indigenous army.
The initial cadre of this force consisted of some 3,000 former soldiers of
the Korean Volunteer Army, an exile column which had fought with
distinction as part of the Chinese Communist forces since 1939. These
and other Korean veterans—including some, now Soviet citizens, who
had served as far afield as Stalingrad—were received by the USSR
occupying authorities in 1946 and 1947. Under a long-range program,
some ten thousand North Korean young men were phased into Russian
schools in Siberia for technical training in ordnance, armor, communications, and aviation maintenance.

Within two years, by late 1948, the Russians had forged a North
Korean mobilization base 60,000 strong. During the year which followed,
this force was doubled by an increment of 40,000 carefully selected
conscripts and, more important, by over 20,000 more Koreans who had
served in the Chinese Communist armies. These latter represented the
intact transfer across the Yalu River of two Chinese divisions from the
so-called "Korean Volunteer Corps" to the Russian-controlled NKPA.
Redesignated respectively as the 5th and 6th NKPA Divisions, they were

rearmed with Russian weapons—and their Yenan-trained senior officers were promptly and prudently dispersed elsewhere by widespread transfer.

In April and May 1950, building its weapons, equipment, and reserve stocks to war levels, the Russians completed final re-equipment of the *In Min Gun*. By this time several thousand North Korean junior officers and enlisted men had completed their USSR schooling in virtually all the military specialties.

In equipment and organization, and in military style, the army which had been brought into being was as Russian as Beluga caviar: 150 T-34 medium tanks; almost a hundred Yak and Stormovik tactical aircraft; 122mm howitzers and 76mm divisional howitzers and guns; 76mm self-propelled guns; 120mm mortars; the whole family of Soviet antiaircraft weapons, and every requisite infantry weapon from antitank rifles to burp guns. Supervising this array were eight USSR advisers per division and many more at higher staff and command levels. When summer came in 1950, the *In Min Gun* was, among the armed forces of the Far East, probably better trained and equipped for its intended work than any other army but Russia's.[9]

While Defense Secretary Louis Johnson was energetically hewing away, indiscriminately, at U. S. Armed Forces "fat" (and muscle, too), nine divisions of the *In Min Gun* were, in mid-June 1950, deploying to invade the Republic of Korea.

C

2 *WE SHALL LAND AT INCHON*

~~~~~~

. . . A bold plan worthy of a master strategist

HARRY S. TRUMAN

BEFORE DAWN on June 25, 1950, as MacArthur later recounted, the *In Min Gun* "struck like a cobra."[1] Within 72 hours North Korean Communist soldiers were in Seoul and the shredded remnants of the ROK (Republic of Korea) Army were in hard-pressed retreat down the long road southward.

That same morning, June 25, Admiral Doyle, Colonel Forney, and Amphibious Group 1 were under way for Chigasaki Beach, near Yokosuka in Tokyo's great bay. The amphibious experts were about to supervise a landing exercise by the 35th Infantry.

The first exercise went off as planned on June 26. The second was begun on the morning of the 28th, but a message came in canceling the air support and withdrawing all Fifth Air Force units and observers. Soon afterward, the destroyers, too, were withdrawn by Admiral Joy, and nobody will ever know how the exercise might have gone.

For the time being, much else was unknown. For example, that at three in the morning, Washington time,[2] June 25, the United States had called for an immediate session of the United Nations Security Council; that, in due session 12 hours later, the Russian delegate (and his veto) being absent on boycott, the Security Council had called on U.N. member states to "render every assistance"; that President Truman had forthwith committed U. S. naval and air forces against North Korean military forces south of the 38th parallel or in the sea approaches to Korea; or that, in the early hours of June 30, President Truman would direct General MacArthur to send U. S. Army ground forces to South Korea.

When soldiers of the 24th Infantry Division—406 officers and men—
debarked on July 1 at an airstrip outside of Pusan, America was at war.

In Washington it was hard to believe that we were in a war, even
harder to acknowledge that we were being soundly beaten. Yet the ever-
receding front lines told the story: American regulars, garrison-soft from
occupation duty, were in headlong flight before a trained, tough, well-
equipped cocky little Oriental army with the bit in its teeth.

One officer in Washington had no illusions. In World War I—during
which he received ten wounds—he had commanded a platoon at Belleau
Wood and a rifle company in later actions. By the end of World War II,
he had successively commanded (in combat) an infantry battalion, then
a regiment, finally a division, his latest battle being Iwo Jima. Now,
this officer—General Clifton B. Cates—was Commandant of the Marine
Corps. To General Cates, the oddest thing about the outbreak of trouble
in Korea was that nobody in the Defense Department, let alone Secretary
of the Navy Matthews or Admiral Forrest Sherman, Chief of Naval Operations, had any time to see the Commandant of the Marine Corps.[3] Some
of the more outspoken young planners on the Pentagon's Joint Staff
were even suggesting that we could probably settle the Korean "emergency" without any Marines at all. When General Cates finally did get
past the aides into Secretary Matthews's office on June 30, the Secretary
remarked that the possibility of employing Marines in Korea really
hadn't come up in any conference he could recall.[4]

But this subject, nonetheless, had arisen elsewhere. On June 29, after
fruitlessly seeking an interview for four days, General Cates ran into
Admiral Sherman in a Pentagon hallway. According to Cates the conversation was as follows:

CATES: "Things look pretty grim over there. Why doesn't Mac-
Arthur ask for Marines?"

SHERMAN (after a pause): "What do you have?"

CATES: "I can give you an RCT [regimental combat team] and an
air group from the West Coast."

SHERMAN (another pause): "Leave it to me—I'll send a 'Blue Flag'
to Joy."[5]

There was one more pause: as the situation in Korea steadily
worsened, Sherman waited two days—until after lunch on July 1—
before taking any action on Cates's offer.[6]

The results of Admiral Sherman's highly confidential "Blue Flag" message, when finally sent to Admiral Joy in the Far East, were not long in forthcoming. On July 3, not to their unqualified satisfaction, the members of the Joint Chiefs of Staff—General Bradley, Chairman; General J. Lawton Collins, Army Chief of Staff; General Hoyt Vandenberg of the Air Force; and Admiral Sherman—had before them a dispatch from General MacArthur, asking for immediate movement of a Marine regimental combat team, with supporting Marine aviation, to the Far East.[7] Another message they had before them (at least those who read the New York *Herald-Tribune* that morning) was from David Lawrence, the highly informed Washington columnist:

> General MacArthur . . . has no trained amphibious forces. The United States Marines are at San Diego, all packed up ready to sail, and will be invaluable as reinforcements for MacArthur's troops. . . . Ships must be gotten out of "mothballs" immediately, though no such orders had been given, up to today at least. It takes weeks—not days— to transport men and supplies across the Pacific.

While the Joint Chiefs of Staff (who had reluctantly agreed to let General Cates join them in "The Tank" for this one meeting) debated whether to let the Marines go to war, General MacArthur, 8,000 miles away, was proposing a seaborne attack against the communications of the *In Min Gun*.

On July 4—no day for American celebration in the Far East—when a weak battalion was all that Far East Command could then improvise for field service in Korea, General MacArthur called a conference in his viceregal headquarters, the Dai Ichi Building. The purpose of the General's conference, convened with Admiral Doyle and Colonel Forney in attendance, was to speak of an amphibious counterstroke far behind the enemy flank on the west coast of Korea. Kunsan might be the place, but he inclined to Inchon. The 1st Cavalry Division, MacArthur said, could land at Inchon, attack inland to seize Seoul, cut the NKPA communications which were concentrated in the capital city and, as Admiral Doyle's plans officer put it, "hammer and destroy the North Koreans." Anticipating the requirements for such an operation, MacArthur had already (the day before) radioed Washington to ask for 1,200 specially trained amphibious engineer troops.

Operation *Bluehearts*—the code name for MacArthur's audacious concept—was to take place in exactly 18 days, on July 22. During the frantic interval (according to accepted doctrine the planning of a divisional amphibious assault requires 60 to 90 days), Admiral Doyle was to work up the naval plan, not to speak of reactivating rusting landing craft and jury-rigging MSTS (Military Sea Transportation Service) transports into proper amphibious ships. Colonel Forney, head of the Marines' training team, would become Deputy Chief of Staff of the cavalry division, and selected Marine officers would assume key planning billets in the Army organization. The remainder of Doyle's and Forney's people would try to make amphibious troops out of the soldiers.[8]

Although, for a variety of reasons, the Joint Chiefs of Staff had small stomach for the decision, their July 3 session on sending a Marine air-ground brigade to Korea could have but one outcome: after checking with the White House (where President Truman himself had to approve), they ordered the Marines to mount out. To the last, Air Force General Vandenberg tried to strip the force of its aviation, but July 1950 was no time to be playing inter-Service politics.[9]

The orders from Washington that the 1st Marine Division form and dispatch a brigade to the Far East did not come as a complete surprise. While General Cates was still in the dark as to what Admiral Sherman might be doing on what the latter afterward described as his "Cates to Sherman, to Joy, to MacArthur, to JCS" play, the Marine Commandant had, on his own responsibility, sent a war alert to the 1st Marine Division. By "just playing a strong hunch," as Cates put it, he had gained more than a day's precious lead time for organization of the 1st Provisional Marine Brigade and its aviation, Marine Air Group 33.

Another Marine officer who was taking time by the forelock was Lieutenant General Lemuel C. Shepherd, Jr., USMC. General Shepherd was en route to a new command—Fleet Marine Force Pacific, at Pearl Harbor—as the war exploded. Interrupting his fishing at Yellowstone Park when he learned what was happening, the general reached Honolulu before breakfast on July 2. There, even before he could report in to Admiral Radford, the Pacific Fleet Commander, he found General Cates's warning message and another (from Sherman to Radford) also in the nature of an alert to prepare forces for service in the Far East.[10]

Taking time only to call on Admiral Radford later that morning, General Shepherd worked his staff all day and much of the night to organize and activate the Marine brigade which had been ordered into being on July 7. Its commander was to be Brigadier General Edward A. Craig, an officer of high reputation in World War II. As soon as the brigade's orders were completed, General Shepherd, accompanied by his operations officer (Colonel Victor H. Krulak), set out for Japan. Their mission was to establish liaison with General MacArthur and make arrangements for employment of the brigade.

How the 1st Provisional Marine Brigade, 6,534 strong, mounted out and sailed from San Diego on July 14; how it reached Korea on August 2; how it was immediately committed in defense of the desperately held corner of Korea that was all we could cling to; and how, a month later, after steady fighting, it had, in the words of the London *Times* (September 18, 1950), "saved the day many times"—all these are matters of great import in the story of the Korean War. But the fact that the Marine brigade, magnificently supported by its aviation (". . . some of the best squadrons we will ever have," Admiral Struble later said),[11] saved the perimeter at Pusan is not, directly speaking, part of the story of Inchon, except that the gallant defense of that perimeter bought time for a counterstroke. And time, above all, was General MacArthur's need.

MacArthur Conceives a Counterstroke

The notion that Operation *Bluehearts* would take place at Inchon on July 22, and that the 1st Cavalry Division would thereupon liberate Seoul and shatter the NKPA, lasted less than a week. During those days, on July 7, MacArthur told the Joint Chiefs that "his basic operating plan would be . . . to strike behind the mass of the enemy ground forces."[12] Such a stroke, as he saw it, would involve two steps: stabilization, somewhere, of an almost nonexistent front; then a vigorous blow to cut the roads and railroads in the enemy's rear.

By July 8, it had become apparent that every soldier available in the Far East would have to reinforce the central Korean front—a front which very shortly would become the Pusan perimeter. Even the Marine brigade, which MacArthur wanted to hold out for his amphibious thrust, had to be rerouted to Pusan, and only got there in the nick of time. As for the cavalry division, they landed behind friendly lines at Pohang on July 18, and ultimately served as one of the anchors of the perimeter.

The strategic situation now shaping up was simple—perilous, too, for the moment, but, as MacArthur saw it, also opportune.

The bulk of the *In Min Gun* was or soon would be concentrated in the southeast corner of Korea, intent on pushing the U.N. defenders into the sea. Since the U. S. Navy controlled the sea, the supply lines of the NKPA ran by land down the length of Korea, with Seoul as the focal point of their communications. Their spearhead was sharp and strong, but their flanks and rear were totally exposed.

The day after the cavalry's Inchon landing was shelved, General Shepherd and Colonel Krulak arrived in Tokyo. Next morning, July 10, General Shepherd was escorted by MacArthur's chief of staff (Mayor General Edward M. Almond, USA) into the presence. After compliments to the Marine Corps, paid with the graciousness of which he was master, MacArthur (as Shepherd recorded in his journal) said, "I wish I had the entire 1st Marine Division under my command again, as I have a job for them to do."

Rising from his king-size desk, General MacArthur pointed the stem of his corncob pipe at Inchon on a map, and continued: "I would land them here and cut the North Korean armies off from their logistic support and cause their withdrawal and annihilation."

General Shepherd reacted immediately. "Why don't you ask for the 1st Marine Division, General?"

"That's the kind of talk I like to hear," said MacArthur. "Do you think I can get it?"

Surely, the Marine general responded, MacArthur could get the division if he were to ask it from the Joint Chiefs of Staff. In his own capacity as the division's higher commander, General Shepherd went on, he could, if ordered, have the unit—at full peace strength, less the units in the brigade already committed—ready by September 1. Could Shepherd take this up with General Cates, asked MacArthur. No need, was the reply; he would assume the responsibility. Good, said MacArthur, "You sit down and write me a dispatch to the JCS."

Looking at the General's great desk and chair, and imagining the General's glance over his shoulder, General Shepherd decided he could do a better job elsewhere. Excusing himself, he went into the office of General Almond, a fellow alumnus of the Virginia Military Institute, and drafted MacArthur's message on a government interoffice memo pad. When he took it in, as Colonel Krulak recalled, the General already seemed to be exuding "enthusiasm and resolute confidence."[13]

"One of MacArthur's greatest attributes," according to his future naval commander at Inchon, "was to get going, *and to hit quick*."[14] The message which General Shepherd had drafted was in Washington within hours.

General Collins's reaction to MacArthur's proposal was conveyed in person since the Army Chief of Staff and his Air Force colleague, Vandenberg, were poised for a trip to Tokyo when the General's message arrived. Admiral Sherman felt he should remain in Washington but asked Admiral Radford to go along from Pearl Harbor and represent him.

At the Tokyo meeting on July 13, MacArthur confirmed that Operation *Bluehearts* was no longer feasible, but that he still intended to attack the North Korean lines of communication on the west coast as soon as the *In Min Gun*'s advance could be brought to a halt. Inchon, he thought, was the best place, but he was also considering Haeju and Chinnampo. Then, and during staff talks next day, General Collins was dubious as to the proposed amphibious counterthrust, especially when the troop requirements were explained. Still trying to guess whether the Russians would seize this convenient moment to march on the Rhine and points west, Collins told MacArthur, "General, you are going to have to win the war out here with the troops available to you in Japan and Korea."

MacArthur, Admiral Radford recounted, smiled and shook his head. "Joe," he said, "you are going to have to change your mind."

Later, at an opportune moment, MacArthur turned to Radford (the two theater commanders were side by side) and, apparently testing General Shepherd's offer, asked what he thought the Marines might be able to contribute. Radford, who had seen Shepherd hurriedly on the latter's return from Tokyo, had the right answer: "A brigade rapidly; and probably in the fall, the rest of a division."

Still later, before leaving, speaking at least for himself rather than the Chiefs, Collins did change his mind: privately, he told MacArthur, he thought a full Marine division could be sent to the Far East. Thus encouraged, as soon as the visitors left, on July 15, the General sent his second request to the JCS for the 1st Marine Division and supporting aviation.[15]

While these developments were in progress, General Shepherd was on the West Coast. After briefing Admiral Radford ("I feel that there is a serious war in progress in Korea . . . for which Marines are trained and constituted,"[16] he said), Shepherd felt it imperative not only to see how the Marine brigade was mounting out, but, more important, to meet General Cates, there for the same purpose.

At Camp Pendleton, California, the rattlesnake-ridden West Coast Marine base, General Shepherd disclosed MacArthur's plan. Cates, whose knowledge of the Korean situation and of the Joint Chiefs' deliberations was only what Admiral Sherman, a taciturn man, chose to disclose, was initially hesitant. An alluring offer was pending to commit Marine forces to NATO in the Atlantic. "Clifton, you cannot let me down on this," said Shepherd. "This is a hot war. We ought to be in it."[17]

For a fighter like Cates, that clinched it. The two then conferred much of the afternoon and all evening on July 12, and when Cates took off next day for Washington, he knew what had to be done. At his immediate orders the staff at Marine Corps Headquarters prepared plans to organize a war-strength Marine division or, alternatively, to bring General Craig's brigade to war strength. To attain either, let alone both objectives, the Corps (which Louis Johnson had whittled to 74,279 officers and men) would need major augmentation. This would mean mobilizing the Marine Corps Reserve.

General Craig, his brigade once embarked and underway at best speed for the Far East, had on July 16 flown with his staff to Japan where, on the 19th, he had what he afterward described as "an audience" with MacArthur.

After speaking of the brigade's immediate future in the perimeter with General Walker, the supreme commander, in Craig's account, [18]

> . . . outlined to me his plan for the landing at Inchon . . . that the Marines were going to turn the tide of the Korean War; and then he proceeded to outline in detail his plans for the landing at Inchon. This landing, when it did take place, was more or less similar in all respects to the way he visualized it at that time.

Nine days had elapsed since the General's original request for a Marine division, four days since his reiterated request, and no reply had yet come back. Learning that Craig's brigade, however welcome, was nevertheless at peace strength, MacArthur on July 19 sent the Joint Chiefs of Staff still another message asking (1) that the brigade be brought to war footing; and (2) repeating for the third time that he needed a full Marine division.

As General Cates knew by this time, approval of either request would entail calling the Reserve to the colors, and this answer he quickly gave to the Joint Chiefs of Staff as soon as asked. With the roof falling in—the *In Min Gun* was in the very act of drubbing the 24th Infantry Division out of Taejon—the Chiefs went to Blair House on July 19 and recommended immediate mobilization of the Marine Corps Reserve. Harry Truman nodded grimly, signed the papers, and that afternoon warning telegrams and phone calls alerted the entire ground Reserve for active service.

While the reservists packed seabags, updated death beneficiary slips, signed powers of attorney for their wives, and reassured proud, tearful boys and girls that everything was going to be all right, a shabby tug-of-war was taking place to prevent mobilization of any of the Marine Corps's 30 reserve aviation squadrons.

It will be remembered that Air Force Chief of Staff Hoyt Vandenberg had been unalterably opposed to sending any Marine aviation to Korea (". . . from a sensitive feeling here at the Pentagon," David Lawrence noted in the *Herald-Tribune,* "that the Marines should not have their own aviation"). Now, for reasons nowhere on record, Admiral Sherman —never a Marine Corps enthusiast—joined Vandenberg and on July 20 curtly vetoed General Cates's urgent request that aviation units be included in the Marine call-up for Korea. While it was clear to Cates—and equally so to MacArthur, who had reassured both Shepherd and Craig— that aviation had to be an integral part of the Marine air-ground team, this view evidently was anything but accepted in Washington.

On July 23, under increasingly sharp prods from the press—two days earlier, Lawrence had charged Generals Collins and Vandenberg with "having combined to squelch the opportunity of the United States Marine aviation units to fight in the Far East"—Admiral Sherman told General Cates he could order up six fighting and three ground squadrons. A week later, following what General Cates described in his *Record of Events* as "a plain, forceful, and harsh" session on July 31, between Representative Carl Vinson, House Armed Services Committee Chairman, and Admiral Sherman and Secretary Matthews, the admiral announced that two more reserve aviation squadrons would be mobilized and that the Corps was to be expanded to two war-strength divisions and 18 squadrons. Shortly before this disclosure, General Bradley sought out General Cates and asked if he "couldn't do something to stop Lawrence's critical articles," as, in the Chairman's words, Cates "was the only one that could do it." "I thanked him for the compliment," Cates dryly noted.[19]

Although the dispute over Marine aviation had the center of the stage, a simultaneous contest was in progress as to whether the 1st Marine Division would go to war with only two, or with all three, of its infantry regiments.

By the outbreak of hostilities, Defense Secretary Johnson's "economies" had reduced the division, effectively, to one infantry regiment, the 5th Marines, and the supporting units to back it. The 5th Regiment and nearly everything else at Camp Pendleton had gone to Korea as the 1st Marine Brigade. Then, as a result of MacArthur's pressure, the Joint Chiefs of Staff had authorized activation of a second infantry regiment, the 1st Marines, which, with supporting units, when joined in the Far East to the brigade, would comprise a Marine division but without its third infantry regiment (i.e., the 7th Marines, still on paper).

Here again, MacArthur and Cates wanted a full-strength division, distinctly including the 7th Regiment. Here again—for reasons having nothing to do with the war effort—the Joint Chiefs of Staff and Defense Secretary opposed mobilizing a single Marine or activating a single unit if the step could be avoided. And here again, Chairman Vinson of the House Armed Services Committee was to tip the balance: in early August, Admiral Sherman got his orders—the 7th Marines were to form and go to Korea.

Now that the Marines were mobilizing, the Joint Chiefs of Staff at length—the date was July 20, ten days after the General's initial request —gave MacArthur a reply: yes, he could have a war-strength Marine division but no sooner than November or December. This date represented Marine Corps Headquarters' view of an "orderly" mobilization and buildup, but was very far from meeting the imperatives of war, as General MacArthur quickly pointed out in his fourth message to Washington on this subject:[20]

> Most urgently request reconsideration of decision with reference to 1st Marine Division. It is an absolutely vital development to accomplish a decisive stroke and if not made available will necessitate a much more costly and longer effort both in blood and expense. It is essential the Marine Division arrive by 10 September 1950. . . . There can be no demand for its potential use elsewhere that can equal the urgency of the immediate battle mission contemplated for it.
>
> MACARTHUR

Under the cumulative impact of four dispatches such as only MacArthur could hammer out, the Joint Chiefs of Staff at least gave the General a prompt reply. Within 48 hours, on July 22, they answered that he must give them more information on his plans for the period before September 10 and, by way of encouragement, said orders had been issued to get the Marine brigade, and of course its aviation, up to war strength.

In his response the next day, General MacArthur did not identify Inchon as his objective, although it had been unwaveringly in his mind from the beginning, but he said this:[21]

> Operation planned mid-September is amphibious landing of a two division corps in rear of enemy lines for purpose of enveloping and destroying enemy forces in conjunction with attack from south by Eighth Army. I am firmly convinced that early and strong effort behind his front will sever his main lines of communication and enable us to deliver a decisive and crushing blow. . . . The alternative is a frontal attack which can only result in a protracted and expensive campaign.
>
> MacArthur

The General's *Reminiscences* recount that this final message was greeted by "a silence of three weeks." This is not exactly true. On July 25, the Joint Chiefs of Staff gave in. They directed that the 1st Marine Division (less one regimental combat team) be brought to war strength and mount out from San Diego between August 10 and 15. Included in the JCS directive—another score for General Cates (very likely for David Lawrence, too)—were the words, "with attached air" (actually only one and a half more squadrons, but the precedent had been accepted).[22]

MacArthur's scheme now had its cutting edge.

". . . The Worst Possible Place"

In a remark which no account of Inchon could omit, Lieutenant Commander Arlie G. Capps, gunnery officer on the amphibious staff of Admiral Doyle, said: "We drew up a list of every natural and geographic handicap—and Inchon had 'em all."

"Make up a list of amphibious 'don'ts,' and you have an exact description of the Inchon operation," was the almost equally quoted statement of Doyle's communication officer, Commander Monroe Kelly.[23]

To understand what "don'ts" Commander Kelly and many another planner had in mind during July and August 1950, let us see what the Navy's amphibious warfare instructions of that day—and, for that matter, this day, too—give as the criteria for a suitable area in which to make a landing. Then, as we look at Inchon, we can visualize the problems which confronted Admiral Doyle and would very soon face the 1st Marine Division.

Amphibious doctrine sets out seven criteria for a landing area. As given in the 1952 edition of USF-6, then the Navy's amphibious bible, these are:

1. Ability of naval forces to support the assault and follow-up operations;

2. Shelter from unfavorable sea and weather;

3. Compatibility of the beaches and their approaches to the size, draft, maneuverability, and beaching characteristics of the assault ships and landing craft;

4. Offshore hydrography (i.e., water depths and bottom configuration);

5. The extent of minable water (any depth less than a hundred fathoms—600 feet—is considered minable, although currents also affect minability);

6. Conditions which may affect the enemy's ability to defeat mine-clearance efforts by the attacking force;

7. Facilities for unloading shipping, and how these may be improved.

Against this list, General MacArthur's chosen objective presents aspects which are bleak and discouraging indeed.[24]

Inchon is an Oriental seaport of about the same size and general attractiveness as Jersey City, New Jersey. Its harbor is well protected and ice free even when winter howls down the Yellow Sea from Siberia, and this is about the best that can be said for Inchon as an amphibious target, except that it is the seaport and nearest landing area to Seoul, 25 miles inland, beyond the Han River, and, only less important, that Korea's best airport, Kimpo, lies but 16 miles distant.

The tidal range at Inchon—about 32 feet—is among the highest in the world, being greatly exceeded only by the 45–50-foot ranges in the Bay of Fundy. As these tides race in and out via tortuous channels, they alternately disclose and hide wide, gray, oozing mud flats, backed at high water in some places by seawalls, in others by salterns (salt pans) and swampy bottomland. Currents in the channels rarely drop below three knots and in the main ship channels (there are two, which join below Inchon in an inverted Y) may run as high as 7 to 8 knots, close to the speed of a landing craft. The approach channel to Inchon is a dead-end street with little if any sea room to facilitate turning or maneuver. There are many points in this channel at which one sunken or disabled vessel would pen in all above and block the approach of those below. Despite the currents, Inchon's waters are eminently minable, and are commanded

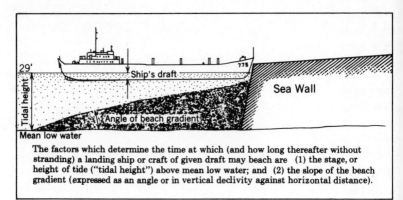

The factors which determine the time at which (and how long thereafter without stranding) a landing ship or craft of given draft may beach are (1) the stage, or height of tide ("tidal height") above mean low water; and (2) the slope of the beach gradient (expressed as an angle or in vertical declivity against horizontal distance).

at several points by heights or islands well suited for batteries which could shoot a minesweeper out of the water.

Inchon is a harbor of projecting moles, breakwaters and seawalls. As one comes up-channel, the port is dominated and the city almost masked by a mile-long island with the same unlovely, menacing toad shape as Iwo Jima. This island—Wolmi Do ("Moon Tip Island")—looms like a barrier dead ahead, dividing the harbor in two and blocking the way to Inchon. No Marine or soldier would think of landing at Inchon until Wolmi Do was safe in hand.

Of beaches, in the common usage of the word, Inchon has none. In the military definition of a beach (". . . that portion of the shoreline designated for landing of a tactical organization") the Inchon of 1950 had three, spread on a four-mile arc around the waterfront and consisting mainly of piers and seawalls. Naming these as Admiral Doyle's planners did, the beaches are:

Green Beach: a 200-yard strip on the northwest shore of Wolmi Do, described in one intelligence study as "sand, with patches of rocks," but more truthfully, rocks with patches of sand, backed by a low revetment and a ridge.

Red Beach: 220 yards of seawall, running north from the mainland root of the causeway which joins Inchon to Wolmi Do; immediately inland is a dismal industrial area with a tangle of railroad yards, a tank farm and a Japanese-baroque brewery overlaid with the grime of decades. At low tide, Red Beach's 1,000-yard mud flats have the crust and underlying gooey consistency of solidifying chocolate fudge, but the smell is different.

Blue Beach: an area on the other side of Inchon—four miles southeast of Red Beach—with a 14-foot seawall, backed by salt pans or by a precipitous, terraced though partly eroded hillock, approached over some 4,500 yards of mud flats.

Taking into consideration the underwater gradients approaching the foregoing beaches, a tidal height of 23 feet would be required to get Navy landing craft—the trusty LCVP (landing craft, vehicles and personnel) and LCM (landing craft, mechanized) of World War II—ashore, while 29 feet would be needed by LST (landing ships, tank). Tidal height of such magnitude prevails at Inchon but once a month, for a space of three to four days. At no other time could a landing be made.

If the problems posed by conditions in the inner harbor might daunt the most expert (in fact it was the most expert who would be most daunted), those of the approaches to Inchon were hardly more encouraging.

As noted, two approach channels lead eastward from the Yellow Sea toward Inchon. These converge about nine miles below Inchon at a tiny island, Palmi Do, which juts up perilously in mid-channel just where the two approaches join. East Channel, mainly used by shipping today, is shorter, more direct, somewhat less constricted and tortuous, but it runs nearer to shore and passes close aboard two large islands, Yonghung Do and Taebu Do, about 25 miles south of Inchon. Flying Fish, the northernmost, more circuitous and more difficult channel, comes in on an almost east-west parallel toward Palmi Do and thus offers less likelihood that an approaching force would be spotted from ashore.

Although most accounts describe the common channel above Palmi Do as "Flying Fish," this is not strictly accurate. Flying Fish proper ends there. Of this channel (properly entitled the Salee River), and of the final approach to Inchon, too, Captain Norman W. Sears, USN, an experienced amphibious officer who would lead in the Advance Attack Group, said afterward,[25] "Flying Fish Channel was well named. A fish almost had to fly to beat the current, and check his navigation past the mudbanks, islands, and curves in the channel." In addition to natural difficulties, Inchon and its approach channels were made for mines. Channel configurations and depth were ideal for modern ground mines while the Yellow Sea's muddy waters render visual mine spotting or sweeping unusually difficult. "If ever there was an ideal place for mines, it was Inchon," said Admiral Struble.

Although not an amphibious expert, General Almond characterized

Inchon accurately when he called it ". . . the worst possible place we could bring in an amphibious assault." But because it was the worst possible place, it was, in a sense, the best possible place: there is an ancient Chinese apothegm that "the wise general is one able to turn disadvantage to his own advantage." In any case, whether worst or best or a combination of both, strategically speaking, in Admiral Struble's phrase, "Inchon was the jackpot spot."[26]

The region of which Inchon is the seaport, as Kimpo the airport, forms part of the western lowlands of Korea, whose name means "High Mountains and Sparkling Streams." Seoul, the ancient capital, is not only Korea's first city but the most important communications center in the country. The excellent railroad net left by the Japanese fans north and south from Seoul, as do the less excellent highways. The central valley of southern Korea runs down the peninsula from Seoul, while the Uijongbu corridor north may lead to Pyongyang or, angling northeast, across the 38th parallel toward the east coast and Wonsan. Paralleling these routes, Korea's national telephone and telegraph systems radiate from Seoul.

The Han River, beyond which Seoul lies, forms the principal barrier between Inchon and the capital city. The current is swift, the channel, when in spate, may be a thousand yards wide. At other times sandy river bottoms are exposed to the sun, and in summer and early fall Koreans bathe and swim on the sandbars. At any season, however, the Han is a military obstacle of importance.

West of the Han the terrain is relatively gentle, with valleys and lowland paddies interrupted by rolling hills 300 to 1,500 feet high, becoming more rugged as one moves east and inland. In addition to omnipresent rice fields, one sees neat patches of soybeans, potatoes, corn, sorghum, truck vegetables well fertilized with fragrant human manure, and ginseng —money crop of the Far East because of its legendary aphrodisiac properties. The main roads leading from Inchon toward Seoul—one directly to Yongdungpo, the other via Kimpo—are bordered by poplars and sycamores and follow the bases of the hills, avoiding the paddies.

Kimpo airfield, to the north of the main Inchon-Seoul axis, is about a mile inland from the left bank of the Han, downstream (i.e., northwest) of Seoul. Adjacent to a mud and brick village from which it takes its name, Kimpo was, at the outbreak of the Korean War, a 6,000-foot, hard-surfaced runway, 150 feet wide, with a load capacity of 120,000 pounds, the most important field in Korea. From Kimpo, the road to Seoul runs along the riverbank across the Kalchon, a tributary stream, into the unlovely industrial suburb of Yongdungpo, which squats behind tall levees across the Han from Seoul, as Camden scowls across the Delaware at Philadelphia. At Yongdungpo also, the direct road comes in from Inchon on the west side of town. The Kalchon (meaning "Middle-Sized River," a slight overstatement at most times of the year) is the moat of Yongdungpo and must be crossed no matter whether you come from Kimpo or direct from Inchon.

Until 0215, June 28, travelers from Inchon or Kimpo would have entered Seoul via the highway bridge at Yongdungpo or one of three railroad bridges which also span the Han. At that hour (unfortunately for three ROK divisions on the wrong side of the river), all four bridges were blown as the North Korean invaders converged on Seoul. Although engineers of the *In Min Gun* made temporary repairs on the least damaged railroad span and decked it over for tanks, air attacks took the bridge out again, and the principal means of getting over the Han was by ferryboats.

Seoul had a 1950 population of some 2,000,000 persons who inhabited the mountain-rimmed basin in which the city is set. Although craggy pinnacles wall the city except on its riverfront, the dominant terrain feature is Nam-San (South Mountain), a 900-foot peak, highest within Seoul proper, which juts into the center of town from the bottomland of the Han. Ordinarily a bosky, breezy park with striking views and winding trails and roadways, Nam-San was, after the Communist capture of Seoul, a hiding place for refugees, for officers and soldiers cut off from their units, and for underground resistance fighters who refused to admit that the war was lost.

Never generous in their colonization of Korea, the Japanese had not done much for Seoul. The red brick railroad station, the block-shaped Government House (Changdok Palace), the Chosun Hotel whose brocaded halls had survived Japanese and Communist conquest and American liberation—these were the principal monuments of nearly 50 years of Japanese occupation. Despite the wide avenues and the ancient grace of the Duksoo Palace and the Namdaemun (the city's old South Gate), Seoul in 1950 was often shabby, almost always old-fashioned and poor; yet the setting was beautiful, and the spirit of the people—said to be the Irish of the Far East—resolute and fiery. There is a Korean proverb which says that the sky is blue everywhere, but that it is bluer over

D

Korea, and this is the way the South Koreans felt about their homeland and their capital.

". . . Capable and Tough"

On August 6 General MacArthur, conferring with Averell Harriman, whom President Truman had sent out to Tokyo for a look around, remarked that the NKPA were "as capable and tough" as any army in his military experience. Fortunately for the United Nations, however, most of the capable and tough North Korean soldiers were far south of Seoul and Inchon by August 1950. This is not to say that either place was denuded of troops; it was not. Headquarters of the *In Min Gun* were in Seoul, as was all the motley of line-of-communication troops required to keep supplies and replacements moving south. And Seoul was infested with the police and political cadres charged with re-educating the inhabitants of the South Korean capital.

The military garrison of Seoul, the 18th Rifle Division ("Seoul Defense Division") numbered some 10,000 officers and men. This division was reinforced by the Seoul City Regiment, an infantry unit 3,600 strong. In keeping with Communist practice, the city had a proficient antiaircraft defense force, the 19th Antiaircraft Artillery Regiment, a 1,200-man unit armed with Russian 85mm guns, 37mm automatic cannon, and the 12.7mm machine guns used with painful effect against U. S. aircraft in Vietnam. Principal among the logistic troops was a 900-man railroad security and operating regiment (10th Railroad Regiment), while the hated 36th Battalion, 111th Security Regiment, pried, proselyted and purged as seemed best in the interests of the Korean Peoples Republic.

Aside from some 19 propeller-driven Yaks and Stormoviks which were all the *In Min Gun* could still operate at increasing peril, the North Korean forces at Kimpo were what might be expected: an Air Division—the 1st (likely the only)—providing base personnel and services; the 107th Security Regiment, a 2,500-man guard force here rather than a political unit; and the 877th Air Force Unit, 400 people whose exact function will never be clear because they went their separate ways soon after battle was joined. The Kimpo base commander was a tough, Chinese-trained brigadier, Wan Yong.

At Inchon, that "worst possible place," the extent of the defense forces and their preparations—at least as of August 1950—indicated that the NKPA's intelligence staff must have shared the views of many American opposite numbers as to the feasibility of a landing. The garrison of Inchon consisted of two raw battalions of new conscripts, some 2,000 of them, in the 226th Marine Regiment, and two harbor-defense batteries of 76mm guns (eight in all) manned by 200 gunners of the 918th Coast Artillery. The engineers had worked out plans for eventual development of suitable defenses at Inchon and Wolmi Do, Russian land mines were being laid, trenches and emplacements dug, training was proceeding, and additional weapons and ammunition were coming in via the railroad yards just ashore from Wolmi Do. While Inchon harbor was to be mined, work had not yet commenced.[27]

Although G-2 estimates of the American forces underestimated the enemy numerical strength in the Inchon-Seoul area, especially early in the planning, the general conclusion, or at least the hopeful impression, of unawareness of the weighty stroke which MacArthur was preparing is supported by the actual picture of the enemy defense forces which has just been drawn.

But if the North Korean enemy seemed unaware of what was shaping up, one large question nagged the U. S. planners: Would Russia and/or China intervene, and, if so, when and under what conditions?

Port Arthur, Russia's major naval base at the head of the Yellow Sea, is little more than 200 miles northwest of Inchon. The flank of any force moving up the Yellow Sea would be exposed to Port Arthur, as Task Force 77—the Seventh Fleet's carrier striking force—learned on September 4, when Russian reconnaissance bombers approached and made the literally fatal error of firing on Corsairs from the combat air patrol of USS *Valley Forge*. One bomber turned tail and the other went down in flames, which settled matters for that day, but did nothing whatever to ease the planners' minds.

While at this time Russia was the main worry, China could not be brushed aside. During August, intelligence sources (including many taken over intact from the Japanese military) reported that forces of China's Peoples Liberation Army were being reinforced along the Manchurian border of Korea—a development which clearly suggested China's sensitivity to events in progress. Our own sensitivity is demonstrated by the fact that, among the "EEIs" ("essential elements of information"— critical items of needed information about an actual or potential enemy), all plans for landing at Inchon accorded high priority to any indication of Chinese intervention in the Korean War.[28]

But Japan, too, was critically important to the planners—not, of course, as an enemy, but because MacArthur's basic and paramount mission (at least as a U. S., as distinct from a United Nations commander) was the defense of Japan. This problem was kept from becoming academic by the ever-threatening presence of substantial Russian forces only a few miles north of Hokkaido.

Looking at things from the enemy's point of view, as intelligence planners must, what—aside from obliteration of the Pusan perimeter— were the most damaging Communist capabilities to be foreseen in early August as thinking began to focus sharply on Inchon?

Obviously, heavy reinforcement of the Inchon-Seoul area and intensification of fortification activities would unbalance General MacArthur's strategic equation. Equally obvious, the intervention of Russian air or submarines, or of Chinese ground forces, with or without Russian support, would not only jeopardize Inchon but would in reality initiate a new, perhaps even a nuclear war. Most obvious—and most feared—the enemy could step up mining.

If General MacArthur had known that the Russian naval mine depot at Vladivostok already had instructors and several trainloads of mines at Chinnampo (west coast) and Wonsan (east coast), even his confidence might have wavered. Yet, unknown to the U.N. headquarters, some 4,000 Russian mines were south of Wonsan by early August and were being hauled by rail, truck and sampan from Chinnampo to Inchon, Kunsan, Haeju and Mokpo.

This development, something the American planners did not know, could indeed hurt them. If undertaken quickly, minelaying could take Inchon out of play entirely. What the odds on this might be, neither General MacArthur nor Admirals Joy and Doyle could then say, but it did mean that the sooner MacArthur could collect his forces and strike, the more favorable his odds would be.

Chromite

Undaunted when the original version of Operation *Bluehearts* collapsed, General MacArthur kept his planners working on the project of some later amphibious thrust which would cut the enemy communications and reverse the situation with a single stroke. Like Jervis before Cape St. Vincent in 1797, the General could realize that "a victory is very essential at the moment."

MacArthur's chosen instrument for this amphibious plan was the Joint Strategic Plans and Operations Group (JSPOG), an elite interior staff group in FECOM headquarters that dated from 1949. Throughout

World War II—unlike Nimitz in the Pacific Command—MacArthur had refused to organize a joint staff. After the war, although a unified commander, he had continued to operate what was effectively a uni-Service (Army) headquarters. Under heavy JCS pressure for "jointness," the organizational infatuation of the day, MacArthur had formed an inner joint staff cell—the JSPOG—which conceded the question in principle while allowing the remainder of the headquarters to continue undisturbed. Though small, the JSPOG was staffed by able officers, and it was headed, under a second "hat," by MacArthur's capable G-3 (Assistant Chief of Staff for Operations), Brigadier General Edwin K. ("Pinkie") Wright, USA.

By July 23, drawing together the operational, intelligence and logistic data available, General Wright's planners had worked up three possible variants for a September landing which, in the form of draft plans, he circulated to the Far East Command staff. One plan contemplated Inchon; the second, Kunsan; and the third, Chumunjin on the east coast. Kunsan, Wright later said, "really had very little to offer" while Inchon, he added, "stood out like a sore thumb." And there was little doubt among officers in immediate touch with MacArthur that Inchon remained his choice, even though he had still not disclosed this to the Joint Chiefs of Staff.[29]

General MacArthur's two "earliest and most important decisions," said Admiral Struble, were to (1) go into Inchon, and (2) do it as soon as he could.[30] Both decisions were embodied in Far East Command Operation Plan 100-B (code-named *Chromite*) which MacArthur issued on August 12, 1950. Three days later the General set up a planning staff, essentially a cadre for future operations, to proceed with *Chromite*. Soon afterward, since he envisaged operations by a corps, he asked the Department of the Army to activate X Corps headquarters for the purpose.

To MacArthur, as soon as possible meant just that. More specifically, it meant September 15. The extreme high tide on that day—the only such in September—would put maximum water over Inchon's mud flats, a tidal height of 31.2 feet. Twelve days later, on the 27th, there would be 27 feet (two feet short of what the LSTs needed). Not until October 11 would there again be 30 feet of water. September 15 was therefore not only the earliest possible date to land, but the best, too.

But there was one hitch: morning high tide that day came at 0659, just 45 minutes after sunrise (hours too soon for the less maneuverable transports to make a daylight approach up Flying Fish Channel). The next high tide would not crest until 1919, 37 minutes after sunset, hardly an orthodox hour for an assault landing. Intractable as the terms of the problem seemed, Navy and Marine planners would have to find some solution; in Douglas MacArthur's sweeping thoughts, September 15 was the day.

While General Wright's group was sketching Operation *Chromite* with the broad strokes of a high-level brush, Admiral Doyle and Amphibious Group 1 were seeking to fill in the details. Among many at this stage, the most crucial were accurate information on tides and currents (example: Japanese and American tide tables differed for Inchon— which to use?); mud-flat gradients and trafficability (and would the Wolmi Do causeway support tanks?); and the existence and height of seawalls.

Although Inchon had been occupied and used by the U. S. Army after World War II, intelligence information on the port was conspicuously lacking. At the insistence of Doyle's chief of staff, Captain Norman Sears, USN (and later of Colonel Bowser, landing force operations officer), frantic search turned up an Army warrant officer, W. R. Miller, who had lived on Wolmi Do and operated Transportation Corps boats all over Inchon Harbor. Mr. Miller, discovered in Yokohama, forthwith joined Admiral Doyle's staff. In Colonel Bowser's later words, Miller

> . . . was the very first person who could give us sufficient detail on which to make firm plans. He was intelligent, willing to work around the clock, and served as the real key to unlocking a lot of closed doors.

To supplement Miller's firsthand information—particularly with regard to seawall heights at various tidal stages—aerial photographs were needed.

The only available photo aircraft in the Far East Command turned out to be a pair of photo-configured Marine Corsairs assigned to a team aboard USS *Valley Forge,* commanded by Major Donald Bush, USMC. Flying as many as 13 sorties in four days, with only two airplanes, Bush and his pilots delivered complete coverage of Inchon's mud flats, beaches, islands, and the seawalls. To read the resulting pictures, most taken from an altitude of 200 feet (lower than the top of Wolmi Do), experts were flown straight to Japan from the Air Force Photo Laboratory at Dayton, Ohio. And plans were soon going ahead to verify all that Warrant Officer Miller and Major Bush's photo-strikes had revealed, by the surest means of all—personal reconnaissance.[31]

What the staff studies and the accumulating intelligence showed Admiral Doyle was hardly encouraging. As the only professionals on the scene, at least until the 1st Marine Division arrived, it was not the naval staff's job to paint a rosy picture: just because General MacArthur wanted a landing at Inchon didn't necessarily guarantee its accomplishment. Rather, it was up to Doyle and his people to discover the problems and, if possible, how they could be solved.

An amphibious plan can progress only so far without the landing force, and it is therefore time to see what success the Marine Corps was having in its race against tide and time to raise and mount out the division and supporting air which MacArthur had been promised.

Camp Pendleton, north of San Diego, largely represents the domain of Santa Margarita, a vast Spanish ranch which the Marine Corps obtained in 1942 as its West Coast operating base. Back at the ranch, things were humming.

When the 1st Brigade shipped out for Pusan on July 14, an aching void was about all they left behind. While the Marine unit at Camp Pendleton in June 1950 was still called a division, Louis Johnson's surgery had effectively reduced it to the bare strength of a brigade. Moreover, while the depleted headquarters of the nominal 1st Marine Division stayed behind, even this was in the hands of a caretaker. By ironic coincidence, only days before Korea exploded, Major General Graves B. Erskine, the division's steely commander and one of the Corps's most distinguished World War II tacticians, had just been dispatched on secret orders to find out what was happening to the French in Indo-China. Training and readiness were Erskine's fortes, and, although he had little to work with in 1948–49, what there was at Pendleton had been superbly prepared. Now, having fashioned a well-tempered weapon, it was Erskine's ill fortune not to wield it.

At war strength a Marine division included 22,343 officers and men of the Marine Corps and the Navy. The 3,386 people remaining when the 1st Brigade sailed represented fragments of the headquarters and service elements of a division, and little more. The 1st Marine Aircraft Wing, stationed at El Toro, California, northwest of Camp Pendleton, was in similar shape; less than 2,500 officers and men remained as the base on which the wing must be rebuilt to whatever level Washington intended to allow. The day the brigade left, the division's new commander was still winding up his duties in Washington, and the commander of the wing had as yet no idea whether he and his headquarters might get into the war at all.

Major General Oliver Prince Smith, under orders to take over the 1st Marine Division, was an unusual Marine in many respects. The contrast between him and his predecessor could almost be called startling. Despite the fact that, in a career going back to 1917, he ultimately commanded every type of unit from platoon to army corps, O. P. Smith had the reputation of being a school man and a staff man. In pre-war days when only the Corps's most studious officers ever got to the Army's Infantry School at Fort Benning, Captain Smith had been there. One Marine officer was selected every two years to attend France's École Supérieure de Guerre in Paris; Major Smith went there, too. In the war he saw much combat—New Britain, Peleliu, Okinawa. By temperament he was a mild, kindly, ascetic thinker and teacher, a practicing Christian who smoked only a pipe and drank sparingly. In physique, General Smith was tall, slender, a little rawboned, with a fine aquiline face and a shock of prematurely white hair. That General Cates, active, practical, sanguine, gregarious and extroverted, a man who played his hunches (and usually won), had had O. P. Smith as his Assistant Commandant of the Marine Corps and then sent him west to command the new 1st Marine Division on its way to war, possibly revealed more about the man than his externals suggested.

On July 25, 1950, the morning General Smith broke his flag at Pendleton, there remained but 21 days before the division must be prepared to mount out. During those three weeks, the 2d Marine Division, at Camp Lejeune, North Carolina, would be stripped to the merest cadre by bodily transfer and redesignation of East Coast units. From some ten thousand mobilized reservists, who began flooding in on July 31, 91 officers and 2,800 enlisted men were to be absorbed. From over a hundred posts and stations, Navy Yard Marines to the number of 130 officers and 3,500 enlisted were to join General Smith's command. In fact, during one frantic four-day period, August 1–5, 9,000 officers and men reported for duty.[32]

Amid this Niagara of people, the division staff had to plan for movement to the Far East, receive war stocks of ammunition from depots as far away as New Jersey, and, not least, get units equipped. Fortunately, there was Barstow to call on. The Marine Corps Supply Depot at Barstow, California, reminded logisticians of a war surplus shop. After World War II, unlike other forces which left their gear where it stood, went home and disbanded, the Marines of the Pacific had cannily salvaged every weapon, every truck, every tank, every amtrac within reach (and without too much nicety as to original ownership, either). All this trove had eventually reached Barstow where, from 1946 to 1950, items had been patiently overhauled, mothballed, assigned serial numbers and painted Marine Corps green when the OD or gray showed too conspicuously. "From this miser's lair at Barstow," recounted Andrew Geer in *The New Breed*,

> . . . came the trucks, DUKWs, jeeps, trailers, and amphibian tractors that were to go once more to war. There were more veterans of Iwo and Okinawa among the vehicles than among the men who would drive them.

The day after General Smith took command, General Shepherd, his immediate superior, arrived from Honolulu for a visit. Characteristic of his drive and enthusiasm, General Shepherd recorded that he "gave General Smith and his staff a pep talk" after inspecting the smart-looking honor guard which, amid chaos, the 1st Division had paraded for him. Shepherd also telephoned his own boss, General Cates, in Washington. During this call he made two important points: (1) that 1st Marine Aircraft Wing headquarters, with Major General Field Harris, the wing commander, ought certainly to go to Korea and assume command of tactical air operations; and (2) that, somehow, the division must get its third infantry regiment (the 7th Marines). Both suggestions bore fruit. After tussles, first with Admiral Sherman, then with the JCS hatchet man, Air Force Lieutenant General Joseph T. McNarney, "who personally checked every figure submitted and questioned many in detail,"[33] General Cates won approval (which the JCS again had to get from the President) for inclusion of the 1st Wing, as such, in the Inchon force, and got the 7th Regiment onto the troop list. Following this final effort, General Cates on August 9 jotted in his journal: "Surveyed personnel situation. . . . Can do. Few cadres left."

Few indeed. The 2nd Marine Division in the east was so stripped that, on September 15, 1950—D-day at Inchon—it had but 3,928 officers and men on board. The 2d Wing, also in North Carolina, had bodily transferred Marine Aircraft Group 15 to El Toro; this, with 1,230 pilots and ground crews added from the Reserve, completed the tactical air command which would support the assault at Inchon. To denude the East Coast and the Atlantic Fleet of its Marine expeditionary force was a risk;

but so, to say the least, was the impending operation. Back in Washington, a planner in the Pentagon said, "The only thing left between us and an emergency in Europe are the Schools Troops at Quantico."[34]

"... I Shall Crush Them!"

The transports taking the Marine division and air wing to war sailed from San Diego between the 14th and 18th of August. After the last ship cast off her lines and stood down the channel, General Smith and a staff group [35] enplaned and took off for Tokyo.

During this week, it seemed, all roads led to Tokyo.

General MacArthur, never the most pliant of Washington's subordinates, had not fully disclosed—at least not officially—his conception of an assault at Inchon. Troops were moving, ships were on the seas, and it was obvious that the cards were being dealt for a game in which the stakes were high. But the Joint Chiefs of Staff, military advisers to the President, did not yet know the name of the game.

"Frankly," General Collins said in 1952, "we were somewhat in the dark."[36]

Thus, on August 20, General Collins, accompanied by Admiral Sherman and by Lieutenant General Idwal H. Edwards, Air Force operations deputy on the JCS, was sent to Tokyo, in Collins's words, "to find out exactly what the plans were." General MacArthur, as he put it in his *Reminiscences,* viewed the visit in a somewhat different light. "The actual purpose of their trip," he wrote, "was not so much to discuss as to dissuade."

In addition to the delegation from the Joint Chiefs of Staff, Admiral Radford and General Shepherd were both on their way to Tokyo; Admiral Doyle and his staff were already there, with *Mount McKinley* lying alongside a Tokyo pier; and, as we have seen, General Smith would shortly arrive. Alone among the key figures of the forthcoming operation, Admiral Struble, soon to be designated as overall commander, was absent at sea, conducting bombardment and air strikes along the west coast of Korea.

There can be little doubt at this time that General MacArthur looked on Admiral Sherman, top officer of the U. S. Navy, as the man he had to convince, and therefore as the key figure among all the admirals and generals converging on Tokyo. The operation which MacArthur had in mind was, above all, a naval operation; without the Navy's ships and support, without the Marines' amphibious troops, and without the pro-

fessional know-how of both Navy and Marines, the landing at Inchon—
however brilliant a concept—could never become reality.

Moreover, General MacArthur already knew, there were serious reservations as to the Inchon scheme, not only in his own headquarters[37] but
most certainly on the part of Admiral Doyle and his planners and generally among most senior Navy and Marine officers privy to the plan. In
fact, the more the experts—and Doyle's people were that in the most
real sense—looked at Inchon, the more pessimistic they became.

For these reasons—and also because Sherman, at the height of his
powers, was an officer of tenacious mind and purpose, professionally
respected even by those who disliked him most—the admiral, short of
MacArthur himself, was the dominant figure. And Sherman, in accordance with habit, was keeping his own counsel.

Those who knew, or thought they knew, this complex, incisive, ambitious admiral, had little doubt that he was deeply concerned over the
risks MacArthur seemed so bold to confront. General Collins, for one,
has no doubt that this was his feeling.[38] General Shepherd's journal, on
August 21, describes Sherman as "unquestionably opposed to the proposed plan."

The conference at which Inchon was to be thrashed out was scheduled
for August 23 at MacArthur's headquarters. On the preceding day,
Admiral Sherman, who with General Collins had reached Tokyo on the
21st, flew down to the U. S. Naval Base at Sasebo, having first been
thoroughly briefed by Admiral Doyle in Tokyo. Late that afternoon,
Sherman boarded USS *Rochester*, Seventh Fleet flagship, which only a
few hours earlier had returned with Admiral Struble. During two months'
wartime operations the ship, her people, and their admiral had dispensed
with peacetime protocol. When Sherman, in crisp khaki blouse and
gleaming shoulder boards, reached the quarterdeck, there was no guard
and band; stickler that he was, Sherman allowed a flash of momentary
displeasure to show, then went below with Struble.

Once clear of the quarterdeck in admiral's country, Sherman spoke
long and in deep confidence about the war—and about Inchon—to the
officer who had been his deputy in Washington. "Rip," he said, using
Struble's Navy nickname, "I'm going to back the Inchon operation
completely. I think it's sound. If it is approved, it will be held very soon,
and you will recognize the importance of the Navy's doing everything
possible for its success." After a moment Admiral Sherman continued,
"You are to command the operation, and I will want you to get up to

Tokyo as soon as you can, with a staff, and get the best possible plan prepared. You'll find many problems up there, but you'll be able to handle it."[39]

Departing for Tokyo next forenoon (he got the full guard, band, "Admiral's March," eight side boys and a 17-gun salute when he left *Rochester*), Sherman joined Admiral Joy and proceeded to the Dai Ichi Building, where the stage was set.

The paneled sixth-floor conference room lay between the offices of General MacArthur and Almond. At 1730, August 23, when the supreme commander entered the room, there were assembled: Admiral Sherman and Generals Collins and Edwards, representing the JCS; Admirals Radford, Joy, and Doyle; Generals Almond, Hickey, Ruffner, and Wright, all of MacArthur's staff; and three officers from General Wright's JSPOG. Curiously (it was Almond who had made arrangements) neither Marine general then in Tokyo (Shepherd and Smith) was invited to attend, so the landing force interest was unrepresented save for a Marine lieutenant colonel among Doyle's briefers. As General Shepherd later remarked,[40] "Marines weren't *persona grata* in Tokyo in those days."

A day or so before, concerned because MacArthur seemed oblivious of the enormous technical hazards posed by a landing at Inchon, Admiral Doyle had insisted to General Almond that MacArthur be briefed on exactly what the Inchon landing involved. Almond demurred: "The General is not interested in details." Doyle shot back: "He *must* be made aware of the details."

Now, following an introduction by General Wright, MacArthur puffed reflectively on his pipe for 80 minutes while nine officers of Amphibious Group 1 proceeded to give their audience little else but details—details of intelligence, aerology, beaches, tides, currents, channels, communications, pontoonery, landing craft, boat waves, naval bombardment and air strikes. As the last speaker, Commander T. H. Moore, the aviator, uttered his last detail, Admiral Doyle rose and in one sentence gave General MacArthur the broad picture: "General, I have not been asked nor have I volunteered my opinion about this landing. If I were asked, however, the best I can say is that Inchon is not impossible." Then he sat down.

After a pause, MacArthur replied, "If we find that we can't make it, we will withdraw."

"No, General," said Doyle, "we don't know how to do that. Once we start ashore we'll keep going."

General Collins, who had "wanted to be sure just what these plans were," now knew and now took the lead, "but not," he later said, "in any contentious way, as has sometimes been pictured." Why not Kunsan, to the south? Or Posun-Myong, just below Seoul? Sherman, said one account, was at first "lukewarm." However, when Doyle pointed out some of the dangers of the Inchon approaches, asserting that enemy shore batteries could completely command the dead-end channel, Sherman sniffed, "*I* wouldn't hesitate to take a ship up there."

"Spoken like a Farragut!" exclaimed MacArthur.[41]

History must regret that the conference room had no tape recorder. Since it did not, we shall never know exactly what the General said when the discussion had run its course. The several versions (including his own, in his *Reminiscences*) are at odds. But everyone who heard him that evening (dusk had fallen when he began to speak) agrees that his 45-minute reply, extemporaneous, without a note, was one of the compelling declarations of his career. Remembering that scene, Admiral Doyle said, "If MacArthur had gone on the stage, you never would have heard of John Barrymore."

The bulk of the enemy, the General said, were committed against the Pusan perimeter. Frontal attack out of the perimeter would cost a hundred thousand casualties. The North Koreans were unprepared for an enveloping attack, least of all at such a place as Inchon. To land at Kunsan would be easier, to be sure, but the results would be "ineffective and indecisive." Nothing in war, he underscored, is more futile than short envelopments. With a deep cut across the Communists' lines of communications, they would soon be deprived of munitions and fighting power, and Inchon would become the anvil upon which the Eighth Army would smash the enemy from the south. "The amphibious landing is the most powerful tool we have. To employ it properly, we must strike hard and deep!"

Adverting to what Wolfe's contemporaries in 1759 had termed "a mad Scheme," MacArthur likened the Inchon assault to Wolfe's surprise landing at the Anse du Foulon and his subsequent capture of Quebec. "Like Montcalm," MacArthur says he said, "the North Koreans would regard an Inchon landing as impossible. Like Wolfe," he continued, "I could take them by surprise."

As for the Navy's objections, he recognized their validity. They were not, however (it was nearly Doyle's phrase, but a different ring), insuperable. Perhaps he had more confidence in the Navy than the Navy had in itself. "The Navy has never let me down in the past, and it will not let me down this time," he said, looking at Sherman.

"I realize," he concluded, "that Inchon is a 5,000 to 1 gamble, but I am used to taking such odds. . . ." Then his voice dropped so that the listeners strained to hear him: "We shall land at Inchon and I shall crush them!"

The effect was mesmeric. It might have been a minute before anyone spoke. Then Sherman said, "Thank you. A great voice in a great cause," and the meeting broke up. At dinner afterward, when all the Navy and Marine flag officers foregathered at Admiral Joy's, Sherman said to General Shepherd that MacArthur's oration had been "spell-binding."

"I wish," the admiral observed next day, "I had that man's optimism."[42]

Once the MacArthur spell wore off, some listeners had second thoughts. As the group broke up for dinner, General Collins took Wright aside and asked, "Pinkie, if this plan doesn't work out, are you prepared for an alternate?" Wright truthfully assured the Army Chief of Staff that a thorough plan for Kunsan had been worked out. What he omitted to say was that the JSPOG had "never really considered Kunsan except as a feint and a deception."

After sleeping on the matter, the admirals and Generals Shepherd and Smith foregathered in Joy's office for what O. P. Smith described as "an indignation meeting." The consensus was that Army planners were giving insufficient, if any, weight to the naval considerations that loomed so large to the eyes of experience, and that another, more feasible landing area must be found, from which enemy communications could be just as effectively severed. However, as General Shepherd noted, "Nothing of a concrete nature developed."[43]

Lack of concrete developments in any situation frustrated General Shepherd and the opportunity to press for such developments, at the highest level, presented itself that morning. Almond phoned and asked that Shepherd come to the Dai Ichi Building. General MacArthur wished to see him.

Before his appointment with MacArthur, General Shepherd (accompanied by Colonel Krulak) had 45 minutes with Almond. The conversation was revealing. The first matter raised by the Marine was to urge that the brigade, which had been heavily engaged in the Pusan perimeter, be withdrawn from action, "as in my opinion," he recorded, "they had one more good fight in them and that if [General Walton H.] Walker threw them into another tough battle . . . they would not be capable of combat effectiveness on D-day." Almond replied shortly that the Marines could not be withdrawn until just before Inchon, as General Walker couldn't spare them.

General Shepherd then voiced the apprehensions he felt about Inchon and, as he had several times previously during this visit to Tokyo, urged that Posun-Myong be substituted. Almond then disclosed that "the real objective" of the Inchon assault was to take Seoul, "that Inchon had been decided upon and that was where it would be." He added that he didn't believe there were any troops in Inchon, and dismissed the amphibious landing as "a simple mechanical operation." General Shepherd now could better understand Admiral Doyle's umbrage at what the latter had described as Almond's "most dictatorial manner."

At this juncture, perhaps fortunately, MacArthur entered the room and took General Shepherd and Colonel Krulak into his office. Here the supreme commander asked if the Marine could temporarily join his staff as an amphibious adviser and see the forthcoming operation through the critical period. Wisely and tactfully, General Shepherd suggested that such a post would carry much responsibility and no authority, but countered that he would be happy to accompany MacArthur as an observer, since the landing force would be composed of troops—the division and wing—still under administrative command of Shepherd's headquarters.

Then, grasping the nettle, General Shepherd spoke earnestly about Inchon and once again urged an alternate objective. Instead of cutting off discussion with a sentence, as Almond had done, MacArthur launched into a 30-minute analysis of the strategic importance of capturing Seoul which, he said, "would quickly end he war."

"For a five-dollar ante," he concluded, "I have an opportunity to win $50,000, and I have decided that is what I'm going to do."[44]

Landing at Washington's National Airport in a pouring rain, Sherman and Collins flashed brief smiles for the photographers while Pentagon PIOs—news managers before their time—continued to assure reporters there was "nothing extraordinary" about the trip. Then, with more pensive mien, the two chiefs described to Bradley and Vandenberg, there to meet them, MacArthur's plans and his unswerving determination to go through with them. On August 28—there seemed nothing else they could do—the Joint Chiefs of Staff transmitted a message of tepid approval to Tokyo:[45]

We concur in making preparations for executing a turning movement by amphibious forces on the west coast of Korea, either at Inchon in the event the enemy defenses in the vicinity of Inchon prove ineffective, or at a favorable beach south of Inchon if one can be located. We further concur in preparations, if desired by you, for an envelopment by amphibious forces in vicinity of Kunsan. We understand that alternative plans are being prepared in order to best exploit the situation as it develops.

Just 17 days remained until September 15.

Final Plans and Preparations

General Smith had landed at Tokyo's Haneda airport on the afternoon of August 22 and was welcomed by Admiral Doyle, who took him on board *Mount McKinley* and made him comfortable in the landing force commander's capacious cabin forward on the port side of the superstructure. Here he was immediately waited upon by his G-3, Colonel A. L. Bowser, USMC. Bowser, who had flown to Japan in the forward echelon of the 1st Marine Division staff, confirmed what General Smith had, at least in part, heard on August 8 from Brigadier General W. S. Fellers, just back from Tokyo—namely, that the division was to land in assault at Inchon on September 15 and that, to put the matter mildly, there were serious and complicated tidal problems to be solved. Before Smith left to report to MacArthur, Doyle put his head in, "not happy over the whole affair," to reinforce what Bowser had said about the problems that confronted them. But, as he would later tell MacArthur, he refused to say the operation was impossible.

Smith's initial meeting with Almond was not an auspicious one. Major General Almond, fifty-eight years old, addressed Major General Smith, age fifty-seven, as "Son." Employing the same unfortunate adjective that General Shepherd later noted, he spoke of the amphibious problems as "purely mechanical." Then, having disposed of these matters, he got up, went across to General MacArthur's office, where he spent a few minutes, no doubt conveying his first impressions, and finally ushered in General Smith.

MacArthur (looking his seventy years, thought Smith) shook hands cordially in the Latin fashion, left hand to elbow, lit his pipe and spoke of Inchon. This landing, he said, would win the war in a month, and it would be the Marines who had won it. Unknowingly echoing Forrestal's comment when he saw the colors rise atop Mount Suribachi in 1945,

MacArthur continued that there could never again be any question as to the future of the Marine Corps after such a victory. He appreciated that Marines strove for perfection, and that the forthcoming operation might be "somewhat helter-skelter," but (here he was firm) the landing had to be made on the 15th. Then he got up, grasped Smith's hand, and bade him good-by.[46]

Next day was a whirl of conferences. First came a briefing by what in a few days would officially become the staff of X Corps, higher headquarters under which operations ashore would ultimately be conducted. Almond, still MacArthur's chief of staff, was corps commander designate. This morning's briefing, however, was presided over by Major General Clark L. Ruffner, USA, the capable, tactful officer who was to be Almond's deputy.

As, in Admiral Doyle's subsequent words, "the corps staff, with very few exceptions, had no amphibious training, experience, or basic understanding of amphibious operations," the briefing conveniently skirted the amphibious part of the operation and dealt at length on how the land battle would be conducted once X Corps was ashore and Inchon behind them. But even here, it seemed to General Smith, there appeared some lack of realism. For example, he noted, the Engineer spoke at length about crossing the Han River, then admitted that no bridging equipment or materials were yet to be had. (In contrast, while mounting out of San Diego, Lieutenant Colonel John H. Partridge, the Marine division's Engineer, had seen to it that the Marine engineer battalion was fully equipped with Bailey bridge and 50-ton floating bridge sections, too.)[47]

Then there was another briefing, and after that—now it was afternoon —General Almond called in General Smith and Major General David G. Barr, USA, commander of the 7th Infantry Division which, once the beachhead was secure, would land behind the Marines.

At this conference (apparently Smith was unaware that MacArthur's showdown with the Joint Chiefs of Staff delegation was scheduled shortly afterward), Smith adverted to the doubts that were troubling all the naval people and spoke to the Posun-Myong concept. Almond cut him off. "Not interested," he said, and reiterated that the landing would take place at Inchon on September 15, and that the real objective was to take Seoul anyway, not avoid it (as the Posun-Myong maneuver would). "I saw no point in pursuing the matter further . . . ," recorded Smith, and later in the day told his staff to get to work on a scheme of maneuver which would enable the 1st Marine Division to take Inchon.[48]

At this point the thorough spadework of Admiral Doyle and his staff, and of General Wright's JSPOG, paid off. The Marine planners, arriving late and even then split three ways between Tokyo, Kobe, and Pusan,[49] at least had information on which they could rely.

The nub of the problem has already been stated: how to land a Marine division on two separated tides, the one so early that normal assault shipping could not get up the tricky channels in time for the flood at Inchon, the second so late that landings would have to be made by twilight if not darkness.

Paradoxically, recognition of still another problem pointed the way to solution of the others. Wolmi Do, as we have seen, is the tactical key to Inchon. Its peak commands the harbor and the city. General Smith's planners, recognizing Wolmi Do's importance, quickly concluded that the island—which must be captured first—should be taken with a separate landing on the morning tide, and that the main landings at Inchon proper could then proceed in the evening. In this way, by solving the Wolmi Do problem first, the Inchon landings could be simplified and streamlined.

But how to get the Wolmi Do landing force—on the scale of a battalion, the planners calculated—up for landing on the morning flood just after sunrise? The usual amphibious shipping, slow and cumbersome single-screw APAs (attack transports), AKAs (attack cargo ships) and LSTs were not built (or in those days radar-equipped) to negotiate Flying Fish Channel by night.

"The first examination of the night approach through the tortuous channel," said Colonel Bowser, "resulted in the general conclusion that it could not be done. Captain Norman Sears, Admiral Doyle's chief of staff, was just about the lone dissenter." The force, Sears reasoned, would not be large or laden with much gear. Let the assault battalion be embarked on board high-speed transports (APDs, destroyer escorts rebuilt for raiding and landing light forces), and an LSD (landing ship, dock). These ships were maneuverable, equipped with modern navigational instruments, and powerful enough to stem the currents of Flying Fish Channel.

The Marines worked out a minimum load for the battalion—to be selected from the experienced troops of the 1st Brigade—while Admiral Doyle and his people found the ships. As finally visualized, the landing force (3d Battalion, 5th Marines) would include one infantry battalion, some engineers and shore party, tanks, and reconnaissance parties for division artillery (the 11th Marines) which it was hoped might support the main landings from positions on Wolmi Do. Three APDs and one LSD, with destroyers and rocket ships for close-in naval gunfire support, would suffice. Concurring in the calculations, Captain Sears then convinced Admiral Doyle of their soundness and promptly volunteered to command the Advance Attack Force which would execute this hazardous operation.

The Wolmi Do landing, as we have seen, would take place over Green Beach on the morning tide. During the day, Wolmi Do would be occupied, mopped up, and organized. Although cut off from its ships by the ebb, the battalion on the island would be capable of protecting itself against anything the NKPA was thought to have at Inchon, and would be ready before nightfall to support the main landing on the Red beaches to the immediate northeast.

As for the main landings—those in the twilight—the remaining two battalions of the 5th Marines would attack Red Beach, extending north from the root of the Wolmi Do causeway, would capture a necklace of abrupt hills that curve through Inchon, and would link up by daylight with the 1st Marines. The latter regiment, landing over the Blue beaches south of town, would seize a cutlet-shaped beachhead, hook left and north to join the other regiment, and attack east toward Yongdungpo. Throughout the night, which surely, in MacArthur's phrase, would be "helter-skelter," the Navy would have LSTs beached—stranded, really— while vital supplies and vehicles were unloaded into the 5th Marines' beachhead.

To get these LSTs, restricted to 500 tons' load apiece, onto the beach near flood tide would be a neat trick. They would have to beach in semi-darkness, side by side like cars in a parking lot, avoiding landing craft of the assault waves, and do so while battle raged a street or so inland. Once on the ground, ramps down, there they would stay, come what might, until they could retract on next morning's tide. Besides the ordinary burden of the LST—vehicles, engineering equipment, shore party gear, etc.—each would bring 50 tons of ammunition, 30 tons of rations, 15 tons of water and five of fuel. And two of the eight were rigged for hospital duties, with doctors, corpsmen, and medical facilities to handle the night's casualties until they could be gotten off the beach next morning.

Finding the 47 LSTs required for the Inchon operation was one of Admiral Doyle's most intractable problems. From all sources, the Navy could provide only 17, and many of these hardly in prime condition. The balance—30 ex-USN ships on loan to the Japanese government for inter-island shipping—were available because of the foresight of MacArthur's FECOM planners. Maintaining and supporting these grimy rust-buckets had been a constant drag on Naval Forces Far East, which had repeatedly attempted to scrap all or part of them. Mindful of MacArthur's primary mission—defense of Japan—General Wright, backed by the G-4, had prudently insisted that these ships be kept in active status and—whether the Navy liked it or not—given minimum mechanical maintenance.[50]

For its reserve, the landing force would be stretched thin indeed. Only two of the Marine division's three infantry regiments would land at Inchon. (The 7th Marines, which Cates and MacArthur had pried from the Joint Chiefs of Staff, could not even reach Japan until September 17.) To provide General Smith the minimum reserve and—no small task—to mop up Inchon, an ROK infantry regiment was at first allocated to the landing force. Subsequently, on a happy suggestion by Colonel Edward W. Snedeker, USMC, the 1st Regiment, Korean Marine Corps (KMC), was substituted. These spirited, though as yet ill-armed and partly trained Korean troops were in the Pusan perimeter, and it would be up to General Craig and the Marine brigade to train, arm and embark them—an ambitious project which fell upon the broad shoulders of Lieutenant Colonel J. L. Stewart, USMC, Craig's imperturbable operations officer and onetime nationally famous college quarterback from Auburn.

Thus, then, the plan for landing and the initial scheme of maneuver of the landing force as finally composed.

Within four days after General Smith boarded *Mount McKinley*, his staff and Admiral Doyle's had agreed, and a draft plan—substantially that finally adopted—was on paper and in circulation.

To work up such a plan (or any plan) in any such time was a virtuoso performance even though it played hob with established procedures. Nevertheless, as O. P. Smith later pointed out when briefing the correspondents en route to Inchon:

> With additional time, the operation could be executed with more precision, but the availability of additional time would not materially change the character of the operation.

The comments and recommendations of key subordinate commanders and their staffs could neither be solicited nor obtained. While General Smith's people in Tokyo were working out detailed, rigidly organized plans for the 5th Marines' landing at Inchon, that regiment was fighting in another campaign 500 miles away. The 1st Marines, whose landing was being similarly planned, were not yet even in Japan. "Both regimental commanders were surprised, and, indeed, somewhat taken aback," recounted Colonel Bowser,

> . . . at the detail into which the division staff had gone, particularly with respect to landing plans. They both felt that we were usurping their prerogatives and binding them to predetermined courses of action in the initial stages of the landing. Be this as it may, they both also quickly grasped the cold, hard fact that had the division staff not done this for them, it would not have been accomplished.

No experienced officer, in command or on the staff, subscribes to this way of having to do things. Only common background, well-tested standard doctrine and long experience could render viable a plan so conceived.

The plans and orders of the 1st Marine Division and Amphibious Group 1 broke precedent in another respect: instead of responding to directives from higher headquarters apportioning, as is the normal process, missions and tasks to be carried out, the landing and attack force plans anticipated and in fact largely dominated the plans of the high naval headquarters, Joint Task Force 7, and of General Almond's X Corps. For example Smith issued his first Inchon operation order on August 27, whereas the corresponding X Corps Operation Order No. 1 (which in theory should have been the starting directive for the Marine division's plan), although dated August 28, was not issued until the 30th (after General Smith had sent a copy of his completed order to the newly formed X Corps staff).[51]

Until Admiral Struble entered the picture on August 26, what General Smith and Admiral Doyle had to go on were verbal directives of MacArthur, somewhat amplified during General Ruffner's conference on the 23d, and of course by free and frequent access to General Wright. From these sources it was concluded that the forthcoming campaign would require accomplishment of the following missions:

1. Seize the port of Inchon and capture a beachhead line.
2. Advance rapidly and seize Kimpo airfield.
3. Cross the Han River.
4. Seize and occupy Seoul.
5. Occupy blocking positions north, northeast, and east of Seoul.

All the foregoing were assigned to the Marines. In addition, the 7th Infantry Division, landing behind the leathernecks, would advance along the Marines' right (south) flank and, eventually, form with them the anvil on which Eighth Army was to smash the *In Min Gun*. Elements of General Harris's 1st Marine Air Wing—temporarily designated "Tactical Air Command, X Corps"—operating at first from carriers, then from Kimpo, would provide tactical air support.

". . . A Damn Good Unified Command"

While Admiral Struble was still at sea harrying the Communist flanks, Admiral Joy, MacArthur's naval commander in Tokyo, had on August 20 issued orders forming a force—Joint Task Force 7 (JTF-7)—which would carry out the Inchon operation. Joint Task Force 7, as the name suggests, was something in the nature of a falseface designation for the U. S. Seventh Fleet, and it was that fleet's commander, Admiral Struble, who was assigned duty as Commander Joint Task Force 7. Until the conclusion of the amphibious phase of the campaign, General Almond's Corps was to come under Struble, as of course were Doyle's naval attack force and Smith's landing force.

The question may be asked, and has been, why—if JTF-7 and its commander were in fact the Navy's Seventh Fleet and its admiral—these familiar entities were given new labels? Further—why, in the organizational structure for the landing at Inchon, were the well-understood command titles normal to an amphibious operation, each with defined prerogatives based on World War II experience, avoided?[52] In the case of Admiral Struble under a joint "hat," the answer is that, as a joint task force commander, so designated by MacArthur, he would thereby extend his authority to forces of all Services and, most notably, could control (or restrict) Air Force operations within stipulated areas and on missions related to the Inchon assault. Since control of Air Force operations by a naval commander (and vice versa) is, even today, occasion for inter-Service heartburn, the practical usefulness of Struble's joint command ought not to be overlooked and ought not to be regarded, as some writers have suggested, as a politic device to mask and minimize the dominance of naval command and participation in the Inchon operation.

On the other hand, after thorough study of the Inchon plans, it is hard to avoid the impression that, within the Army and Air Force headquarters involved, there did exist a desire where possible to bypass Navy/

Marine doctrines, terminology and command relations—recognizable trademarks of the Navy's World War II march across the Pacific—thus clothing this latest operation in the high-fashion garb of "jointness" (and also incorrectly suggesting a coequality of participation and joint contribution from all Services which did not in fact obtain).

None of this worried Admiral Struble then or now. Mindful of Sherman's injunction, he was concerned for the success of the operation and thus with the substance of authority, not its symbols, and was prepared, as he later said, "to throw the book away." What he intended to forge for the forthcoming invasion was ". . . a damn good unified command," and it was in this mood that he gathered his staff after Admiral Sherman left Sasebo for Tokyo on the forenoon of August 23.[53]

Struble rightly recognized, after almost two months of action along the east and west coasts of Korea, that his joint task force headquarters must include well-qualified gunnery and air officers. On 30 minutes' notice, while the young officer "kicked like a steer," the admiral conscripted a promising destroyer squadron commander, Captain U. S. Grant Sharp, USN, as JTF-7 gunnery officer. In the same breath he ordered Rear Admiral John ("Peg-Leg") Hoskins, his fast-carrier commander, to yield up "his best aircraft planner." As for mines, Admiral Struble knew the subject: he had experience in mine warfare.[54] With his staff filled out, the admiral hastened to Tokyo on August 25 while *Rochester* steamed thence from Sasebo at best speed.

Struble reached Tokyo in time for lunch with Admiral Joy and General Shepherd (and speculated between bites on the possibility of the latter's getting command of the expeditionary troops—i.e., X Corps—in the amphibious operation). Briefings followed from Doyle and Smith. From these it was clear that planning for the assault was in skilled hands and progressing well; Struble largely accepted what they had accomplished and said he would provide any further required decisions orally (there never was or will be such an operation as *Chromite* for concurrent, word-of-mouth planning). Written orders would eventually catch up.

Now to the Dai Ichi Building for a call on MacArthur and talks with Almond and the Far East Command planners about top command relations (the military equivalent of corporation law in Wall Street). While some matters—particularly air plans and operations—could not be settled immediately, Struble, as a joint task force commander, enjoyed direct entrée to MacArthur when he wished to discuss high-level decisions.

Aided in this by earlier service and acquaintance with the General, the admiral could thus talk things over privately and without the official constraints of the staff machine.

Considering the haste with which it had to be improvised, Struble's command was an impressive one. This invasion task force, for such it truly was, would lift, land and support a Marine division, an infantry division, the bulk of a Marine air wing, and all the myriad special and supporting troops for a major campaign—71,339 officers and men of the Marine Corps, Navy, Army, and Korean Marines.[55]

The armada for this expedition exceeded 230 ships: U. S. Navy, Royal Navy, Royal Canadian, Australian, and New Zealand Navies, ROK Navy, French Navy, MSTS, chartered merchantmen pressed into the breach, and 34 Japanese vessels, mostly ex-U. S. Navy LSTs commanded by ex-Japanese Navy officers, at least one a former battleship captain. Admiral Struble's force was divided into six major task forces:

TASK FORCE 90.* *Attack Force*
                              Rear Admiral J. H. Doyle
TASK FORCE 91. *Blockade and Covering Force*
                              Rear Admiral Sir W. G. Andrewes, RN
TASK FORCE 92.* *X Corps*
                              Major General E. M. Almond, USA
TASK FORCE 99. *Patrol and Reconnaissance Force*
                              Rear Admiral G. R. Henderson
TASK FORCE 77. *Fast Carrier Force*
                              Rear Admiral E. C. Ewen
TASK FORCE 79. *Service Squadron*
                              Captain B. L. Austin

The question of how to staff and organize the corps headquarters—and, most important, who would command it—went unsettled until mid-August. Early that month, Sherman had suggested to MacArthur that General Shepherd and his headquarters (Fleet Marine Force Pacific) be given the command. Such an assignment would have made sense not only because Shepherd, a lieutenant general and thus of corps-command

---

*During the assault and until General Smith assumed command of operations ashore, the 1st Marine Division, as the Landing Force, came under Admiral Doyle, the attack force commander. Ultimately, when General Almond assumed command of X Corps operations ashore, the Marine division would revert to the corps command.

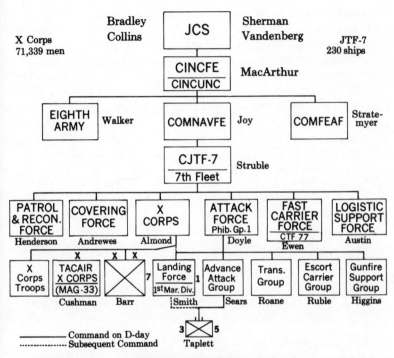

X Corps
71,339 men

JTF-7
230 ships

MAJOR FORCES AND COMMAND RELATIONS
Operation "Chromite", D-day

rank, was a veteran amphibious commander, but also because his headquarters, composed of Marines, was organized for amphibious warfare and, above all, was a going concern. General Wright, MacArthur's G-3, made these points in a memorandum of August 7, urging that the Marine headquarters be employed:

> This headquarters must be one that can operate in the field as a going concern with such things as situation reports, operations reports, communications, etc., happening automatically. A provisional command group selected from GHQ officers will not be a going concern . . . no matter how efficient the individual officers are.

Major General Hickey, the deputy chief of staff, concurred emphatically and warned against ". . . the hasty throwing together of a provisional corps headquarters . . . at best only a half-baked affair." These recommendations stopped at the chief of staff's desk and were sent back with the notation, "Return without action."

Three days later, when Wright again urged the prompt formation of a corps headquarters, a provisional staff for this group was selected by General Almond. About August 15, General Almond has related, he asked General MacArthur who was to command the corps, and was, he says, startled to hear the General reply, "It is you." The reasons Almond has given for MacArthur's (and his) preference for a provisional corps headquarters made up of Army officers were that *Chromite*, ". . . definitely a land operation, *once the landing was made,*

> . . . would require a Headquarters for a lightning-like strike which could be handled by the personnel then available to the Far East Command . . . many able, experienced and senior officers who had commanded in Europe and in Italy. *Once the force had been landed* the principal problem would be a land operation over some 18 miles of terrain involving a river crossing. . . . *The real essence of the Inchon landing was not merely to land and form a beachhead* but to drive across difficult terrain 18 miles and capture a large city and thereafter properly outpost and protect that city. [Italics supplied.]

And so it happened that, on August 26, when Washington authorized activation of X Corps, Major General Almond (who by dispensation retained his post as MacArthur's chief of staff) was named to command it.[56]

Edward Mallory Almond, a Virginia officer of distinguished record (he lists 12 lines of decorations in his *Who's Who* biography), entered the Army in 1916 after turning down a commission in the Marines. Besides combat service in both World Wars, he was a graduate of the Air Corps Tactical School and of the Naval War College, which later prompted him to say: "I had to do some fast talking to get into the Air and Navy Schools. I had seen some Army officers in Washington who just didn't know what it was all about when the discussion turned to planes or ships." Trim, iron-gray-haired, ruddy-faced, impetuous and impatient, Almond was no man to trifle with. In a cover story (October 23, 1950), *Time* said of him:

> . . . A whip-cracking officer, he never compromises with discipline, drives himself hard and his subordinates only a shade less hard. To some he seems an insufferable martinet. Those who know him best say his

professional manner, as tough as armor plate, is only the protective covering. . . . If MacArthur has any subordinate who qualifies as his trusty right hand, it is Almond.

General Almond's Army division, the 7th Infantry, was commanded by an old friend and service contemporary, Major General David G. Barr, USA, of Alabama. A bullet-headed, graying blond, General Barr enjoyed a reputation throughout the Army for his courtesy, practicality, and down-to-earth common sense.

Through no fault of General Barr's, his division was in sorry shape. One of the occupation divisions in Japan, the 7th had been used as a replacement pool during the fighting in Central Korea and the perimeter. Following an initial bite in July of 130 officers and 1,500 enlisted men—naturally the best and most experienced—the division had been gutted to less than half strength, with far more serious shortages among officers and NCOs in the fighting jobs. On July 26, the day this unfortunate unit was alerted for the campaign ahead, it was short 416 officers and warrant officers and 8,701 enlisted men. Soon after, frankly stating his predicament, General Barr told Colonel Forney that the division wasn't even ready for amphibious training, let alone an amphibious mission.

To get the 7th Division back on its feet demanded heroic measures. Throughout August—over cries of anguish from General Walker's Eighth Army—the entire flow of infantry replacements from the United States (390 officers, 5,400 enlisted men) was transfused into the division. When it could be foreseen that even this would not suffice, General MacArthur ordered Walker to sweep up South Korean replacements—8,637, they finally numbered—to fill the 7th Division's ranks. This expedient was described in MacArthur's *Reminiscences* as "the so-called 'buddy system' which proved so successful." In less sanguinary vein, the Army's official history says bluntly, "They were civilians—stunned, confused, and exhausted. Only a few could speak English." Mainly garbed in the shirt, shorts, sandals, and cloth shoes they had on when caught by Walker's press gangs, these pitiful refugees were dealt out, a hundred in a batch, to each infantry company and artillery battery in the division. Such fundamental problems as the use of western-style latrines had to be explained in sign language and then demonstrated, by the numbers, by American instructors.

Fortunately for General Barr, the Stateside replacement drafts in August contained a compensating element: virtually the entire school troops, highly qualified NCO instructors and demonstration personnel from the Infantry and Artillery Schools at Forts Benning and Sill had been uprooted and sent to war. One of the 7th Division's artillery officers, Colonel Patrick Welch, described the artillery replacements as "virtuosos of the FDC [fire direction center]—Paderewski couldn't have done any better."

These experienced soldiers were a godsend to General Barr. The fact remains that an 18,804-man division, more than a third composed of non-English-speaking, civilian levies, is not the likeliest material for an invasion less than a month hence.[57]

To complete the X Corps troop list, General Almond had two additional 155mm howitzer battalions, an antiaircraft battalion, an amphibian tractor battalion, and an engineer brigade (mostly for port operations at Inchon). Not under General Almond, but in theater reserve subject to MacArthur's control, was the 187th Airborne regimental combat team (RCT). It was planned that these parachutists might be airdropped in conjunction with the amphibious assault, a favorite World War II tactic of MacArthur's and much in vogue during the European landings of that war, but rarely productive of military results commensurate with either the effort or publicity involved.

The Tactical Air Command, X Corps, under Brigadier General Thomas J. Cushman, USMC, was composed of Marine Aircraft Group 33 and headquarters and service units from the 1st Wing. To reinforce the shore-based Marine air, which would base at Kimpo, Marine Aircraft Group 12 would be afloat in the jeep carriers *Sicily* and *Badoeng Strait*—the latter well known to Korean veterans as "the Bing-Ding." General Cushman and MAG-12 represented major assets. Cushman was deputy commander and senior aviator in the 1st Brigade, where MAG-12, under his direction, had been winning laurels for its tank-busting close air support in the battles at Obong-Ni and along the Naktong. Support for the Inchon assault would be the main responsibility of Cushman's proven squadrons.

Fire Support

Unlike battles ashore, assault landings have to rely during the most critical phase, that of initial lodgment, on fire support from ships and aircraft. Only when the beachhead is established can artillery assume its role. Thus naval gunfire and air support were matters of great concern to Admirals Struble and Doyle, and to General Smith.

The Marine Corps, habituated to hard fighting in opposed assaults, confident and knowledgeable in the Navy's gunfire support and in the precision support of Marine and Navy aviators, believed in these weapons and liked to use them generously. Army staffs, having less experience in this type of work, hesitated to rely on the Navy's guns in the absence of their trusted artillery, and knew little of air support as the Marines practice it.

Thus, when General Smith first reached Tokyo, he found that the Army planners, hoping somehow for total surprise (usually a will-o'-the-wisp in amphibious planning), wanted little or no naval gunfire support. To Smith the Marine, and to Doyle, veteran of the Central Pacific, which had been one long smash by carrier air and heavy naval guns, such a view seemed unbelievable. If only to reduce Wolmi Do—Corregidor of Inchon Harbor—ample naval gunfire and air would be needed. Thus the attack and landing force commanders set to work in close concert on fire support plans more realistic in character.[58]

As soon as *Rochester* reached Tokyo (on the 26th) and moored alongside *Mount McKinley* (thus bringing the key commanders, Struble, Doyle and Smith, into close proximity), Admiral Struble took thought to his air plan.

To support Inchon, the following air tasks would have to be performed: preparation of Korean west coast areas (as in surgery, "preparation" is the military term for the painful preliminaries of an operation) 150 miles north of Inchon and 100 miles south; diversionary strikes to keep the enemy deceived and confused; preparation of Inchon proper and Wolmi Do; support of the landings; air defense of our forces at sea and ashore; and at least five days' air interdiction of the Inchon-Seoul area until shore-based air could be established (initially Tactical Air Command, X Corps, later Fifth Air Force).

One highly important decision regarding the air effort had already been made. "Although," General Wright later wrote, "we were all under great pressure in early August to utilize Air Force elements in the operation," MacArthur (Wright further stated) had approved a recommendation that the campaign be supported entirely by Navy and Marine air. One reason for the General's decision was the obvious one that, since the Navy and Marine squadrons which had been providing most of Walker's close air support in the perimeter would have to be withdrawn for Inchon, Fifth Air Force should properly take on the entire support of Eighth Army. It may also be conjectured that the excellent performance of the Navy and Marine aviators, working with a superior doctrine (which, by the days of Vietnam, had been accepted even by the Air Force), prompted Wright, Almond and MacArthur to insure that *Chromite* received what, at the time, was admittedly the best tactical air support in the theater. As might be expected, MacArthur's exclusion of the Air Force from the forthcoming operation met resistance not only from his own air commander, but from Air Force Headquarters in Washington, and was one reason why General Vandenberg had elected to send a deputy rather than attend the August 23 conference in Tokyo with Sherman and Collins.[59]

Besides the factors which prompted MacArthur's decision, Admiral Struble, like most naval commanders, was in any case wary of the elaborate coordinating arrangements which always seemed necessary when Air Force units took part in invasions. As a veteran of Normandy he could well remember that, despite all the weight of Eighth Air Force and its promised commitments before the landings, it failed completely over Omaha Beach, where the air effort against the beach defenses was practically nil.

Thus, one of Struble's first actions as joint commander was to reaffirm independently that air tasks in and around Inchon would be handled by Navy and Marine air under JTF-7, although he remained willing to accept any practical Air Force assistance that would serve his objectives. Naturally, however, any final decision on Air Force participation would have to come from MacArthur.

Attempting to reopen MacArthur's decision, General Stratemeyer, the Far East Air Forces commander, conferred with Struble and General Almond soon after the former's arrival in Tokyo, but from Stratemeyer's viewpoint the meeting went badly. As Admiral Struble pointed out, Air Force planes operating from inconveniently distant shore bases would have very little time over targets and small bombloads as compared to the carrier-based Navy and Marine squadrons close at hand in the Yellow Sea.

Ultimately, Struble assented to Far East Air Force operations around Kunsan as part of the deception plans, but from September 12 (D—3 day), unless requested by Joint Task Force 7, there should be no Far East Air Force sorties at all within a specified radius of the Inchon-Seoul area. The final conference aboard *Rochester* at which these decisions were announced was stormy: they were not, in the words of Colonel Bowser, a participant, "happily accepted by the Air Force." As always, however,

Struble knew what he wanted (which here coincided exactly with what MacArthur wanted) and would not be swayed.

These measures attended to, the joint task force commander set his air planners to work on wide-ranging strikes against Chinnampo, Ongjin, Inchon and Kunsan—each a west coast port at least conceivable as the site of an amphibious descent. These strikes would accomplish planned destruction, reconnaissance and photography at Inchon, slow down defensive construction and mining along the entire coast and, perhaps most important, prevent the enemy—if suspicions became aroused—from knowing which shell the pea would be under. However, as D-day approached, from August 30 on, 40 per cent of the sorties by Task Force 77 (Admiral Ewen's fast carriers) were to hit Inchon-Seoul, while 30 per cent of Ewen's effort was to hit north, and the remaining 30 per cent south of the objective.[60]

Sifting the chaff from reconnaissance reports, studies, stereo pairs and all the grist of the intelligence mill, the naval gunfire planners could tell Admiral Doyle and General Smith that they had 106 hard targets—enemy weapons or fortifications—and about three miles of entrenchments already dug on Wolmi Do, throughout Inchon, and near Blue Beach. Of these, over four-fifths were sited so that they could fire on or command one or more of the three beaches or the related movement from ship to shore.[61]

Commander Capps (Doyle's gunnery officer) and Bowser (landing force G-3) were highly qualified amphibious gunnery officers with extensive World War II experience. It was their conviction, based on targets already counted plus more to be conjectured, that the landing at Inchon would require a methodical naval gunfire preparation, and this view was shared by Doyle and Smith. Such a bombardment, coordinated with air strikes and napalm defoliation of Wolmi Do, would ideally commence several days before the landing and would, it is true, likely disclose Inchon as the objective.

The crux of the problem, therefore, was to balance out opposed considerations of surprise and of guaranteed destruction of enemy targets which could jeopardize the assault by shooting landing craft out of the water and raking the beaches.

At three conferences (on the 1st, the 3rd, and—right down to the wire—the 8th of September) the tug of war went one way or the other. The first decision (it caused "much unhappiness" to Doyle and Smith, said Struble) was to have destroyers pirouette up to Wolmi Do on the day before the landing (D—1) deliver a light bombardment with their 5-inch guns, following a morning's shooting at long range from cruisers downstream. In the eyes of the Marines, this was hardly enough to lift the dust on Inchon's streets, and Admiral Doyle thought so, too. Struble, however, was adamant that there could be no bombardment before D—2, and inclined to less rather than more of it in any case.

Finally on September 8, with D-day a week off, Struble agreed to make Wolmi Do a test case. On the forenoon of D—2 (the 13th) destroyers would close Wolmi Do, bombard at close, nearly point-blank range, and try to goad Inchon's defenders into action. That afternoon the cruisers would shoot from downstream. If the enemy showed his hand, one more day—D—1 (the 14th)—would remain to soften up Inchon and Wolmi Do.

So, at length, the essential elements of the plan to seize Inchon were completed. The landing on the two tides had been worked out; so had the scheme of maneuver for the Marines ashore. And finally, the all-important plan of supporting fires—including napalm strikes on Wolmi Do and a crisply coordinated D-day sequence of air strikes, rocket barrages and ships' gunfire—was agreed to.[62]

Only two pieces of business remained outstanding—one almost bizarre in its lack of realism, the other possessing grave implications for the success or failure of the campaign.

Crackpot Schemes

During a weak moment in August, General Shepherd had committed the 1st Marine Division to provide 100 volunteers, he believed, as a raiding detachment under Admiral Doyle. This had been a proposition made by General Almond, who was raising an Army Special Operations Company for the same purpose, to be commanded by an intelligence specialist, Colonel Louis B. Ely, USA. When, on arriving in Japan, General Smith learned that his hundred Marines (whom the division could ill spare, anyway) were now earmarked to join Ely's Special Operations Company, he felt less inclined than ever toward the idea.

On September 8, the day the bombardment controversy was settled, with plans complete and D-day just a week off, General Smith was thunderstruck to learn that, unbeknown to the Marines, Colonel Ely, planning separately under X Corps, was working on a scheme to capture

Wolmi Do by landing his company on the night before D-day (to make sure things came off, two Marine companies from unspecified sources in the 1st Division would land at dawn and finish the job, under Ely's command). As this visionary project cut squarely across the assault by the 3d Battalion, 5th Marines, on the morning tide, it withered on exposure to daylight. "There were quite a few details left out of his plan," noted General Smith.

But Ely had another plan. Within forty-eight hours, he told General Smith and others present (the conference was chaired by General Hickey of MacArthur's staff), he would embark his company aboard a British frigate, debark in rubber boats north of Inchon, paddle ashore amid tides strong enough to stem a landing craft, and capture Kimpo airfield. Here again, there seemed to be certain impracticalities: more than a thousand yards of mud flats to cross, not to speak of adverse tides; an enemy garrison at least four times larger than the 124-man Army company; only three days' rations and radio sets inaudible beyond three miles. Aside from these snags, General Smith pointed out that it was one of the Marine division's main missions to take Kimpo airfield, and that, when they did so, they would take it for keeps; also, that he didn't propose to have the Special Operations Company at large in his zone of action, underfoot but not under command, restricting maneuver, naval gunfire and air support. General Hickey quickly saw the point and the raid was thought to be dead. But on September 10 on orders from General Almond, not only was the question reopened, but the 1st Marine Division was ordered to give Ely the original 100 Marines. With the landing only five days off, and with much of his division already at sea, it was simply too late, replied Smith (with support from General Shepherd), and the order was rescinded.

Afterward, General Almond admitted he had gone along with this scheme simply "to spur the Marines on to capture Kimpo." As General Smith remarked years later, "He didn't understand Marines."[63]

Disengaging the 5th Marines

It will be remembered that the 5th Marines, scheduled for the landing force main effort over Red Beach, was playing a role of its own in the Pusan perimeter. The 5th Marines' performance with the Eighth Army had in fact been so stellar that the troupe was being held over by popular request.

As early as August 23, General Shepherd had suggested to Almond

F

that the 5th Regiment "had one more good fight in them" and ought to
be disengaged so they could plan and regroup for Inchon. On the same
day (which must have been irritating to Almond) General Smith had
raised the identical point. Like General Shepherd, he too was brusquely
turned down: it would be bad for Eighth Army morale to see the
Marines depart (which was no doubt true), and their withdrawal would
betray the impending operation.

For a week Smith bided his time, then raised the point again. This
time the answer was that General Walker would of course be reasonable
and would release the 1st Brigade when General Craig, the brigade
commander, asked. Smith reflected that this was putting Craig in an
intolerable position—that of having to ask himself out of fighting in
progress—and sent Almond an official message requesting that the
brigade be disengaged. With D-day little more than a fortnight ahead,
the request could hardly be turned down: on September 4, Far East
Command directed, the Marines would be released.

But while Far East Command proposed, events disposed. Hardly had
the brigade been ordered released than the *In Min Gun,* with 13 divisions, hit the Pusan perimeter on September 2 in what was to be its
final attack. Faced with grave emergency, Eighth Army was allowed
to hold the Marines as its mobile reserve. While General Smith wondered
exactly how Inchon would be taken 13 days later, he received word that
X Corps had a solution to his problem: if General Walker felt he simply
had to hold the Marine brigade down south, Inchon or not, General
Almond would provide the Marine division a substitute assault regiment
—the 32d Infantry from the 7th Division, a unit without amphibious
training and with about 40 per cent of its ranks filled by non-English-
speaking Korean civilians.

"It became apparent to me," General Smith noted at this point, "that
there was a complete lack of understanding at GHQ concerning the
manner in which amphibious forces were mounted out."[64]

Once again the Navy and the Marines held an indignation meeting.
Afterward, at Joy's request, Almond agreed, this time as MacArthur's
chief of staff, to consider General Smith's appeal against the X Corps
proposal, and to settle the matter in conference on September 3.

"There was a rather heated discussion," said General Smith. Admirals
Joy and Doyle took the lead for the Navy, while O. P. Smith spoke for
the landing force and Struble listened quietly. The naval and landing
force arguments were restated—shipping already under way to Pusan;

brigade planning going full tilt; D-day but 12 days distant; the 32d Infantry's utter lack of qualifications—each was brushed aside. When O. P. Smith said he would cancel Blue Beach and land only the 1st Marines (over Red Beach) rather than have the 32d Infantry in assault, Almond said MacArthur would be present and take that risk.

As voices rose and fell, Almond retired periodically, as if to consult MacArthur or phone Walker (though without ever saying so specifically). Finally Struble, who felt that the weight of professional opinion had Almond in a corner, offered a solution designed to get the Marine brigade while allowing Almond to back down gracefully. The whole discussion, said the admiral, boiled down to General Walker's requirement for an emergency reserve—why not load an infantry regiment aboard ship immediately and send it down to Pusan, where it could remain in floating reserve until the Eighth Army's crisis was past? This neat solution, which gave General Walker an Army unit for his reserve while permitting the Marine brigade to resume its role as amphibious troops, could hardly be resisted. General Almond withdrew and this time did go in to see MacArthur.

Although Walker had already said, "If I lose the 5th Marines I will not be responsible for the safety of the front," MacArthur quickly sided with Struble and the Navy. "Tell Walker," he told his chief of staff, "he will have to give up the 5th Marines."

And so it happened that, within an hour after Almond had broken the news to General Walker, the 1st Marine Brigade was ordered detached from Eighth Army the night of September 5–6. This left the 5th Marines nothing to do during the next nine days but complete planning, embark aboard ship, and be ready to lead a major amphibious assault on the morning of the 15th.[65]

"There Is No Question in My Mind . . ."

After the Tokyo conference on August 23 the Joint Chiefs had guardedly acquiesced in the Inchon landing, but Washington's reservations had by no means been disposed of. That MacArthur, keeping his counsel as before, had wisely but irritatingly not disclosed his detailed plans for nit-picking by the Joint Staff, did nothing to allay the doubts held by many. These doubts came to a head on September 5, when the Joint Chiefs of Staff sent their Far East commander a request for details on the pending operation; MacArthur blandly replied that his plans remained unchanged.

Thereupon, MacArthur's *Reminiscences* recorded, "At this eleventh hour . . . I received a message from the Joint Chiefs of Staff which chilled me to the marrow of my bones." For once the florid rhetoric of the *Reminiscences* lives up to its topic; what the JCS said, in part, was:

> We have noted with considerable concern the trend of events in Korea. In light of the commitment of all the reserves available to Eighth Army, we desire your estimate as to the feasibility and chance of success of the projected operation.

Would General MacArthur please—it was now September 7, D—8 in other words—reconsider the whole question and give them his views?

General Bradley and the Chiefs should have known that in any such exchange they were outgunned. MacArthur's pencil slashed out a reply:

"There is no question in my mind," he began (there never had been), "as to the feasibility of the operation and I regard its chance of success as excellent. I go further and believe that it represents the only hope of wresting the initiative from the enemy and thereby presenting the opportunity for a decisive blow . . . I and all of my commanders and staff officers, without exception, are enthusiastic for and confident of the success of the enveloping movement."

Gloomily the Chiefs conferred over the great man's message, drafted a brief one of their own, and Bradley went to Blair House to see the President. After he returned, the Joint Chiefs of Staff handed the Joint Staff Director an outgoing dispatch for the Far East: "We approve your plan and President has been so informed."

Wider at this point even than the Potomac, the Rubicon was at last behind. Ahead lay Inchon and the Han.[66]

ENEMY VESSELS APPROACHING

~~~~~~

[The North Koreans] cannot possibly have guessed at the strength of the blow. That had to be seen to be believed.
VICE-ADMIRAL SIR WILLIAM G. ANDREWES

THE ATMOSPHERE of Tokyo and Kobe was grim, unremitting and urgent. That in Sasebo, Kyushu's remote navy-yard town where the Seventh Fleet had its base, was exciting and, to the end of the war, rather jolly.

When on July 29, France's contribution to the Inchon landing, the aging frigate *La Grandière,* steamed into Sasebo Wan with five months' supply of wine but no coding machine, she found the largest international fleet that had assembled in the Far East since the days of the Boxer Uprising. Besides the mounting strength of the Seventh Fleet, there were, counting herself, warships present from six foreign powers and the place had the feel of a regatta. "Truly the Korean war was *très dure* [very hard] at Sasebo," recorded *La Grandière's* captain:[1]

> Drinks flowed without stopping from the moment of arrival. *La Grandière* had to uphold the reputation of France by gulping down great quantities of whiskey, gin, horse-neck, and other mixtures, and, above all, by entertaining when our turn came. The flowing tide of cocktails and champagne quickly cleared the air of the protocol which sometimes prevailed at first. . . . We shall always remember the atmosphere of camaraderie among the Navies of the United Nations."

Besides the usual conviviality whereby bone-dry American wardrooms provided steak dinners and foreign ships provided the cocktails, there was, observed the French, "a lively struggle" among the smaller, less dignified destroyers and frigates to get prints of a certain photograph of

Miss Esther Williams, the luscious American starlet whose charms made her the favorite pin-up of the Korean War.

Senior foreign officer present, and commander of the British Empire's substantial contribution to the United Nations forces afloat, was Rear Admiral Sir William G. Andrewes, RN, who, with three cruisers, a light carrier, and three destroyers and smaller ships, had provided welcome reinforcement to the Seventh Fleet since the dark days of early July. By the same kind of good luck that brought Admiral Doyle and Colonel Forney to the Far East just ahead of the storm, the Seventh Fleet and the British Far East Fleet had held combined exercises in March 1950. "As a result," Admiral Andrewes later wrote, "we were already in possession of the United States [code and signal] books and many of us had had recent experience in their use. . . . It all seemed familiar, joining up in Formation Four Roger, as it was just what we had done so often during the exercises in March."[2]

The Pirates of Yonghung Do

While the allied navies were living it up in Sasebo, a tiny U.N. task force was getting in some shore duty under rather different circumstances.

Commencing in mid-August, with Commander M. J. Luosey as his adviser, Rear Admiral Sohn Won Yil, ROK Chief of Naval Operations, had begun a campaign of harassment along the west coast of South Korea. Admiral Sohn's program included raids, evacuation of loyal Koreans, and, as it picked up momentum, occupation of some of the numerous islands which girdle the coast. In this he received enthusiastic support from Admiral Andrewes and H. M. ships in these waters.

On August 19, an ROK landing force was put ashore from ROKN *PC-703* (Lieutenant Commander Lee, ROKN) on the island of Yonghung Do. Just 14 miles south of Inchon, Yonghung Do lies on East Channel below Palmi Do, where Flying Fish Channel comes in. At this time Communist detachments from the West Coast Regiment (a "Marine" coast defense formation) garrisoned three neighboring islands (Taebu Do, Taemuii Do, and Yongyu Do). Yonghung, with a loyal South Korean population of several hundred, was unmolested. Lee accordingly left a small garrison commanded by Lieutenant Commander Ham Myong Su.

When the intelligence community in Tokyo learned that friendly forces held an island only a few miles down-channel from Inchon, it was

obvious that this capture must be exploited. Working in conjunction with
CIA, MacArthur's intelligence staff laid on Operation *Trudy Jackson*.
Trudy's object was to verify by personal reconnaissance the vital details
of intelligence—the seawalls, the mud flats, the tides, the defenses—on
which the Inchon plan was premised. The team selected to carry out
Trudy Jackson was headed by Lieutenant Eugene F. Clark, USN; it
included an unidentified U. S. Army Officer, three Army enlisted men,
and two Korean interpreters.

Lieutenant Clark, a former chief petty officer and longtime Asiatic
sailor with 16 years' service, was especially fitted for this mission because
he had extensive amphibious force background together with experience
as a military government officer in the fishing villages of Okinawa. Moreover, from inception in July, he had worked in General Wright's special
planning group at GHQ in Tokyo and—this made the thing bigger than
the mere gamble of a few lives—knew the *Chromite* plan. As insurance
for the security of the operation, Clark later related, he kept a grenade
on his person, night and day ("A grenade," he said, "is a lot more
certain than trying to shoot yourself with a pistol").

Profiting by a Swiss Family Robinson mountain of supplies—fish, rice,
DDT, radio, whiskey, halazone tablets, medical gear, a million ROK
won (₩1,800 = $1), two .50-caliber machine guns, a squad tent and
cots (everything, in fact, but a wardroom steward)—Clark's team
landed on September 1 and quickly established a snug and secure base.
Lieutenant Commander Ham had already mobilized the boys and young
men of Yŏnghŭng into a private army which Clark christened "The
Young Men's Association." This band of franc-tireurs manned observation and listening posts, spotted infiltrators crossing the mud flats from
Taebu Do at low tide, and commenced infiltrating on their own.

The island boasted one powered sampan, an ancient one-lunger "with
a cylinder better than a foot across" (as Clark tells it). In waters where
sail still reigned, this boat gave Clark the means to raid adjacent islands
and harry Communist sampans in the channels. With a machine gun
for main battery and Thompson submachine guns as the secondary, Clark
took his first three prizes in one morning on September 3. Thereafter he
raided regularly, the object of course being to take and interrogate
prisoners, not to blockade Inchon.

Between prisoners (many of whom turned out to be loyal South
Koreans) and reports from the Young Men's Association, Clark's nightly
radio transmissions began to provide interesting reading. The Japanese

tide tables for these waters, he reported, were dead on; ours were off. Fortification was in progress at certain points. Inchon's seawall heights at various tide stages were checked by Korean urchins and, on one exciting night, by Clark himself in a rowboat (he also squished about the mud flats and reported them impassable). Some of his agents made their way to Kimpo and Seoul, returning with word of enemy strengths and locations. One boy even wormed onto Wolmi Do, although the island was restricted to troops and laborers working on defenses.

As the team had gone ashore in broad daylight from a naval vessel and were carrying on a vigorous raiding program, their presence was hardly unadvertised. On September 8 (two days after Admiral Andrewes had bombarded Inchon), the 300-man garrison on Taebu Do launched an attack. The NKPA landing force, embarked in sailing sampans, was supported by a motor sampan with a 37mm antitank gun lashed in its bows. As soon as his observers spotted the enemy putting out from Taebu, Clark and his people got their own sampan under way and stood out to meet the hostile flotilla. While the 37mm banged futilely at long range, Lieutenant Clark closed in Nelson's style, let go a sustained burst with the .50-caliber machine gun ("it was sheer murder"), first disabling, finally sinking the NKPA gunboat in a cloud of blood and splinters. Then he turned on a sailing sampan with 18 reds aboard and sank her, too. As soon as he got back ashore, he radioed an action report and asked for support.

The arrival next day of destroyer *Hanson,* with two sections of *Badoeng Strait* Corsairs aloft from MAG-12, was the reply to Clark's call. When Commander C. R. Welte, *Hanson*'s rangy, blue-eyed skipper, offered to take them off, Clark demurred but suggested a strike against Taebu. For the next 31 minutes *Hanson* put 212 rounds of 5-inch onto Taebu, after which the Corsairs unloaded bombs, rockets and cannon, and returned on board with all ordnance expended. "We had no more trouble from Taebu for a long time," Clark later related.[3]

The day after Commander Welte's bombardment (September 10), the lieutenant chugged up-channel for a look at Palmi Do, the island pinnacle that juts up where East and Flying Fish Channels join. After a breathless climb up Palmi Do's 219 feet, Clark entered the lighthouse, darkened since the early days of the war. Evidently expecting to have it in routine service before long, the North Koreans had not damaged the machinery but had merely disconnected the battery-powered rotor of the reflector and snuffed out the ancient, French-made oil lamp. The damage

inflicted by an August landing from HMCS *Athabaskan* was also superficial. With a bit of tinkering, Clark ascertained that the reflector would
rotate if reconnected, and there were oil and a wick in the lamp. That
night's radio report (with Admiral Struble about to sortie from Yokosuka) asked: Would it be helpful if Palmi Do were relit on the night
before the landing? Decidedly yes, came the answer.

As always, the last days were the hardest. The intelligence missions had
been carried out. Clark and his team now had time to ponder their own
situation on this remote, tide-washed, sunlit island framed by the
horizon of enemies who well knew they were there. Expendable when
they landed, now with their job done they were trebly so. The sense of
being expendable, with plenty of time to reflect on it, is an uneasy one.

On the 14th (after they had seen Inchon's preliminary bombardment
forces come and go for the second day), Clark made ready to strike camp
on short notice; the team's plan was to spend that night on Palmi Do,
where the light was to be turned on at midnight to greet the Wolmi Do
attack force.

Well that they were ready: goaded and worried by the imperialist
pirates of Yonghung Do, the defense commander at Inchon had shifted
part of his reserve down to Taebu with the idea of liquidating these
troublemaking provocateurs. As dusk fell, the Yonghung Do observation
posts reported infantry wading across from Taebu and many sampans
approaching the south beach. Leaving their gear and all the weapons
they could, Clark and his team decamped in the one-lunger and made
it to Palmi Do. Behind, on Yonghung, troops of the 226th Regiment
were shooting down more than 50 villagers—men and women, boys and
girls—to demonstrate what happens to those who aid the Americans.
Clark got the Navy Cross.[4]

The Expedition Embarks and Sails

The days of wine and roses ended for *La Grandière* on September 6.
That day, she sailed as escort for the first movement unit—a gaggle of
tugs, LSUs (landing ships, utility—the LCT of World War II) and
minesweepers whose collective speed of advance was five knots. For this
reason, *La Grandière*, which could make 12 knots on all boilers and a
fair wind, was selected to shepherd them onward.

An amphibious assault, most complicated of all operations in war,
ordinarily demands painstaking rehearsal. For Inchon, time permitted no
such luxury. (Speaking wryly of his amphibian tractor battalion, O. P.

Smith later said that when the amtracs dipped into the water off Blue Beach on D-day, "That was the rehearsal.") The transports bearing the Marines from the West Coast did not begin reaching Japan until August 28, and the last ship docked on September 3.[5]

The landing force—that is to say, the 1st Marine Division—mounted out from Kobe and (the brigade's units) Pusan. Their transports, the assault shipping, were, except for some Japanese-manned LSTs, U. S. Navy entirely. The 7th Division and X Corps troops mounted mainly from Yokohama; having no assault landing to make, these embarked in MSTS vessels or chartered merchantmen. As always in an amphibious operation, the ships of the attack force were divided into movement groups according to speed and roles, sailing from different ports, proceeding by different routes at carefully regulated speeds so as to reach the objective, without getting in each other's way, by the time when needed. To arrange all this, together with the plans for the assault itself, is no small matter: when the aircraft carrier *Boxer* entered Sasebo to pick up her copies of the operation plans, she was greeted by 185 pounds of secret and top-secret documents which had to be hoisted aboard in a cargo net.[6]

Although not hoisted in with cargo nets, still another important component of the expedition was embarking along with the troops. Eighty-six correspondents, assigned to 19 ships, representing (besides U. S. media), journals of France, the United Kingdom, the British Empire, Scandinavia and Taiwan, were covering Inchon. To serve and yet curb this mettlesome crew (including such names as Jim Lucas, Howard Handleman, Carl Mydans, Joseph Alsop, Bill Blair, Homer Bigart, Keyes Beech, and Marguerite Higgins) Joint Task Force 7 alone had 17 PIOs, besides an even larger delegation of Army information officers with X Corps. One merchant ship assigned to the 7th Division happened to be SS *American Press;* considering the scope of press arrangements for Inchon, perhaps she should have been set aside as a headquarters ship for the correspondents.[7]

While the press corps in the Far East were bidding farewell to the GHQ Officers' Club and the Correspondents' Club in Tokyo, their colleagues in Washington were having a saturnalia at the expense of Harry S. Truman.

Irked by mounting Congressional pressure and White House mail, all to the effect that the Marine Corps was getting less than a square deal at the hands of the administration, President Truman rounded on

Representative Gordon L. McDonough, who had the temerity to suggest that the Marine Commandant should be a member of the JCS. In a testy letter of August 29, 1950, the President (no doubt echoing sentiments he had imbibed from his adviser, Fleet Admiral W. D. Leahy, no Marine admirer) dismissed the Marines as "the Navy's police force" and went on to say, "They have a propaganda machine that is almost equal to Stalin's."

On September 5—when, in the Far East, the Marines were girding for battle and, in Washington, the Marine Corps League was holding its annual convention—the story broke. Public reaction hit Blair House like the Johnstown flood. By five next afternoon, President Truman sent for General Cates and handed him a written apology: "I sincerely regret the unfortunate choice of language which I used. . . ." Next day, arm in arm with Cates (after General Bradley had glumly attempted to dissuade him), Truman manfully faced the Marine Corps League and set things right.

For the 1st Marine Division, the episode was a final spur to valor and glory. In General Cates's view, it was one of the luckiest things that ever happened to the Corps.

Aside from the fact that everything connected with the embarkation had to be done at a dead run with no rehearsals and no time for mistakes or false starts, two big problems confronted the landing force: transshipping the West Coast contingent (some of which had crossed the Pacific in merchantmen) to the transports and LSTs from which they would land; and (an unforeseen, last-minute contribution by Navy Secretary Francis P. Matthews) transferring to noncombatant duty every enlisted Marine whose age was less than eighteen. With ten days to go until D-day, this political propitiation of Mom cost the 1st Division more than 500 trained Marines and caused severe headaches at every level, even though it did insure that none of "our boys" would be shot at Inchon unless he was eighteen.

While embarkation arrangements for the brigade troops at Pusan were excellent, their problems—including the seventeen-year-olds—were most pressing of all. General Craig's brigade was, as we have seen, detached from Eighth Army on the stroke of midnight, September 5. On that dark night, in a streaming rain with no letup, the 1st and 3d Battalions, 5th Marines, in actual combat up to the moment of relief, were relieved in the front lines by Army troops, mud-marched for four miles to truck convoys in the rear, and jolted their way to Masan. Their shipping must sail for Inchon on the morning of the 13th; even at this late hour the rank and file and most of the officers had no idea where their next battle would be.

Leader that he was, the brigade commander put first things first. As the weary troops reached Pusan, they found not only clean clothes and a roof but, in Korea's humid heat, a warehouse full of iced beer, bought from copious Army stocks with Marine post exchange funds.

The whispered night relief in the front lines, the weary slog through the mud, the truck columns winding rearward, the imminence of another battle in some unknown place—all this might have been France in 1918 (where the 5th Marines fought from the Chemin des Dames to the Rhine), rather than Korea 32 years later. In the style of France (but even there, the Marine brigade had 20 days after Belleau Wood to refit for Soissons) these Marines had just six days in which to reorganize, re-equip, absorb replacements to fill battle's gaps, embark in their appointed shipping, learn what and where the next battle was and how they would fight it—and supervise the same process for 3,000 new Korean Marines.[8]

Despite problems of his own, General Smith well knew what the brigade was up against, and found time to say so in a hurried note to Craig on September 8:

> I appreciate the beating you are taking in coming out of action and mounting out. Only Marines could do what you are doing. We had a narrow squeak in getting you at all. We had 100 percent backing of the Navy in finally putting it across. . . . The Brigade has done a splendid job in South Korea and we are all proud of you. You have put the rest of us on the spot. . . . I am looking forward to seeing you on Wolmi Do.

With the same number of days before D-day, General Smith had one last X Corps improvisation to contend with: on September 9, he was visited, on General Almond's instructions, by Brigadier General Henry I. Hodes, USA, of the 7th Division. Hodes presented a scheme to have an infantry battalion of the 7th Division land on Wolmi Do on the evening tide of D-day (at the same time and over the same beach already scheduled for two battalions of the Marine division artillery), "borrow" tanks from the Marines, and "barrel down the road" (the phrase was Hodes's) in a deep thrust through pitch-darkness to take the high ground south of

Seoul, some 20 miles inland. Aside from interrupting the artillery's landing and the fact that the landing force had ample work for all tanks, it was logistically out of the question to support an isolated force of this kind, and General Smith said so. (As things turned out, it was two days after D-day before the unit in question got ashore, and several days later—definitely not barreling—before it got abreast of the 1st Marines as ordered.)[9]

The man-made problems of mounting out should have been enough, but nature took a hand as well. September is the typhoon season in Asiatic waters, and on September 3 Typhoon Jane, screeching in on 100-knot winds with 40-foot waves, put four feet of water over docks covered with cargo, parted $2\frac{1}{2}$-inch wire hawsers, tore seven ships from their moorings, carried away a 200-ton crane, and nearly capsized the ship carrying the landing force signal gear. The 24 hours required to tidy up after Jane was 24 hours' lost time from a schedule with no time to spare.

There is a Japanese saying that when you have one typhoon, another follows within ten days. Seven days on the heels of Jane, a storm-hunter aircraft spotted Kezia; the weatherman said she would hit Kobe on the 12th. This meant Admiral Doyle must have his ships at sea by the 11th, even though the embarkation schedule ran through the 12th. Could this be done? Answer: it was done. At 1030 on the 11th, after the last transport had sailed, *Mount McKinley* put out from Kobe, wearing Admiral Doyle's blue flag, butting her way southwest into mountainous seas and gales of wind.

Admiral Doyle's destination was not Inchon, at least not yet. General MacArthur, accompanied by five other generals, aides and suite ("They all wanted to travel in the light of the sun," said Doyle), had determined to observe his battle from the amphibious command ship and was going down to Kyushu, where *Mount McKinley* was to embark them. When, on August 28, he learned of this decision—in the Dai Ichi Building it must have seemed no more than hailing a staff car—"Admiral Doyle," wrote O. P. Smith, "was rightfully concerned."

Besides diverting the flagship from her station with the attack force, losing precious hours working in and out of harbor and docking, there was only so much space in the ship. An amphibious command ship is not a royal yacht: she is built for specific functions, with accommodations and work space—skimpy at best—for the large staff of officer and enlisted experts who must coordinate the landing. Every square foot of deck space and every bunk (not a few in rotation around the clock) has its use. Where and how he was to sleep, feed, and keep from underfoot, nine senior officers plus a coterie of the General's favorite correspondents might well give the admiral cause for concern.

On the other hand, oblivious of the ship's stringent space limitations, MacArthur and his staff considered *Mount McKinley* as an advance command post afloat for Far East Command. From her bridge, Douglas MacArthur proposed to be the first (and to date, only) U. S. unified commander to take the field tactically.

The original plan had been for the General to fly to Fukuoka, which has both airfield and port, and join the flagship there. But Typhoon Kezia, which had upset other plans, imposed its will even on MacArthur. To beat Kezia, the party left Haneda Airport in *Scap* (acronym for "Supreme Commander Allied Powers"), the General's new Constellation. In company was his former plane, *Bataan,* loaded chockablock with favored members of the press. (MacArthur had called in this select group and announced, "I'm going on a little operation and I'd like to have you boys with me.") Departing on September 12 for Itazuke, on Kyushu, the entourage faced an 86-mile drive to Sasebo, better sheltered and more suitable for embarkation but without an airfield.

For the ride down via dusty, beautiful, bumpy back-country Japanese roads, the General asked General Shepherd to join him while Almond sat up front with the driver. As the talk turned to and fro ("MacArthur made himself most agreeable," General Shepherd noted in his journal), the General spoke of his tussle with the JCS to get the Marine division, remarking that, "for political reasons," the Army was loath to let the Marines get into the war. Then the cavalcade pulled to the roadside and an MP strode smartly up to the sedan, clashed heels, saluted and announced, "It's a pee stop, General." Untroubled by the exigencies of lesser men, the General replied, "Thanks. I don't need it." ("MacArthur had remarkable kidneys," commented INS's Howard Handlemen, who caught the moment for history.)

At Sasebo, which they reached after dark, the General's arrival took the place by surprise. A large party was going full blast in the officers' mess prior to departure of ships to the wars, and some difficulty was encountered in getting anyone to take care of the group during the two hour wait for *Mount McKinley*'s arrival.

We finally found one young officer and a CPO [General Wright later recalled] who apparently had scorned the grape and, with their assistance, managed to scrounge up some sandwiches and coffee and some seats at the club.[10]

Admiral Doyle's passage had not been an easy one. The seas outside Kobe were the worst he had ever encountered in a ship of *Mount McKinley*'s size. Even the redoubtable Captain Virginius R. ("Gus") Roane, commodore of the APAs and AKAs, despairing of a way through the typhoon, had come about. With 35 years at sea behind him, Doyle pondered the weather map at length and consulted with his aerologist.

I felt [he later wrote] there was a reasonable chance that the typhoon would curve north and pass along the east coast of Korea and that it was worth the risk. I must admit that I applied a little body English.

Thus, when Doyle made contact with the transport group on the 12th —while MacArthur was making his way to Sasebo—he ordered them up into the storm in the flagship's track, flying that signal which antedates even Nelson: *"Follow the movements of the senior ship."* Without this action there would be no landing force at Inchon on D-day.

Without equally bold seamanship from USS *Conserver* this same morning, there assuredly would have been no headquarters, 2d Battalion, 1st Marines, at Inchon. Buffeted by 90-knot winds blowing a full gale, *Conserver* came upon *LST 1048,* port engine dead, wallowing as only an LST can, with a shipload of seasick Marines and their battalion commander (Lieutenant Colonel Allan Sutter). Repair was out of the question— main blower gone and no spares on board—so *Conserver* got to windward and floated down a hawser, *1048*'s boatswain's mates and forecastle gang chocked it down, and on to Inchon they staggered.

When *Mount McKinley* reached Sasebo, turned hard to port inside the entrance and made her way alongside, Generals MacArthur, Almond, Wright, and A. P. Fox and Courtney Whitney came on board, together with aides and reporters. General Shepherd and Colonel Krulak also boarded. Doyle gave MacArthur his own quarters and retired to the emergency cabin on the bridge; the rest of the generals were double-bunked, two to a room. Krulak said, "You had to be a captain or a colonel even to get a bunk, and two stripes or below couldn't even get a cot." Admiral Doyle ordered that O. P. Smith was to retain the landing force commander's cabin and mess, no matter how many stars were embarked. Then the lines were cast off, *Mount McKinley* put out into the waning typhoon and headed for the Yellow Sea. It was the 191st anniversary of Quebec.[11]

At breakfast next morning, following the invariable rule of a Navy mess, Doyle took the admiral's seat at the head of the table, courteously beckoning MacArthur to the guest's place of honor on his right. As if unseeing, the General moved to the opposite, theoretically junior end, seated himself and presided graciously. His Irish sense of humor tickled by the General's aplomb, Doyle reflected, "Where Murphy sits is the head of the table." And so it was.

During the forenoon—it was D—2, and already the advance force destroyers were shelling Wolmi Do—there was a tour of the ship for the visitors. This was a device of Admiral Doyle's, with the object of suggesting some of the complexities of an assault landing. A command ship, or "AGC," such as *Mount McKinley,* is an intricately tiered mechanism, ranging from bowels packed with hundreds of radio and relay positions to photo darkrooms, a printshop capable of producing four-color maps and charts, joint operations room jumbled with display boards, radiotelephones, H-tables for air and gunfire controllers, and air-defense gear flickering with fifty PPI-scopes relaying information from the ship's myriad radars.

All this the generals saw; then the correspondents were briefed. Russell Brines, Earnest Hoberecht, Howard Handleman, Roy McCartney, Carl Mydans, Percy Wood, Richard Rendell, Julius Zenier, Gordon Walker, and Charles Jones—AP, UP, INS, Reuters, ABC, NBC, *Life, Chicago Tribune, Christian Science Monitor*—all sat around the green baize wardroom tables while MacArthur and Almond expounded the battles to come. As described by O. P. Smith, "This briefing covered the broad strategical plan in which the landing was merely a small incident. . . ." The part best remembered by Howard Handleman was MacArthur's exposition of his strategy:

> We could commit 150 million Americans, and they could still put in four Asiatics for every American. I therefore made the decision I would not fight a war to the enemy's strength, but would fight a war to my strength. We have devised a plan where we can get away from his advantages and use our advantages. . . . If the Chinese do intervene, our air will turn the Yalu River into the bloodiest stream in all history.[12]

Aboard other ships there were less exalted briefings. Officers and NCOs studied maps and photographs, drivers checked the waterproofing on their vehicles, weapons were field-stripped, cleaned and oiled for the hundredth time, coxswains and boat engineers tinkered with their LCVPs and LCMs. Once the storm abated, physical drills shook the cataleptic pallor off Marines who had ridden out a typhoon in bunks four deep at the bottom of a battened hold. Recognition drills on Russian aircraft and tanks were held daily. In one Marine fighting squadron a thoughtful CO had the surgeon talk to all hands on VD and venereal prophylaxis.

Intelligence briefings were not always cheerful; it is not the S-2's function to be a pollyanna. After one such session for the field officers of the 1st Marines, Colonel Puller, the regimental commander, cut his intelligence officer short: [13]

> We'll find out what's on the beach when we get there. There's not necessarily a gun in every hole. There's too much goddamned pessimism in this regiment. Most times, professional soldiers have to wait 25 years or more for a war, but here we are, with only five years' wait for this one. . . . We're going to work at our trade for a little while. We live by the sword and if necessary we'll be ready to die by the sword. Good luck. I'll see you ashore.

From home, besides other news, came one cheering item. Defense Secretary Louis Johnson had resigned. Defense Gain Is Seen in Johnson Exit, headlined the New York *Times,* above a September 14 Hanson Baldwin article which stated:

> Mr. Johnson was never fitted by character, intellect, or vision for the job. Mr. Forrestal was a man of intellectual humility. Mr. Johnson was one of intellectual arrogance. Forrestal was a selfless public servant; Johnson was a selfish public servant. Forrestal possessed moral integrity and he was not a politician. Johnson often appeared to be careless of the truth and he was preeminently a politician.

With George C. Marshall as the new Secretary of Defense, all hands felt easier.

Air Operations

As the amphibious ships made their way south of Kyushu through Van Diemen Strait, the air effort stepped up against both coasts of Korea. Between September 5 and 10, planes from HMS *Triumph* and USS

Badoeng Strait attacked roads, railroads, supply points, and the electric power system between Kunsan and the 38th parallel. On the 8th, USS *Sicily* joined up. Train-shooting provided a change of pace and considerable sport for the Marine squadrons, VMF-214 and VMF-323, whose Corsairs had been the mainstay of the brigade's air support in the south: putting a rocket into the boiler of a steam locomotive highballing south from Pyongyang was considerably more exhilarating than peacetime gunnery at El Toro. Seoul, Haeju, Pyongyang, Kaesong and Kumchon took the brunt. Amid these high jinks, Second Lieutenant D. H. Cole shot the "Bing-Ding's" 10,000th landing, on return from an interdiction strike; but, on the business side, Inchon got 36 sorties, while Wolmi Do received 42.

The last day the escort carriers were on station, the 10th, both Marine squadrons armed with double loads of napalm: two 150-gallon tanks per plane, 95,000 pounds in all. Then every Corsair that could fly took off for Wolmi Do and tumbled its load of fire onto the wooded seaward (south and west) faces of the island.[14]

While the ship-based Marine squadrons worked close in, Task Force 77, Rear Admiral E. C. Ewen's fast carriers, commenced sealing off the Inchon-Seoul objective area. At the same time, a precaution against unlooked-for surprises, the Navy's Panther jets, still something of a novelty in those days, raked every known Communist airfield northward up the coast. Although Admiral Ewen and two officers of his staff had only 40 minutes' briefing on the Inchon operation, this sufficed for the spirited fast carriers *Valley Forge* and *Philippine Sea,* both of which, not to mention their admiral, had been hammering the *In Min Gun* since the early days of the war. To these naval aviators, whose backs, like the Marines', had been against the wall ever since unification, the Korean War offered an opportunity to prove, as it seemed to them, the unsurpassed quality of U. S. naval aviation, and its unique capabilities in all types of precision attack. With Inchon but two days ahead, they were on their mettle.[15]

On D—1, the 14th, the escort carriers were back from Sasebo, replenished and rearmed. While the Fleet Air Arm pilots of HMS *Triumph* jabbed at Kunsan to keep enemy intelligence guessing (they hoped), the Marine squadrons from *Badoeng Strait* and *Sicily* lashed Inchon and Kimpo. As a dividend Admiral Ewen backed them up with three hefty sorties, each of 16 ADs, the superb single-engine carrier attack planes that could carry more bombs than a B-17 and that 17 years later were still workhorses of Vietnam.

Feints and Demonstrations

"Security," mused Admiral Andrewes after the operation, "was sadly lacking . . ."

> I do not believe, however [he wrote], that such a plan could possibly have been produced and put into operation so quickly had not a huge army of people worked at it, and there is no doubt that in one respect the enemy must have been completely wrong. He cannot possibly have guessed at the strength of the blow. That had to be seen to be believed.

Although the Tokyo press club's nickname for the forthcoming landing was "Operation Common Knowledge" (and Syngman Rhee had blurted, "We are about ready to go"), General MacArthur had one advantage, and this was the inherent improbability of Inchon as an objective. Admiral Struble's air plan was shaped, as we have seen, to maintain enemy uncertainty as to where the blow would fall. (That a blow was poised could scarcely be denied: "An amphibious landing on the Korean coast well behind the enemy's front lines is an obvious and possible strategy," the New York *Times* remarked on September 14.) In line with HMS *Triumph*'s Kunsan strikes the same day, the Marine brigade, mounting out at Pusan, were given an open-air lecture, complete with p.a. system for the benefit of Korean onlookers, on the beaches, terrain and defenses of Kunsan. To lend still further realism to the Kunsan idea, Far East Air Force had, since September 5, been bombing and strafing railroads, highways, junctions and bridges within a 30-mile radius of the port, while on the 11th heavy bombers of the Air Force delivered a major bombardment of military installations at Kunsan.

On the other side of Korea, a cruiser, destroyers, and the august *Missouri,* called to war from summer midshipmen's cruise in the Atlantic, took part in an unplanned diversion on September 14 and 15. Without thinking to let Admiral Joy know what was afoot, General Walker's headquarters attempted to land 800 Korean guerrillas from a Korean LST at Samchok, due east of Inchon, on the east coast. The LST broached, all was revealed (even, eventually, to the Navy), and five days of shooting and air strikes were needed to cover the withdrawal.

Meanwhile (based on a suggestion by Colonel Bowser), on the night of September 12–13 Colonel Ely's special operations company, together with highly trained Royal Marines of 41 Commando, under Lieutenant E. G. D. Pounds, RM, landed from the British frigate *Whitesand Bay* and hit the waterfront of Kunsan, where a confused fire fight resulted in three American dead but helped to maintain the Kunsan illusion.

A further contribution to enemy unrest in these waters was a series of ROK Navy raids and landings—code-named Operation *Lee,* in honor of the aggressive Korean naval officer who commanded ROKN *PC-703* (the ship that had landed Lieutenant Clark and his team on Yonghung). Commencing in late August, Lieutenant Commander Lee (forever after known as "Inchon" Lee) first hit Tokchok To, an island near the mouth of Flying Fish Channel. His next objective, on August 19, was Yonghung (Clark's island). Then, on September 8, he landed ROK troops on Yonpyong Do, south of Haeju. And, as D-day approached, *PC-703* harried the sampans that crept among the coastal mud flats.[16]

"... Enemy Vessels Approaching Inchon"

On September 10, when "Inchon" Lee, bold as Drake at Cadiz, sailed right into Haeju Bay, he caught a North Korean sailboat and put a 3-inch shell into her. Laden with Russian mines, she blew up with a thunderous crash that was heard for miles around. A week earlier, USS *McKean,* destroyer, on patrol southwest of Chinnampo, had spotted seven mines. Haeju was the next port down from Chinnampo, as well as the next up from Inchon. The mine problem was rapidly ceasing to be academic, though how much so was yet to be disclosed, for no one knew yet that, on August 29, a shipment of Russian magnetic mines had left Chinnampo for Inchon. All that was keeping them out of the water was one of those mix-ups which are the frustration of armies: whoever packed the mines had left out cable harnesses.[17] These the supply officer had on requisition.

At seven in the morning the cruisers and destroyers entered Flying Fish Channel. The day was D—2, September 13. Before dawn, wearing the flag of Admiral Struble, *Rochester* had joined the darkened, radio-silent column and formed on *Toledo,* flagship of Rear Admiral John M. Higgins's Gunfire Support Group. Astern of *Rochester* were HMS *Jamaica* and *Kenya,* British light cruisers. Ahead were five destroyers: *Mansfield, DeHaven, Lyman K. Swenson, Collett,* and *Henderson.* A sixth destroyer, *Gurke,* broke across the dark western horizon and cut into the formation; amid a flurry of blinker signals she closed *Toledo*'s starboard quarter, expertly sent over a heaving line, and transferred a canvas pouch. This was "the late dope": last-minute target information, yesterday's aerial photos, and the latest intelligence, obtained only two hours earlier from *Valley Forge,* flagship of the fast carriers. Then the bombardment group turned east toward Flying Fish Channel as the sun, red and round, broke through the gray haze of mist and woodsmoke from cooking fires ashore.

The tide was still ebbing as the leading destroyers poked into the channel. At full low as they passed Palmi Do, it would be flooding when they reached bombardment stations at Inchon. Here was another of the infinite expert calculations required to make the operation succeed: with scant turning room up-channel, the rising tide would keep the anchored destroyers stemming it, bows downstream and full broadsides uncovered toward the enemy throughout the shoot. When the moment came to retire, even to slip anchor if need be, they would be headed out.

Overhead, covering the advance, were the Panther jets of Task Force 77's combat air patrol, or "CAP." In addition, a strike group of heavily armed ADs had reported in to Admiral Higgins at 0700. Aboard the destroyers final preparations were in progress: additional boilers being lit off and put on the line for full power on short notice; fenders and towing gear being rigged out in case a cripple needed help; repair parties being armed, not with cutlasses but with rifles (the world's most ludicrous sight: a sailor with a rifle), so as to repel boarders or suicide sampans; then an early steak dinner for all hands before the covering air strike and the clangor of General Quarters.[18]

Now the time was at hand to see whether Admiral Doyle and General Smith had been right in their insistence on a methodical naval gunfire bombardment. Would the destroyers goad the gunners of the 918th Coast Artillery into disclosing themselves?

Meanwhile, there was another disclosure. At 1145, as *Mansfield,* first in column, approached Pukchangjaso, an islet below Palmi Do, the port bridge-wing lookout sang out, "Mines!" Moments later the same report came from *DeHaven,* next in column. Riding on the muddy surface, exposed by extreme low tide, were the ugly black casings of 17 Russian contact mines.

Momentarily, perhaps because it was so ominous, the sight was unbelievable; *DeHaven*'s skipper, Commander O. B. Lundgren, a mine-warfare expert, had no doubts and quickly confirmed *Mansfield*'s tentative report. The three leading ships opened fire with rifles and 40mm and 20mm guns, seconds later there was a thudding explosion and geyser of mud—"After that, nobody doubted me any further," recollected Lundgren.[19]

Here was a turn of events, conceivably the very worst turn of events, for which preparation had not been made. The few minesweepers in the Far East had been pressed into service as escorts, and were far behind with the transports rather than ahead of the destroyers in the Salee River. For the four cruisers, there was no problem: their bombardment stations —at very long range for such work—were down-channel just below the mines. For the destroyers it was another matter; if more mines lay in the channel higher up, they would soon find out. Meanwhile, Captain Halle C. Allen, USN, the destroyer squadron commander, detached his rear ship, *Henderson,* with orders to destroy the mines by gunfire, and pressed on in the brilliant morning sunshine toward Wolmi Do.

Fortunately the channel was clear. Douglas MacArthur's luck had held. What had happened was that, after the British had shelled Wolmi Do on September 5 and 6, using the area now mined, the North Koreans had planted two fields of contact mines in case the Royal Navy came back. These fields were also located so as to commence closure of the junction of Flying Fish and East Channels. Later, when the harness cables arrived for the more dangerous ground mines, general mining would proceed at Inchon, and the cork could be put into the bottleneck between Pukchangjaso and Palmi Do.

As the cruisers' anchors clattered down from the hawseholes and the destroyers moved up, the ADs from the fast carriers shrieked down on Wolmi Do. At headquarters in Inchon the defense commander reached for a message blank and his ink block. Quickly brushing in the characters, he wrote:[20]

> Ten enemy vessels approaching Inchon. Many aircraft bombing Wolmi Do. Every indication enemy will carry out a landing. All units my command are directed to be ready for battle; all units will be stationed in their assigned positions so they may throw back enemy forces when they attempt their landing operation.

The report was a good one. Alas for the Communists, there is no evidence that higher headquarters accepted it. In any case, even if the harness cables had arrived that very afternoon, time had run out.

At 1242, *Gurke*'s anchor went down. Six minutes later, three miles upstream, north of Wolmi Do and Inchon, *Mansfield* anchored at the other end of the line. It might have been—in a very real sense it was— a visit by the Fleet. Aboard sampans in the harbor and the channel, white-robed Koreans in black hats stared at the warships as the 5-inch mounts and directors trained out to port. Even though *Philippine Sea*'s AD Skyraiders slugged and swooped at Wolmi Do, a Los Angeles *Times* correspondent, observing from the bridge of *Rochester,* said the island "looked like a picnickers' paradise, green-wooded and serene."

A signal—"Commence scheduled mission"—fluttered at the dip from *Mansfield*'s starboard yardarm. In 12 minutes Commodore Allen would two-block his signal just as the last AD pulled out of her dive. Then the destroyers would open fire. At the root of the Wolmi Do causeway, beside a railroad siding, Commander Lundgren could see a pyramid of black cylinders—Russian contact mines. That was how close it had been.

From *DeHaven*'s director, Lieutenant Arthur T. White, USN, the gunnery officer, could see something else. On the tongue of land north of Red Beach in Inchon proper, a gun was being run out and uncovered. "Captain!" he reported over the battle phones. "They're running out a gun. . . . Captain! They're loading the gun. . . . Captain! Request permission to open fire."

"Permission granted," came the word, and seven minutes early, before the anchor windlass detail could clear the forecastle, *DeHaven*'s 5-inch guns began the battle. The forward mount's blast nearly blew the chief boatswain's mate overboard while he was stopping down the starboard anchor. It also disconcerted Commodore Allen, a man who went by the book and kept a weather eye on how things might look to higher authority. But Lundgren had a good excuse, or so Admiral Struble thought when he heard the story, and there the matter rested.[21]

Just as *DeHaven* ceased fire (target destroyed), the other four ships opened. Firing deliberately, from ranges as close as 1,300 yards, under the muzzles of masked enemy guns, the destroyers commenced to probe.

For just eight minutes the Communist gunners held fire. Then they took the bait. A 76mm gun barked and flashed from a cave on the slope of Wolmi Do. Seconds later a high-velocity antitank shell hulled *Collett.*

"A necklace of gun-flashes sparkled around the waist of the island," reported the Associated Press man (Relman Morin) aboard *Rochester.* "The flashes were reddish gold and they came so fast that soon the entire slope was sparkling with pinpoints of fire."

Within the next few minutes intense automatic-weapons and mortar fire were directed at the ships above Wolmi Do (*Mansfield* and *De-Haven*) while *Swenson, Collett* and *Gurke* (off Wolmi Do or immediately downstream) came under hot fire from the 76mm guns on Wolmi and heavier weapons on Observatory Hill in Inchon.

Collett took the punishment. Five hits by armor-piercing shell, at close range, smashed into her hull. The wardroom was hit (this, a dud,

came to rest on the transom), fuel lines were cut, the plotting room damaged and the main-battery computer put out of action, guns had to go
into local control, and old-style pointer fire, telescope cross-hairs on the
targets, kept the ship fighting. Three minutes after *Collett* took her first
hit, *Swenson,* next upstream, came first under mortar and heavy small-
arms fire, then from the 918th Coast Artillery's heavily revetted 76mm
guns on Wolmi Do's northwest face. *Gurke,* below *Collett,* was straddled
by an enemy salvo at 1330, then by another and another. At 1346,
within the space of two minutes, three shells hit home: a 40mm gun was
knocked out, a torpedo tube jammed, a stack punctured—all superficial
to the ship's fighting power.

As the enemy showed his hand, the destroyers hit back. Between 1253,
when *DeHaven* opened fire, and 1347, when Commodore Allen signaled
retirement, they fired 998 rounds of 5-inch onto Wolmi Do and parts of
Inchon. Now, with the hornet's nest buzzing, it was time to head down-
channel, and in reverse order, under full power, the "sitting ducks" swept
through the shell splashes, dueling the enemy with after mounts as forward
guns ceased to bear. *DeHaven* and *Mansfield,* which had been above the
coast artillery arcs of fire, ran the batteries at 25 knots, swamping small
craft and sampans with their bow waves and nearly broaching *Henderson* as they raced by, fantails low, guns still blazing and black smoke pouring from stacks.

Although *Swenson*'s bridge had rung up turns for 31 knots, 23 was all
she could get in the muddy shallows. With Blue Beach two miles abeam
at 1402, she came under fire—a departing salute—from the battery on
Observatory Hill. A two-gun salvo hit close aboard, 25 yards to port.
On the ship's 40mm director, a junior lieutenant two years out of
Annapolis was ripped by fragments and fell dead. His name was David
H. Swenson. He was the nephew of Captain Lyman K. Swenson, USN,
killed in the South Pacific, the destroyer's namesake.

The salvo that killed Lieutenant Swenson was the enemy's final blow.
Now the reconnaissance mission was accomplished—"Successfully, the
Navy will say," wrote a correspondent. "Gloriously is a better word."

Below Palmi Do the cruisers opened up with 8-inch and 6-inch guns
to cover the destroyers' withdrawal. As they were anywhere from seven
to ten miles from Inchon and Wolmi Do, and air-spotting arrangements
had been badly muddled, the heavy ships' counterbattery fire, while loud
and rapid, was far from precise or accurate. Then the planes from the
fast carriers raked Wolmi Do again and the destroyers' dead (1 only,

Lieutenant Swenson) and wounded (8) were transferred by whaleboat to *Toledo,* whose sick bay could best handle them. As the planes headed out to sea, the cruisers fired for another half hour and stood down Flying Fish Channel for the night.[22]

Off the channel entrance with deep water and sea room, the fire support group took night dispositions and prepared to darken ship. In the twilight, while there was still light to come alongside, Admiral Higgins's barge and Commodore Allen's gig closed *Rochester* for conference with Admiral Struble.

Two matters dominated the discussion. Point 1—the 918th Coast Artillery had amply justified the apprehensions of Admiral Doyle and General Smith. Obviously Inchon was defended—Wolmi Do most evidently so—and those defenses were far from neutralized. A full day's work ("a real working-over," said Struble's report) would be required tomorrow for the destroyers, cruisers and Task Force 77's aircraft. And on that last subject, air spotting had better improve—communications between planes and ships had been terrible, and the pilots (theoretically supposed to have basic qualifications as gunfire spotters) were wholly unfamiliar with the process.

Point 2—mines—nagged at everyone who had seen those shapes between Pukchangjaso and Palmi Do, let alone those who, like Commander Lundgren, had actually observed piled mines ashore. Admiral Struble could well remember a conversation[23] in Tokyo when MacArthur had said, "You're confident, aren't you?" and he had replied, "Yes— the worst hazard, except for large Russian air intervention, would be mines." Now nothing could be done, mines or no, but to send an urgent dispatch telling the minesweepers to abandon their charges and hasten forward. Just before midnight the meeting broke up. By the time Higgins and Allen were back on their flagships, it was D—1.

In the morning, again screened with planes from the carriers (and this time with a fleet salvage tug in company), the cruisers and destroyers stood in toward Inchon. Out in the channel mouth, at eight bells, the formation hove to, colors at half-mast, Marine guards paraded on the cruisers, crew at quarters in all ships, while in *Toledo* the boatswain's mate piped the word, "All hands to bury the dead." After the padre's simple, immemorial sentences of committal, the volleys from the Marines and the poignant strains of "Taps," Lieutenant Swenson, in a sailor's shroud of canvas, was given to the deep. Ten minutes later column was formed and the force was steaming toward the enemy.

At 1116, as the destroyers picked their way up the Salee River, the cruisers opened fire. This time the spotters were on station and their radios worked. Even so—the *In Min Gun* still had plenty of fight— a shore battery promptly took on HMS *Kenya,* the inshore cruiser, prompting Captain Brock, her CO, to remark, "The enemy gunners were either very brave or very stupid. . . ." In either case they paid for their bravery (or stupidity) by a heavy air strike as the destroyers closed in. One *Valley Forge* pilot reported that there was no more vegetation left on Wolmi Do:[24] "The whole island looked like it had been shaved."

There were no niceties today about destroyers opening fire. Again *De-Haven* opened the ball: at 1242 she took on one of the cave-mounted 76mm guns on Wolmi Do's southwest face. Four minutes later, *Swenson*'s 5-inch mounts went to work against a target from yesterday—a gun emplacement on the west tip of the island. Reflecting her lack of familiarity with the target areas, *Henderson,* which had replaced *Collett,* waited until 1305 to be sure she had a target, and then joined in. For 75 minutes the destroyers hammered away, and it was 40 minutes before they drew a feeble reply. As they withdrew, the shore batteries remained silent; the five destroyers had fired 1,732 rounds at Wolmi Do—barely less than the number of 5-inch shells that hit Omaha Beach before the Normandy landings.

Overhead, the air spotters (Marine pilots who knew how to shoot) brought in the cruisers' guns for a useful hour's work on military targets now disclosed in Inchon (Admiral Struble had underscored that he wanted no indiscriminate bombardment of the crowded town) and on battered Wolmi Do. Then, covering the fire-support ships' retirement, the airplanes went to work again. The final report, from one of the Marine pilots of VMF-323, said Wolmi Do was "one worthless piece of real estate."[25] So the island looked from the air. How would it look to the 3d Battalion, 5th Marines?

4   *ABOUT AS PLANNED*

The Navy and Marines have never shone more brightly.
DOUGLAS MACARTHUR, September 15, 1950

THE DAY BEFORE the landing, as *Mount McKinley* steamed north by east up the Yellow Sea, General MacArthur was in great form. With Kezia behind, even the Army officers had regained their appetites, and lunch in Admiral Doyle's mess—iced tea and purple fruit drink, chilled olives and celery in relish trays, jellied consommé, an entrée, chopped tossed salad with bottled dressing, ice cream and coffee—was the last unhurried meal most of those present would eat for some days. When the white-coated stewards had cleared the table, passed cigars and cigarettes, and refilled coffee cups, the General held forth.

Averell Harriman?—very likely the next Secretary of State: many social graces, a good troubleshooter and pacifier, but not enough iron in his veins. . . . Chiang Kai-shek?—Mr. Truman detests him cordially and will never give him any support. . . . Louis Johnson's resignation?— "Everybody seemed happy," recorded General Shepherd; MacArthur thought George Marshall's choice a good one. One Army general ventured that Eisenhower had failed the Army in leadership?—Not so, the General said, and rather surprisingly came to Ike's rescue.

So the talk went for more than an hour. To General Shepherd "it was a most illuminating conversation." O. P. Smith (perhaps because he had more on his mind) found "the pomposity of his pronouncements a little wearing." Afterward, following the fixed regime of many years, the General retired for his siesta.[1]

Aboard a much humbler flagship, so small that her name was merely a number—USS *LSMR-401*, a bombardment rocket ship—there appeared a cheering sight just about the hour that General MacArthur was stirring. From the bridge, a large smoke formation was sighted looming high up from behind the horizon, dead on the bearing of Inchon, 65 miles ahead. Commander Clarence T. Doss, Jr., commander of the three rocket ships, had word passed to all hands. The pillar of smoke spoke for itself. "It was welcome news," said Doss.[2]

Night fell—"Dark as the inside of a cow's belly," recollected Captain Sears, in command of the advance attack group headed for Wolmi Do. The advance group (three light transports and an LSD, carrying the 3d Battalion, 5th Marines) was the detachment of fast, maneuverable ships capable of moving up Flying Fish Channel by night and arriving off Wolmi Do at dawn in time for the morning high tide.

Commanded by Lieutenant Colonel Robert D. Taplett, a tall, wiry, dark-haired Marine, the 3d Battalion, 5th Marines, were crammed sardinelike (at 200 per cent capacity, reported one skipper), one company to each of three destroyer escorts rebuilt as light, fast transports. The two assault companies—G and H, the most experienced—were in USS *Diachenko* and *H. A. Bass*, respectively. Taplett's new, third rifle company, I (the battalion had fought through the perimeter with two companies), would land in reserve from USS *Wantuck*. The tanks, vehicles, engineer equipment, shore party gear and battalion headquarters were in Captain Sears's flagship, the LSD *Fort Marion*.

It was past midnight when the ships joined up, a perfect rendezvous amid the blackness, at the entrance to Flying Fish Channel. In the van of the 18-ship column was Commodore Allen with his leading destroyer division—*Mansfield, DeHaven* and *Swenson*, veterans already. Then came Captain Sears and the advance group (*Diachenko, Fort Marion, Wantuck* and *H. A. Bass*). Astern of *Bass*, boxlike, clumsy, wallowing, followed Commander Doss's Rocket Division 11—*LSMR-401, 403,* and *404,* loaded with bombardment rockets, the shotguns of an amphibious assault someone called them. In the second destroyer division, USS *Southerland* now replaced wounded *Collett,* whose plotting room had been wrecked, and then came *Gurke* and *Henderson,* followed by *Mount McKinley,* where Admiral Doyle, General Smith and General MacArthur were up and about for the passage of Flying Fish Channel. In the rear, because they would drop off first in downstream fire-support stations, were the cruisers, Admiral Higgins leading in *Toledo,* then Admiral Struble, on whose back the enterprise now rested, in *Rochester,* and finally the smart, seamanlike British light cruisers *Kenya* and *Jamaica.*

For two dark hours ("Boy! It was a dark night in that channel," said
Lundgren of *DeHaven*) the captains and navigators peered at radar
screens while lookouts could hardly tell sea from sky.[3] Then a welcome
sight showed ahead: a quick flash of light, then another, and still another. . . . *Mansfield*'s quartermaster clicked a stopwatch: at the fortieth
second, the light flashed again, and twice more. There was no mistake.
It was Palmi Do. On the stroke of midnight, Lieutenant Clark had re-
lighted the old French lamp and connected up the batteries. Although
the lookouts couldn't see him in the gloom, he was perched on top of
the lighthouse, wrapped in a blanket, watching the ships file by in the
fitful gleam of the light. So closely kept had been the secret of Clark's
foray that both General MacArthur and General Smith thought the
enemy had left the light burning. To MacArthur it seemed, as he related
in his *Reminiscences,* "We were taking the enemy by surprise. The lights
were not even turned off. I went to my cabin and turned in."[4]

The General had one hour and 33 minutes to sleep before *Mount
McKinley*'s anchor rattled from the hawsepipe at 0508. Up ahead, steering by Palmi Do and the light of fires still burning in Inchon, the
destroyers had reached their now familiar stations. By first light Marine
Corsairs from *Sicily* and *Badoeng Strait* were already commencing runs
on Wolmi Do, and observers on *Mount McKinley*'s bridge could hear
the quick thud-thud-thud of bombs, the ripple of rockets, and tearing
bursts of 20mm strafing.

Up-channel, across from Wolmi Do, Captain Sears positioned his
ships. At 0520, having earlier confirmed that L-hour (the time Taplett's
first wave would hit Green Beach) would be 0630, Admiral Doyle broke
the traditional signal, "Land the landing force." When this signal
reached the yardarm, Marine boat teams commenced embarking, landing craft went into the water, and chaplains stood by embarkation stations to wish the troops well. "It was a beautiful morning," General
Shepherd mused in his journal, "and as the first pink streaks of dawn
broke in the east my thoughts went back to other dawns when I had
watched preparations for similar landings. . . ."

At 0540 the destroyers opened fire. Seconds later (the time of flight
from downstream was longer), 6-inch and 8-inch salvos crashed in from
the cruisers. "I have never seen any better shooting," noted General
Shepherd. "The entire island was smothered with bursting shells from
the cruisers and destroyers."

To this welcome music, as sunrise outlined Wolmi Do, waves of loaded
LCVPs circled in the rendezvous area, less than a mile off Green Beach,

wave commanders watching the control vessel flying a red and white flag at the dip. At 0615, with a tremendous hiss and swoosh and thunderous roar, the rocket ships joined in. Two, lying north of Wolmi Do off Red Beach, began dumping each a thousand 5-inch rockets on the rear, east slopes of Moontip Island, where the North Koreans might have mortars or reserves. The third, *LSMR-403,* belting Green Beach and the high ground to the right, jockeyed against the 3-knot current which had almost dragged her aground, and took station for a special maneuver.

On the control vessel the red flag rose to the yardarm and the leading wave—LCVPs bearing the assault fire teams of Companies G and H, 5th Marines—formed in line. Up to the left, the stubby rocket ship, wreathed in smoke and flame, moved into the boat lane, steaming dead across the bows of the landing craft, scourging Green Beach with rockets and 40mm shell. Now the flag was down and coxswains were steering under full power toward the beach. With two minutes until L-hour, ships' guns suddenly quieted, and down shrieked the Corsairs. Twenty aircraft from VMF-214, led by Major Robert P. Keller, and 18 from VMF-323, with Major Arnold A. Lund in the lead, covered the final run-in of the boats. Only *LSMR-403,* now clear of the boat lane, and four destroyers kept up the fire. As the Marine aircraft hammered the north end of Wolmi Do, the destroyers, shifting to VT-fuzed shell, lashed the Inchon waterfront and forward slope of Observatory Hill with a curtain of air bursts whose wicked crack, boiling black smoke, and rolling clouds of dust and debris churned the town into a foul haze.

At 0633—three minutes late because the airplanes ran a little overtime (no cause for complaint in the landing force)—the first wave touched down. Suddenly there were no bow ramps to shield the crouching Marines—ahead a low seawall backed by a ridge, on the right a smoking, charred, pitted steep hillside which a week ago had been covered with pine and locust. With a grunt and a shout and a few oaths to mask their tenseness the green-clad riflemen burst out of the LCVPs, unlocking the safety catches on their weapons.[5]

The mission of George Company, on the right, was to pivot sharp right and storm Radio Hill, the 351-foot peak of Wolmi Do still marked by its wrecked radio towers. As the company commander, First Lieutenant Robert D. Bohn, breasted his way ashore (he had stepped off the ramp

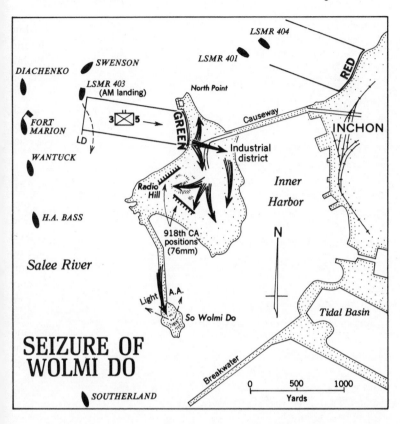

LSMR 404

LSMR 401

SWENSON

DIACHENKO

LSMR 403
(AM landing)

North Point

RED

FORT
MARION

3 ⊠ 5 →

GREEN

Causeway

INCHON

LD

Industrial
district

WANTUCK

Radio
Hill

Inner

Harbor

H.A. BASS

918th CA
positions
(76mm)

N

Salee River

Light

A.A.

So Wolmi Do

Tidal Basin

**SEIZURE OF
WOLMI DO**

Breakwater

0   500   1000

SOUTHERLAND

Yards

into water over his head), he found Second Lieutenant John D. Counselman forming his platoon for the uphill charge, while Lieutenants Lawrence O'Connell and Roger W. Peard, Jr., with the other two platoons,
were preparing to advance along the west shore of the island and seal
off the causeway leading south to So Wolmi Do. There was hardly any
enemy fire—nothing to compare to the shriek and rat-a-tat-tat-tat of the
Corsairs which kept a curtain of cannon fire 50 yards ahead of the
Marines.

How Company, on the left, under Captain Patrick E. Wildman,
attacked straight forward in line of platoons over the low ridge to the
front. Peeling off a couple of squads to clear North Point on the left,
Wildman quickly worked his people to the opposite shore, immediately

blocked the base of the causeway from Inchon, and sent out a team of engineers who laid a field of antitank mines to prevent counterattack from the city. Then Wildman swung his company to the right, too, picking his way through the rocket-shattered Esso compound and industrial facilities along the east shore. Here, too, firing was scattered, desultory and inaccurate.

While the two assault companies moved on their objectives, the LSUs had crunched onto the beach with tanks from the 1st Tank Battalion— six M-26 Pershings, one flame-thrower tank, two tankdozers, and one retriever. While the tanks lurched ashore and stood by for orders, the final wave, with Item, the reserve company, made the debris-strewn beach. Just before, at 0650, Colonel Taplett landed and was greeted within five minutes by the sight of a set of American colors flying from the top of Radio Hill.

The tanks got their first call from Captain Robert A. McMullen, of Company I, which was mopping up North Point in the wake of How. Although the area was supposed to be secured, an enemy platoon had been overlooked on the reverse slope facing back toward Red Beach. Now, the air and naval gunfire neutralization wearing off, they came to life, greeting Item Company's fire teams with a shower of hand and rifle grenades. McMullen spoke into the transmitter handed him by his radioman and, within minutes, Pershings and a tankdozer clattered up. While the riflemen kept the North Koreans' heads down and the M-26s covered, the dozer blade shoveled the enemy emplacement over its defenders. Than, working from cave to cave, the tanks put rounds into each, flushing out stunned, deafened and bleeding prisoners or, when they refused to come out, entombing them with the dozer. To provide the tank gunners more excitement, an enemy armored car sortied onto the causeway from Inchon. Without waiting for it to hit the engineers' minefield, the turret of an M-26 swung around, tracked it an instant, the long-barreled gun barked and snapped rearward in recoil, and the armored car was blown open like a sardine can.

Before eight o'clock, Lieutenant Bohn—a hard charger twice wounded already during the fighting in the perimeter—had George Company in complete possession of Radio Hill. Only So Wolmi Do ("Little Moontip Island") remained to be taken.

Now it was Colonel Taplett's turn to reach for his radio transmitter. "Isherwood . . . Isherwood . . ." he said, calling division headquarters. "This Glove . . . Wolmi Do secured at 0800."[6]

. . .

Veteran seagoing Marine and connoisseur of landing operations that he was, General Shepherd had had his eye-opener of thick black Navy coffee and come onto *Mount McKinley*'s flag bridge at 0530. O. P. Smith, also a seagoing veteran, was of course there already and had been since before dawn. General MacArthur, snoozing after the passage of Wolmi Do, was awakened by the naval gunfire preparation and joined the two Marines. "Just like Lingayen Gulf," he remarked. Then he settled into the admiral's chair and watched the sun rise over the jagged Korean hills. "His staff," General Shepherd recorded,

> . . . was grouped around him. He was seated in the Admiral's chair with his old Bataan Cap with its tarnished gold braid and a leather jacket on. Photographers were busily engaged in taking pictures of the General while he continued to watch the naval gunfire—paying no attention to his admirers.

From joint operations below, from the control vessels and from air observers reports flowed in: waves forming, initial landing, progress inland, colors atop Radio Hill. Soon Taplett's reports were added to the flow of good news: "Have captured 45 prisoners . . . light resistance . . ." Imperturbable, smiling and satisfied that events were going as he had known they would, Douglas MacArthur listened and observed the landing. When word came in at 0800 that Wolmi Do had been taken, he asked about casualties. Perhaps a half dozen dead, 15 or 20 wounded, was someone's guess. "More people than that get killed in traffic every day," observed the General.

Turning to Admiral Doyle, he directed, "Say to the Fleet [an echo of Nelson?], 'The Navy and Marines have never shone more brightly than this morning.' " The admiral's pencil hovered until he knew from context whether it would be "shown" or "shone," then he finished the sentence and handed it to a staff officer. With a broad smile MacArthur glanced around at Generals Shepherd, Smith and Almond, and the admiral, and said: "That's it. Let's get a cup of coffee."[7]

In the cabin below, over the coffee cups, the General's thoughts turned to Washington. Reaching for a pad, he drafted a message for Bradley, Collins, Sherman and Vandenberg: "First phase landing successful with losses slight. All goes well and on schedule."

While all hands breakfasted, some on wardroom scrambled eggs, some on C rations, the tide began to recede, leaving Taplett and his battalion very much on their own. Physically cut off from the fleet which sur-

H

rounded them in plain view, confronted across the causeway with un-known enemies, they could count on overwhelming air and gunfire sup-port but, beyond this, until the afternoon tide, only on their own weapons. Fortunately they had much to keep them occupied. And so did General Smith and Admiral Doyle.

The first order of business on Wolmi Do was to deploy the Marines for defense against counterattack from Inchon. George Company held the crest of Radio Hill, where Colonel Taplett had his observation post. How overlooked the industrial area, and Item held North Point and the ridge behind Green Beach. Major McMullen had already converted North Point swimming pool into a stockade for the 136 prisoners who were being herded in, some showing little discomfiture at their changed lot.

From Radio Hill—militarily, at any rate—the view is spectacular. Inchon is spread out like a map. To the left, beyond the causeway, lies Red Beach; to the far right, Blue Beach. Immediately to the front, key terrain feature of Inchon proper, rises Observatory Hill, which dominates the town as Radio Hill dominates Wolmi Do. Really two hills joined by a saddle and crowned by the concrete cylinder of the Japanese weather station, Observatory Hill appears from Taplett's vantage point as a long, steep, tree-crested ridge (well battered on September 15, 1950). Around it, with their Oriental curves and pointed eaves, the tile roofs on lesser hills resemble the chop of a swelling sea.

Intently surveying this scene for signs of enemy activity, intelligence observers took notes while the naval gunfire spotter searched for targets. In radio contact with *Mansfield,* assigned to support the battalion, this young Marine lieutenant had superb observation, a wide selection of targets, and all day to shoot at them.

Closer at hand was ample evidence of what the Marines might have encountered. Radio Hill was covered by trenches, caves and emplace-ments. More than 300 antipersonnel mines and booby traps were sown on the hill's west face. In addition to weapons and gun positions wrecked by the bombardment, intact 76mm guns were found. In defenses which General Shepherd later described as "truly impressive," these guns, served by more resolute crews less thoroughly pounded, could have played hob with the 3d Battalion's landing craft and assault waves. Fortunately, as Taplett wrote in his action report, the enemy—about 400 men of the 226th Regiment and 918 Coast Artillery—were in the main "newly inducted, poorly trained, and unable to use the weapons provided them."[8]

Perhaps because their backs were to the wall, the North Korean platoon on So Wolmi Do put up a better fight. Little Moontip is a tiny knoll about 500 yards square, with a lighthouse and a couple of storage buildings, joined to Wolmi Do in 1950 only by a narrow causeway ominously like that between Gavutu and Tanambogo in Tulagi Harbor, which 1st Division Marines had stormed in 1942. Besides individual weapons, the So Wolmi Do people had some dual-purpose light antiaircraft guns, always bad news when used against infantry.

As soon as Wolmi Do was mopped up, Taplett ordered Company G to seize So Wolmi Do. Bohn turned the job over to Lieutenant Counselman, who was given a rifle squad, reinforced by tanks, machine guns, and engineer mine-clearance teams whose unsought honor it was to precede everybody else. From back on Wolmi Do, the battalion's 81mm mortars began dropping rounds on the little hummock as the assault group, feeling rather conspicuous on the narrow, elevated, 900-yard causeway, made its way forward.

The enemy held fire until the Marines were well within range and a long way out from the main island. Then they cut down with a withering blast of automatic-weapons fire and musketry. The advance halted. On Radio Hill, with a perfect view of what was happening, Taplett turned to his forward air controller, a Marine pilot assigned to the infantry "crunchers." Within moments the controller was talking by radio to the tactical air coordinator, Lieutenant Colonel Norman J. Anderson, circling aloft, then giving instructions to the VMF-214 strike leader, Major Robert Floeck (who that morning had eight days left to live before being shot down near Pyongyang). Coached on target by the aviator on the ground, eight Corsairs roared down on Little Moontip, stitching it right and left with 20mm cannon and then searing it with napalm. Although Counselman's people, hugging the deck, couldn't see them, enemy soldiers dived into the channel to take their chances with the tide when the Corsairs attacked.

The riflemen lifted their heads, hunched forward toward the enemy, and advanced with the tanks while the 81mm mortars pounded away. When the mortars lifted, the tank guns began to bark and snap, the machine-gun bursts lengthened, and the fire-team automatic riflemen hammered in. The flame thrower spurted and flared two or three times. There was a brief, rising sound of battle, then firing abruptly slackened until the occasional shots sounded more like those on a rifle range at midmorning. Seventeen enemy were killed, 19 gladly surrendered.

With the capture of So Wolmi Do at 1115, the 3d Battalion, 5th

Marines, had accomplished its mission. Not a single Marine had been killed; only 17 had been wounded. Now, all they had to do was wait for the tide to rise again.[9]

Not long before Lieutenant Counselman was preparing to advance along the causeway, the quartermaster of the watch on *Mount McKinley*'s quarterdeck spotted a trim, blacked-hulled barge heading for the ship. Her coxswain held up six fingers, signal that his passenger was a vice-admiral. Admiral Struble was coming over from *Rochester* to see MacArthur, Doyle and Smith.

After completing his business and making sure there were no changes in the general situation or plan, Struble told MacArthur that he planned to take a close-hand look at Wolmi Do and the beaches from his barge. Did the General care to come along? As MacArthur's instincts always took him toward the enemy, the invitation was welcome. Gathering his retinue with a glance, the General headed for the quarterdeck and Admiral Struble's barge. Besides General Shepherd, whose trained eye the General particularly valued, the admiral invited Generals Almond, Whitney, Wright and Fox. An aide asked if a few reporters might accompany the entourage. Why not? In the ensuing scramble "about one-and-a-half boatloads" of correspondents elbowed in, Struble recalled, and the barge shoved off.

Since 4,000 yards of exposed mud flats lay between the channel and Blue Beach, the admiral had his coxswain head directly up toward Wolmi Do, not as brightly outlined now as at daybreak, for clouds were coming in and beginning to lower. Green Beach was carefully examined. Eager to see (and be seen), the General stood tall in the forward part of the barge, "in a Napoleonic pose," related one of the destroyer commanders whose ship the party passed. From Wolmi the barge steered for the Red Beach boat lanes and lay to less than a thousand yards from enemy gunners. At this point, having already earned four Purple Hearts since 1917, General Shepherd said to MacArthur, "General, you're getting up pretty close. Somebody's liable to take a pot shot at you." The advice was eminently sound: Struble had the coxswain put about, and the party made their way back to the command ship unscathed.[10]

As the Attack Force and the Landing Force made their thousand final preparations for the afternoon assault, what was happening ashore?

Even from Radio Hill, little could be discerned. A few squads of enemy troops on Observatory Hill, a tank down in town, some suspected gun emplacements behind Cemetery Hill, a red-clay eminence hard by Red Beach—these and a random flow of civilians, some scooping up rice from unguarded stores along the waterfront, others clustering on the mud flats where few shells would fall, were the only visible activities in Inchon.

In Seoul, near-panic reigned, at least among the *In Min Gun*. Despite early and accurate warning from Inchon, the NKPA were utterly surprised. Although there was talk of a possible landing at Kunsan, one at Inchon had seemed impossible. Busy with the "re-education" of Seoul, the North Koreans hardly had time to desist from political slaughter[11] before the Landing Force was ashore. But from September 15 onward, the *In Min Gun* forgot about indoctrination and prepared to fight for its life. Security Police press-gangs roamed Seoul, coercing "volunteers" into the ranks of militia units. The 70th Regiment was ordered to Seoul from Suwon and, even more important, the 18th Division, which had been headed for the Naktong, was immediately recalled to the capital. At Inchon, however (especially with local reserves depleted by the NKPA landing of the 14th on Yonghung Do, described in Chapter 3), the time for reinforcement was past. The 226th Regiment and the remnants of the 918th Coast Artillery could only await the impending blow.[12]

The Assault on Red Beach

While the victors of Wolmi Do spent a warm and pleasant afternoon watching Inchon, the preliminaries were going ahead for the main assault.

At midday the transports and LSTs for Red Beach came up to Wolmi Do. At long last, steaming four bells and a jingle, the minesweepers arrived and were combing the approach channels. (In addition, there was another mine scare: frogmen in the water around Wolmi Do reported mines on Red Beach; *DeHaven*'s Lundgren, a former mine specialist, observed carefully through powerful glasses, worked over the area with 40mm fire, and reassuringly reported that it was nothing but fish stakes.)

To keep Inchon sealed off, Admiral Ewen kept flights of Task Force 77 ADs hitting targets and interdicting hostile movement within a 25-mile radius of the landing area. He could be generous with aircraft this important day because he was about to receive a third fast carrier, USS *Boxer*, which, despite a broken reduction gear, was approaching Task Force 77 on three shafts at 26 knots. *Boxer* had made three transpacific runs since mid-July, ferrying 161 badly needed Air Force airplanes on her first trip west (besides nailing up a Pacific blue ribbon that still stands, for an eight-day crossing from San Francisco to Tokyo); then flashed back to embark an Atlantic Fleet air group ferried in from Norfolk, and returned to Korea. Past due for overhaul when the war began, battered by Kezia and limping though she was, *Boxer* joined up proud as *Oregon* at Santiago and launched planes on schedule.

Inshore of the fast carriers, the jeep carriers *Sicily* and *Badoeng Strait* were carrying out a flight schedule that taxed every resource. Limited by pilot rather than plane availability, the schedules worked out by Lieutenant Colonels James L. Neefus and Norman J. Anderson, the two senior Marines afloat, called for at least two missions per pilot and, in many cases, three. Anderson, a short, alert twinkly-eyed pilot, was, as tactical air coordinator, aerial ringmaster of all close support for the ground Marines. This day and the next, he flew five sorties, totaling 16 hours in the air.[13]

At 1430 the tempo of bombardment picked up. The scheduled pre-H-hour fires commenced. *Toledo* and *Rochester,* again relying on Marine air spotters, began to drop 260-pound 8-inch shells into the eastern part of Inchon and the northeastern outskirts. *Jamaica* and *Kenya,* today using Royal Navy Fleet Air Arm spotters from *Triumph,* whose spotting procedure (not to mention their English) was more intelligible, covered areas around Blue Beach with their 6-inch guns. *DeHaven* and *Swenson* —which could support the assault battalions of the 5th Marines on Red —methodically worked over the beach area (railroad yards, brewery, gas tanks, factories, godowns) with 5-inch. As the naval gunfire intensified, fires began to break out in the lower town, adding their smoke to the dull overcast.

Fifteen minutes after the fire-support ships resumed work, Admiral Doyle two-blocked the expected signal from *Mount McKinley*: "Land the Landing Force." Soon afterward, he signaled that H-hour (the hour the first waves were to hit Red and Blue Beaches) would be 1730.

Now heavy-laden ADs and Corsairs from Ewen's fast carriers concentrated on Red Beach with 500- and 1,000-pound bombs, 5-inch rockets, and strafing. More fires broke out. The butane tanks north of the beach flared with fierce white flame and black smoke. A nearby factory flamed up. Watching from *Mount McKinley*'s bridge, Captain Martin J. Sexton, General Smith's aide, saw an unforgettable panorama. "The whole area for miles," he remembered, "was obscured by smoke and debris and burning fires."[14]

Aboard attack transports *Henrico* and *Cavalier,* the assault battalions of Lieutenant Colonel Raymond L. Murray's 5th Marines were boating. It may seem strange that a regiment assigned the main effort—and that into the bowels of an Oriental city on a dark night—should be commanded by a lieutenant colonel. But Murray, burly, forceful and tenacious, had fought the 5th Regiment with distinction all through the perimeter, and General Smith would not have traded him for most colonels.

If there could be any such single unit, Murray's regiment was traditionally thought of as the elite of the Corps. Aside from the compelling military factors of seasoning and recent victorious battle experience, it seemed altogether appropriate for the 5th Marines to be in the forefront of the battle. Its colors heavy with battle streamers from France, from Nicaragua, from Guadalcanal, New Britain, Peleliu and Okinawa, and with unit honors ranging from the French *Fourragère* to our own Presidential Unit Citation, the 5th Regiment held a special position in the mystique of the Corps.

In the forefront of the 5th Marines, its 1st and 2d Battalions (under Lieutenant Colonels George S. Newton and Harold S. Roise, respectively) were to land abreast—each in deep, narrow column of companies— across the left and right portions of Red Beach. The latest aerial photographs of this narrow, 650-foot quay, with its stone seawall, showed only too clearly a cluster of bunkers and trenches on the left, while the whole beach was dotted with emplacements, more bunkers, and connecting trenches. In the words of Captain Frank I. Fenton, one of Newton's company commanders:[15]

> It really looked dangerous. . . . There was a finger pier and causeway that extended out from Red Beach which reminded us of Tarawa, and, if machine guns were on the finger pier and causeway, we were going to have a tough time making that last 200 yards to the beach.

At 1704, with rain squalls beginning to pelt the landing craft, the LCVPs carrying the assault platoons of the leading companies (A from the 1st Battalion, E from the 2d) were at the line of departure a mile offshore. Even from this distance, amid smoke and haze, the initial objectives stood out clearly: Cemetery Hill (foreign burial ground of old

Chemulpo), key to Red Beach, a sheer reddish cliff to seaward but sloping down to the right; Observatory Hill, the observatory tower sharply defined, a lunette-shaped redoubt commanding the inner harbor and city; and, to the right and lower, British Consulate hill, overlooking the harbor master's deserted, riddled headquarters. Newton's battalion must seize Cemetery Hill, then the northern horn of the Observatory Hill lunette; Roise and the 2d Battalion were to take British Consulate hill, then the southern horn of Observatory Hill. In regimental reserve, Taplett on Wolmi Do would bring his 3d Battalion across the causeway and support the attack as needed.

Observing intently from *Mount McKinley*—he had commanded a platoon of the 5th Marines in France—General Shepherd caught the scene for his journal:

> We watched the troops disembarking in small boats from the transports around us and their movement to the Line of Departure. It was overcast and smoke from the burning city made it difficult to observe the final run for the beach. As H-hour approached, the crescendo of fire increased. . . .

Toledo now began dropping 8-inch shells on Observatory Hill while *Rochester* interdicted the outskirts and approaches to the town: no reserve units must be allowed to enter, no artillery batteries to occupy positions from which to shell the beaches. *Mansfield* began raking Red Beach with airbursts. *DeHaven*'s 5-inch guns shelled the north face of Observatory Hill while *Swenson* worked on Cemetery Hill and the jumble of gas tanks, chimneys and railroad yards to the left. Hard by *Mansfield* up-channel, *LSMR-403* roared, hissed and shook as she began to loose off 5-inch rockets (a hundred a minute for the next 20 minutes) at the beach and north flank.

The red and white 1-flag was at the dip on *H. A. Bass* from which each boat wave would be dispatched; now it went up. Two minutes later, at 1724, the flag went down and the first wave—eight LCVPs, carrying four platoons of Marines—gunned across the line of departure toward the beach.

As the landing craft forged in, Taplett's mortars, machine guns and tanks opened up from Wolmi Do on the right. Able to observe their own tracers and fall of shot, as well as the advancing waves, gunners on Wolmi Do could fire on Red Beach until the last instant without endangering the assault troops. By way of a bonus to this planned fire

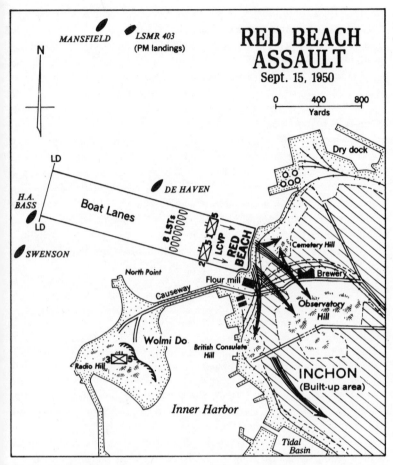

RED BEACH
ASSAULT
Sept. 15, 1950

support, enterprising Marines of the 1st Tank Battalion turned an un-
damaged Russian 76mm gun on its former owners and pronounced it
a good-shooting weapon.

When the leading LCVPs were midway to the beach, the naval guns
fell silent. For the next five minutes VMF-214 and 323 had their turn.
Led by the two squadron commanders (Lieutenant Colonel Walter E.
Lischeid and Major Lund), the Corsairs gave the beach its final treatment. Like Major Floeck who had attacked Wolmi Do in the morning,
Lischeid was an aviator whose days were numbered: within ten days,
again supporting the 5th Marines (and flying a Corsair numbered 17,

the same unlucky number as Floeck's) Colonel Lischeid was destined to crash flaming into the outskirts of Seoul.

Besides the Corsairs, Navy ADs joined in. First Lieutenant James W. Smith, forward air controller with the 1st Battalion, 5th Marines, spotted a target as his LCVP neared the beach, called in a strike and had it under attack by Skyraiders before the leading wave was ashore. The support was so close that the boats were pelted with spent 20mm empties as the ADs roared past.

The wind was blowing directly along the beach so that the heavy smoke from fires ashore provided a screen as effective as if it had been put down by ships' guns and aircraft. On the point to the left a large fire was sending up dense black smoke. Behind, beyond the drydock, a huge, bright, hot fire shone through. All along Red Beach, amid the drifting smoke were angry red pinpoints of spreading flame. To the *Herald-Tribune*'s Marguerite Higgins, landing with the 1st Battalion, 5th Marines, Wolmi Do "looked as if a giant forest fire had just swept over it. . . ."

> Beyond was Red Beach [she continued]. As we strained to see it more clearly, a rocket hit a round oil tower and big, ugly smoke rings billowed up. The dockside buildings were brilliant with flames. Through the haze it looked as if the whole city was burning. . . . The strange sunset, combined with the crimson haze of the flaming docks, was so spectacular that a movie audience would have considered it overdone.

Observatory Hill, hammered by the 8-inch shells and the strafing, was masked in a solid black cloud rising high above the town. Against this backdrop of havoc, Cemetery Hill stood in clear relief.

So did the Red Beach seawall, which *Time*'s James Bell said "seemed as high as the RCA Building." The LCVPs (some painted TRUMAN'S POLICE FORCE, for the famous letter had not gone unnoticed) drew near. In the boats, gunnery sergeants rasped, "Lock and load. Runners out first. Keep your goddamned heads down." As they saw the stone wall ahead, officers and NCOs looked for breaches while others readied scaling ladders—mostly homemade by the 1st Engineer Battalion—or (in later waves) stood by furled cargo nets with steel pickets and sledges to anchor them atop the wall. Underfoot, each boat had two long planks so that Marines could get across mud flats in case of grounding.

Coxswains jockeyed for final positions—there were no soft spots on this ironbound beach. Then, as the boats crunched against the seawall and hung in place with engines, leaders sprang up the rickety, bobbing ladders, over the top like a trench assault on the Somme, and the riflemen followed them into the smoke. Flying low and slow over the beach in his blue Corsair, Norm Anderson flashed word back to *Mount McKinley*: "Scaling ladders are in place and Marines are over the wall."

The time was 1733 when Company A, 5th Marines, hit Red Beach. At the seawall was a trench, on the left a bunker spitting burp-gun slugs, and from back in the smoke, farther left, heavy rifle and machine-gun fire. To the front, across 200 yards of flat, only 130 feet high but looking like a miniature Suribachi, rose Cemetery Hill. This was the objective of Technical Sergeant O. F. McMullen's 1st Platoon, one of whose boats (McMullen's own) had conked out offshore and, with the half-platoon cursing to no avail, was drifting gently in with the tide. The other half-platoon, led by Sergeant Charles D. Allen, got over the seawall only to be pinned to the deck, with casualties, by heavy fire from the bunker.

On Allen's right, Second Lieutenant Francis W. Muetzel found a breach and led the 2d Platoon through it. Stopping to toss grenades into a pillbox whose silent machine gun stared at them coldly, the leading fire teams advanced smartly around the right of the hill, for Muetzel had no mind to be stalled against the face of the cliff. While the support collared six groggy prisoners from the pillbox, Muetzel headed across the railroad yards, veered right and made for his objective, the Asahi Brewery. This compelling objective was high in the minds of A Company because Colonel Newton had promised the 1st Battalion a heroic beer bout if the brewery and contents were taken intact.

While Muetzel advanced on his brewery, things went from bad to worse on the left. First Lieutenant Baldomero Lopez (a World War II Navy veteran who graduated into the Corps via Annapolis) landed the 3d Platoon amid the 1st. Hurling in a grenade, he took out the bunker to the front, then pulled the pin and drew back to throw a second into another bunker. A burst of fire caught him, right arm and shoulder, and he toppled. The grenade's striker flicked up, the primer popped, sputtered and smoked beyond reach of his wounded arm. "Grenade!" he cried (the last word he spoke); then, lurching toward the deadly thing, got it crooked in his elbow, cradled it into his body and so died.

All these events took place during the first five minutes of the landing. Then, exactly at H+5, Captain John R. Stevens (who had commanded Able Company unscathed all through the perimeter) landed through the same breach as Muetzel. Receiving word of Lopez's death, he turned to his exec, First Lieutenant Fred F. Eubanks, Jr., and said, "Lope is dead —take over there and get them organized and moving."

When Muetzel reported that the brewery was his, Stevens ordered him back to the beach. Without Cemetery Hill there would be no landings over Red Beach.

As Muetzel led his people back again, he got a better look at the hill. Its south and rear (east) faces sloped easily up. Quickly the twenty-four-year-old lieutenant changed direction, re-formed for attack, and moved onto the hill. Taking a surprised cluster of infantry prisoners as they advanced, the Marines drove into the emplacements of the 226th Regiment's mortar company, bagged the surviving members of the company, and herded them downhill under guard. From the crest, now theirs uncontested, they could see a grenade duel around an enemy bunker on the north flank. Just as Muetzel was issuing breathless orders to wade in, he saw a long burst of flame envelop the bunker, and the Marines below clambered to their feet and advanced. Cemetery Hill was taken, the beach was clear and Red was open. But there were eight dead Marines on the flat, and the Navy corpsmen had 28 wounded from A Company to transfuse, ligate, splint, patch, tag and evacuate.

To the right, the first wave of Captain Samuel Jaskilka's Easy Company, landing at 1731, beat Able Company onto the beach by two minutes and thus could claim to be the first Marines in town. Lieutenant Edwin A. Deptula, a Basic School classmate of Muetzel's, got his platoon up and over the wall, covered the landing of the rest of the company and then, with little opposition, headed down the railroad tracks to the right, past a five-story factory with every window aflame, toward British Consulate hill. At 1845, still almost unopposed, Company E held this objective and the lower face of Observatory Hill to the left. Rearward, Colonel Roise had the rest of the 2d Battalion ashore in position around the Nippon (now the Dae Han) Flour Mill at the base of Wolmi Do causeway. The 5th Regiment's right was secure, and the 2d Battalion could now prepare to take its share of Observatory Hill.[16]

Because infrequently exposed—at least on the receiving end—American troops, even Marines, sometimes underestimate the deadliness of naval gunfire. Soon after 1800, as the eight LSTs approached Red Beach at flood tide, men of the 5th Marines had a vivid opportunity to correct misapprehensions on this score.

Among many daring features of the Inchon plan the landing of eight

LSTs on a rigid schedule of time and tide within 60 minutes after H-hour was one of the boldest. Audacious in any circumstance, this maneuver was trebly so for the rust-eaten ships and novice officers and men to whom the job fell. The LSTs were mostly repossessed from Japanese island trade, stinking, said the captain of *LST-799*, "with a penetrating odor of fishheads and urine." Only one LST skipper had previous experience: he had actually beached his ship twice before D-day; crews and officers were mainly mobilized reservists.

Soon after six in deepening twilight the boxlike, single-screwed arks waddled in column toward Red Beach. Large, slow, conspicuous, they presented admirable targets for everything the NKPA could still shoot. In a shower of mortar and machine-gun fire, *LST-859* led the way into a beach far from secure. Gun flashes—theirs? ours? whose?—still sparkled atop Cemetery Hill and on the left half of the beach. Following the *859* at five-minute interval, *LST-975* and *857,* loaded, among other combustibles, with gasoline, ammunition and napalm, took mortar hits. Ammunition trucks on the *914* were hit and caught fire, but sailors and Marines knocked down the flames with fog and CO_2. Eight drums of gasoline on the *857* were punctured in one machine-gun burst. Small-arms fire ricocheted, pinged and clanked on bow doors, ramps and superstructures.

Nobody can really blame the sailors for firing back but their choice of targets was not very discriminating. Shooting up all Red Beach in a fireworks display of unaimed, high-intensity, short-range fire from 3-inch, 40mm and 20mm guns, seven LSTs (the eighth, *914*, held fire) briefly made Inchon harbor unsafe for friend or foe. The 2d Battalion, 5th Marines, crouching for dear life in the lee of the Nippon Flour Mill, took more casualties that day from the LSTs' guns—one dead, 23 wounded—than it sustained from the enemy. Lieutenant Muetzel and his platoon were blasted off the crest of Cemetery Hill toward the enemy, whose machine-gun fire from Observatory Hill they found preferable to the hail of naval gunfire.

By 1900, when all LSTs had beached, Marines, braving the friendly guns, managed to stem the torrent, and peace returned to Red Beach.[17]

Observatory Hill

The job of taking the north half of Observatory Hill (Objective A) was assigned to Company C, 5th Marines; the south half (Objective B) fell to Company D. With this redoubt in hand the 5th Regiment could feel secure in its beachhead.

Despite the action reports, most of which convey the impression that everything goes according to plan, battles rarely in fact do, a circumstance which C Company learned as its LCVPs approached the beach behind the assault waves of Able.

Nobody is more powerless than troops in landing craft: they land when and where their coxswains drop the ramps and are entirely subject to the wave commanders and control officers through whom the Navy coordinates the ship-to-shore movement. First Lieutenant Poul F. Pederson, commanding C Company and boated with the Navy wave commander, learned how powerless he was when the latter pulled out of formation to assist a broken-down LCVP from an earlier wave. It would be hard to criticize the wave commander's good intentions, but they prevented the CO of a unit with a critical mission from reaching his beach until chaos had arrived first.

Pederson, a rawboned Dane who 15 years later would land a battalion of his own on an equally dark and stormy night in Santo Domingo, finally got ashore. But C Company, landed hit or miss, was already at sixes and sevens. For that matter, so was the beach: fire-swept by the intense fight on the left, bombarded by the massed friendly guns of seven LSTs, and still receiving mortar incoming from Observatory Hill. "Bullets were whining persistently," wrote Marguerite Higgins, who landed in the fifth wave,[18]

> . . . spattering the water around us. We clambered over the high, steel sides of the boat, dropped into the water and, taking shelter beside the boat as long as we could, snaked on our stomachs up into a rockstrewn dip in the seawall. . . . Whatever the luck of the first four waves, we were relentlessly pinned down by rifle and automatic weapon fire coming down on us from another rise on the right. . . . A sudden rush of water came up into the dip in the wall and we saw a huge LST rushing at us with the great door half down. Six more yards and the ship would have crushed 20 men. Warning shouts sent everyone speeding from the seawall, searching for escape from the LST and cover from the gunfire.

While Miss Higgins was dodging the LST and Pederson was trying to sort out Charlie Company, two of his lieutenants did some sorting on their own. Second Lieutenant Byron L. Magness got his 2d Platoon in hand and was joined by Second Lieutenant Max A. Merritt with the company's 60mm mortars. Fresh from Basic School and well imbued with the necessity to do or die, these young men moved out their troops and headed for Observatory Hill. Checked in the darkening streets by a machine-gun nest in a church, Technical Sergeant Max Stein, disregarding wounds, smothered the gun in a shower of grenades. Bearing right, past Muetzel's brewery and a battered cotton mill, the Marines panted up the steep slope and at 1845 found themselves on the saddle that overlooks what is now Inchon's municipal stadium and joins the north and south horns of Observatory Hill. When Magness tried to fire the amber star cluster that would signal "Objective taken," the result was a dull click: his lone flare was a dud.

Down below, Colonel Newton had no knowledge that a unit of his battalion was up the hill. With the beach in disarray and darkness descending, he ordered his reserve company under Captain Fenton (son of a distinguished Marine officer) to take Observatory Hill. As Fenton later recounted:[19]

> Darkness was more of an aid to me than to the enemy, and the cover and concealment that the town afforded aided. . . . The men had been very well briefed; they knew all the streets, knew where each house was, and consequently, even in darkness, were able to make their way with good speed.

Hooking around to the left with one platoon, moving straight ahead with another, "Ike" Fenton encountered intermittent resistance from remnants of the 226th Regiment (which had a battalion command post on the hill) but got to the top by 2000. As his left platoon extended around the inner slope of the bowl behind Observatory Hill, they were greeted by the 2d Platoon of Charlie, and Colonel Newton's worries were over.

First Lieutenant H. J. Smith (nickname: "Hawg Jaw"), whose Company D was to take the 2d Battalion's half of the hill, emerged from cover when the LSTs ceased fire, headed across the railroad yard toward the electric company, and thence followed a road leading up the side of Observatory Hill. In the confusion of battle, Lieutenant Smith had gotten the impression (incorrectly) that E Company was already on the hill. Consequently he led his people up the road in route column so as to get there quicker. Unfortunately, the troops he encountered at the top were not Marines but NKPA. An enemy squad with machine guns opened on the head of column with no warning whatever. Marines hit the deck, went into firing positions or heaved grenades across the road and a general melee ensued. The Navy corpsman was hit but in the tradition of his kind, stayed on to handle the Marine casualties. When Colonel Roise plowed up the road with Lieutenant Michael J. Dunbar, the company exec, the latter was wounded beside him.

But surprise could only delay, not change the outcome. Dog Company, thoroughly experienced from the perimeter, pressed the attack and soon pushed the defenders off the hill into the smoke and blackness of the town.

Night had fallen by the time all units on Observatory Hill had reorganized and groped into defensive positions. Even with light from *Swenson*'s star shells it was dark indeed, and Roise felt it would be crowding the 2d Battalion's luck to try to advance down from his portion of the hill to secure the godowns, wrecked railroad yards and waterfront alleys that extended right and forward to the tidal basin. From the regimental command post near the flour mill, Colonel Murray, who had landed at 1830 amid the red glare of LSTs' tracers, ordered that, where the objective line could not be tactically defended, it must be outposted. Sending forward a two-squad patrol from his reserve company (Fox), augmented by a squad of Korean Marines (no small asset for a night patrol in their home town), Roise learned that all was quiet. Thereupon he sent in F Company, less a platoon already committed on Observatory Hill, to set up a blocking position along the east end of the tidal basin.

To the left, a final action took place after midnight. Outside his CP on the hill, Captain Fenton stood poised to relieve himself by the light of a star shell. As he did so, the hole at his feet came alive and a frightened Communist soldier, armed with burp gun and grenades, sprang out and cried for mercy. Momentarily transfixed, Fenton shouted for his runner, who disarmed the drenched captive.

And back toward the beach, there was no paean of victory from the 1st Battalion. During the night, the brewery caught fire and burned itself out to the melancholy thud of bursting kegs and bottles, and the gutters flowed with good Asahi beer.[20]

The Capture of Blue Beach

Among many complicating factors of the Inchon landings was the necessity to deliver two widely separated simultaneous regimental assaults. With the 5th Regiment in possession of its objectives, let us see how the 1st Marines fared on the Blue beaches.

Compared to the 5th Marines, a going concern when war broke out, the 1st Regiment, organized in ten days and thereupon embarked for Korea, was, to say the least, untried. But the regiment's history went

Louis Johnson, Secretary of Defense, confers with General Omar N. Bradley who in October 1949 predicted, "large-scale amphibious operations . . . will never occur again." Below, the Joint Chiefs of Staff in 1950 (left to right): General Omar N. Bradley, Chairman; General Hoyt S. Vandenberg, Chief of Staff, U.S. Air Force; General J. Lawton Collins, Chief of Staff, U.S. Army; and Admiral Forrest P. Sherman, Chief of Naval Operations.

Maj. Gen. O. P. Smith, left, Commanding General, 1st Marine Division, and Lt. Gen. Lemuel C. Shepherd, Commanding General, Fleet Marine Force, Pacific, study defense map on bridge of *Mount McKinley*. Below, General Douglas MacArthur, with, left to right, Maj. Gen. Courtney Whitney, Brig. Gen. Edwin K. Wright, and Maj. Gen. Edward M. Almond on D-day morning. "Just like Lingayen," MacArthur said.

General Smith, left, confers with Admiral Doyle and Colonel Krulak, Marine Corps operations officer, prior to invasion. Below, MacArthur inspects the beaches before landing, accompanied by, left to right, General Shepherd, Admiral Struble, Generals Whitney and Wright.

(U.S. Marine Corps Photo)

Marine flame thrower sears an emplacement on Radio Hill, Wolmi Do. Below, Marine roadblock on Wolmi Do causeway. Cemetery Hill, Red Beach, rises abruptly to the left. Observatory Hill is at far right.

(U.S. Marine Corps Photo)

"It looked as if the whole city was burning," reported correspondent Marguerite Higgins. Above, Red Beach is blanketed by smoke and flame prior to H-hour at Inchon. Below, leading waves of the 5th Marines pass destroyer *De Haven* on the way to Red Beach.

Moments before touchdown on Red Beach, first wave approaches Cemetery Hill under smoke pall as second wave follows it in.

Soon to give his life, for which he won the Medal of Honor, Lt. Baldomero Lopez, 5th Marines, leads his platoon onto Red Beach.

Admirals Struble, left, and Doyle receive a progress report from Lt. Cdr. M. T. Jacobs. Below, "fierce and utterly fearless," Col. L. B. "Chesty" Puller, Commanding Officer of the 1st Marines, prepares to land at Blue Beach.

(U.S. Army Photo)

Amphibian tractors carry the 1st Marines toward Blue Beach. Below, Navy
rocket salvos plaster Blue Beach.

(U.S. Navy Photo)

LST and assault craft beach at H+30. Note Marines hugging captured trenches in foreground as Nippon Flour Mill burns brightly. Wolmi Do rises on right horizon. Below, on the bridge of his flagship, Admiral Doyle, whom General Shepherd called, "a great commander and the best amphibious naval officer I have ever met."

(U.S. Marine Corps Photo)

Marines bring in communist prisoners while Inchon burns. Below, "The best publicity the Marines could have put on," said General Wright after viewing gutted Russian-made tanks knocked out by the 5th Marines' dawn ambush on D+2.

(U.S. Marine Corps Photo)

Greeted by General Smith, MacArthur comes ashore at Yellow Beach, D+2.

General MacArthur is briefed at the Marine division command post. Seated with MacArthur, left to right, General Smith, Admiral Struble, Generals Whitney and Wright. Below, MacArthur and Admiral Struble, to his right, visit Col. R. L. Murray, 5th Marines. General Shepherd stands with cocomacacque stick, souvenir of Haitian campaigns.

Maj. Gen. Frank E. Lowe, President Truman's personal representative in Korea, chats with Admiral Struble. Below, Marine carrier pilot Lieutenant John Hanes explains to skeptical Generals Cushman and Harris why he had to land at Kimpo while the field was still out of bounds.

LSTs resting on mud flat discharge supplies at Red Beach with Wolmi Do at left, background. Below, Colonel "Chesty" Puller, with pipe, waits impatiently for the 32nd Infantry to come up, D+4.

On the road to Yongdungpo, Brig. Gen. E. A. Craig, foreground, checks situation-map with Colonel Puller. Below, 1st Marines work their way through Yongdungpo.

Seoul and its wrecked bridges as seen by machine-gunners from across the Han. Below, amtracs cross the Han to capture Hill 125.

(U.S. Marine Corps Photo)

Returning to Tokyo, General MacArthur lights pipe aboard his plane, the *Scap*.

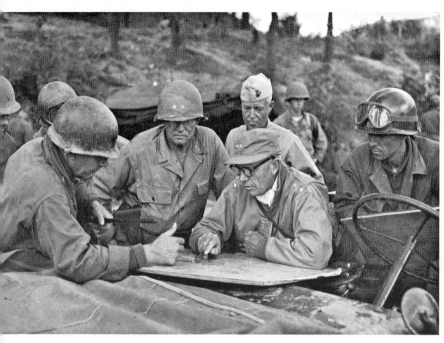

General Almond gives instructions to Col. Charles Beauchamp (hand on map board) as Generals Hodes, Barr, and Craig look on. Below, Generals O. P. Smith, Barr, and Col. A. L. Bowser, right, at Yongdungpo Circle.

(Photo by Larry Keighley)

Col. R. L. Murray beside his battered command post at Sojong.

5th Marines in heavy fighting north of the Han. Below, "One of our beloved Corsairs," as a grateful ground officer described them.

(U.S. Marine Corps Photo)

Ridges northwest of Seoul, where communist General Wol made his stand.

Marine tank at a barricade, central Seoul.

Seoul and its fire-blackened capitol.

Litter bearers under fire carry a wounded Marine to an aid station in Seoul.

Marine riflemen and tank advancing up Ma-Po Boulevard, Seoul.

Korean Marines herd prisoners rearward while U.S. Marine tanks support the action.

Hastily abandoned schoolroom provides cover for Marine rifleman as he fires.

"It looks like the Fourth of July," said a 5th Marines gunnery sergeant as the colors went up over the Korean national capitol.

"To Harry from his M.P.'s," reads the Marines' inscription on Stalin's picture in liberated Seoul.

In his third shooting war, General C. B. Cates visits a 7th Marines machine-gun position north of Seoul.

In the capitol of the Republic of South Korea at Seoul, General MacArthur, on behalf of the United Nations, restores the seat of government to its president, Syngman Rhee.

back to the Boxer Uprising, to Veracruz, to Nicaragua, Haiti and Santo Domingo, and to a succession of battles in World War II: Guadalcanal, New Britain, Peleliu and Okinawa. Disbanded after the war, with their colors barely furled, the 1st Marines were abruptly shaken together again in August 1950 from East Coast Fleet Marine Force units, from navy-yard Marine guards, and an infusion of reservists. Regardless of origin, a high percentage of the officers and men, reserves included, were World War II veterans, and, as their regimental commander observed, "As usual when war comes, some of the best fighting people came out of the brig."

This regimental commander, whom troops in the field often mistook for an old gunnery sergeant, had commanded the 1st Marines during World War II and had them now by virtue of $19 worth of commercial telegrams beseeching General Cates to detach him from a snug barracks command to lead the regiment again. For, if the 5th Marines could claim to look down their noses at any other regiment in the Corps, the colonel of the 1st Regiment was an officer on whom no Marine could look down.[21]

Colonel Lewis Burwell Puller, fierce and utterly fearless, was entitled to almost as many battle stars as the regiment he commanded. Winner of two Navy Crosses before World War II, and of two more during the war, Puller was one of the great fighting soldiers of American history: resolute and intrepid in battle, an iron disciplinarian, yet, under the armor plate, simple and kindly hearted. Above all, "Chesty" Puller was a leader, a warrior-legend among the troops, a man whose command post was always in the front lines, a terror to staff officers, communicators and quartermasters, and most of all, to the adipose, the incompetent, or the fainthearted.

Puller's mission was to land south of Inchon and seize a beachhead covering the main approach to the city proper, from which the regiment could advance directly on Yongdungpo and Seoul. To do this, the 1st Marines were landing two battalions abreast over Blue Beach—2d Battalion (Lieutenant Colonel Allan Sutter) on the left, Blue Beach 1; 3d Battalion (Lieutenant Colonel Thomas L. Ridge), on the right, Blue Beach 2. Puller's reserve (1st Battalion, Lieutenant Colonel Jack Hawkins) would follow the 3d Battalion over Blue 2.

No planner with any freedom of choice would have selected the Blue beaches for a landing operation. Aside from the two-and-a-half-mile approach over mud flats (a 45-minute run for the amphibian tractors

I

landing the troops), the so-called beaches were, in their way, about as bad as the 5th Marines'. Blue 1 was a mere shelf overlooked by an abrupt hillock only a few yards inland; its only exit was a dirt road winding around the left shoulder of the hill. On the right side of the hill, a fetid drainage ditch ran inland and divided Blue 1 from Blue 2. Sea-walled Blue 2 ended in a square-cut point with a large cove running back over more mud flat. Nobody could make out, either from intelligence or aerial photos, but Colonel Ridge, who would come in over Blue 2, speculated that the shoreline of the cove (which was also the south flank of Blue 2) might be usable as beach.

Tactically speaking, the main advantages of Blue Beach over Red Beach were that the former allowed the attackers more elbowroom, more beach, less town; and of course (at least as far as anyone knew) that Blue was not defended in anything like the density of Wolmi Do or Inchon Town. This latter proposition it would, however, be up to the 1st Marines to confirm. Simply as a map exercise, the planners could hardly overlook that the beaches lay within a bight—a miniature Salerno—flanked by two jaws little more than a mile apart—Tok Am Point to the south, backed by steep and commanding Hill 233,[22] and less forbidding but practically alongside the Blue 1 boat lanes, Won Do, an island joined to Blue Beach by a causeway-breakwater. Determined fire from well-emplaced antiboat guns on either or both jaws of the bight could shoot the amtracs out of the water.

To avert any such development, the two British cruisers were dropping 6-inch shells in the rear of Blue Beach and on that menacing promontory, Tok Am, and Hill 233, down to the right. Destroyer *Gurke,* whose 5-inch guns would support Colonel Ridge's landing, was working over Blue 1 and 2 and Won Do, the abrupt little island that flanked the boat lanes on the left. *Henderson,* bearing the name of a Marine officer killed at Midway, was to support Colonel Sutter's battalion. Her guns were shelling Blue 2 and the deep cove to the right. Demonstrating that these preparations were not idle, *Jamaica* touched off an ammunition dump whose thunderclap was heard for miles.

As for the Red Beach assault, the troops for Blue Beach commenced boating (though in amtracs) at 1445. Their H-hour was 1730, too. While boating progressed, Task Force 77 Skyraiders swooped and hammered. Then, at 1705, the final gunfire preparation began, *Jamaica* continuing to cover high ground behind Blue Beach, *Gurke* and *Henderson* the immediate rear and flanks. Flying battleship-size American colors to

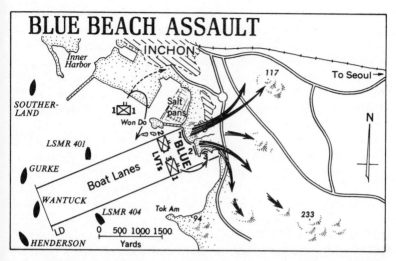

prevent unfortunate mistakes in identity due to their odd configuration, two of the LSMRs, *401* and *404,* were well inshore on either side of the boat lanes. Now, with asbestos-suited "goon-men" gunner's mates moving among the flaming launchers on their smoke-wreathed decks, each of these let go 2,000 5-inch rockets on the beaches themselves and on the menacing jaws of the bight.

Despite all this firepower, the enemy still had fight left in him. At 1555, *Gurke,* on station a mile below Wolmi Do, was shot at by batteries in Inchon and responded. Less than an hour later, as Blue Beach control vessel *Wantuck* was marshaling boat waves at the line of departure, shells began to fall among the LVTs and armored amphibians which would lead in the first wave. Again, destroyer 5-inch guns stopped the hostile fire. The LSTs launching amtracs came under fire and, in the words of General Shepherd's journal, the LST flotilla commander ". . . sent a frantic message for permission to launch the LVTs [amphibian tractors] and pull out. Admiral Doyle indignantly gave him a negative." An equally pointed negative came from the fire-support ships which, General Smith noted, "put down a terrific barrage."[23]

By now the amtracs, 172 in all, had commenced churning in on their long run to the beaches. And it was about this time, as Lieutenant Theodore B. Clark, USN, Blue Beach Control Officer, later wrote,[24] that there came ". . . the beginning of the end of the well-planned ship-to-shore movement for Blue Beach." Plans or no, two factors had taken charge: (1) Only four Navy guide-boats were available to shepherd in 25 boat waves whereas existing doctrine called for a minimum of 32 such guides for a landing on this scale; and (2) Blue Beach was precisely downwind of battered, burning Inchon, whose smoke and gloom mingled with the rain squalls to blanket boat lanes and beaches in impenetrable, mustard-colored haze. Under such conditions, 32 guide-boats would hardly have sufficed; with decent visibility, even four could have averted much of the chapter of accidents which ensued.

Essentially what happened was that the first three waves of both assault battalions, capably led through the murk by the guide-boats, reached their beaches on time (at H-hour exactly, in the case of the 2d Battalion) and generally in proper formation. For succeeding waves, utter confusion reigned. Waves without guide-boats, amphibian tractors without compasses or serviceable radios, the primary control vessel unable to see the beach or even learn whether the leading waves had landed, an unforeseen crosscurrent which set amtracs off course at a rate equaling their speed of advance—these were some of the ingredients of disorder which prompted Colonel Puller (truthfully but somewhat unfairly) to report, "The naval control of the ship-to-shore movement was very poor and almost non-existent."[25]

The waves which landed more or less as planned contained, as it happened, the troops and leaders required for success. On Blue 1, Companies D and F, Sutter's assault companies, landed without opposition. The exit road, around to the left, was blocked by a slide resulting from air strikes or gunfire, so advance inland aboard their tractors was likewise blocked for Company D. Fox, however, debarked as planned and quickly clambered to the top of the yellow clay hillock overlooking Blue 1. With about 600 of his people ashore, Sutter landed, set about reorganizing what he had, and wondered where the rest of the 2d Battalion might be.

To the right, on Blue 2, the Army armored amphibians (gun-carrying LVTs, sometime miscalled "amphibious tanks") which comprised the first wave had failed to go onto the beach and lay offshore firing at random on small groups of NKPA infantry who were attempting to oppose the landing. Churning past the Army LVT(A)s, the leading wave of Marine amtracs waddled up to the seawall, guiding on a large burning building back of the beach, which was the only visible landmark. The five tractors carrying the left assault company, George, plashed up the drainage ditch until the lead tractor bellied down in the muck; others, carrying Item, the right assault company, lay alongside the wall while

Marine riflemen staggered up the scaling ladders (some of which buckled) or staked in the cargo nets up which others would clamber.

Moderate fire was encountered. Occasional mortar rounds flung up geysers of water and mud. Small-caliber airbursts cracked overhead. From a tower or some industrial structure 500 yards inland, a machine gun played long-range bursts over the beaches.

Like Sutter, Ridge, the 3d Battalion commander, landed early. With his executive officer, Major Reginald R. Myers, Ridge immediately headed for the cove around the point on his right flank to see if it could be used to land tractors. A quick look showed that the answer was yes. Within minutes, a third beach, Blue 3, came into being, at right angles to Blue 2, when Ridge and Myers began directing incoming LVTs to turn the corner and land via the cove. Virtually all the remaining amtracs came ashore over Ridge's impromptu beach.

Thus by H+30 minutes (1800), despite incredible confusion, gloom, foul weather, tide and current, each battalion had its respective assault companies ashore, and both battalion commanders were on the beach and taking charge. To complete the picture, Colonel Puller (making his fifth major assault landing since Guadalcanal) brought in his own amtrac amid the third wave, and the 1st Marines, skeletonized, so to speak, were in business.

Reading from left to right the regiment had four objectives lettered A, D, C, and B. For reasons not now clear, A and D—respectively a key road junction and a hill (117)—were the letters given to the objectives of the left battalion; B and C—Hills 94 and 233, on the promontory to the far right—belonged to the 3d Battalion. In addition, though not a formally lettered objective, an avenue of approach along low ground leading inland to the southeast from the center of Blue Beach was to be blocked by G Company. With these five positions in hand, the 1st Marines' initial beachhead would be secure.

Colonel Sutter waited a while for the remaining waves of the 2d Battalion, but none appeared through the wall of smoke which curtained off the beaches from the transport areas. Finally, as twilight came on, he realized that there could be no more delay. Without a reserve, with only parts of his headquarters and weapons companies ashore, Sutter ordered Dog and Fox—his whole fighting force—to advance on their respective objectives: the road junction a half mile inland on the left (objective A); and Hill 117, the commanding ground farther inland which overlooked the road from Inchon to Yongdungpo. With only scattering resistance,

Company D had its road junction just as night fell, and by 2200 Fox was on Hill 117, prepared to block the highway. Fifteen prisoners were in hand, 50 enemy dead were estimated, and the 2d Battalion had lost one killed and 19 Marines wounded.

In the 3d Battalion on the right, much the same process was taking place. Captain George C. Westover led Company G forward from the amtracs stalled in the ditch. Soon after dark he had them in their blocking position in the corridor leading into the beach. Even earlier, First Lieutenant Joseph R. Fisher, a six-feet-two, 235-pound veteran of Iwo Jima, had swung Item Company to the right and headed south along the railroad tracks and coast road to occupy the western nose of Hill 233 before night fell. Company H, Colonel Ridge's reserve, which had ultimately gotten in over Blue 3, was ordered to take up two outpost positions and to cover the gap between Westover in the corridor and Fisher on Hill 233. The first platoon of How moved to the right, down past Hill 233, and worked its way up Hill 94 (Objective B, on Tok Am Point). Near the top they hit an NKPA company which abandoned well-constructed defensive positions when the Marine platoon closed in. How Company's second platoon was to have outposted the rugged east end of Hill 233, some distance inland from Lieutenant Fisher's strongpoint at the seaward end, but the nighttime going was too difficult in this precipitous, confusing terrain. Well on to his objective, the platoon leader was allowed to halt for the remaining hours of darkness on a position which served the tactical purpose.

Thus, with light casualties, against negligible human opposition, the forward elements of the 1st Marines gained the regimental beachhead. Colonel Puller satisfied himself that things were in hand, and so reported to General Smith at 0130, then got a few hours' sleep under a poncho in a gulley. His last act before settling down was to reach into his pack and pull out a neatly folded set of colors. Handing them to his runner, he said, "You keep this. . . . We're going to fly it over Seoul."[26]

The 1st Marines secured their beachhead, essentially, with the first three assault waves. The main struggle for the remaining 22 waves was simply to get ashore and join their parent organizations.

It will be remembered that there were only four guide-boats for the whole Blue Beach landing, and these led in the first three waves. Trying to act as signposts in the gloom, these boats took station on either side of the boat lanes offshore. Succeeding waves had to do the best they could. The experience of Major Edwin H. Simmons, a dark-haired, handsome professional in Ridge's battalion, gives the picture:[27]

> We had been told that a wave guide would pick us up and lead us to the line of departure. . . . Two LCVPs did come alongside our wave. The first was filled with photographers. The second was loaded with Korean interpreters. Two of these were hastily dumped into my LVT apparently under the mistaken notion that I was a battalion commander. Both interpreters spoke Korean and Japanese; neither spoke English. Time was passing and we were feeling faintly desperate when we came alongside what apparently was the central control vessel. I asked the bridge for instructions. A naval officer with a bull horn pointed out the direction of Blue 2, but nothing could be seen in that direction except smoke. We were on our way, and our path crossed that of another wave. I asked if they were headed for Blue 2. Their wave commander answered, "Hell, no. We're the 2d Battalion headed for Blue 1." We then veered off to the right. I broke out my map and asked my LVT driver if he had a compass. He looked at his instrument panel and said, "Search me, six weeks ago I was driving a truck in San Francisco."

Like orphans in the storm, waves straggled past the control vessel, whose officers were powerless to direct the landing. However, someone on *Wantuck* got the idea of turning on the ship's searchlight and leveling it into the smoke on course to Blue Beach. The thought was good but the execution fell short: the beam was aimed far northeast of the correct bearing and only compounded the confusion.

It was this errant gleam that mislanded Colonel Puller's reserve, the 1st Battalion, under Lieutenant Colonel Jack Hawkins, two miles to the left of the beaches on the outer seawall of Inchon's tidal basin. Two of the battalion's four waves got over the wall thinking it was the Blue 1 revetment they expected to encounter. Puller's exec, Lieutenant Colonel R. W. Rickert, in a free boat, discerned landing craft crossing his bow nearly perpendicular to the boat lanes and feared the worst. First calling Hawkins by radio and then finally intercepting him about 50 yards off the tidal basin seawall, he reoriented the battalion. Hawkins told the boat group commander they were in the wrong place. He insisted, Hawkins said, "that we were at Blue Beach, but that if I wanted to land somewhere else, that was up to me. He then departed·in his boat and I did not see him again."[28]

Rounding up the waves still afloat and ranging the length of the wall to recapture his troops, Hawkins was able to get Company A, part of Company B, and other units over to Blue Beach, but some of the battalion spent the night by the tidal basin, having first killed or captured most of an NKPA platoon. Next morning, hiking back to the beachhead, they mopped up as they went and arrived with a long file of enemy prisoners. Of the entire battalion, only Company C (". . . due to a combination of luck and an especially good coxswain," said its CO, Captain Robert F. Wray) landed at Blue Beach as planned, and was ashore and waiting when Hawkins finally got there.[29]

While these events were taking place, the defenders managed to keep things stirred up by continuing to shoot at ships downstream from Wolmi Do. At 1732, *Gurke,* which had already received fire that afternoon, was shelled by an NKPA tank or high-velocity gun on the south face of Observatory Hill. With shell spouts boiling up and splinters singing around the ship, *Gurke*'s 5-inch battery went into continuous rapid fire, 20 rounds a minute from each of six guns. Within minutes the air coordinator had a strike down on the same target. The fire ceased. Soon afterward, *LSMR-401*, rather conspicuous with her billowing colors, especially after spewing 2,000 rockets over the heads of the assault waves, came under fire from a gun in Inchon. Unlike the trigger-happy LSTs on Red Beach, the little rocket ship, thin-skinned and ugly, was proud to consider herself a fighting ship, and promptly took on the NKPA with her lone 5-inch gun. When the power rammer went out of kilter, the loading crew served their piece so enthusiastically that, even with hand ramming, they burned the paint off the gun barrel and silenced their foe in a 112-round duel.[30]

As daylight faded, the literal and figurative obscurity of what was happening on Blue Beach prompted Admiral Struble to see for himself. Inviting Generals Shepherd and Almond to come along, together with a few correspondents (including the AP man, Russell Brines), the admiral took his barge in.[31] Just before they entered the wall of smoke, the setting sun and a rain squall framed Inchon in a magnificent rainbow that dulled even the 13 large fires General Shepherd counted in the city. One factory in the industrial area inland of Blue Beach, he recorded, "was going like an inferno."

Despite occasional mortar rounds still falling, Admiral Struble had his coxswain lay the barge right alongside Blue 2 seawall. Then a Marine noncommissioned officer gave a stentorian hail: "Lay off, you stupid bastards! We're going to blast a hole in the wall!"

With some umbrage the coxswain replied, "*This* is Admiral Struble's barge."

"I don't give a shit whose barge it is," said the Marine. "Get it clear before I blow the seawall!" At this point, Struble, who had been listening with some amusement, ordered the coxswain to back off without further parley. Thirty seconds later a heavy explosion blew the wall sky high.

"As we pulled out to sea," General Shepherd's journal noted,

> . . . we could hear machine-gun and mortar firing all around the shoreline. The various fires were burning fiercely and occasionally some oil stowage would go off and flames would leap way up in the air. It was a terrific sight and one I shall long remember.

The Follow-Up

The object of the fighting on Red and Blue Beaches was to uncover the port of Inchon as rapidly as possible and make it available to support the campaign for Seoul. Intricate and carefully organized as were the details of the assault, those of the immediate follow-up were equally if not more so.

Artillery had to be landed and registered. All the tanks had to come in. Beaches had to be marked, opened, cleared and organized. Dumps had to be set up. Prisoners of war and Communist sympathizers had to be corralled. A division command post, with all its communications, had to be established. The wounds of Inchon had to be repaired and its civil administration reconstituted.

Ideally, it would have been most desirable to land at least part of the 11th Marines (the division artillery, commanded by Colonel James H. Brower) on Wolmi Do on the heels of the morning assault. This would permit artillery support from the island for the afternoon landings by the 5th and 1st Marines. But the plan was complicated enough without this added feature, and the final decision was to send in artillery reconnaissance parties with the morning attack and land the light (105mm howitzer) battalions that afternoon.

Landing the two 105mm battalions (1st and 2d Battalions, 11th Marines) in amphibian trucks (DUKWs) proved to be a hard job. The DUKWs were underpowered for the racing tides in the channel off Wolmi Do; some were virtually swept off the ramps of their LSTs and orderly formation of waves was impossible. But batteries got ashore somehow, and by 2150 were in position, registered, and ready to mass fires. Regimental headquarters had landed an hour earlier and the battalions were under regimental control. As it turned out, the lack of serious resistance combined with the gloom and dark to produce few targets for the artillery.[32]

Built-up areas, especially those with winding narrow streets and steep hills, such as Inchon, are not well suited to tank operations, so General Smith decided to land only one tank company (to support Colonel Murray's Red Beach assault) and bring in the other companies of the 1st Tank Battalion over Green Beach on Wolmi Do. What actually happened was that the entire battalion didn't get ashore and in its assembly area in Inchon's outskirts until September 17, nonetheless in good time to do yeoman's service in the advance on Kimpo and Yong-dungpo.

Opening the beaches, making order out of seeming chaos, was the job of the 1st Shore Party Battalion, whose redheaded commander, Lieutenant Colonel Henry P. Crowe, was on his third war. "Jim" Crowe, hero of Guadalcanal, Tarawa and the Marianas, was almost as much of a Corps tradition as Lewis Puller—a broad-shouldered, poker-playing, mustachioed onetime gunnery sergeant who spurred a Guadalcanal charge with the bellow: "Get up, you sons of bitches, you'll never get Purple Hearts laying in those god-damned foxholes!" As the combat moved clear of Inchon, Crowe's Shore Party Battalion would be absorbed into a larger port-operating organization composed of the Army's 2d Engineer Special Brigade, a Marine Combat Service Group (which the troops persisted in chaffing as "the Combat Nervous"), and a Marine motor transport battalion.

Leading elements of the shore party—beachhead bridge between land and water—hit Red Beach with early waves of the 5th Marines. With enemy machine guns stitching bursts through the billboard-sized beach-marking placards run up like giant targets, the shore party men guided in the eight LSTs on the heels of the assault. These ships must be completely unloaded during the night, no matter what conditions might be on the beach, then they must retract empty on the morning tide, and make prompt way for eight more ships bearing still more beans, bullets and equipment.

As ramps clanged down and bow doors swung open, bulldozers charged out into the pandemonium. Then, reversing course, operators dropped blades into the rear side of the seawall and shoveled sections into the sea so that the 450 vehicles aboard the LSTs could roll ashore. If this description makes the operation seem smooth and uncomplicated, that impression is false. While all this was going on, the LSTs were draw-ing enemy fire, with mortar rounds going off amid drums of gasoline, machine-gun bullets zinging high and low, and the LSTs making it worse by firing back. It was, in fact, just the environment for Jim Crowe.

Within four hours, heaving, shouting, bull-horning, bulldozing, string-ing communication wire—all under brilliant floodlights which gave the beach the air of a shooting gallery to enemy snipers in the dark town— the shore party and the engineers were well on top of the situation. When the morning tide flooded in with the dawn, the battered LSTs were empty. After a night of thrills and with a crucial mission accomplished, the young skippers, a lot more experienced now than 12 hours earlier, clawed off the beach and gave place to their incoming successors. In the heartfelt words of O. P. Smith, "Those eight LSTs were a godsend."[33]

Establishing the landing force command post ashore was in the capable hands of General Craig, whose former 1st Marine Brigade staff now served as the forward echelon of 1st Division headquarters. In accordance with arrangements previously worked out between the two generals, O. P. Smith sent instructions to Craig about noon on D-day, confirming that he was to land on Wolmi Do with the evening tide and open the advance command post. One night on the island, jam-packed with artillery, vehicles and supplies, convinced Craig that it was no place for the CP; next morning, he and Lieutenant Colonel Stewart, both of them veteran operations officers, found a better spot in southeast Inchon and began readying it for General Smith.

By the end of D-day, Admiral Doyle had landed 13,000 troops and their weapons and equipment. Nineteen more fully loaded transports and cargo ships, and 8 more LSTs had arrived on schedule and were being unloaded. With both assault regiments on their objectives, the total cost to the landing force had been 21 killed, 1 man missing, and 174 wounded. What D-day cost the *In Min Gun*—besides Inchon—will never be accurately known. In the hurly-burly there seems to have been no precise count of prisoners taken that day; at least three hundred would be a fair guess.

Much has been made in accounts of Inchon of seeming disorganization and confusion (the Blue Beach assault, especially) in this unrehearsed landing under difficulties without parallel. The fact remains that landings were made on time, objectives were captured on schedule and the enemy was struck so hard and so quickly that he was incapable of organized resistance or reaction until too late. As General Smith matter-of-factly put it in his log, "D-day had gone about as planned."

If, however, after the events of this long day, there were any, like General Almond, still prepared to view the landing as "a purely mechanical operation," O. P. Smith had a final word.[34] "The reason it looked simple," he later observed, "was that professionals did it."

General Shepherd also had a final word. Of the officer who would never admit that the landing was impossible and who, in the final analysis, had orchestrated the operation, the Marine general wrote, "Doyle is a great commander and is the best amphibious naval officer I have ever met."[35]

5

‚‚‚‚‚‚‚‚‚‚‚‚‚‚‚‚‚‚‚‚‚‚‚‚‚‚‚

Attack, push, and pursue without cease.

MAURICE DE SAXE

FLIGHT QUARTERS, then General Quarters, sounded before dawn on D+1 aboard the jeep carrier *Sicily*. Scarlet-shirted ordnancemen completed arming VMF-214's strike Able with bombs, rockets, napalm and 20mm magazines; gun switches, sights and arming mechanisms were checked. Gasoline crews, also in red, topped off the barrel-nosed Corsairs. Yellow-jacketed taximen and blue-clad plane handlers, obeying the air officer's bullhorn commands, stood by aircraft. As the eastern horizon lightened the word came, "Pilots, man your planes!" Plane captains in brown fussed over their airplanes, helped pilots into cockpits, and handed up "yellow sheets" for signature.

Eight pilots, mostly wearing the green "dungarees" of Marine infantrymen—a better bet on the ground than flight suits if worst came to worst —expertly worked through pre-flight checklists, tugged seatbelts, shoulder harness and parachute harness, patted .38s in shoulder holsters, and looked down at kneepads with gridded target maps. "Start engines!" the bullhorn rasped. Propellers jerked as starters whined, then spun with the cough, belch and blast of well-primed engines. Purple-coated chockmen crouched beside landing gear, keeping warily clear of propeller arcs. ("Nobody ever won a battle with a prop," goes the saying).

On a signal halyard the red and white "Fox" flag flies at the dip. The ship heels and turns into the wind. Fox is two-blocked at the yardarm, signal that flight operations have commenced. The morning wind whips along the flight deck. While taximen nod, gesture and beckon, the flight-deck chief supervises the spotting of aircraft and the flight-deck officer, checkered black-and-white raceway flag in hand, stands beside the island superstructure. When the lead Corsair is on "the spot," the flight-deck officer gives his circular hand signal to rev up. Feet hard down on brake and rudder pedals, the pilot eases his throttle forward. Now the engine roars. The pilot nods; the flight-deck officer snaps down his flag; and at 0550 this September 16, 1950, VMF-214's first airplane rolls ahead, gains momentum at the very edge of the flight deck, lifts tail and wheels, levels off to gain speed, then climbs to starboard waiting for the others to join up.

Once aloft and formed, the eight blue Corsairs head eastward toward the sun and the smoke columns still rising from Inchon. Today's battle-field and tomorrow's and the day after's are laid out like a terrain model.

Inchon sits on a peninsula. About three miles inland, beyond the smudge, the neck of land narrows, indented to north and south by estuaries, mud flats and salt pans. Then it widens out, the ground rises a little (not much from the air but enough for the "crunchers" of the in-fantry), there is a town to the left with many quonset buildings—"Ascom City," onetime U. S. occupation forces supply depot ("Ascom" = "Army Service Command"). From Ascom the railroad and highway bear due east toward Yongdungpo and.Seoul on the horizon, and a corridor of paddy and truck gardens angles left (northeast) toward the cement run-ways of Kimpo.

The place where the neck of land narrows beyond Inchon is also the neck of the tactical bottle. Here the *In Min Gun* has a three-mile line on which it might contain the landing force. In possession of this line, the 1st Marine Division can thrust at Kimpo, Yongdungpo, or both. Colonel Bowser, landing force operations officer, has designated this line as Objective "O-3." Beyond it, in grease pencil on Bowser's map, and spread out on the deck below VMF-214, an imaginary arc of almost 90 degrees, passing through Ascom City and terminating on blue water at each end, marks the force beachhead line. Attainment of the FBHL is General Smith's first main objective: once in Marine hands, this line insures that Admiral Doyle can land troops and material without inter-ruption and gives O. P. Smith maneuver room for his advance on Kimpo and Yongdungpo.

Aviators like nothing better than a highway and a railroad to steer on, and both, linking Seoul and Inchon, lay below. Now it was seven, a fine morning, breakfast was digested, formation tight, engines smooth, props in high pitch, and the strike leader, Major Floeck, was looking for trouble.

Just forward of Colonel Bowser's O-3 line, near some huts marked Kansong Ni on the target map, six Russian-built T-34 "Caviar Cans" were clattering down the highway toward Inchon. Late yesterday, elements of the 22d Regiment had headed that way from Seoul, but turned back abruptly when they learned of the afternoon landings on Red and Blue Beaches. This morning the T-34 tanks were pressing on. In a mile or so, unchecked, they would encounter leading riflemen of Colonel Sutter's 2d Battalion, 1st Marines.

Floeck spotted the tanks, spat out a radio transmission, pulled up sharp, then rolled down, straight down, as his wingman and the others followed. Toward the bottom of his run, close to the deck, he leveled off.

Floeck hit the lead tank square with a container of napalm. Drenched with "cooking oil," the tank burst into orange flame topped with black smoke. A rocket salvo ripped the tracks off a second tank, while a third, spurting hydraulic fluid and fuel, jolted to a stop but failed to burn. Antiaircraft tracers arced up (like its Russian masters the *In Min Gun* was highly indoctrinated in AA defense). A bullet pierced the oil cooler of Captain William F. Simpson's Corsair. If peacetime economy directives had not stripped the armor from F4U oil coolers, Simpson might still be flying.[1] But his cooler was unprotected, the airplane failed to pull out, and Simpson crashed to his death with a screaming thud and a fireball as bright as his enemy's.

VMF-214's second flight, which had gotten off at 0650, came in soon afterward. With bombs and rockets they knocked one T-34 off the road and blew another to pieces. Then they spotted NKPA soldiers diving for cover into nearby huts, and discovered camouflaged vehicles. Napalm drops incinerated the huts, and bombs and 20mm strafing did for the vehicles and most of the soldiers. The flight leader reported three tanks killed which, added to the first strike's score, seemed to make six. In fact, however, the tanks which the second attack smashed were those already stopped by Major Floeck—an overkill of which the 5th Marines would soon become aware.[2]

Winning the Force Beachhead

As these things go, the first night ashore was quiet. The enemy had been completely surprised, his local defenders wiped out or routed, and his high command was still in the dark as to what might be happening, other than trouble, at Inchon.

Inchon, in fact, was being zealously mopped up by the Korean Marines, who had come in over Red Beach. Using these troops on a difficult job for which they were uniquely qualified, General Smith could quickly get the 1st and 5th Marines out of town and on the way to the O-3 line. While the rest of the KMC Regiment, commanded by Lieutenant Colonel Shin Hyun Jun (later commandant of his corps and ultimately a distinguished Korean diplomat), remained in landing force reserve, Major Kim's 3d Battalion, attached to the 5th Marines, gave Inchon a thorough going-over.

Impetuous, victorious, fiery as their beloved *kimchi,* and still pretty green, the Korean Marines have been teased over the way they cleaned out Inchon. One account says neither friend nor foe was safe while they were in the town. No doubt this is so. But they knew from every loyal tongue in Inchon what the Americans did not yet know of the terrible crimes perpetrated by the Communist invaders, and they left no stone unturned. If the performance lacked professional smoothness, who could blame a new unit whose lone U. S. advisers were a Marine lieutenant who spoke no Korean and a sergeant who did know Japanese? In the words of the 5th Marines' operations officer, Major C. H. Brush, this lieutenant, Davis by name, "achieved a quite remarkable success. . . . They moved rapidly through the city, which they knew, and saved us a lot of trouble."[3]

The 5th Regiment was moving rapidly, too. Ray Murray's first job was to link up with Puller, then to bring his regiment abreast of the 1st Marines. With Roise's 2d Battalion in the lead, the 5th Marines were a mile out of town and in touch with Sutter's 2d Battalion, 1st Marines, on Hill 117 a half hour before morning colors on the stroke of eight bells aboard every warship in the harbor.

With no more opposition than the 5th Marines—that is to say, practically none—Puller's regiment had much more ground to sweep, and more complicated terrain, too. Until the 7th Infantry Division could get ashore, the 1st Marines had to cover the wide-open right flank of the landing force, and this entailed sweeping Munhang Peninsula, the rugged ground south of Blue Beach, to make certain it was clear of lurking Red units. Ridge, the wary and meticulous CO of the 3d Battalion, 1st Marines, and between wars a Jesuitical propagator of Marine amphibious doctrine, got the Munhang assignment. With his battalion all in one place after the night's turmoil around Blue Beach, he advanced south from Hill 233, rolling ahead in amphibian tractors which shook the mud huts of fishing villages. Looping south, then swinging north again along the peninsula's curve, he bagged prisoners, found an abandoned coast-defense battery covering the transport and lower fire-support areas where the mines had been, and garnered in rifles, machine guns, and a battery of the vicious 120mm Russian mortars so well known to Korean War veterans.

Five miles north, on the opposite side of the 1st Marines' zone, Puller kept Sutter and the 2d Battalion alongside the highway to Ascom City, advancing beside the 5th Marines' 2d Battalion. In the large gap between his far-flung assault battalions, Colonel Puller used his reserve battalion in characteristic fashion—well forward and virtually committed. When General Craig, up early and active as usual, got to the 1st Regiment command post, he found Puller drinking scalding black coffee out of a canteen cup, "very calm and collected for the first morning after a landing."[4]

By midmorning the battalions astride the highway were on the O-3 line. With the sun not yet over the yardarm, no prolonged deliberation was needed to evoke General Smith's next order—advance immediately and seize the force beachhead line.

About the time Colonel Bowser was putting the finishing touches on this order, the advance guard of the 2d Battalion, 5th Marines, was approaching Kansong Ni, with the 3d Platoon, Company A, 1st Tank Battalion, in the point. Here the highway veers north around the shoulder of a high knoll, built up with mud-walled thatched houses. Knowing his business, the platoon leader, Second Lieutenant Joseph Sleger, Jr., halted short of the knoll, looked it over intently, then sent one section (two of his Pershings) up a dirt track on the left to secure the hilltop and guard against unpleasant surprises from around the bend, and also to cover a steep hill (186) due east of the road.

As the two tanks reached the crest, they sighted three T-34s on the highway below. The Communist tanks were "buttoned up," hatches closed and guns horizontal, obviously expecting contact with the Marines. While the North Koreans frantically tried to hand-crank manually powered turrets onto the Marine tanks, the Pershings' hydraulic-drive turrets whipped toward the enemy, and before the North Koreans could get a round off, slammed 20 90mm armor-piercing shells into them. The three tanks exploded one after the other in a shower of fragments, broken

K

tracks and red dust and black smoke, then burned fiercely, and joy filled Lieutenant Sleger's heart.

Not far away were the hulks of two more T-34s, still warm and smoking, evidently VMF-214's quarry. No sign was seen of the third tank wounded by the aviators; probably it got away to the rear.[5]

When Colonel Murray received word to continue the advance, he swung Taplett's battalion—in reserve since its capture of Wolmi Do—into line on Roise's left. Both battalions moved out at 1330. Since contact did not exist with the enemy main force or, for that matter, with any organized enemy, the advance posed no problem more serious than flushing out the occasional sniper or herding in prisoners, some of whom were stripped naked in the search for concealed weapons. On the other hand, precisely because the enemy was not yet found or fixed, unremitting alertness and security were at a premium. But Taplett got the 3d Battalion on its objective before four o'clock with 12 prisoners and no casualties, and Roise had one company on each of two hills covering the highway and railroad defiles before the sun was down.

Still spread out and with the larger zone, Puller's regiment didn't cross the O-3 line until 1600. Along their side of the highway the 2d Battalion, 1st Marines (Sutter), had begun to develop resistance. The ground here would strongly have favored the *In Min Gun*. Both the highway and the railroad pass through defiles; the observation toward Inchon and Kansong Ni is all with the defender; the rugged ground south and west of Ascom City abounds in excellent blocking positions. That the Communists were still too shaken to make use of this terrain by anything but the scantiest screen of skirmishers is the measure of their loss of control. But it was a portent that all four 1st Division Marines killed on D+1 came from Sutter's battalion, as did ten of the division's 21 wounded.

To all intents and purposes, General Smith had his beachhead line when night fell. No unit was quite on the line physically, but the 5th Marines held high ground that overlooked Ascom City and commanded the FBHL. Colonel Puller still had more than a mile to go, but his 2d and 1st Battalions were also on key terrain features. Ridge had completed the 3d Battalion's sweep of Munhang Peninsula and was assembled in reserve. To take over the flank guard, Captain Kenneth Houghton's Division Reconnaissance Company had landed in the afternoon via Green Beach after a wearying time in their boats before the control vessel would let them go in. Reporting to Colonel Puller, Houghton was ordered to cover the 1st Regiment's far right flank and, next day, give the Namdong Peninsula (east of Munhang) a sweep. At both ends of the line, enemy dumps had been overrun. Houghton's people, making up for lost time, promptly located a seaside schoolhouse converted into a factory for wooden box mines. The building contained 40 tons of flaked TNT and almost 2,000 cases of other explosives captured from the U. S. Army. Taplett, on the extreme left of the 5th Marines, found a large vehicle park west of Ascom City and another dump stocked with captured U. S. ammunition.[6]

Everyone in the high command had the urge to get ashore. By afternoon the KMCs had done their work and Inchon had quieted down. Accompanied by Colonel Krulak and the aides, Generals Shepherd and Almond landed over the new beach—Yellow—now opened in the inner harbor. First they looked over Red Beach and Wolmi Do and visited wounded on one of the hospital LSTs, then there was a chat with Jim Crowe and, when Almond decided to get back to *Mount McKinley* for dinner, General Shepherd borrowed General Craig's jeep and went forward in search of "Chesty" Puller. Admiral Struble also came in later in the afternoon for a firsthand view of the beaches.

General Craig and Colonel Stewart had finally located the advance command post in the quonset huts of what had been a U. S. Army port installation during the postwar occupation. The generals' mess and quarters were to be in the remains of the officers' club, where the stewards were busily cleaning up and reactivating the galley. A fallen flagpole had been hoisted up, and the Stars and Stripes was flying.

With a good command post ashore, with the fighting units deployed, and with the force beachhead in sight, the time had come for General Smith to leave the command ship and assume command of operations ashore. There was a heartfelt handclasp for Doyle, and a certain wrench of parting: much had been compressed into the 25 days since O. P. Smith had arrived in Tokyo; few attack force and landing force commanders could have had a more harmonious relationship. Then General Smith called on MacArthur. "Be sure to take care of yourself," was the General's injunction, "and—capture Kimpo as soon as you can."

Clad in khaki garrison cap, green utilities and the Navy-style canvas leggings by which friend and foe came to recognize Marines during the South Korean fighting, the general went down *Mount McKinley*'s starboard accommodation ladder into the waiting boat. "Shove off, coxswain, take General Smith to Yellow Beach and return to the ship," came the officer-of-the-deck's hail, and, with his jeep and trailer, aide, map board and driver, the landing force commander headed for the beach.

Craig, minus his jeep, was waiting with Colonel Snedeker, a brave, quiet, skilled officer who had been the brigade's chief of staff. Admiral Struble chanced to be at Yellow Beach, too, and it surprised General Smith that the invasion commander should be ashore so soon.[7]

While Generals Smith and Craig jolted along the waterfront road, General Shepherd had missed Puller's unpretentious CP and ended up with Allan Sutter's battalion along the Ascom City road, where enemy resistance was beginning to show. While the general watched, Marines "dug a couple of North Koreans out of a hole in the side of a hill and polished them off in short order with a flame thrower." Then he returned rearward, located Colonel Puller, and stopped by the landing force CP for a final chat with O. P. Smith and to return Craig's jeep. While General Shepherd was on his way back to the flagship, at 1800, General Smith assumed command of operations ashore. Within 24 hours, with light casualties, the amphibious objective had been won.

Tanks at Dawn

Although NKPA Headquarters in Seoul still had no clear idea of the strength or location of the American forces ashore, the Communists were trying to regain their grip on the situation. Their immediate problem was to find and then either fix or delay the advancing U.N. columns until the defense of Seoul could be organized.

During the night of September 16–17, the 2d Battalion, 1st Regiment, Seoul Defense Division, with a tank platoon from the 42d Mechanized Regiment, advanced from Yongdungpo along the highway toward Ascom City. Beyond Sosa, a market town on the road, the battalion went into an assembly area in a hilly area southeast of Ascom City. Though the Communists did not realize it, they were in the zone of action of Sutter's battalion of the 1st Marines.

The North Korean battalion commander planned to advance his left company across the ridges, including Hill 186 to his front, toward Kansong Ni. His right company, working with the tanks, would have easier going with a rapid advance down the highway through Ascom City and thence, who knows how far? If his infantry could get onto the ridgelines beyond Ascom City, they would provide a base of fire for his tank-infantry maneuver unit, which was now drawing near, dangerously so, to the outposts of the 5th Marines.

Company D, 5th Marines, had halted at dark on a hill with the highway on its right and the Inchon–Seoul railroad line on its left. About 300 yards northeast the highway makes a sharp jog to the right (east) as one goes into Ascom City. Overlooking this jog, a natural blocking position in either direction, is another hill forward of Dog Company's position. To the practiced eye of Lieutenant H. J. Smith, the company commander, this hill was important. Instead of sending a squad to outpost it, "H.J." gave his 2d Platoon leader, Second Lieutenant Lee R. Howard, a machine-gun section and a 2.36-inch-bazooka man, and ordered the platoon to dig in where it could command the road.

Back toward Kansong Ni, in the defile between the main Dog Company position and Fox Company, 1st Marines, on the other side of the road, Colonel Murray had posted the regiment's 75mm recoilless rifles (the "75 Reckless" to the troops) hard by the new heavy 3.5-inch rocket launchers of Roise's 2d Battalion, 5th Marines. A little farther back but tied in with the 75 Reckless and the 3.5 bazookas were all five Pershings of the 1st Platoon, Company A, Tank Battalion. These powerful deployments, equally with the deep, tidy foxholes on the hills, were the routine precautions of trained, disciplined soldiers, different in form but no different in purpose or doctrine from the fortified *castra* of. Caesar's legions in Gaul.

It was a beautiful, sunny dawn with a breeze and a little chill in the air. While some of Howard's riflemen spooned into dense cylinders of cold C-ration corned beef hash or meat and beans, a few tried to warm up canteen cups of powdered coffee, or drank the juice off cans of pears or pineapple. Some reached into helmet liners to see if they had enough toilet paper for the day, and whether it was dry and serviceable. Empty cans were pitched over foxhole parapets, ration-component cigarettes of obscure brand were lit off, and the troops awaited the platoon sergeant's word to saddle up.

From up the road, through the patches of ground fog not yet burned off, came the sound of a tractor, more like several tractors, the steady clank-clank-clank of metallic treads and the growl of heavy-duty engines. Replacements fresh from the States would say it was tractors; Dog Company knew this morning that it was tanks. Lieutenant Howard passed word to hold fire, regardless of temptation. As the first T-34 nosed into sight, he could see it loaded with heedless infantry while less fortunate comrades hiked along, equally heedless, cracking jokes, munching rice balls and keeping up with five more tanks. Howard notified H. J. Smith, who relayed the report to battalion—six tanks and at least an infantry company strolling down the highway.

The approach side of Howard's knoll was a good ambush site—a ridge looking straight down the highway—but the reverse side was even better. Like a veteran ("Chesty" Puller couldn't have done it better) Howard held fire until the tanks and infantry had passed across his front, passed his crouching outposts, were beyond him and headed for Company D's position. Then, only then, did he let go. Every rifle, automatic rifle and machine gun loosed off in a hurricane of aimed fire. The NKPA soldiers were blasted off the tanks, dropped in the road, and cut down in swaths.

The bazookaman, Corporal Okey J. Douglas, ran downhill to within 75 yards of the lead tank, within killing range of his 2.36-inch rocket, blasted off, and set his target afire. As the next tank tried to dodge the wreck, Douglas reloaded and slammed in another rocket. Wounded but still moving, the T-34 tried to get onto the dried paddy beside the road.

Then all hell broke loose. The high-velocity 90mm guns of the Marine Pershings opened fire. The 5th Marines' recoilless rifles zeroed in with loud blasts; so did those from the 1st Marines across the road. Roise's 3.5-inch rockets whooshed. A private first class in F Company, 1st Marines, Walter Monegan, dashed down like Corporal Douglas, and hulled a tank with point-blank rocket fire.

Who did exactly what, and with which, and to whom in this ambush will never be known. After Douglas's unquestioned kill, the remaining T-34s were blown to pieces by a storm of shot and shell. More than 200 dead infantry cluttered the road. Probably the 45 90mm shells fired by the tank platoon accomplished most, but there was glory and honor for all hands—even glory enough to satisfy Douglas MacArthur.[8]

"... A Good Sight for My Old Eyes"

The General had breakfasted early and was eager to get onto the beach. Accompanied by Admiral Struble, by General Shepherd, by Generals Almond, Ruffner, Hodes, Fox, Wright and Whitney, and by a train of reporters including Marguerite Higgins and Carl Mydans, MacArthur

was greeted at Yellow Beach by O. P. Smith. First they visited the landing
force CP; Colonel Holcomb (intelligence) and Colonel Bowser (operations) were briefed smoothly and General Smith privately noted that
he was pleased. Then the jeep caravan set out up the highway looking
for Lewis Puller (who had been in the same class at Fort Benning with
General Wright back in 1931). As might have been expected, Colonel
Puller was commanding the 1st Marines from the front lines and had no
time to go back to meet MacArthur—"If he wants to see me, have
him come up in the front lines. I'll be waiting for him," was the word
he reportedly sent.[9]

Never one to avoid bullets, MacArthur went forward. Passing a dead
enemy, he spoke to a medical officer. "There's a patient you'll never
have to work on." Then, as he climbed back into his jeep, ". . . a good
sight for my old eyes."

Puller was on top of Hill 186, a steep enough climb for a young man,
when the supreme commander caught up with him. "We thought we'd
find you back in the CP," an officer expostulated. Puller gestured toward
his battle map: "That's my CP." MacArthur studied the scene. The 2d
Battalion, 1st Marines, was working its way forward up the next ridge,
Hill 132, having easily turned back the earlier infantry probe by the left
company of its counterpart battalion and regiment in the Seoul Defense
Division.

Abruptly General MacArthur said, "Colonel, your regiment is per-
forming splendidly, and I am gratified to present you with the Silver
Star." His aide having omitted to stock his jacket pocket with the usual
supply of decorations carried on these occasions, he dug in vain, then
ordered, "Make a note of that." Moments later, no doubt to avoid any
appearance of discrimination, the General presented Silver Stars to
Colonel Shin of the KMCs and Admiral Sohn, both of whom were
fortunate enough to be present.

Down on the road again, they came on the previous day's bag of tanks,
killed by VMF-214 and the Marine tankers. "Considering they are
Russian," the General grinned, "these tanks are in the condition I desire
them to be."

About this time (at least in General Smith's view) Colonel Murray of
the 5th Marines put his foot in his mouth. Seeing MacArthur's pleasure,
Ray Murray said that if the General wanted to see fresh-killed tanks,
there were some just up the road. As small-arms fire was still sputtering

audibly from the scene of Lieutenant Howard's ambush, O. P. Smith thought it was anything but a good idea to get General MacArthur killed that morning and in the Marine division's zone.

There was no stopping MacArthur. As he forged ahead, a young Marine officer ran up in a state of agitation and said, "General, you can't come up here!"

"Why?" asked the General.

"We've just knocked out six Red tanks over the top of this hill," the officer replied.

"That was the proper thing to do," rejoined MacArthur and strolled onto the crest for a look. General Shepherd recorded the moment:

> [The tanks] were still burning and dead North Korean troops were all around them. The occupants lay half cooked on top of several of the tanks. . . . The turrets had been punctured by clean hits. It was truly a very realistic battle picture.

Beyond the pass a fire fight was in progress as Roise's battalion advanced past Ascom City. MacArthur dismounted again and watched for a while. Kimpo airfield was clearly visible up ahead. Finally, to General Smith's everlasting relief, he consented to head rearward. Walking back from the hilltop, he said a downhill grade was easier on old legs like his, awarded Murray a Silver Star, and drove back to have a look at some of the 671 prisoners in the 1st Division's stockade. On the way back, Wright, always sympathetic toward the Marines, leaned over to General Shepherd and said, "That was the best publicity the Marine Corps could have put on."

And, by way of proof that O. P. Smith's apprehensions weren't idle, no sooner had the caravan departed than Lieutenant George C. Mc-Naughton's platoon poked seven NKPA riflemen, fully armed, out of the very culvert atop which MacArthur had parked his jeep while admiring the gutted tanks.[10]

Kimpo Captured

Although the capture of Kimpo airfield was his most important business that day, O. P. Smith spent much of the 17th coping with high-level visitors. In addition to the morning visit of the supreme commander and entourage, when he got back to the division CP in the afternoon General Smith found a Washington delegation awaiting him: Major General James M. Gavin, USA, and a civilian Ph.D. (Edward

Bowles of M.I.T.) from the Pentagon's Weapons Systems Evaluation Group. They were interested in Marine tank-killing techniques which had abruptly reversed the widespread assertion, dating from early panics in the perimeter, that American weapons somehow couldn't stop Russian tanks. Even more, they wanted to talk about Marine close air support. The striking, widely reported success of Marine tactical air in Korea— coming within less than a year of Louis Johnson's nearly successful attempt to abolish Marine aviation—was a subject of controversy and, indirectly, inter-Service recrimination. The Navy and Marines were not reticent over their battlefield vindication in this field, while the Army, which only three years before had sired the separate Air Force, was getting little or no effective tactical support from its former comrades, who looked on the business as a tiresome waste of air power. The Army power structure in Washington, which had a heavy stake in unification, could hardly afford a spitting row with the new Air Force but found it increasingly difficult to muffle nonsupport complaints against the airmen from the Army in the field. Aside from many points of technical interest involved, Gavin's visit resulted from this situation.[11]

Other visitors of importance were General Ruffner, X Corps Chief of Staff, and General Hodes of the 7th Infantry Division. The Army generals were there to coordinate the landing of the 32d Infantry and ultimate landing of the parent division. News that the 32d would soon be ashore was welcome to the Marines since the landing force right flank was covered only by the Marine reconnaissance company; and, while Eighth Army in the south had not yet responded very vigorously to the Inchon stroke, enemy reaction to General Walker's pressure, once aggressively exerted, would come against General Smith's right.

But the most colorful visitor (eventually a very welcome one) was a National Guard major general in the war zone with a personal *laissez-passer* from President Truman, to whom he submitted handwritten personal reports which were delivered unopened on the desk in the Oval Room.

Major General Frank E. Lowe, a fellow battery commander with Harry Truman in France, had been active in the Guard (and in Guard and American Legion politics) and later served as military liaison officer for the World War II Truman Committee of the Senate (because of whose disclosures and strictures a decade earlier, the Marines at Inchon had Higgins-design boats in which to land).

Tall, straight and vigorous for his sixty-five years, General Lowe wore a personal field uniform topped by a two-starred elephant-hunter pith helmet, and traveled with a Filipino striker, an aide, an interpreter, and a jeep fearsomely armed with a .50-caliber machine gun. Arriving at the Marine division CP, the striker picked out a corner in General Smith's billet, set up Lowe's cot and mosquito frame, unstrapped his bedroll and lugged in a water can. Less even-tempered generals than Smith and Craig might have taken umbrage at this proceeding, but they awaited their new messmate with equanimity and soon took him in. As O. P. Smith later wrote.[12]

> He got well up front and became a familiar figure to company commanders in the Division. His frank and disarming manner made him welcome throughout the Division. As to personal danger, his claim was that the safest place in Korea was with a platoon of Marines.

Whether or not this view was wholly welcome in the White House or the Pentagon, Lowe faithfully so reported throughout his months at the front. GHQ in Tokyo understandably found his presence trying. (In October, when General Cates called on MacArthur, the supreme commander confided, "A General Lowe is up there, who is a pain in the neck to me.") Another senior Regular commander dismissed Lowe as ". . . a National Guard windbag."[13] Actually, Lowe performed a useful function and did much (often over anguished Pentagon denials and reclamas) to give President Truman home truths about the atmosphere of the war.

Before the assault on Seoul could be launched, several intermediate objectives would have to be taken. Kimpo airfield, a prize in its own right, and Yongdungpo were the most important. As these two places were widely separated, the landing force would have to advance on two diverging axes (5th Marines to Kimpo, 1st Marines to Yongdungpo), with a final converging attack on Seoul. From here on, for a time, as the 1st Marine Division debouches from the Inchon peninsula via Ascom City, we will advance with Colonel Murray toward Kimpo.

Since about 12 miles of the division's 19-mile frontage on attaining the next objective (or "phase line") would be in the 5th Marines' zone, Murray's advance itself fanned from an attack due north by Major Kim's 3d Battalion, KMC, to an attack due east along the highway and railroad by Newton's 1st Battalion. Up the center, on a northeasterly axis from Ascom City, headed toward Kimpo, Roise and the 2d Battalion would make the main effort. Taplett, with the 3d, was in reserve.

After the tank ambush, Murray formed his regiment in column of battalions, Roise leading, Newton next, and Taplett off the road west of

Ascom City. The KMC battalion had already struck out north through Roise's initial positions. The advance jumped off at 0900.

Getting past Ascom City was slow work. The place was a shantytown surrounding many acres (two square miles, roughly) of warehouses, dumps, caves, fences and barriers. At its featureless edges the thatched huts and lean-tos of the poor gave way to equally featureless, flat paddy. The town itself was a natural collecting point for stragglers or retreating units from Inchon.

With Captain Jaskilka's Easy Company and correspondents Jim Bell and Joseph Alsop in the van, the 2d Battalion worked its way past the southern edge of town, encountering pocket after pocket of disorganized North Korean troops. Then, in much the same fashion, Roise headed his column northward to the left, still following the edge of town and also looking for a secondary road which was supposed to lead to Kimpo, clearly visible from the hills around Ascom City. As Jaskilka pushed along, he was aided by Company A of the tank battalion, and his left flank in the town was covered by a platoon of Fox Company under Second Lieutenant Tilton A. Anderson. Anderson had the unenviable job of working his way up the center of Ascom City, but hit relatively little resistance.

By noon Roise was at the northeast corner of town, looking for the dirt road which meanders out toward Kimpo and is as hard to find today as it was then. Newton, meanwhile, had struck out along the regiment's right, advancing rapidly on the highway to Seoul. Although the 1st Marines, on Newton's right, were meeting fairly stiff resistance that morning, Newton's battalion encountered only occasional small-arms fire, took a few prisoners, searched a few houses and kept going.

From Roise's corner of Ascom City an absolutely flat, broad corridor runs directly to Kimpo. It is mainly paddy (but the rice had mostly been harvested by September and the ground was solid) with occasional gardens of cabbage and leeks. Beyond Kimpo, two large hills of future interest to the 5th Regiment—131 and 125—dominate the left background. Beyond the Han, the mountains rise hard and sharp on the horizon. This corridor, with its shoulders and a few knolls toward the farther end, was the 5th Marines' zone.

Up ahead and to the right of Kimpo lay two bare knolls, arbitrarily named Able and Baker. These were the 2d Battalion's initial objectives. Once secured, they would provide a base for Roise's jump-off toward Kimpo, three miles north.

"At each small village," wrote Jim Bell in *Life*, "the citizens came out to meet us waving flags, clapping their hands and bowing. One of the most unexpected and pleasant experiences of this operation has been the genuine enthusiasm which has greeted the Marines."

No resistance was encountered during the hot, dusty three-mile advance on Able and Baker. "The newspapers will say this was a flying column knifing across Korea," one rifleman said to Bell. "Look at my tired feet. Do I look like a flying column?" At 1600, after two more hours for tired feet, the 2d Battalion was at the base of knoll Baker. A rifle platoon— Deptula's—scouted the hill, found only empty trenches, got a good look at Able, and reported it empty, too. Then Roise faced his battalion left to advance in line of companies on the airfield.[14]

While Roise's flying column knifed wearily along toward the two knolls, his supporting tank platoon, under First Lieutenant William D. Pomeroy, found the dirt road out of Ascom City untrafficable for the Pershing tanks. Reconnaissance to the north disclosed a far better road (the Kimpo–Inchon highway) which approximately paralleled the 2d Battalion's advance, but about two miles north. Picking up Anderson's detached platoon of Company F, Pomeroy formed a tank-infantry team and rolled forward. The rifle platoon was not all Pomeroy picked up. First he was joined by the 2d Battalion's combat train, which had also found this road, and then by another tank platoon and his own company commander, Captain Gearl M. English. English's tanks were accompanied by a jeep bearing Marguerite Higgins and Keyes Beech (himself a World War II Marine). Miss Higgins had vowed she would be the first to set foot on Kimpo field and tried to outrun the column until Captain English, not to be outdistanced, firmly positioned his own jeep in the van. By 1600 the tanks— the nearest thing to a mechanized thrust that occurred during the campaign—had come up on Roise's flank and were in position to swing north and support the 2d Battalion's push toward Kimpo.

Properly anxious to capture Kimpo and keep the advance rolling, the assault battalions of the 5th Marines had gotten past Ascom City as quickly as they could, but the place proved to be a hornet's nest. The Korean Marine battalion, which had jumped off northward at 0700, found itself unable to get through the western outskirts of the town, while Taplett's battalion, in regimental reserve, discovered that the origin of the resistance holding up the KMCs was the initial assembly area of the 3d Battalion. Having to attack to capture an assembly area is a novel operation for an infantry battalion in reserve, but this is what Taplett did. First committing G Company, then Item and How, the battalion knocked out North Korean machine-gun nests, killed 18 Communists, and had to mop up much of Ascom City's unfashionable northwest section before it could settle down to await further orders. With this help the KMCs broke loose and advanced rapidly without further difficulty.[15]

But Ascom City still had some sting. In the afternoon, just as Roise was forming the 2d Battalion to seize Kimpo, Colonel Murray's command post displaced into town and set up near the railroad station. As the ordnance officer, Marine Gunner Parrish, reconnoitered a site for his dump, he was cut down and killed by a blast of small-arms fire which wounded two of his NCOs. First Lieutenant Nicholas A. Canzona (later an able Marine historian) came to the rescue with his platoon of engineers, who swept through the adjacent paddies and orchard, killing 10 enemy and taking prisoners. Then, when Major James D. Jordan, China hand and Oriental linguist, led in the battery detail of A battery, 11th Marines, they too were fired on, and the artillerymen, like the engineers, had to ground their aiming circles, grab their rifles and wade in as infantry (killing four more NKPA die-hards) before A Battery could rightfully claim its new position-area.[16]

Colonel Krulak, General Shepherd's skilled operations officer, spent the afternoon ashore while the 5th Regiment was closing in on Kimpo, but had to make his way back to Inchon and the command ship before sunset. His report that Kimpo was still in enemy hands dampened General Shepherd's spirits, for he was anxious to be able to tell MacArthur that the Marines had swept over still another major objective. "I confess I hated to go in to dinner," he recorded, "as I knew MacArthur would ask me if we had taken Kimpo."

General Shepherd might have spared himself his worries. As he was cleaning up for dinner, Roise had completed the northward realignment, forming the 2d Battalion on left into line, with D and E Companies in assault, and moved out toward the airfield. Up to his left front, English's tank company and its infantry support were advancing across country while the shadows lengthened.

The tankers hit resistance about a half mile south of the field. An NKPA combat group opened up with machine guns and small arms. Tanks buttoned up, Anderson's riflemen deployed into fire teams, and English ducked out of his jeep into a ditch to coordinate the attack. "Not far away," recounted one of English's officers,[17]

. . . was the most beautiful press correspondent this writer has ever seen and she too had assumed the position of a good wise combat Marine when he comes under unexpected fire.

Neither English nor Higgins stayed pinned down. With the tanks' 90mm guns barking and machine guns hammering, the riflemen attacked briskly and drove in the enemy picket, for it was only that. About this time the assault companies of the 2d Battalion came level with the armor. English assigned one of his platoons to each, and the two companies raced each other for the edge of the airstrip. Before sunset (there was still light enough for *Life*'s Hank Walker to catch the scene), U. S. Marines were on Kimpo field.[18] After night had fallen, O. P. Smith had the pleasure of phoning *Mount McKinley* to notify General Shepherd that the 2d Battalion, 5th Marines (in which Shepherd had served, war and peace, as platoon leader, company commander and battalion commander), had secured the field at 2005. Beaming, General Shepherd, who had turned in early, rushed across in pajamas to give MacArthur the news; equally pleased, the supreme commander penned a dispatch to the Joint Chiefs.[19] He could have been forgiven had his last sentence read, "I told you so."

Counterattacks on Kimpo

The night dispositions of the 5th Marines were these: Newton's 1st Battalion held Objective E, a hill mass east of the road linking Kimpo and the town of Sosa, almost four miles southeast; Roise, as we have seen, was at Kimpo; and Taplett, with the 3d Battalion, still in reserve, was a mile back on the Ascom City–Kimpo highway.

At Kimpo field the 2d Battalion had formed three company perimeters ("goose-eggs," the tacticians call them, from their symbol on a map) about the southern half of the field and its base installations. Fox Company's goose-egg, including an engineer platoon and an antitank platoon, covered the southeastern approach; Easy, the northeast. Lieutenant Deptula's platoon of Company E outposted the north end of Soryu Li, a brick-walled village which straggles around the approach roads northeast of the airfield. Dog Company had the rear position along the west side of the main runway, and had both English's tanks and Roise's command post within its lines.

The North Korean dispositions, such as they were, were not quite so tidy.

The defenders of Kimpo had been the thoroughly bombed and strafed 1st Air Division, an infantry formation, the 107th Regiment, and beaten remnants of the 226th. The field's ground security troops, the 877th Air Force Unit, were the ones who had pinned down Maggie Higgins, but had lost their commanding officer in English's attack. The leadership of the 107th Regiment is open to some question, as their colonel, one Han Choi Han, slipped from his headquarters on the night of September 17 and was last seen crossing the river on an important mission to Seoul. Those unable to emulate this prudent officer milled about the flatlands and river bottoms that lie between the Han and Kimpo. By dint of furious labors to the tune of occasional pistol shots, the surviving officers and the political cadres inspired the troops for one final effort.

At 0300 Lieutenant Deptula's people on outpost in Soryu Li heard the sound of enemy approaching. As happened often during this campaign, the Marines coolly held fire. Advancing down the road toward Kimpo, an NKPA company was allowed to penetrate to the center of the outpost. The platoon sergeant, Richard L. Martson, stood up, shouted the war cry "United States Marines!" and commenced firing. In the blast of rifle and automatic-rifle fire that followed, 12 enemy died before the rest of the company could scuttle back into the darkness.

In the succeeding hour the North Koreans made three more probes. Each was repelled. Then, as dawn drew near, the Marines discerned the growl of a tank approaching. As the platoon had no tank-killing weapons, Deptula felt the time had come to fall back onto E Company's goose-egg. Carrying one wounded Marine and the body of another who had been killed (the platoon's only casualties) the platoon made it back by 0500, having stopped four attacks. The tank—it was a T-34—chose not to pursue and neither did the Communist infantry. Captain Jaskilka, the company commander, who had begun to wonder if he had lost a platoon, breathed easier.

Jaskilka's relief at seeing Deptula didn't last long. Just before daylight, from the west (somewhere toward the center of the airfield) small-arms fire began to play on Company E. Since this came from the direction of D Company's goose-egg, Jaskilka jumped up and shouted, "Hey, you guys! Cease fire! This is Easy Company!"

When the guys failed to cease fire, the captain realized that the bullets zinging by came from Moscow, not Rock Island or Springfield, and that his company was being attacked by enemy squads who had infiltrated the battalion area during the night. Shortly afterward a second, heavier attack came in from the east in company strength. Second Lieutenant Charles Christiansen's platoon caught the brunt, but with mortar fires expertly called in by Sergeant Marvin Eggersgluss and a grenade charge by Corporal Russell House (who was killed as the attack ebbed), the position held.

Describing the Communists' final effort, Bell wrote in *Life:*

> In the first light of morning I saw one Red officer, a Japanese sword in his hand, leading a group of 30 men. He was hit once but got up and rallied his men, screaming at the top of his voice. His men dropped about him until he was the only one left. Hit again, he struggled to his feet and stumbled to within 15 yards of Jaskilka's hole. There he fell for good, a victim of company gunnery sergeant Bob Barnett, a fiercely bearded old pro.

Soon afterward, Captain Fenton of B Company, atop the high ground south of Kimpo held by the 1st Battalion, saw about 200 enemy soldiers filing across his front in the direction of the airfield. Holding fire though the target was tempting, he notified battalion and word was quickly relayed to Roise that another attack was coming in.

The night had not been quiet southeast of Kimpo. Soon after midnight an NKPA demolition team had been stopped by F Company's outpost (actually the engineer platoon and the assault platoon from regiment.) Later, another probe had been halted at the same point, an overpass crossing the Ascom City highway.

Unaware that Fenton was watching them or even that Marines were on the ridge to their left, the enemy trudged past while forward observers from the 11th Marines and the infantry mortars depressed microphone buttons and transmitted the command: "Fire Mission . . ."

Simultaneous with the opening volleys from the 1st Battalion, 11th Marines, Roise's and Newton's mortars crashed down, while Peters's F Company riflemen and machine gunners joined in. From his vantage point on the flank, Fenton directed enfilading fire into the Communists.

Save for a sharp fight at the overpass, where one North Korean platoon hit the outpost (their third attack since midnight), it was over almost before it began. At the outpost, however, Second Lieutenant James E. Harrell, with his assault platoon and the engineers, fought a spectacular point-blank battle using white-phosphorus incendiary rockets to the tattoo of the engineers' machine guns.

As the enemy scattered and fell back, Roise launched the tank company in a cruising attack across the fields while Companies E and F mopped up, and Newton sent in his reserve company, Charlie, when the Communists straggled into the 1st Battalion's zone.[20]

Later in the morning, while the rest of the 2d Battalion secured its grip on the field and on Kimpo village, Soryu Li, and the surrounding hamlets, Lieutenant Smith's Dog Company, innocent victims of Jaskilka's wrath, advanced without opposition onto Hill 131, overlooking the banks of the Han, and thus became the first Marines to reach the river.

The next step was to get across.

". . . Our Beloved Corsairs"

Just about the time that Communist tanks were advancing into the 5th Marines' trap near Ascom City early on the 17th, the North Korean Air Force delivered its only blow during the campaign.

At 0555 that morning, *Rochester*'s fantail sentry, a sailor armed with a rifle, heard the sound of aircraft engines. Buzzing low out of the sunrise and just over the hills ashore, a YAK-3 and a Stormovik IL-10 made for the flagship. Each plane let go a string of four 100-pound bombs, all but one of which burst close aboard in the water (the one that hit glanced off the ship's aircraft crane and failed to detonate). Caught flat-footed (which mightily displeased Admiral Struble), *Rochester*'s antiaircraft battery was silent, although the fantail sentry got off eight .30-caliber rounds from his rifle.

Five thousand yards astern of the flagship, HMS *Jamaica* was next. Raking her bridge and topside with machine-gun and cannon fire, the Communist pilots killed one and wounded two of the ship's company. But the alert British gunners got their 4-inch antiaircraft and pom-poms smartly into action and downed the Stormovik—to that time the only instance in the war of an aircraft being brought down by ship's antiaircraft. But the attack was ill conceived; it was, as Captain J. S. C. Salter, *Jamaica*'s captain, observed, ". . . foolhardy of them to go for two cruisers when they had a choice of transports and freighters galore."[21]

Within 24 hours, aside from having lost its major airdrome, the NKAF was short several other aircraft though not from U.N. fire. Part of the rich haul at Kimpo was an intact YAK-3 (possibly the villain of the day before) and two more Stormoviks. Other YAKs and Stormoviks had been destroyed or damaged by the retreating defenders. The intact YAK was immediately painted with U. S. markings by MAG-33, delivered to Air Force technical intelligence crews and flown to Japan.

The first American aircraft to land at Kimpo after its capture was a

L

Sikorsky HO3S-1 helicopter from cigar-chewing Major Vincent J. Gott-schalk's Marine Observation Squadron 6 (VMO-6). It is a common-place today to speak of helicopters; it was anything but a commonplace in 1950. There were only eight helicopters in Korea then, and all were from the Marine Corps. The Brigade's helicopter detachment, flying in the perimeter, and now with the 1st Marine Division, was the first heli-copter unit ever to fly in combat.[22]

Even had the landing of a Marine helicopter at Kimpo been a routine matter, this HO3S-1 had no ordinary passengers. Piloted by Captain Victor A. Armstrong, it was carrying General Shepherd and Colonel Krulak. As they debarked, surprised and pleased to have made the first touchdown on the recaptured field, they were spotted first by General Craig, who had just arrived by jeep, then by reporters and photographers. Characteristically, General Shepherd's first action was to seek out Roise and congratulate his old battalion on its newest feat.

The field was in fine shape, and Company A of Colonel Partridge's engineers was already getting minor damage patched up when Generals Cushman (tactical air commander, X Corps) and Harris (1st Marine Air Wing) flew in by helicopter during the afternoon. While looking around, they heard the familiar roar of a Corsair with prop in low pitch and saw one of VMF-323's *Badoeng Strait* airplanes on final approach with flaps set at 30 degrees and landing gear down. Although the field was still closed and thus distinctly off limits, Lieutenant John V. Hanes had decided he would be the first pilot to land a high-performance plane at Kimpo. His joy was dampened when, on clambering out of his cock-pit, he had to explain to two Marine aviation generals and well-known disciplinarians why he was playing hookey. Mumbling something about his engine running a little rough, he quickly enplaned and stood not on the order of his going. When they saw him safely airborne and headed for the "Bing-Ding," the two generals grinned at each other. And, back aboard the "Bing-Ding," his messmates in the wardroom presented him a ceremonial cake baked in honor of the first landing.

One other witness—Captain Pomeroy of the tanks—who had watched the expert fashion in which Major General Harris assumed the role of taximan and spotted his victim into the visiting pilots' space beside the tower, recorded the "comfort" of seeing "one of our beloved Corsairs" land nearby, "though we all suspected the pilot of feigning engine trouble."[23]

Rather than break up a going concern on the two escort carriers, which up to now had provided tactical support for the landing force, General Harris had planned to leave the original Marine squadrons afloat, flying in additional squadrons and ground units to Kimpo from Japan. General Cushman's Tactical Air Command (TAC), X Corps (in reality the headquarters and service elements of MAG-33, with ground control intercept and tactical air control squadrons attached), would take over Kimpo and use it as a base for close support of the advance on Seoul. General Almond approved this decision and ordered Cushman to land MAG-33 on September 19. At the same time, in the usual way of an amphibious operation, control of tactical air operations in the objective area passed from the Navy (afloat in *Mount McKinley*) to the Marines ashore at Kimpo.

Restoring Kimpo to life as a functioning base required more than arrival of tactical squadrons. Kimpo's logistic problems highlighted a serious deficiency in the logistic arrangements of X Corps. As highest ground echelon in the *Chromite* operation, X Corps had the responsibility of combat support for all corps units, including the 1st Marine and 7th Infantry Divisions, and the Tactical Air Command. Unfortunately the corps staff failed to provide for sufficiently early landing of the vehicles needed to operate the port, clear beach dumps, and move supply inland from Inchon. ("The impetus of supply must always be forward," runs the soldier's maxim.) As a result, robbing Peter to pay Paul, General Almond pre-empted General Smith's 7th Motor Transport Battalion for rear-area port operation, thus stripping O. P. Smith of essential combat transportation and thereby burdening a frontline division with the support of X Corps in the rear.

One consequence of this breakdown was that aviation fuel which was to have been trucked to Kimpo from Inchon could not, even with the extra capacity provided by the Marine motor transport battalion, be delivered. Instead, Colonel K. H. Weir, General Cushman's chief of staff, worked out impromptu arrangements with Far East Air Forces to fly in over a thousand tons of avgas and more than four hundred tons of ordnance, which gave the Tactical Air Command a stockpile to go on. Even so, initial missions from Kimpo had to be flown by arriving squadrons from gas remaining in their tanks, and refueling had to be accomplished by hand. As of the end of the campaign, responding generously to the emergency, Far East Air Forces Combat Cargo Command had lifted 3,338 tons of all classes of supply directly into Kimpo for operation of the air base, while only 1,450 tons ever got there via the

X Corps pipeline from Inchon. As General Cushman's Tactical Air Command action report tersely observed, "Comparatively little supply support was obtained from X Corps."[24]

Operation of the field—as distinct from flight operations therefrom —was supposed to be an Air Force responsibility, but it turned out that Fifth Air Force had no equipment available for this expeditionary work, so MAG-33 provided ambulances, crash trucks, refuelers, water purification units, and Marine crews. When the Fifth Air Force communication center arrived, they lacked the correct cryptographic publications and equipment, so MAG-33 took on this chore, too. Field security was another chore, and a necessary one. When it turned out that this elementary requirement had not been anticipated in base planning, General Cushman, in the tradition of Marine aviation, activated a 120-man infantry company from his ground crews and mechanics, who downed tools, slung rifles, mopped up, patrolled and challenged, and serviced airplanes in between. Within 24 hours the base even had its newspaper, the first such published ashore: the Kimpo *Pioneer Press,* put out by the group information officer with a 400-copy mimeo run and two ambitious Korean urchins as newsboys.

While General Cushman was reactivating Kimpo, calls for tactical air support were mounting, mainly from the 1st Marines, whose operations we will soon see. On September 18 and 19, over 50 requests for tactical air were handled by the carrier squadrons. Just before nightfall on the 19th, Lieutenant Colonel Max J. Volcansek, Jr., a short, blond, cheerful, cocky aviator brought in the first tactical squadron, Marine Night Fighting Squadron 542 (VMF(N)-542), from Itami in Japan. Ironically, for a night-fighting outfit, "Maxie" Volcansek's first strike— and the first such from Kimpo since recapture—came by daylight next morning when four of his F7F's blew up two enemy locomotives, always favorite targets for aviators.

On the following day, Volcansek was followed by VMF-212 and VMF-312. And thus, in less than two days after its capture, General Cushman had Kimpo in full operation with a strength of 2,051 people, three tactical squadrons and more to come. With a major seaport and a major airdrome securely in hand, the U.N. forces could proceed with the liberation of Seoul.[25]

Rubber-Boat Raiders

Only one part of the operation had fizzled so far. In some way not yet wholly explained, Colonel Ely had secured permission to go ahead with his commando-style grab for Kimpo, and tried to execute it on the night of September 16–17.

In a complicated series of movements, Ely transferred his 124-man Army special operations company from HMS *Whitesand Bay* to an ROKN frigate, which cast them loose north of Inchon, in rubber boats with canoe paddles, at dusk on the 16th. They were to paddle three miles against the tide, land by night, march 12 miles across enemy country, seize Kimpo from its 500 or more defenders, and then deliver the field to the Marines on arrival. As noted in Chapter 2, General Smith and his staff had little confidence in the scheme and felt, to say the least, that it had not been fully thought through.

Ill-planned (". . . a manifest attempt to make headlines," General Smith called it), this operation was finally canceled because no amount of breathless paddling against the tide could get Ely's rubber boats within a half mile of shore. Maybe this was just as well: one member of the party who thought so said afterward, "Every night for the rest of my life I'm going to get down on my knees and thank God for that tide."

Yet even if Ely's landing had gone according to plan in every respect, Kimpo would have been captured during the day of September 17— the day the 5th Marines took the field anyway. Obviously, Almond's design for "early seizure" of Kimpo would therefore not have achieved its stated purpose even if it had succeeded.[26]

The In Min Gun *Revives*

On September 18 Pyongyang first admitted publicly that something might be happening at Inchon: an official communiqué stated that two American aircraft had been shot down there by coast artillery units. Next morning *Jen Min Jih Pao* (*People's Daily*, Peking) disclosed to its readers that the American imperialists had made still another mistake. There had been a landing at Inchon, but it was "a gamble . . . completely lost." Evidently unfamiliar with the 1st Marine Division, *Jen Min Jih Pao*'s military editor went on to say that the Americans were weakened by "low fighting spirit . . . distant reinforcements. . . . If the fighting lasts any length of time, they will surely be defeated."[27]

Closer to home, as we have seen, the 18th (or Seoul Defense) Division had been immediately withheld from its Naktong assignment in the south, and the 70th Regiment ordered north to Seoul from Suwon. The

18th Division, in fact, had been ordered to retake Inchon, a mission the difficulties of which had already been underscored.

Just about the time of Pyongyang's gingerly inference of trouble at Inchon, Colonel Holcomb, the landing force G-2, began to perceive the first signs—and evidence mounted quickly—that the *In Min Gun* was reviving from shock and making ready to fight for its life.

Infantry, armor and many vehicles were spotted by division air observers on the 18th (D+3) moving north from Suwon (the 70th Regiment, no doubt), not only toward Seoul, but also into Yongdungpo, in the path of the 1st Marines. Heavy traffic was also seen crossing the 38th parallel south from Pyongyang and Kaesong.

That same day, pilots of VMF-214 and VMF-323, the two highly experienced carrier squadrons, reported and attacked tanks near Yongdungpo, as well as large accumulations of supplies on the sandspit river bottom between Yongdungpo and Seoul. Intelligence informants said NKPA engineer troops were heavily mining the Sosa–Yongdungpo highway and all approaches to Yongdungpo. Mortar positions were reported there, too, and another source disclosed that the 87th Regiment, 9th Division (a new formation), had been ordered to make an all-out defense of the town.

Upstream (northwest) of Yongdungpo, a commanding hill mass (Hill 118) was being organized by enemy troops swept eastward by the 5th Marines. Across the Han, Haengju and Hill 125, both of which the 5th Marines would soon know well, showed signs of occupancy in force. On the landing force left flank, up the Kumpo Peninsula, division air observers and Navy pilots from Task Force 77 had spotted about a thousand enemy troops.

In addition to all these signs and portents of trouble, Colonel Holcomb did not yet know that still further enemy reinforcements were on the way: the 105th Armored Division moving north toward Suwon; the hardened 25th Brigade, mainly composed of troops with Chinese experience, had been started to Seoul from Chorwon the day of the initial landing. The 78th Independent Regiment, another strong infantry formation, would reach Seoul on the 19th.

Thus the NKPA had commenced its struggle to contain the U.N. thrust. On the right, reinforcements were moving up from Suwon; in the center, Yongdungpo and Seoul were being organized for defense behind holding forces; on the left, reinforcements were on the way from Pyongyang, Chorwon and Kaesong, the Han crossings were being covered, and the northwest approaches to Seoul were being stoutly fortified.[28]

The fighting spirit of Koreans, South and North, is well known to all who have fought beside or against them. The ferocity of Communists in defense of cities—Madrid, Leningrad, Stalingrad, for example—is equally well known. By D+3, could fighting spirit outweigh the momentum of MacArthur's thrust—and was Seoul destined to know the agonies of Madrid or Leningrad?

Eighth Army Begins to Move

During dinner on the 19th, the General was quiet and noncommittal —a role sufficiently unusual to be immediately remarked by his messmates. When coffee was finished, MacArthur led the way down to *Mount McKinley*'s joint operations room, three decks below. On the display board on the forward bulkhead was a large map of Korea; around the table were Admiral Struble, General Shepherd, Admiral Doyle, and Generals Almond, Fox, Whitney and Wright.

After general remarks about the course of the campaign, MacArthur said gravely that he did not believe General Walker would be able to break out of the Pusan perimeter with sufficient strength to make the requisite juncture with X Corps. Continuing, the General said that the Eighth Army had been on the defensive so long that he doubted their ability to attack forcefully (a new army commander might well be needed), and the distance between Eighth Army and X Corps might be too great for them to link up.

It therefore appeared to him, said MacArthur, that there might have to be another amphibious thrust farther down the coast in order to join forces. Kunsan was the place he had in mind. Struble replied that the Navy could find the shipping; Doyle said the beaches were feasible. As always when MacArthur proposed, Almond agreed. Then followed the usual discussion of details—beaches, hydrography, road net, beach exits, possible schemes of maneuver, troop list (would it be the Marines again? —no, said MacArthur, they were his best division and should cover Seoul, the vital spot). What about Posun-Myong instead? ventured Struble with Shepherd's support. Doyle was tentative, evidently preferring Kunsan. When the meeting adjourned MacArthur directed Wright, the G-3, to have a study of the operation ready within a week. Wright's first action was to send a message to General Hickey (standing in for Almond as chief of staff in Tokyo) relaying MacArthur's instructions and directing that the pre-Inchon plan for a Kunsan landing be dusted off and activated.[29]

In his impassioned sales talk to Sherman and Collins in Tokyo, Mac-Arthur had pointed to Inchon on the map and declared, "This is our anvil, and Johnnie Walker can smash against it from the south." What was worrying MacArthur now was that, although the Eighth Army had jumped off—at least nominally—on September 16, in four days' fighting it had not secured even a proper bridgehead across the Naktong, and its farthest advance had covered a bare handful of the 180 miles that separated Eighth Army and X Corps. MacArthur had visualized Walker's attack as a blitzkrieg up the axis Taegu-Kumchon-Taejon-Suwon, but it was advancing more like a tortoise than a tank.[30]

Walker's problem—admittedly difficult—was to shift gears from a hard-pressed defense to a driving attack, and that without replacements or even (as Walker felt) an adequate reserve. In plans it had been contemplated that news of Inchon would buck up the Eighth Army and demoralize the Communists. Neither result took place. For four days after the 1st Marine Division's landing, this ominous news was withheld from all but the highest levels of the NKPA, which continued to fight with accustomed tenacity, thus quenching the Eighth Army's cautious optimism. As late as September 22, when the 1st Marine Division was hammering at the gates of Seoul, the farthest advance of Eighth Army was still less than 25 miles ahead of its positions on the 15th.

In fact, however, even while MacArthur was planning a Kunsan landing, the Communists were commencing redeployments for a stubborn withdrawal from the south. When the tidings of disaster finally reached the rank and file, the *In Min Gun* began to disintegrate and—eight days after the landing at Inchon—the Eighth Army began to roll northward. Kunsan went back to the files.

Behind the Front

Although every commander's heart is on his front and flanks, many of his most serious concerns lie in the rear. Thus, while the 1st and 5th Marines were pushing on toward the Han, O. P. Smith had much to occupy him in Inchon.

His logistic situation, thanks to prodigies by Admiral Doyle and Jim Crowe on the beaches, was better than anyone could have hoped. Both Blue and Red Beaches had been closed out (the former on the 16th, when the assault had rolled past; the latter, next day). Green Beach, on Wolmi Do, and Yellow, essentially the Inchon inner harbor, now were carrying the load. Getting the inner harbor and tidal basin in operation was a race against time: the last of the spring tides came on September 18; after that the beaches could not be used by LSTs. But Captain W. T. Singer, USN, the naval beachmaster and Crowe's opposite number, landed heavy cranes over Green Beach and had them working by the 17th (D+2) in time for arrival of Rear Admiral L. A. Thackrey, with the headquarters of Amphibious Group 3 in USS *Eldorado*. Thackrey and his group, ultimately to relieve Doyle and Amphibious Group 1, had as their first job operation of the port of Inchon.

General unloading had now begun. This meant that all ships could be emptied of cargo as fast as it could be discharged, rather than having specific items and units called in as needed. On the 19th, every ship in the first echelon had been unloaded; only three days later, 25,512 tons of cargo had been unloaded (twice the amount projected in corps logistic planning), and 53,882 troops and 6,629 vehicles were on the beach. Surveying the mountain and variety of X Corps supplies piling in, Jim Crowe growled, "If porcelain crappers will win the war, those guys had better quit now."

Moving in behind the Marine shore party, the Army's 2d Engineer Special Brigade assumed shore operation of the port on September 18. One early achievement of the brigade was to get the trains running. As early as D+1, the engineers patched up a switch engine and six cars and put them to work in the port area. By the 19th the road was operative to Ascom City, where the first train highballed in with 1,200 Marine replacements. Before the campaign was over, the railroad hauled 350,000 rations, 315,000 gallons of fuel, 1,260 tons of ammunition and over 10,000 troops.[31]

But the most welcome event of the 18th was the landing of the 32d Infantry, first Army regiment ashore and precursor of the 7th Infantry Division, which had reached Inchon on D+1. This regiment was temporarily attached to the Marine division, and its 2d Battalion was to go into line on the right flank next day. For the left flank there would be another battalion, too: the Engineer Special Brigade assumed responsibility for Inchon and thus released the 2d Korean Marine Battalion, commanded by a second Major Kim, which went forward to join its regiment north of Kimpo. One more welcome arrival was the 96th Field Artillery Battalion, an Army medium howitzer outfit commanded by

Lieutenant Colonel Richard T. Knowles, USA (who as a general 17 years later would lead his brigade beside the Marines in Vietnam). The 96th (which was attached to the 11th Marines) had been a schools battalion at Fort Sill, the Artillery School, and quickly won the admiration of the Marines by its accurate, practiced gunnery.

A somewhat unexpected responsibility for O. P. Smith materialized on September 17 when he received instructions to restore civil government in Inchon. Inchon was a shambles. Much of the city had been burned or blasted to the ground. During pre-D-day operations, many inhabitants had fled. Even earlier, when the Communists originally arrived, most city officials had been killed or had, if lucky, escaped south.

Putting the whole problem of military government in a nutshell, General Smith later wrote, "The proper procedure was to find loyal officials, clothe them with authority, and support them in reestablishment of law and order."

Fortunately Admiral Sohn, the Korean Chief of Naval Operations, was at hand. He recommended that Pyo Yang Mun, a loyal man who had narrowly missed pre-war election as mayor, be appointed now.

On September 18, under the shell-shattered portico of the town hall, General Smith proclaimed Pyo mayor of Inchon. The KMC Regiment provided a guard of honor, schoolchildren and prominent citizens were in attendance, the Korean national anthem was sung, and Admiral Sohn concluded the proceedings by leading the people in six *"mansaes."*[32]

Pyo's appointment proved wise. With help from the American forces, teams were set up to bury the dead, hospitalize the sick and wounded, police the town, re-establish sanitation, distribute food, and care for homeless waifs and orphans.

With his logistics secure, with reinforcements arriving, with civil government coming to life in the rear area—and with his assault regiments forging ahead—General Smith decided that the time had come to move his command post forward. On September 19, in preparation for the advance across the Han, landing force headquarters therefore opened at Oeso-Ri, just outside Kimpo airfield.

6

INTO YONGDUNGPO

*Get up, boys, Get up and go. That's the
quickest way to get it over.*
—Colonel Lewis B. Puller

It had been 56 years since United States Marines marched on Seoul
over the highway from Inchon. In July 1894 the Japanese seized Seoul
and the American Minister asked for Marines to protect the legation.
On the evening of July 24, commanded by Captain George F. Elliott
(later tenth Commandant of the Corps), the ship's guard landed in
pulling boats from USS *Baltimore,* then lying at Chemulpo, marched all
night in their dress blues (the only Marine uniforms in those days) and
were in Seoul next morning.

Now in 1950, Puller's 1st Regiment was following Elliott's route but
the going was harder. The reason, as we have seen, was that the *In Min
Gun*'s first coherent reaction to the landing at Inchon was to push troops
forward toward Ascom City along the Inchon–Seoul highway. After the
Communists' tank-infantry thrust was obliterated on the morning of
September 17 (D+2) it was clear that the 18th Division had no hope
of retaking Inchon, but it was well within enemy capability—and on
favorable ground—to delay the 1st Marines' push toward Yongdungpo.

General Smith's scheme of maneuver for the capture of Seoul re-
sembled the pincers of a giant Korean king crab. One claw—Murray
and the 5th Marines—had reached around Kimpo and was preparing
to hook across the Han and right toward the city. The other claw—
Puller and the 1st Regiment—was probing forward to grasp Yongdungpo and then to stab into the vitals of Seoul.

The Inchon–Seoul highway, as it leaves Ascom City, runs for a time

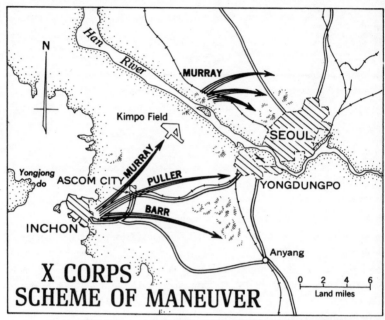

along the south shoulder of the flat, cultivated corridor leading toward Kimpo, then, striking eastward beside the railroad, cuts through the belt of abrupt ridges and hills that lies athwart the approaches to Yongdungpo. Where not dusty and eroded, these red hills are covered with scrub pine and brush. Poplars and sycamores border the roadsides, and the round mounds of ancient tombs rise from sodded clearings on the hillsides.

It was in this terrain—increasingly rugged and difficult along the Marine division's still-open south flank—that Colonel Puller launched his regiment on September 17 (D+2). His dispositions that morning, after the tank battle short of Ascom City, were these: 2d Battalion (Allan Sutter) initially advancing along the highway, then ahead into a jumble of high ground (Hill 208) south of Ascom City and the highway. Hill 208 had been the point of departure for the early morning probe by the 2d Battalion, 1st NKPA Regiment. Behind Sutter, ready to come into line on his right, was the 3d Battalion (Ridge), as well as Company B of the tank battalion, under Captain Bruce F. Williams. Far to the south, covering the regiment's and the division's right flank, was Hawkins's 1st Battalion and the reconnaissance company, neither confronted with opposition of any consequence.[1]

Sutter jumped off at 0700, companies in line. Easy pushed along the highway; Fox and Dog, south of the highway, working onto Hill 208. Here the Communists were holding; to shake them loose, the 2d Battalion, 11th Marines, commanded by Lieutenant Colonel Merritt Adelman, a thoughtful, scientific artilleryman, worked over the ridges and draws with 105mm concentrations that enabled the riflemen to push forward.

On the highway, Easy Company (First Lieutenant Johnny L. Carter) hit its first resistance—a roadblock west of the mud village of Mahang-Ri, which was apparently the right flank position of the defenders of Hill 208. Outflanking the roadblock in an assault that killed 20 enemy, Carter attacked Mahang-Ri, the entrance to which was defended by a group of Communist diehards entrenched in a hedgerow ("Every time we threw three or four grenades in the hedge, we received six or seven back in return," Carter recalled).[2]

Meanwhile, in an attempt to effect a deep penetration, Colonel Puller attached the tank company to Ridge's battalion which, embarked in amtracs, was to launch a mechanized column up the highway. Sutter's battalion sideslipped left, leaving the road to Ridge, who moved out at about 1000 and was soon engaged in the noonday fight for Mahang-Ri.

The first contribution of the tank company was to ride down the hedgerow that was holding up Carter. Then, nosing into Mahang-Ri, much of which was afire, a Pershing tank of First Lieutenant Robert L. Gover's platoon spotted the snout of a Russian 85mm gun protruding from a hut. The long-barreled 90mm gun on the Marine tank barked twice; mud and thatch flew in all directions, and the camouflaged Communist T-34 blew up before its crew could aim or fire. Soon there was another explosion: a house blazing merrily just south of the road had been stacked ceiling-high with ammunition. Just as a file of 12 captured enemy was being hustled rearward, the building went up with a roar and a blast that shook the earth and killed the entire batch of prisoners.

Mahang-Ri was finally secured in midafternoon, and a less energetic commander than Colonel Puller might have been tempted to halt and dig in, but this was not Lewis Puller's style. About a half mile east of the village a ridge lies square across the highway, which runs through a defile. Here the NKPA formed for a stand; troops retreating from Mahang-Ri rallied and reinforcements came up from Sosa, the next town eastward. Antitank guns were brought forward and rapidly emplaced.

During this burst of enemy activity, when the situation demanded prompt attack, the American tanks, which had had no opportunity to refuel earlier, began to run out of gas and the mechanized column ground to a halt midway between Mahang-Ri and the ridge. There, perforce, they sat until a truck loaded with fuel drums and a hand pump could be brought from the rear. Captain Westover, G Company commander, later wrote:[3]

> While we sat awaiting gasoline the NKPAs had every opportunity to fortify that area beyond the defile and outside Sosa—*which they did!*

Perhaps emboldened by this delay, the Communists ventured a small counterattack. As riflemen of the 2d Battalion advanced across country toward the ridge, they were startled by the sight of NKPA infantry charging to meet them, with fixed bayonets. In a tradition going back to Belleau Wood, a platoon of Company E dropped down on the embankment beside a rice paddy, unslung packs, adjusted rifle slings, clicked off elevation and windage, and picked off the attackers with aimed fire. Watching approvingly, Captain Carter said it "reminded me of the firing line on the rifle range back at Parris Island."

When the tanks' thirst was quenched, the 3d Battalion's advance resumed. In the mouth of the defile the lead tank, that of Second Lieutenant Bryan J. Cummings, rumbled in. Westover's riflemen worked forward on each side of the cut. Then came a sudden blast of fire: small arms, mortar, and antitank guns. Pinned flat, the infantrymen were helpless; an instant later, so was Lieutenant Cummings: his engine went dead.

Cummings's first thought in this tight spot was to see if any of the Marines who had been riding his tank were still outside. Unbuttoning momentarily as NKPA infantry charged into the cut, he collared a rifleman and got him inside. Outside, the Communists began to pry and hammer at the hull; with no blower inside, the tank filled with fumes from the breech of the gun. Then the rescued rifleman went crazy until his screeching was abruptly halted by a knockout clip from one of the half-smothered tankers. Groggy with the heady cellulose fumes, Cummings opened the pistol port for a gasp of air—a grenade was shoved in. It went off with an ear-splitting clap, wounding Cummings, one of the crew, and the limp rifleman.

Then the tide turned. A second Pershing moved up, raking the hull and turret of Cummings's tank with machine-gun fire that sprawled the NKPA attackers in the road. Moments later, in response to a call from the battalion's forward air controller, five Corsairs from VMF-214

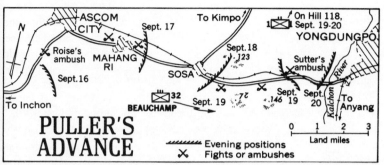

screeched in with rockets and bombs, and cannon blazing. With this support, Westover got his people onto the ridge on the right of the highway, while the 2d Battalion pressed the attack to the north. Cummings opened up and his beleaguered crew gulped the fresh air oblivious of bullets zinging in all directions. When more tanks crowded in, the Communist antitank gunners furiously returned fire, blowing a track off Cummings's battered M-26 and damaging two others.

Even though the defile was blocked by wounded tanks (until a retriever tank got up and towed them clear), the infantry forged ahead. When they reached the crest the NKPA—a regiment of the 18th Division—gave way and pelted for Sosa, leaving the field to the 1st Marines, together with 250 killed and wounded, 70 prisoners and six guns. And here, at 1830, having fought steadily since seven that morning, Puller's Marines dug in for the night. Considering the regiment's long gains against steady opposition—in fact, the stiffest yet encountered by the landing force—casualties were still negligible: one killed and 34 wounded.[4]

After the 1st Regiment's hard fight the day before, the action on September 18 (D+3) was almost an anticlimax. Typically an early riser in garrison or the field, Colonel Puller had his battalions moving before seven. As Sutter and the 2d Battalion advanced up the highway, Ridge and the tanks thrust forward again behind a thundering attack preparation from the main battery of HMS *Kenya* (Captain W. P. Brock, RN) which put down over 300 rounds of 6-inch onto the 3d Battalion's objective—Hill 123, a commanding ridge east of Sosa and north of the highway.

Passing through Sutter's infantry, Ridge veered left against slight opposition. (The worst difficulty that morning came from American guns: an artillery concentration dropped short, killing two Marines and wounding three more in the 2d Battalion.) By noon the mechanized column had pushed into Sosa, a flat, drab, dusty town ornamented by several Christian churches. Digging in on Hill 123 while the sun was still high, the 3d Battalion had in effect exchanged zones with the 2d. As Sutter brought his companies up, the 2d Battalion went into line on the 3d's right, astride the highway. To the south, still unopposed, Hawkins's 1st Battalion and the Reconnaissance Company continued to beat the bushes and covered the Marine division's flank.

Although the *In Min Gun* had to yield Sosa that morning, it did so with ill grace. Revealing something of the shape of things to come, Communist gunners and mortarmen began dropping concentrations on Hill 123 at 1415. For an hour the 3d Battalion's positions were blanketed by fat, evil 120mm mortar projectiles interspersed with artillery. Amid the shelling, which wounded 44 men in Ridge's and Sutter's battalions and named Hill 123 "Shrapnel Hill," Lieutenant Robert J. Fleischaker, USN, the 3d Battalion's surgeon, moved about as calmly as if he were administering APCs and "black-and-white" at sick call in San Diego. Not at all the field soldier ("He was completely naïve on Marine matters," reminisced a regular officer), Dr. Fleischaker won unstinting admiration then and throughout the campaign for his devotion and fearlessness.[5]

The Army Arrives

While Puller's regiment was consolidating east of Sosa and the 5th Marines were extending their control from Kimpo to the left bank of the Han, the 32d Infantry, under Colonel Charles E. Beauchamp, USA, landed at Inchon. (History sometimes does repeat: on September 10, 1945, five years almost to the day, this same regiment had landed at Inchon to receive the port from the Japanese.) By afternoon on September 18, the regiment was ashore in an assembly area, attached to the Marine division until General Barr could get the rest of his division unloaded and deployed.

Arrival of Army combat troops was important not only because the 7th Division would cover the wide-open south flank of the landing force (a cause of continuing anxiety to O. P. Smith and to Puller) but also because it would permit the Marine division to effect deployments necessary to cross the Han and to capture Yongdungpo.

On the evening of the 18th, General Smith directed the Army regiment to commence operations in the 7th Division's zone, to advance to X

Corps phase line C-C (which would bring the doughboys roughly in line with the 1st Marines), and relieve Hawkins's battalion and the Marine Reconnaissance Company in the morning. It was expected that this would be a normal passage of lines at the time of the 1st Marines' morning jump-off, but, with the sun already high, the 32d Infantry was still not ready. Puller, not the most patient officer on the battlefield, fumed sulphurously on his stub pipe until 1030. Then, with some of the day's best fighting hours spent, he launched the 2d and 3d Battalions, leaving Hawkins to await the Army regiment, which finally came up and relieved the Marines during early afternoon.

This slow advance and delayed arrival by the 7th Division caused impatience and caustic comment among the 1st Marines, from privates to colonel. What it really reflected, however, was not ineptitude or overcaution among the soldiers but lack of effective liaison between the two divisions and, behind that, failure by corps headquarters to insure positive coordination. O. P. Smith fully understood the problem of the 7th Division and, as he later wrote, made allowance for them: [6]

> General Barr was confronted with an almost impossible situation. . . .
> Although he landed at Inchon with a full-strength division, its quality
> was in no way comparable to that of the 1st Marine Division.

Doing his utmost, General Barr had his division headquarters ashore by afternoon on the 19th (D+4) and assumed responsibility for operations in the 7th Division's zone that night. With the landing of the 31st Infantry next day, a substantial part of an Army division would join the campaign.

Although X Corps headquarters had not yet assumed control of operations ashore (and would not do so until the 21st), General Almond was now beginning to influence events. Commitment of the 32d Infantry on the Marines' flank and the prompt landing of 7th Division headquarters reflected Almond's promise to O. P. Smith to get Army troops forward on the right flank so that the Marines could cross the Han. And, as would be increasingly evident during the week to come, Almond was consumingly impatient to capture Seoul not later than September 25, 90 days after the Communist invasion, a magic number which was to dominate much of the operations that lay ahead.

Capturing the Glacis

Like one of Vauban's fortresses, Yongdungo is surrounded by a moat

M

(the Kalchon), by a wide ditch of rice paddies west of the Kalchon, and by a glacis of ridges and hills which range from Tongchok Mountain, southeast of the town, to Hill 123 where Colonel Ridge's battalion stood on the morning of September 19, to Hill 118, which lies directly between Kimpo airfield and Yongdungpo's grimy chimneys.

Hill 118, a key terrain feature called Paeksok by the Koreans, over-looks the Kimpo–Yongdungpo highway and its bridge over the Kalchon into town. It is partly wooded with pines on its precipitous slopes and deeply serrated with draws, ridges, saddles and lesser crests. This tangled massif is not only essential for the capture of Yongdungpo but equally so for the defense of Kimpo airfield, and it was into this area that many defenders of Kimpo fled before the 5th Marines.

Immediately between Paeksok Hill and the expanse of paddy that girdles Yongdungpo are two abrupt lower twins: Hills 80 and 85. These also flank the highway and must be held by anyone who assaults Yong-dungpo from north or west. On September 19 (D+4) the 1st Battalion, 5th Marines, got the job of taking all three hills, after which it was planned that Hawkins's battalion of the 1st Regiment, once relieved by the 32d Infantry, would move north across the rear of Puller's assault battalions and relieve the 5th Marines on these hills. This maneuver was part of the Marine division's northward slideslip out of the 7th Infantry Division's zone and would in turn permit Colonel Murray to concentrate the 5th Regiment for the crossing of the Han. It would also give Yong-dungpo in entirety as an objective for the 1st Marines.

As part of the 5th Marines' consolidation of the Kimpo area, the 1st Battalion—Newton's—had on September 18 occupied two hills (known as Objectives E and F) which lay between Kimpo and Paeksok, and it was from these that Newton planned to attack 118 on the next day.

In war, however, the enemy plays a tune of his own. Just as Com-panies B and C, 5th Marines, were girding themselves for the morning attack on Hill 118, a heavy counterattack by more than 500 NKPA ("gooks," as the average Marine referred to them) hit Charlie Company in a hail of small-arms and mortar fire. Lieutenant Pederson, the com-pany commander, found himself defending, not attacking. Pederson's position (on Objective F) was a low, piny hill which shoulders the Yong-dungpo–Kimpo highway, and the attackers, who had apparently crossed from Seoul during the night, were bent on retaking the airfield. To com-plicate matters, the direct-support artillery battalion of the 5th Marines

(1st Battalion, 11th Marines) was displacing to new position-areas when the attack came in and thus could bring only part of its fires to bear. In the best spirit of the Marine air-ground team, however, the 11th Marines' forward observer with Pederson's company managed to call in and direct an air strike by VMF-214, relaying the mission via artillery communications.

Meanwhile, southeast of Pederson, Captain Fenton and B Company (on Objective E) were untouched by the Communist attack. As Fenton's original mission had been to support Pederson's intended assault from the right flank, Colonel Newton ordered Fenton to advance more or less as planned, capture Hill 118, and hit the enemy in flank and rear. With typical energy and tactical sense, Ike Fenton struck out smartly, advancing more than a mile in an hour, and getting atop Paeksok by midmorning.

The effect of Fenton's maneuver was stunning. Once on the high ground (gained without a single casualty), Baker Company served as anvil for Charlie. With the help of air and artillery, Pederson got moving and drove the North Koreans into Fenton's arms. "We were able to wipe out most of them," Fenton wrote.[7]

> Once again the enemy had failed to watch his flank and was caught with his pants down.

So great was the enemy's confusion—he had not known of B Company's presence at all—that many North Koreans retreated from areas in rear of Fenton into his lines, believing them to be friendly. All told, the 1st Battalion killed over 300 Communists and bagged 150 prisoners that morning.[8]

In late afternoon, Newton's battalion of the 5th Marines held Paeksok Hill (118) and Hills 80 and 85. Hawkins, of the 1st Regiment, had finally been relieved by the 32d Infantry and was making best speed by truck across Puller's rear to relieve Newton on the three hills. However, due to the primitive roads, Hawkins's advance was slow and he was on the point of deciding to detruck and complete the movement on foot.

Even though ejected from the Paeksok complex, the enemy was still showing fight. Some of his people had retreated across the Kalchon bridge into Yongdungpo and could be seen setting up a defense around a warehouse and cluster of buildings on the sandspit where the bridge entered town. Others had dropped down into a small village at the base of Hill 80, from which they kept up intermittent rifle fire at the Marines on the high ground. At the warehouse they set up two heavy Russian Maxim machine guns and an antitank rifle with which they commenced long-range fire onto the captured hills.

Galled by this harassment, the Marine battalion called for artillery support. Lieutenant Colonel Ransom M. Wood, CO of the 1st Battalion, 11th Marines, responded generously. From the fire-direction center came the command *"Battalion, 4 rounds. Fire for effect"* four times. Sixteen times over, each of the battalion's 18 howitzers banged, jumped in recoil, banged again when the lanyard was pulled as sweating, bare-waisted cannoneers checked sights and charges, leveled bubbles, and rammed home the next round. Two hundred eighty-eight 105mm shells crashed down on the warehouse, knocked out the Maxims and the antitank rifle and, as Captain Fenton ruefully added, "much to the disgust of our tankers and engineers the following day, knocked out the bridge, which was hit by a short round."[9]

Night was falling by the time the leading elements of Hawkins's battalion reached Hill 118. Hawkins had detrucked, and sent Company A ahead as fast as its captain, big, hard-driving Robert H. Barrow, could march. The rest of the battalion followed along. Minutes were crucial, not only because of the failing light but, even more important, because the 5th Marines, having to force the Han crossing next morning, had to be relieved and on the way to assembly areas before nine that evening.

When—having covered four miles and climbed a 380-foot hill in less than an hour—Barrow reached Paeksok, he found himself well ahead of Charlie Company, which was supposed to take over Hills 80 and 85 while Barrow relieved Fenton on 118. Recognizing the importance of keeping firm hold on the forward positions, Barrow called Hawkins by radio and asked permission to keep moving and occupy 80 and 85, leaving C Company to close up on Paeksok. In a few minutes, the battalion operations officer called back with word that Barrow was to follow his original orders and stay on Hill 118. Fenton and Barrow conferred briefly, reaching the immediate conclusion that (1) if the two forward hills were to be occupied, there was no time to waste, and (2) if not held through the night, they would surely be reoccupied by the NKPA before dawn. Aghast at the possibility, Fenton came up on the 1st Marines net, out of channels, and pleaded that the positions be secured before dark. The reply was "a firm negative." "Barrow," recounted Fenton, "was really disgusted."

Barrow and Fenton had reason for alarm. Shortly before dawn, in a fierce burst of fire and a shower of grenades, the NKPA charged the abandoned Marine positions on Hills 80 and 85. When the Communists discovered that the hills were undefended, they scrambled up, began digging in, and then tried to push ahead onto Paeksok. Here they hit Companies A and C, 1st Marines, and, with timely help from VMF-214's Corsairs (which raked the reverse slopes of 80 and 85 and then nearby Yongdungpo), were contained to the two hills. Now it was up to the 1st Battalion to get them back.[10]

While Hawkins was countermarching north toward Paeksok on September 19 (D+4), the other battalions of Puller's regiment continued their advance against the glacis of Yongdungpo.

The mission of Ridge's 3d Battalion, on the left, was to strike out northeastward from "Shrapnel Hill" and the Inchon–Yongdungpo highway and secure Sinjong-Ni, a companion hill mass south of Hill 118. Sinjong-Ni was quickly named "Lookout Hill" because it overlooked Yongdungpo and had a good view of Seoul itself. Uphill and downdale for four hot, dusty miles, with clouds of enemy riflemen retiring stubbornly, but retiring, from ridge to ridge, Ridge pushed his assault companies. When night fell, the 3d Battalion held Lookout Hill.

Sutter's advance along the highway with the 2d Battalion was not so simple.

Supported by a new tank company (C, 1st Tank Battalion, under Captain Richard M. Taylor), the 2d Battalion moved out at 1030 when Puller refused to wait longer for the 32d Infantry to come up.[11]

With Taylor's Pershings in the point, the 2d Battalion pushed ahead across low ground and paddies for a quarter of a mile. Suddenly a jolting thud resounded—a thud the riflemen could feel through the soles of their boondockers. The lead M-26 was sheathed in smoke. The right track snapped and whipped into the air; two ground wheels skimmed whirling to the roadside. As the tank listed and settled into the crater, a burst of small-arms and mortar fire beat down on the infantry from a conspicuous knoll to the right front. A thick-sown field of crudely dug-in wooden box mines charged with 15 pounds of high explosive apiece blocked the highway and its shoulders.

Sutter brought his battalion into line but could not work past the hill (72) and its well-defended minefield. Adelman's howitzers began to drop concentrations among the enemy; six Corsairs from VMF-214 responded to the forward air controller's call, first in a straight-down dive-bombing run, then in a succession of flat runs to tumble napalm and spit 20mm bursts onto the hill. While artillery hammered, airplanes swooped and infantry squeezed triggers, engineers came up on the double —a platoon under First Lieutenant George A. Babe, a resolute, impatient, hot-tempered young officer who had no intention of letting a minefield slow the battle. Led by Babe, the engineers hunched forward under the enemy fire, crouched over the ominous mound that marked each mine, cupped down a snowball-charge of composition C-3 (to the engineer what APC is to the corpsman), darted back, and waited for the charge to blow.

Under the sustained firepower of the Marines the defense wilted. As enemy fire slackened, Sutter's riflemen picked their way past the minefield (where the tanks had to halt until Babe completed his work about one o'clock). For a mile, Companies D and F fought forward against retiring infantry of one of the 18th Division's regiments. Up to the right front again, there loomed a long, steep, red-clay ridge higher than 72. Here—the map called it Hill 146—the NKPA had a well-prepared position with artillery support, mortar concentrations that Puller respectfully reported as "deadly accurate," and a roadblock of felled trees, earth-filled rice bags, broken-down carts and the rubble of smashed villages.

To make matters sticky, Hill 146 (like 72 earlier) lay in the zone of action not of the Marine division (which now stopped south of the highway), but of the newly landed 7th Infantry Division, whose leading elements more than three miles to the rear had not yet even finished relieving Hawkins's battalion. One of the most necessary rules in the tactician's book is that units confine their action to their appointed boundaries. But here the 1st Marines were being stopped cold by vigorous resistance from a wide-open flank the Army unit could not possibly protect.

To Puller there could be only one answer. Without hesitating, he ordered Sutter to disregard boundaries and to attack and call fire on anything south of the road that was slowing the battalion's advance. (Perhaps it is just as well Puller had not yet learned that, instead of advancing after going into line, the 32d Infantry planned to stay put all afternoon and jump off next morning, thus exposing the 1st Regiment's flank even further.) [12]

Moving a company (Fox) onto a knoll to the left of the highway to provide a base of fire, Sutter launched Company D in assault to the right front behind successive concentrations from the 2d Battalion, 11th Marines. Six more F4Us, this time from VMF-323, swept the ridge with bombs, napalm and strafing. As Dog Company plowed forward, the tanks rejoined the fight, adding their 90mm shells to the pandemonium while a tankdozer probed, blade down, into the roadblock.

Carts and trees and ricebags gave way as the dozer tumbled them aside. Then came the same seismic thud, the same smoke cloud, the same acrid fumes drifting from the big crater. Again the right track splayed off and a wheel was shattered. The fuel tank ruptured, and the transmission sprung itself from the shock. And once again Lieutenant Babe charged in with his engineers while the frustrated tanks stood fast and the infantry somehow advanced.

And somehow they did take Hill 146 late that afternoon. But the Communists retired reluctantly. Few surrendered (by comparison with Colonel Newton's bag of 150 prisoners that same day from the remnants of Kimpo's defenders, Sutter got only five POWs from the 18th Division). As the NKPA gave ground, they abandoned a truck full of box mines—a minefield that never got laid. Not until seven, with night already falling, did Allan Sutter halt his battalion, after a day's gain of three fighting miles.

Sutter's dispositions for the night—like most such by the Marine division, which was officered by veterans of the Pacific War—were mutually supporting, strong and deep. On a ridge to the right, east of the village of Oryu-Dong, between highway and railroad line, he placed F Company well forward, overlooking the road. Behind Fox, also overlooking the road, was Dog. North of the highway and D Company, in a dogleg extension, stood Company E, facing east, whose fire would cover the front of D and F along the road. Lieutenant Babe mined the highway between Dog and Easy.

After midnight, in the predawn gloom of September 20, an NKPA battalion, with five T-34 tanks, formed up in Yongdungpo to strike the Marines on the highway. Three days earlier they had sallied beyond Ascom City to attempt the same thing; now they had considerably shorter distance to go. As the column moved out, it happened to be behind a supply truck loaded with ammunition and, as it proved, with pyrotechnics, headed for some unit to the west.

Yongdungpo was less than three miles distant. Late in the mid-watch Marines of the 2d Battalion heard the distant drone and slowly rising grumble of tanks. Soon after four, a truck coughed by Fox Company's silent outpost headed, for aught anyone knew, to Inchon. Moments later two T-34s nosed by. Sutter's battalion, trained in ambush, held fire. The truck rattled on.

Behind the T-34s infantry filed along. In E Company's lines, a machine gunner zeroed in down the road, Private Oliver O'Neil, shouting a challenge. His answer, neither password nor countersign, was a fierce burst of automatic-weapons fire from the tanks and their accompanying infantry. As O'Neil fell wounded, the Marine companies returned fire. Seconds later the ammunition truck reached its appointed rendezvous with George Babe's mines. The result was spectacular. The truck blew up in a thunderclap and a sheet of flame accompanied by brilliant pyrotechnic effects which provided perfect illumination for the 2d Battalion.

The tanks halted and commenced firing ahead into Lieutenant Carter's Easy Company, where they thought the trouble lay. But their ammunition was armor-piercing with base-detonating fuze and low bursting-charge: Carter, an experienced regular, coolly noted the zinging ricochet of unexploded shell which did nothing but cut the faces of his machine gunners with pebbles and rock splinters. Carter's fire—and that from the mortars and antitank weapons, and from Companies D and F on the right—had more telling effect.

Enemy soldiers sought shelter and found none. "Those in back cried forward, and those in front cried back." The tanks milled and jerked. North Koreans who tried to retreat up the hillside ran into the arms of Dog and Fox Companies. Those who fled rearward hit a wall of artillery fire, including star shells, from Adelman's battalion, from the 155mm howitzers of the 4th Battalion, 11th Marines, and from Knowles's 96th Field Artillery.[13]

As the melee heightened, Corporal William Cheek, of F Company, led a bazooka team down toward the tanks. His gunner, Private First Class Monegan, fired one round and missed. Closing to killing range, with Cheek beside him, Monegan shouldered the bazooka, aimed in and closed the key. With a blast and a whoosh the rocket went home. The tank flared up. With bullets zapping by, illuminated by the flames of Monegan's kill, the two Marines took cover behind a water tank, where the third crewman, Private First Class Robert Perkins, joined them with additional ammunition. Stepping into the open, Monegan sighted in on another tank. Again the rocket found its mark. Perkins ran forward to reload. In the orange glare, Monegan raised his launcher for the third time. Before he could squeeze the trigger a burst of machine-gun fire hit him square. Not knowing he had won the Medal of Honor, or that fifteen years after his death schoolchildren in Seoul would drape his boot-camp photo with flowers, Private First Class Walter Monegan had killed his last tank.[14]

As day broke, the 2d Battalion inspected their handiwork and made ready to counterattack. More than 300 North Korean dead lay in windrows on the road, its ditches, and the hillside. Monegan's two tanks stood smashed and blackened. A third T-34, slightly damaged, had surrendered. Two others had managed to break out and escape to Yongdungpo. Burned and disabled trucks cluttered the highways; weapons and equipment were strewn hither and yon.

Attacking for the sixth successive day, Sutter jumped off at 0645 and swept in remnants of the battalion he had defeated a few hours earlier. Retiring before the Marines' advance, the Communists pulled back across the west branch of the Kalchon (i.e., "Middle-Sized") River. There they could be seen joining forces with NKPA troops busily fortifying a ridge south of the highway, in the 7th Division's zone, between the western and eastern branches of the river. At 1230, on his day's objective (high ground overlooking the bridge and west branch of the Kalchon), Sutter halted and dug in. Another of Puller's battalions had mounted the glacis and now overlooked the covered way, ditch and moat of Yongdungpo.

While Sutter was surveying a scene of triumph, Hawkins, with the 1st Battalion on Hill 118, was preparing to recoup a setback and regain Hills 80 and 85 overlooking the north end of Yongdungpo.

Leaving Company A, which had originally occupied Hill 118, in position, Hawkins directed Captain Robert P. Wray, Company C, to attack Hill 80 from the south, and then take 85. Major William L. Bates, Jr., the capable, egg-bald, saturnine weapons company commander, was to organize and coordinate the supporting fires from Hill 118, a natural observation post.

Wray's first job was to overrun the small village at the base of Hill 80 from which Fenton had received fire the day before. In this attack, as in all the others ahead, Wray would be advancing north across the front of Company A on Paeksok to the left and could readily be supported by observed fire across his own front.

Despite some artillery support and Bates's weapons, Wray stirred up a hornet's nest in the small village and had to commit his entire company before dislodging the enemy with a double envelopment that took most of the morning. Then, repeating much the same tactic, he enveloped and captured Hill 80.

Having watched Wray's methods in two assaults, the Communist commander on Hill 85 was prepared. With his defense organized in a horseshoe he awaited the attack. Near sundown, Wray left one platoon and his machine guns on Hill 80 to provide a base of fire, then hooked his 3d Platoon (Second Lieutenant Henry A. Commiskey) around to the right while, accompanying his 2d Platoon (Second Lieutenant John N. Guild), he moved up from the left.

Mounting the crest of the hill (Wray recalled), Guild was handling his squads as calmly as if he were running a problem in Quantico, when he was hit full in the chest and abdomen by a burst of machine-gun fire. Despite the shock he stayed on his feet until Wray could reach him, then dropped gasping as he reported the disposition of his squads and urged Wray to keep them attacking. When Wray shouted for a corpsman, he tried to refuse aid until other wounded had been seen. Within moments the brave lieutenant was dead. Captain Wray's radioman had also been hit, though farther back on the hillside; absorbed in the attack, Wray had not noticed. Only after he reached the top did he learn that the painfully wounded radioman had stayed on net and reported the progress of the attack, the company's dispositions, and the hill's capture to Colonel Hawkins.[15]

While Guild was dying at his commander's feet, Commiskey was pressing his attack up the right face of the hill. Here the slope is virtually a cliff running down to the Kalchon, and Commiskey had to veer left to find a better approach, one which goes toward a slight saddle at the top.

As the platoon formed for attack, an automatic rifleman discovered a stoppage that failed to yield to the "tap-pull-push-aim-fire" treatment which keeps most BARs working. Commiskey, correctly preferring to lead rather than shoot, handed the BAR-man his own carbine and ammunition, keeping only the short knife-bayonet. Seeing this transaction, a runner stripped off his belt and pistol and thrust them on his lieutenant. The platoon moved out under heavy fire from machine guns, submachine guns, and everything else that would shoot from the hilltop.

A few yards short of the crest Commiskey saw a Communist machine-gun nest. Shouting to his people to cover him, he charged ahead, leveled his .45, shot the two gunners, and then dropped two more crewmen firing at him with burp guns. Pistol empty, Commiskey, Irishman that he was, waded in with bare fists on the fifth enemy; as the two thrashed in a death grapple, a Marine thrust him a weapon and he killed his opponent. Jamming a fresh clip into his .45, Commiskey went for another machine-gun emplacement and killed the entire crew. Before he could load his last clip for still another attack, the platoon was swarming over the crest and the defenders wilted and scuttled. Miraculously, Lieutenant Commiskey had won his Medal of Honor unscratched.[16]

Assaulting Yongdungpo

The assault impending against Yongdungpo fulfilled Field Marshal Slim's definition of a battle as an event which takes place at the junction of two map sheets: the boundary between the 1:50,000 sheets being used by the Marines nearly bisects the town. Besides this difficulty, however, Colonel Puller had other matters to attend to before the 1st Marines could storm Yongdungpo.

As we have seen, Puller spent all D+5 (September 20) methodically deploying his regiment in an iron ring around the town. Sutter advanced to the west branch of the Kalchon. Ridge was already on Lookout Hill. By nightfall, Hawkins had retaken Hills 80 and 85. Fifth Marines units had been relieved and sideslipped left.

The 32nd Infantry advanced, and did so with a will. Although only lightly opposed, the regiment was faced with difficult terrain south of the Inchon–Seoul highway. At slight cost (seven killed, 36 wounded) and three tanks knocked out by another of the box-mine fields which had hindered the Marines, Colonel Beauchamp brought his regiment in line with, but far south of, the right-flank elements of the Marine division. By nightfall the regiment's left was on Tongdok Mountain overlooking the west branch of the Kalchon. Beauchamp himself had had an exciting day climaxed when his jeep plowed into a minefield; the vehicle was wrecked, the driver killed, his radioman wounded, but he luckily was unscathed.[17]

As the 7th Division began to operate, it became more difficult for Colonel Puller to fire and maneuver against Communist units attacking the 1st Regiment from 7th Division territory. Early in the day, Sutter had observed the strong enemy defenses on the ridge between the two branches of the Kalchon, and had obtained concurrence in shelling them from the commander of the 2d Battalion, 32d Infantry. But the coordinating machinery at X Corps headquarters was so ponderous and inexpert that it was not until seven hours later—after night had fallen—that the necessary clearance was finally given for the Marine artillery to fire on this warren of hostile activity.

Colonel Puller, who, in O. P. Smith's words, "as usual, had his CP [command post] on top of a hill," could clearly see the intense preparations of the 87th NKPA Regiment to defend Yongdungpo. The town, he reported to General Smith, was infested with enemy, and he requested permission, in his usual blunt way, to burn it. Before a decision could come down via channels, Puller had visitors.

General MacArthur, with General Shepherd, Admiral Struble, Almond and others, had spent the forenoon watching the 5th Marines cross the Han. Then the party drove south to visit the 1st Marines and ultimately the 7th Division. When the generals arrived, Colonel Puller's first request was about Yongdungpo. Could he go ahead and put it to the torch? Almond quickly said yes. Before MacArthur departed from the Marine zone, General Shepherd noted, "We could see the town burning fiercely."[18]

Taking leave of Puller, the MacArthur cavalcade met General Barr at the 7th Division boundary on the Inchon–Seoul highway. With two regiments ashore and a good advance in progress, Barr could feel that the visit was opportune. For some members of the party, the most opportune aspect of the journey back was safe arrival. General Almond, acting as his own driver in the lead jeep with MacArthur, drove with a heavy foot. At one point the speeding caravan ran a 6x6 truck off the road, where it overturned (fortunately without killing the driver); after a reluctant halt, Almond sped on. When, at five in the afternoon, the weary passengers reached Inchon, General Wright, with perfectly straight face, asked Almond if he had a driver's license.[19]

Throughout the 20th there was a mounting crescendo of firing from and at Yongdungpo. Communist tanks, mortars and artillery fired steadily into the besieging cordon of the 1st Marines. In return, Colonel Adelman put almost 1,700 rounds of 105mm into the town, while the 155mm howitzers of Major William McReynolds's 4th Battalion, 11th Marines, fired 28 concentrations in Yongdungpo. As soon as he had permission to burn enemy-held sections, Puller had the regimental 4.2-inch mortars ("the four-deuces," as Marines know them) go to work with their heavy white-phosphorous incendiary shell. At noon, six Corsairs of VMF-214 hit the town with rockets and napalm. Spotting a block-long dump stacked solid with fuel drums, the strike leader dropped napalm tanks at both ends. The resulting gush of flame and black smoke mushroomed up 8,000 feet. When eight more F4Us from VMF-323 arrived later, homing in on the pillar of fire, they rocketed the thick defense positions and added their offerings of napalm.

. . .

All through the hours of darkness, while Yongdungpo burned, the 11th Marines "made night hideous" for the 87th Regiment, whose commander had grouped his defending units so as to cover the two highway approaches and their bridges. On the long spit in north Yongdungpo, facing the Paeksok–Hills 80 and 85 massif, much of a battalion was dug in to hold the bridge from Kimpo. In the southern half of town the 87th was prepared to hold the eastern branch of the Kalchon and, as we have seen, had strong forces on the ridge south of the Inchon highway just into the 7th Division's zone. Besides artillery and many mortars, the enemy had tanks, the defensive advantage of a densely built town, moated by a river and walled by levees, and more ammunition than he could shoot. Because the highways and bridges to be defended entered Yongdungpo divergently from opposite ends of town, the NKPA commander tended to split his defense into separate elements beyond the reach of mutual support. This decision proved to be his undoing.

Colonel Puller launched his attack at 0630 on September 21. Holding the 3d Battalion, 1st Marines, in reserve on Lookout Hill, from which it could readily support either of the other battalions, he sent Hawkins against the north end of town, and Sutter eastward across the Kalchon.

At first light, the engineers reconnoitered the concrete bridge by which the Inchon–Seoul highway crosses the west fork of the Kalchon. After removing a few mines, the engineers pronounced the bridge sound for tanks. Then, with C Company of the tank battalion again in support, Sutter and the 2d Battalion moved forward. Companies D and F were in assault. VMF-214 was on hand with a four-plane strike out ahead of the tanks.

As Fox Company advanced along the road (Dog was fanning out to the left), the fortified ridge (named Kuroi-ni) on the right opened up. Stopped cold by this natural roadblock, Sutter called for artillery. But the ridge, though only by a few yards, was in the 7th Division's zone. Once again the staff officers' minuet commenced with the formalities required to secure X Corps clearance to fire, even though 32d Infantry troops were nowhere in sight (and, unknown to the Marines—another liaison breakdown—the Army's scheme of maneuver called for the division to continue its right wheel *away* from Yongdungpo southward toward Anyang).

With no help to be expected from on high, Sutter committed his reserve company and, 7th Division be damned, called the regimental four-deuces onto his tormentors. This helped but not enough. Sutter was facing the bulk of the 87th Regiment dug in for a hard fight. As Lieutent Carter brought up E Company from reserve, he found the highway bridge beaten by heavy machine-gun fire and had to drop his men down into the Kalchon bottoms to wade the stream. As they emerged and joined Fox Company, orders came down not to fire beyond the railroad tracks to the right—Army territory. Besides, came the word, the 7th Division is 40 per cent Korean troops and these gooks may be friendly. Both company commanders replied that there was nothing friendly about the gooks on that ridge, but the order stuck.

Easy's situation was exposed. Going for the enemy's throat, Carter had deployed to the right, south of the highway and along the railroad embankment, which offered cover. Part of his right platoon had worked across the embankment and were already part way up the ridge. That they were in the 7th Division's zone was a remote consideration at this moment. The *In Min Gun* was on that ridge and Marines were going to get him off it.

Carter's company had nevertheless to be disengaged and pulled back to the highway where the mounds and ovens of an old brick factory offered a good position to tie in with Dog, the left assault company.

To cover Carter's involuntary pullback and enable him to get out his dead and wounded, the only solution was an air strike. First Lieutenant Norman Vining, Sutter's forward air controller, was up with E Company and made contact with a six-plane Corsair strike group from VMF-323. Coaching on the tactical air coordinator (Captain J. P. Kelley, Jr.) and strike leader (First Lieutenant J. L. Greene), Vining called for dummy runs to assure the exact line of flight. Then, while E Company hugged the deck in the shelter of the embankment, Vining brought in the shrieking Corsairs with 500-pound bombs, rockets, napalm and strafing—the last within 30 yards of the Marines. As *Badoeng Strait*'s war diary laconically noted, "Four 500-pound GP bombs, 24 5-inch rockets, and 2,400 rounds of 20mm gave good coverage to the target." To Easy Company the coverage seemed a bit better than good: "We crossed the open space to our rear without a single casualty," recounted Carter.[20]

During the fight in front of the ridge, Dog Company on the left of the highway had no bed of roses either. Attempting to advance across paddy and bottomland, they were stoutly opposed from a levee on the west side of the Kalchon's east branch, honeycombed with well-dug-in Communist positions and Russian heavy Maxims. A hundred yards short of this ram-

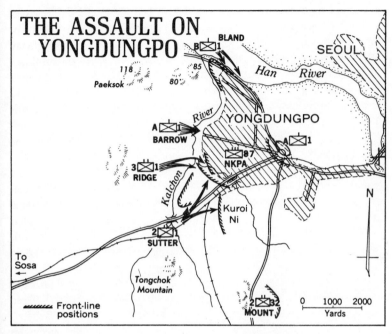

THE ASSAULT ON YONGDUNGPO

part was as far as Captain Welby Cronk could get his company and here they dug in about noon while the tanks slugged 90mm direct fire into the levee. As one tank platoon ran out of ammunition, and withdrew to rearm, another would relieve it on line. Standing still and hammering away with their guns, the tanks became choked with heat and fumes and crews dropped to the deck, gasping for air. Periscopes and radio antennae were shot away; every external fitting was riddled by small arms and antitank rifles.

Crammed into the triangle formed by the forking branches of the Kalchon and the highway, the 2d Battalion's frontal attacks had uncovered well-prepared, strongly defended entrenchments. By midafternoon Colonel Puller felt the time had come to commit his reserve and see whether the enemy could be outflanked.

In his usual way, Puller had his reserve battalion (Ridge's 3d) well forward. (O. P. Smith later remarked that Puller generally put his command post on a forward slope where his OP should be, and kept his reserve in the front lines.) Early in the day, he had moved the battalion down from the bare red clay of Lookout Hill across the paddies and bottoms of the Kalchon, and Colonel Ridge had his companies in the lee of the levee running along the west, left bank of the stream—more like a canal here than a river. Directly across the Kalchon was another levee, and down to the right was the junction of the river's east and west forks (the east fork joins the stream via a water gate, passing through the town levee which continues south along the right bank of the west branch). At this point the eastern branch runs almost at right angles to the western. Along this line, on both sides of the eastern branch, the NKPA had strong defenses, the forward line of which was confronting Captain Cronk and Dog Company.

To pinch out Sutter's battalion and to flank the defenses of the eastern branch, Ridge was ordered at 1530 to cross the Kalchon and attack upstream (southeast) astride the east fork. His objective was the highway bridge crossing the eastern branch.

Since Merritt Adelman already had his gun tubes hot supporting the 1st and 2d Battalions (technically the "assault" battalions of the 1st Regiment), there was no artillery to spare for Ridge. Moreover, his 81mm mortars were low on ammunition. To cover the crossing, Major Simmons, Ridge's Weapons Company commander, therefore set up his heavy machine guns in battery—an antediluvian tactic better known on the Somme, the Aisne, or the Meuse than the Kalchon—and dueled the Russian Maxims, "heavies against heavies," Simmons reminisced. Browning beat Maxim, and the 3d Battalion waded across.

Ridge put Captain Westover and G Company on the east (town) side of the stream, and First Lieutenant Joseph R. Fisher's I Company on the west side. Each company had to attack down the long axis of a heavily fortified levee. Yard by yard, the two companies pushed ahead; just as dusk was descending, they reached the bridge. The battalion's lines for the night were L-shaped—the long leg running precariously along the enemy shore of the eastern branch back to the water gate, the short leg hooking back along the Inchon–Seoul highway to the 2d Battalion's bastion at the brickworks.[21]

While the 2d and 3d Battalions were struggling to establish a toehold at the lower end of town, Hawkins and the 1st Battalion were fighting a hot battle of their own.

From positions on and around Hills 80 and 85, captured the day before, the 1st Battalion overlooked the wrecked Kalchon bridge—a plank and girder structure—and the north entrance to Yongdungpo.

Here, as we have seen, part of one of the 87th Regiment's battalions had manned and fortified the ravelin of levees which come together on the long spit pointing toward Kimpo. One face of the levees is toward the Han, sheltering the main highway to Kimpo, the other runs upstream along the Kalchon, protecting the west face of Yongdungpo. Conforming to the Vaubanesque trace of the town, these dikes are the ramparts of Yongdungpo, which might well have been laid out by some seventeenth-century engineer as a *tête-de-pont* for the bridges into Seoul.

Attacking after some delays, at 0830, Colonel Hawkins sent Company B (Captain Richard F. Bland) across the bridge under cover of mortar and machine-gun fire, and tank direct fire from the west side of the Kalchon. As the bridge consisted in places of only a single girder over which the infantry teetered, tank action had to be confined to long-range fire support.

Once across the bridge and in possession of a carelessly undefended knoll at the far end, Bland's company advanced on the ravelin. Enveloping, he chose to strike the north, Han River face where, between levee and river, he had more maneuver room and no fire on his left or rear. Continually taking the defenders in enfilade and supported by successive concentrations from the 2d Battalion, 11th Marines, Bland punched forward about a mile, capturing the dike as he advanced. Besides continual help from the artillery, Baker Company had two powerful strikes from VMF-214's Corsairs—one about noon, the other in midafternoon.

By early afternoon, although B company controlled the Han River levee, two of Bland's three platoon leaders (Lieutenants Shepherd and Hollingsworth) were down, both wounded. The two platoons—1st and 3d—were equally battered. Bland therefore consolidated them into a single platoon under Staff Sergeant Frank Quadros. He then deployed his people in line facing across town (southwestward) in a hot fire fight with the Communists on the Kalchon levee.

About this time one of the light machine guns ran out of ammunition. Private First Class Albert Collins dashed rearward for more. As he was retracing his steps across an open space, an enemy rifleman dropped him. Still hanging onto the precious boxes of ammunition, Collins crawled to the gun position. The rest of the crew were dead and wounded around the gun. Heaving the box into place, Collins seated the fresh belt, brought the gun back into action, and died of his wound with the final burst of fire.[22]

The anomaly that Bland's exposed position presented on the situation

N

maps was that, while most of the 1st Regiment was attacking northeast, from the west faces of Yongdungpo, Company B was fighting southwest, from the east of town. Once the seeming contradiction got ironed out, Bland received artillery support which had for a while been withheld because the Kalchon levee defenses now looked on the map as if they were 1st Marines rear areas. With Captain Charles M. Cable, Hawkins's artillery liaison officer, directing fire from an OP on Hill 85, Colonel Adelman's howitzers raked the levee with time-fire air bursts and VT-fuzed concentrations. VMF-214's attack was a series of napalm drops, after which observers on the hill could see Communist soldiers, uniforms aflame, jumping out of their holes and rolling on the ground in attempts to smother or dislodge the fiery jelly.

As night fell, Captain Bland was holding a firm position though encumbered by 40 wounded. In the dusk, these people had to be carried on stretchers or ponchos more than a mile, back across the Kalchon bridge and only then placed in jeep ambulances for movement to clearing stations. As these Marines were helped rearward, Company C and Weapons Company moved in the opposite direction to reinforce Bland along the Han. When Lieutenant Commiskey took his platoon over the bridge, he spotted two antitank box mines lurking half under a plank. Like a schoolboy kicking a stone off the sidewalk, Commiskey booted the mines into the streambed and marched on.[23]

Able Company to the Han

While the north and south ends of Yongdungpo were enveloped in furious fighting, a single rifle company—Captain Barrow's A Company, 1st Marines—was in the process, largely unperceived by either set of contestants, of thrusting direct and deep into the heart of the town.

Hawkins had issued his attack order on the Kimpo–Yongdungpo road at 0730. Barrow then had to move his company off Paeksok over a mile of rough going, almost due south, to the jump-off position for a bold attack. What Hawkins ordered was for Barrow to take Able Company through unharvested rice fields to the Kalchon, to cross if he could, and probe what on the map seemed the central bastion of Yongdungpo. At this stage of the battle, Bland and Baker Company were pushing slowly down the Han levee; ahead and to the right of Barrow's route, Ridge had the 3d Battalion along the west shore of the Kalchon awaiting commitment to support the 2d Battalion.

Choosing the time-honored "two up and one back" (i.e., two platoons

in the advance, one platoon in support), Barrow formed his company
and moved out, Major Simmons of the 3d Battalion remembers them
"deployed beautifully as they came across the paddies to our left rear."
Colonel Hawkins—a precise man sometimes inclined to be fussy—said
Barrow's jump-off was "a model of precision." Amid the golden rice
stalks the scene might have been Belleau Wood's wheat field in 1918.
Guiding center on Barrow—all six-feet-four of him and his command
group between the two assault platoons—the Marine riflemen worked
forward expertly over the last levee, squelched into the bottomland, and
waited for the gooks to open up.

Across the Kalchon, the town levee—Yongdungpo's escarpment and
rampart—loomed up. To the right they could hear the 2d Battalion
hammering the ridge. Up to the left came the din of Baker Company's
fight. Concentrations from the 11th Marines hit right and left with the
rippling crack-crump of massed artillery. To the north, low over the
town, they could see VMF-214's gull wings—six Corsairs of the midmorning strike shrieking in to help Bland. Communist mortars, high-
velocity tank guns, artillery and hammering heavy Maxims, everything
the 87th Regiment could throw, were firing into the Marine assault units.

But nothing whatever was firing into Able Company.

Up the escarpment of the levee—scouts over the top, off the skyline
and down the terreplein—still not a shot fired—in the battered edge of
the town not an enemy to be seen—ahead, a wide street running east,
showing surprisingly little damage from the bombardment, and not a
soul in sight.

Barrow could hardly believe his eyes. (As he later said, "We simply
slithered into town undetected.") Searching each house and checking
each side street, Able Company advanced. By noon they were a quarter
of a mile into the town—200 Marines inside the jaws of an enemy
regiment. When Barrow reported his position, Hawkins ordered him to
continue the advance. (Why Hawkins failed to throw his reserve company into the gaping hole Barrow had uncovered is one of the mysteries
of the battle.)

Barrow's wide street is the main street of Yongdungpo. As Able Company was fast learning, this street cuts directly across town and intersects
in a fork with the Han River end of the Inchon–Seoul highway. Captain
Barrow was splitting Yongdungpo in two.

Off to the right, Marines of the 1st Platoon could observe the Inchon–
Seoul highway as it converged. Through the cross streets came the sound

of chanting. A flanker silently lifted his rifle in the signal, "Enemy in sight." The fire-teams halted. Riflemen dropped to their knees in door-ways and beside buildings, checking safety catches on their M1s. The chant grew louder: a detachment of North Korean infantry was tramping up the highway toward the 2d Battalion, singing a proletarian war song. First Lieutenant William A. McClelland, the platoon leader, waited until the enemy were well in view, then made a swift, horizontal chopping signal with his right hand. Every rifle and BAR in the platoon opened fire. Enemy soldiers jerked, crumpled, huddled and sprawled—many very still, some twitching and crying. The Red Army chorus ceased. Shaken survivors scuttled back into side streets. Looking ahead, not down, Marines thumbed fresh clips into the receivers of their rifles.

Now came a sputter of musketry and the hammer of BARs from the front (McClelland's platoon was the company reserve, echeloned to the right rear). The leading platoons had struck the flow of enemy traffic at the hub of the town, some going up the Kimpo highway, some turning onto the Inchon highway.

Without halting, the platoons swept forward, breaking into an open space where their street and the Inchon and Kimpo highways converged. There was a streetcar track: until three months ago, if you had had the fare, you could have boarded a trolley car here for Seoul.

Dead ahead was another levee. Second Lieutenant John J. Swords pushed his platoon to the crest. To the east, at their feet, was a two-mile sandspit crisscrossed with vehicle tracks and a dirt airstrip. Beyond was the Han. Across the Han lay Seoul. But Swords had no time to take in the view. Coming down the levee (here the Kimpo highway) was an enemy company, apparently retreating before Baker Company and de-filing down onto the big flat sandspit. Swords's riflemen and light machine gunners dropped down and commenced firing. The attached section of battalion heavy Brownings puffed up, flung down 60-pound tripods, leveled dials, slapped guns into cradles, yanked ammunition belts through receivers, flipped up sight leaves, and opened fire. Bursts of sand spurted up—up a click, right a click: search and traverse. The Communists broke ranks, fanned out, and those who could, scampered while the riflemen tried to catch them on the rise.

Hastening up with the rest of the company, Barrow was atop the dike not far behind the heavy machine guns. The dike was a natural ram-part, 25 feet high, 30 or more across the top. Sending scouts out into the highway intersection, now no-man's-land, Captain Barrow quickly

organized the levee for all-around defense: two platoons back to back
on opposite faces, Swords above them on his original ground covering
the north end. No more 60mm mortar rounds were left, so Barrow put
the mortarmen in line as riflemen. Before the NKPA could know, or at
least before they could react, Marine entrenching tools were furiously
cutting foxholes and weapons pits out of the levee.

> Being man-moved earth [Barrow recalls] it was comparatively easy
> digging. It was elevated—relatively clean—for short fields of fire toward
> the city and long fields of fire toward the sandspit. The road could be
> easily swept by fire on each end. In other words, we had a strong
> position.

On that position—the sun was now low—Able Company, much on
its own, would have to spend the night in Yongdungpo.

How much the outer world knew of Able Company at this point is
still not clear. Late in the day the batteries on Captain Barrow's SCR-
300 gave out so that he could no longer transmit. Hawkins says he was
in touch with Barrow "until some time after dark." Yet no move was
made to exploit Barrow's gains—enormous gains, as matters stood—or to
reinforce this lone company in the viscera of an enemy city. As late as
noon, Puller's reserve battalion (Ridge's) was still uncommitted along
the west dike of the Kalchon not 500 yards south of Barrow's point of
penetration. Here was an opportunity to reinforce success rather than
battering the reserve battalion headlong into the 2d Battalion's salient.

But Puller says he received no report of Barrow's breakthrough. Did
anyone in regimental headquarters know what was taking place? Did
division? Why, in other words, was Company A, 1st Marines, out on a
long limb as night fell?[24]

Regardless of faulty radio communications, Able Company advertised
its presence. As NKPA skirmishing commenced, with infanty probes
from the south, Marines fired on an enemy squad which took shelter
behind a mountain of supplies heaped in the highway junction. A rifle
grenadier let go a round that fell short. There was the usual pop and
fierce little puff of smoke; a moment later, bright flame radiated over the
huge stack: it was ammunition. Microseconds later came a flattening
wave of concussion, then a doomsday thud, a simultaneous column of
flame and a smoke mushroom that towered up thousands of feet. During
the explosion Barrow's radio still had its voice, and he was in the act of
explaining to Major D. W. Bridges, the battalion operations officer,

where Able Company was exactly. "Do you see that explosion?" Barrow asked. "Yup," replied Bridges. "Looks like an A-bomb." Then, characteristically deadpan, "Didn't know you had one with you." "That's where we are. I'm 75 yards north of there," rejoined Barrow, and his radio quit for the night.[25]

As dusk descended, Able Company scrabbled their cold C rations, climbed out to urinate before nightfall (anyone moving within the Marine perimeter after dark would be an enemy) and added final touches to foxholes. The three Navy corpsmen with the company spread out splints, tourniquets, plasma, syrettes, hospital corps pouches and stretchers, and arranged a trove of medical supplies found in a bulging warehouse across the road along with five floors of other U. S. Army items scooped up by the *In Min Gun* in better days. Seven wounded were made comfortable and dug in on the lee side of the levee. Eighteen prisoners, the day's catch, were glumly herded into a huddle on the west face of the dike.

A last look around served to fix landmarks and aiming points: the five-story warehouse and Yongdungpo's town hall across the open space and highway junction due east, a large school and other municipal buildings to the south, and the clay pipe factory to the north. The last light from the west played over Seoul, South Mountain, the ruined bridges and the Han.

Then came the sound all hands expected—tanks approaching on the Inchon road. Men hunched lower in their foxholes. Bazookamen in the assault squad checked their launchers. In column, five T-34s clattered past the town hall, almost to the levee, then turned left on a dusty road paralleling the foot of the dike. As they made their turn like battle cruisers at Jutland the 85mm turrets trained out to starboard. For awesome seconds the Marines peered into gun muzzles less than a hundred feet away. Then there was a curtain of blinding flashes, the whiplash crack of high-velocity projectiles coming in—close—and the firecracker rattle of tank machine guns.

From McClelland's position came a flash and a blast. In the same instant there was a hollow bang and another flash. The turret of the lead tank, gun, gunner and all, flipped clear of the barbette and caromed onto the road. With a grinding jerk the decapitated tank veered out of column and lurched into a side street behind the town hall. Corporal Francis Devine had just fired his first 3.5-inch rocket in anger.

Up toward the clay pipe factory the four tanks countermarched and stood down again. Turrets trained around to port; again the shock and whip of the close-range fire as Able Company hugged its foxholes. Down by the school the tanks came about for their third pass. This time the bazookamen were lucky, perhaps a little steadier—two of the four were hit, not mortally, but enough to take them off the field. The last two tanks made one more circuit and retired into the shadows beside the clay pipe factory.

When Barrow's squad and fire-team leaders emerged to count noses, the result was unbelievable: Able Company had sustained one single casualty in the entire hurricane of fire. The tanks, armed with base-detonating, delay-action armor-piercing shell, had sunk their rounds deep into the dike which readily absorbed the small bursting charges. In the well-built foxholes the riflemen had escaped the machine guns scot free.

So far, so good. But there was a long night ahead, and only so much ammunition left. Barrow cautioned his platoon leaders to see that every round counted. Thus, after 2000, when McClelland's people heard the sound of enemy moving about the supply warehouse, they held fire until a large carrying party, apparently rummaging for ammunition, exposed itself. With a well-distributed, short burst of aimed fire, the 1st Platoon drove the Communists off; after daybreak 27 NKPA dead were found here.

An hour later, Swords's platoon, on the north end of the position, heard voices, footsteps, the uneasy sounds of an attack forming. The noises increased. Reiterating his orders to hold fire and not disclose their positions, Swords waited. A green flare went up. With shouts of *"Mansae! Mansae!"* a company of the 87th Regiment clumped forward, firing as they came. When the attack was only ten or fifteen yards away, Swords gave the word. Minutes later he told Barrow that the 3d Platoon was having no trouble. Within a quarter hour the Communists pulled back.

On the levee the Marines could hear a North Korean officer rallying his men. In came a second charge. Again the Marines held fire until the last. Again the attack ebbed. From the dark streets and building across the way the leader shouted and exhorted. The enemy company came in a third time; a third time it was stopped.

Taking advantage of his captor's preoccupation, one of A Company's prisoners, an officer, bolted. As he plunged into the shadows, the 2d Platoon's interpreter heard him screech: "Don't attack. . . . They're too strong!"

With more flares, nevertheless, and more *mansaes,* the Communist leader whipped up his people for a fourth try, a do-or-die rush that was halted only amid the 3d Platoon's lower foxholes. Hearing another fight talk in the dark, Corporal Billy Webb gripped his M1. Tall, good-looking in his blues—"a poster Marine," said his company commander —Webb had been recalled to the colors from Oklahoma. Telling his fire team not to fire when he came back, he hoisted himself out of his foxhole and darted across the open space into a side street, rifle at the ready. The voice grew louder. Hugging the side of a building, Webb advanced. Around a corner he saw knots of enemy soldiers: an officer was haranguing them. Taking a good offhand position, right elbow high, butt well into his shoulder, Webb squeezed off a single round. The voice stopped, and Webb made for the dike. "That gook," Lieutenant Swords said, "literally talked himself to death." Years later, when he spoke of Corporal Webb, Barrow had only one thing to say: "A great guy!"[26]

There was a fifth attack anyway, but not to be compared with the previous four. The 3d Platoon held, and that was that. The rest of the night was uneasy, but there were no more attacks. Elsewhere in town, especially to the south, there were sounds of movement. Nobody bothered Able Company again, however. This was just as well because the riflemen were down to their last clips. At dawn, cautiously probing forward in the strangely silent town, Barrow's patrols counted 275 dead enemy and more than 50 automatic weapons in the flotsam about the dike. Four of the five T-34s were found battered and abandoned. When the 1st and 3d Battalions pushed off at 0800, Yongdungpo was empty save for A Company, 1st Marines, and the dead and the jettisoned gear of whatever was left of the 87th Regiment. (One of its battalions, intelligence later disclosed, took 80 per cent casualties in Yongdungpo. The others—these things are relative, of course—got off somewhat more lightly.)[27]

South to Suwon

While the Marines were closing in on Seoul, General Barr and the 7th Infantry Division were occupying the rugged hills south of Seoul and the Han, and blocking the Suwon–Anyang corridor leading into the right flank of the landing force.

When the 32d Infantry advanced, on September 20, it did so on a wide front—more than six miles—in view of the relatively light resistance to be encountered. The 2d Battalion, under Lieutenant Colonel Charles M. Mount, USA, advanced due east, and, while the 1st Marines were hammering at Yongdungpo on September 21, cut the Anyang corridor at Toksan Ni, about three miles south of Yongdungpo.

Unfortunately this battalion failed in one important responsibility whose results we have already seen. The X Corps operation order directed that contact between the 7th Division and the Marines be maintained from right to left (i.e., that physical contact and liaison between the two divisions was the responsibility of the Army unit on the right of the Marines). This vital coordinating instruction was never complied with. As a result, neither Colonel Puller nor O. P. Smith had a clear idea of where the Army units were, nor did the 7th Division deal with enemy resistance in the Army division's zone which was seriously impeding the advance of the 1st Marines on Yongdungpo.

In fact the 2d Battalion, 32d Infantry, walked wide of the hotly contested Yongdungpo approaches, while the regiment's 1st Battalion, still farther to the south, moved directly on Anyang and secured the high ground northeast of that place (Hill 300). With this ground in U. S. hands, the 3d Battalion, 32d Infantry, advanced to Anyang, then took up a blocking position on the highway south of town. The Anyang corridor was now not only cut but sealed off.

One reason why the 2d Battalion tended to swing south of the division's left boundary was a series of attempts to outflank—south and to the right —enemy forces on the high ground south of the Inchon–Seoul highway. The Marines were hitting the north flank of these well-dug-in defenders, while the 32d Infantry relied on a series of company-scale envelopments, short and weak for the forces against them. The NKPA pinned down 32d Infantry companies in succession through most of September 20; when, finally, the infantrymen had flanked far enough to the south to advance with little opposition, there remained a strong enemy wedge between the two divisions. These troops, part of the 18th Division, NKPA, eventually fell back on Yongdungpo and joined the 87th Regiment in its defense of the town.

The operations of the 1st Marines and the 32d Infantry south of Yongdungpo on September 21 produced a seemingly irreconcilable conflict as to where the respective flanks of the two divisions were. Colonel Puller repeatedly complained of galling fire into Sutter's attack from the high ground south of the highway (Kuroi-ni) on the outskirts of Yongdungpo, just inside the 7th Division zone. This was the fortified ridge from which Company E, 1st Marines, had to be disengaged under cover of Lieutenant Vining's air strike.

Puller's complaints reached X Corps headquarters, and General Almond called General Barr. According to the latter's information, the ground from which Sutter was receiving fire had already been secured by the 3d Battalion, 32d Infantry. To be sure, Barr sent Colonel Beauchamp, the regimental commander, to verify in person that this was so, and Beauchamp so confirmed. But there was no letup in the fire coming into the 1st Marines from the position, wherever its coordinates, that was causing the trouble. General Almond thereupon ordered that Barr send General Hodes, the assistant division commander, to double-check Beauchamp's report. Hodes climbed up a church steeple, took a good look, and reported that there was no firing coming from the location in question —all seemed quiet. About this time, in came a radio transmission from Puller saying that, if there were any 32d Infantry people in Kuroi-ni, they should be pulled back as the 1st Regiment was about to place a heavy air strike on it (Vining's strike by VMF-214). Then, said Barr, no air strike was ever run. Soon afterward, Barr took his own jeep and driver and made his way across country to find Puller and iron out the problem between them. As nearly as can be ascertained, the two agreed to disagree; within a few hours the problem became academic with the fall of Yongdungpo which, in General Barr's words, "was just as flat as it could be."

In this head-on conflict of testimony, which generated considerable heat at the moment, certain points stand out.

1. There is no doubt that Sutter's battalion was under heavy fire all day from the fortified ridge south of the highway, which, on the 1950 map, is named Kuroi-ni.

2. The boundary between the two divisions at this point and time was the south (right) edge of the Inchon–Seoul highway, which was physically occupied by Sutter's troops.

3. While map-reading errors, especially in the stress of combat, are always possible, it seems almost impossible that a unit (Sutter's battalion) physically occupying a main highway could have mislocated itself or an immediately adjacent terrain feature, and one which, even today, is as conspicuous and readily located as Kuroi-ni.

4. The 1st Marines did indeed run the air strike (see page 170) of which Puller warned, yet Generals Barr and Hodes were satisfied that no strike was placed on the terrain they had in mind.

5. It seems impossible that soldiers of the experience of Beauchamp, Hodes, and Barr would be guilty of a gross error in map reading.

The most likely conjecture is that both sides were right—i.e., that Sutter was being fired on from Kuroi-ni, and that the ground which the

7th Division people thought in issue was secure and quiet. This could be explained on the hypothesis that, in transmission up and down the chains of command, via X Corps headquarters, a different, erroneous set of map coordinates ultimately reached the 7th Division—an error which, as we shall see, X Corps headquarters would soon commit in transmission of an important attack order.[28]

During September 21 and 22 the 7th Infantry Division secured Suwon, an important town 25 miles south of Seoul, but paid for their capture with the life of one of General Barr's key staff officers.

On the afternoon of the 21st (D+6) the 7th Division Reconnaissance Company was at Anyang, operating under Major Irwin A. Edwards, USA, assistant G-2 of the division. Here orders were received to swing south and secure Suwon and its airfield. Adding a platoon of the 73d Tank Battalion to his force, Major Edwards barreled down the road to Suwon.

Shortly before 1800, on the heels of a strike from the ADs of the fast carriers, Edwards's column entered Suwon. Here, to their surprise, they fell in with another member of the division staff, no less than the operations officer, Lieutenant Colonel Henry Hampton, USA, who followed in from Anyang with a platoon from the 18th Engineer Combat Battalion. Colonel Hampton ("A very Gung-Ho guy," an observer later described him) had, against General Barr's inclinations, persuaded Barr to let him go forward to coordinate operations to secure Suwon.

On arrival in Suwon, some enemy were encountered, mainly from the 105th Armored Division which was reacting north toward Seoul after the landing. A desultory fight took place; one officer and 36 North Korean soldiers were captured. Then the Hampton-Edwards force started for the airfield.

Even though a division G-2 representative was with them, the column had no maps of Suwon. As a result, after reconnoitering several miles south, with night on them, the column halted and formed a perimeter for the night. They had, in fact, well overshot the airfield.

Apparently the night of September 21 was a bad one for radio communication. We have seen how the 1st Battalion, 1st Marines, lost touch with Captain Barrow in the heart of Yongdungpo. At about the same time General Barr lost radio contact with Major Edwards and the reconnaissance company. After waiting fruitlessly until 2100, General Barr, already bereft of his G-3, had good reason for alarm. Organizing a task force of a tank company, an infantry company and a field artillery battery under Lieutenant Colonel Calvin S. Hannum, USA, commander of the division tank battalion, he sent this group ("Task Force Hannum") south toward Suwon as fast as they could roll. To accompany Task Force Hannum, General Barr dispatched another principal staff officer, his G-2, Lieutenant Colonel John W. Paddock, thus leaving the 7th Division command post without its intelligence or operations officers.

Aided by a fine full moon, Hannum got to Suwon about midnight. Edwards's column had seemingly not mopped up Suwon very thoroughly, for an enemy tank promptly opened fire on the command tank of Captain Harold R. Beavers, USA, killing Beavers and destroying his tank. There followed a night melee in which at least one other T-34 made its escape, and Task Force Hannum decided to stay where it was until daylight.

If Colonel Hampton, with Edwards's column, had made the same decision, he might be alive today. During the early hours of September 22, Hampton and Edwards heard the sound of tanks coming down the road from Suwon. Hampton, who knew that Hannum's force was on the way, set out, accompanied by Major Edwards, four jeeps and a Korean guide, intending to meet Hannum and then go back to the division CP. After about ten minutes Hampton saw four tanks headed south. He blinked his headlights at what he took to be Hannum's Pershings. The lead tank—which was not a Pershing, but a T-34—ground forward, opened fire with its machine guns, and the soldiers dived for cover. But Colonel Hampton could not believe they were hostile. Approaching the tank, still waving, he was killed by a burst of fire. Then the T-34s ground south, plowing over the jeeps as the survivors bugged out.

One fugitive made it back to the reconnaissance company perimeter and breathlessly told what had happened. Moments later the lead T-34 hove into sight. Lieutenant Jesse F. Van Sant, USA, the tank platoon leader, had all along suspected that the tanks coming down the road were not American, but, being a second lieutenant, he was not listened to. Now he was ready. Directing the fire of his M-26s into the oncoming T-34s, he blew the two lead tanks off the road in a blast of 90mm fire. This was enough for the remaining two T-34s, which spun about on their tracks and disappeared into the night.

At daylight Edwards staggered into the perimeter, resumed command, and eventually found Suwon airfield. At the same time, Hannum got under way headed for the airfield, and linked up with the Edwards column, recovering the bodies of Hampton and other dead en route. Later in the day, Colonel Richard P. Ovenshine, USA, scion of a distinguished "Old Army" family, brought up the 31st Infantry to Suwon and then the airfield, and relieved the forces there. Even at the price, Suwon field, with a 5,200-foot runway, was a valuable prize: only 21 miles from Seoul, it could take aircraft as large as R5Ds (C-54s). Moreover, Suwon was located on X Corps Phase Line F, ultimate objective line of X Corps for the Inchon-Seoul operation, so it can fairly be said that the soldiers of the 31st Infantry were the first U. S. troops to reach their final objective during the campaign.[29]

North on Kumpo

One confusing aspect of Korea's geography is that Kimpo airfield is located on Kumpo Peninsula; the peninsula as a whole, bounded on the west by the sea and the Salee River (where U. S. Marines made their first Korean landing in 1871) and on the northeast by the Han, takes its name from the town of Kumpo, not the airfield. Most of the U.N. forces, then and now, called it Kimpo Peninsula anyway.

Kumpo Peninsula—as we shall correctly refer to it—while moated by the Han estuary, nevertheless presented the *In Min Gun* with a direct approach from the north into the open flank of the 5th Marines which, in swinging across the Han, was making the main effort of the landing force. Although more attention had been given to the right flank because of the anticipated northward recoil of the NKPA when and if Eighth Army got moving, General Smith—prudent commander that he was— had all along worried about his left flank, too. Characteristically, during the planning, Almond dismissed Smith's apprehensions about the left flank: "There are no enemy there," he said.[30]

As it turned out, Almond was right, or practically so, but the enemy capability of striking the exposed north flank could not be discounted, and the only troops available to cover this flank were the Korean Marines.

Commencing on September 17 (D+2), Colonel Shin, the KMC regimental commander, was given a zone of action whose axis ran northwest up the width of Kumpo Peninsula. It was his job to clear this of enemy and, particularly, to cover the Han River ferry crossing above Kumpo Town, seven miles northwest of Kimpo airfield. Initially, Colonel Shin had his 1st and 3d Battalions and later, when the Army Engineer Special Brigade took over Inchon, got back his 2d Battalion as well. Besides the small cadre of U. S. Marine advisers with the KMC regiment,

Shin also had (like the 7th Infantry Division on the other flank) U. S. Marine air and naval gunfire liaison teams.

Within two days (by September 19) the Korean Marines had worked their way up the peninsula to a line about three miles northwest of the airfield, encountering light resistance but learning their trade as they went. On the 20th, as we shall see in the next chapter, General Smith concentrated the KMC Regiment to cross the Han. To cover the north flank, however, he left the most experienced KMC unit, Major Kim's 3d Battalion, in position.

No sooner had the bulk of the Korean Marines been pulled back for operations ahead than reports came in on the morning of September 21 that NKPA units were crossing the Han at the Kumpo ferry site. By midday, two enemy battalions were reportedly facing the 3d Battalion, and a captured North Korean officer said that the force was to attack Kimpo airfield. Heavy air strikes were directed against the intruders, and cruisers *Toledo* and *Rochester* fired 535 8-inch shells at extreme range in support of aggressive patrols sent forward by the Korean Marines, one of whose company-sized probes killed 40 enemy and took 150 prisoners.

X Corps, which until then had scouted danger from this direction, now hurriedly called on General Smith to advise what measures he was taking to cover his flank (a gratuitous demand since he had been covering the flank methodically ever since landing, and at a time when Almond insisted there was no danger). Smith's reaction was to direct Jim Crowe, whose headquarters was now at the field, to establish a perimeter defense of Marine aviation and service troops already there, and site armored amphibians as covering guns. He also moved in Colonel Ely's Special Operations Company to work with the KMC battalion. These measures, backed by the heavy air and naval gunfire support, sufficed to chill the enemy's ardor and apparently to quiet X Corps nerves. In his log next morning, O. P. Smith wrote, "Nothing happened, of course."[31]

Enter the 7th Marines

Back in August, MacArthur in Tokyo and Cates in Washington had an uphill fight to convince the Joint Chiefs of Staff that the 1st Marine Division should have its third regimental combat team. Now, because MacArthur and Cates had prevailed, the 7th Marines were arriving at Inchon.

Forming a third regiment for the Marine division had strained General Cates's resources to the utmost. About a thousand regulars and two thousand reservists were assembled at Camp Pendleton in mid-August.

To make up the deficit, the East Coast 2d Marine Division was reduced to virtual nonentity: the 6th Marines, an artillery battalion of the 10th Marines, and numerous supporting troops were transferred to Pendleton and redesignated as 7th and 11th Marines respectively. Finally—and here Marine Corps readiness and uniform training paid off—the 3d Battalion, 6th Marines, serving afloat in the Mediterranean, was bodily moved aboard its transports from Crete via Suez to Japan, where it became the 3d Battalion, 7th Marines. In retrospect and on paper all this sounds neat and simple. In the accomplishment it was frantic (for example, the 1st Battalion had five days to organize and draw equipment and get aboard ship). Nonetheless, the 7th Marines reached Japan on September 17, three days before the JCS prediction of the 20th, and were unloading at Inchon on the 21st.

Homer Laurence Litzenberg, Jr., colonel of the 7th Marines, was a compact, sharp-eyed officer with iron-gray hair cropped short. His nickname, "Litz the Blitz," was not an idle one. Colonel Litzenberg was energetic, quick tempered and hard driving. Major Francis Fox Parry, who commanded the new battalion of the 11th Marines attached to Litzenberg's regiment, was a highly trained, resolute and sanguine artilleryman.

As soon as the hook was down, Litzenberg was ashore and headed for General Smith's command post at Oeso-Ri. Having combat-loaded the transports for maximum flexibility in landing, Colonel Litzenberg asked O. P. Smith what unit he would like first. "An infantry battalion," replied the general. What next? inquired the colonel.

"Another infantry battalion."

Before midnight, Litzenberg had his headquarters ashore, two of his three rifle battalions, and Major Parry's gunners. The 2d Battalion was in an assembly area near Hill 131, north of Kimpo airfield (further insurance against trouble on the north flank), while the 3d Battalion was two miles south. The 1st Battalion, still at Inchon, had the onerous job of unloading the transports.

When the entire regiment was ashore, General Smith planned to acclimate them by a day or two of patrolling, and then swing them north of Seoul as the left wing in his envelopment of the city.[32]

X Corps Assumes Command Ashore

The naval aspects of the campaign were rapidly becoming routine. As the Marines pressed inland, fire-support ships began to run out of range:

on the 18th, destroyer support could no longer be used; for a few more days, the cruisers' long-barreled 8-inch guns rendered good service against targets 12 and 15 miles inland; for reasons which are obscure, the great *Missouri* declined fire missions at her extreme range of 20 miles and in return was looked on by naval gunfire officers of the Marine division as a kind of seagoing Ferdinand the Bull.[33]

Inchon's mountains of supplies were being brought low; its crooked roads were being made straight. Supply limitations at the front were no longer measured by what could be brought to Inchon and unloaded but by the X Corps motor transport bottleneck which had already cost General Smith his 7th Motor Transport Battalion.

Up to this time, the role of X Corps headquarters had been nominal. The lack of amphibious knowledge by its commander and staff (noted earlier by Admiral Doyle), together with the lateness in throwing together the headquarters, had precluded meaningful participation in the amphibious phase of the operation.

In the framework normal for landing operations, the corps commander functions under the title "commander, expeditionary troops" as the highest ground forces commander and counterpart of the top naval commander (in this case, Admiral Struble). To perform this role, the corps commander and staff share the flagship communications facilities of the naval commander so that personal liaison may be maintained and the military planners may keep naval and air operations oriented to best support the objectives of the landing forces.

Nothing of this kind was even attempted at Inchon. On the basis of existing doctrine and of experience going back to Wolfe and Saunders at Quebec, General Almond and key members of his staff should have been in *Rochester* with Admiral Struble. Instead, X Corps headquarters was embarked in an MSTS transport, *Buckner*, with none of the complex communications or operations facilities available in a flagship and essential for exercise of command or indeed of any influence over events. Separating himself from his staff and headquarters, General Almond in turn went to Inchon aboard *Mount McKinley* with MacArthur. This may have been the right place for MacArthur's chief of staff; it was surely wrong for the commander of X Corps.[34]

Now, with the campaign rapidly becoming a land operation, with Inchon and Kimpo taken, the Han crossed—in fact, with every objective of the campaign already attained but the capture of Seoul—it was high time for X Corps to assume control of operations ashore. Now it was time to see whether this headquarters, improvised from "many experienced officers who had commanded in Europe and Italy," would justify its commander's hopes or would, as General Hickey predicted, ". . . be at best only a half-baked affair."

As the fighting receded from Inchon, amenities began to reappear. Admiral Doyle found a spare tent and pitched it on Wolmi Do as an oasis for thirsty members of the staff of Amphibious Group 1. The only drawback was that, when the wind was wrong, it wafted in the sweet-and-sour bouquet of some of the island's hastily buried defenders.

When X Corps headquarters began displacing ashore, General Almond asked the captain of one of the transports if his personal van (rigged with refrigerator, hot running water, electricity, shower and flush toilet) could be unloaded. As the van had been spotted well down in a hold below combat equipment, it was not readily available. When the matter came to Admiral Doyle's notice, he told the ship's captain, if pressed on the point, to say that the Navy would cut a hole in the bottom of the ship in order to get the van unloaded soon enough.[35]

Eventually, however, complete with amenities including fine Japanese china, X Corps headquarters landed at Inchon and on September 21, with a spit-and-polish ceremonial honor guard, assumed command of operations ashore. At five that afternoon, Admiral Struble dissolved Joint Task Force 7, which had accomplished so much, and simultaneously donned a new hat as commander of the Naval Support Force for what had now officially become a land campaign.[36]

The Navy's support continued to be of some importance: each day, Almond's mess caterer went back aboard ship to draw fresh food, steaks, ice cream and bread. At the end of the month he was shaken to discover that, instead of dispensing these delicacies gratis, the naval paymaster had carefully kept tally, and presented X Corps with their invoices and bill in triplicate. After that, arrangements were made to have such supplies flown in directly from Japan.

7   *X CORPS OVER THE HAN*

~~~~~~

The passage of great rivers in the presence of the enemy is one of the most delicate operations in war.

FREDERICK THE GREAT

AN INTIMATION that the world would be watching when they crossed the Han came to the 5th Marines on the afternoon of September 19 (D+4). Colonel Murray had his command post in the basement of the administration building at Kimpo, and here, amid a swarm of correspondents, sightseers from afloat, and high-echelon staff officers, Murray and his staff put their plan together. To keep the visitors from driving them crazy, Major Robert M. Calland, the artillery liaison officer, was told off to conduct a briefing.

As Calland, a blunt, burly, active officer, launched into his remarks, the door opened and an apparition was seen—an Army major dressed in knife-creased Class A khaki with blouse, spit-shined shoes and twinkling aiguillettes. Interrupting Calland politely but briskly, the major asked, "Can you tell me where I can pick up a five-star license plate around here?"

"Major," replied Calland, "this is the CP of a Marine *regiment*. Where in hell do you think *we* can find a five-star license plate?"

The aide's jaw dropped. After a pause he gulped, turned on his heel and walked out the door. Calland never saw him again ("Maybe he went around the corner and shot himself," said Calland).[1]

After the capture of Kimpo airfield and its defense against dawn counterattack on the 18th, the 5th Marines had consolidated their hold, patrolled the villages roundabout and established control over Hill 131, a rugged mass which rises out of Kimpo's paddies and overlooks the Han.

Hill 131's counterpart across the river (here more than 400 yards wide) is Hill 125. Precipitous, green, sparsely wooded, tadpole-shaped with a tail of ridge extending northwest along the riverbank, Hill 125 is a key terrain feature. From its top one can see for miles over the Kimpo plain. On September 18 and 19, the *In Min Gun*'s observers on Hill 125 could clearly make out American preparations to cross the Han.

Everyone was anxious to get troops over the Han. On the morning of the 19th, Almond and O. P. Smith conferred.

> He is in a hurry to get across the river [Smith recorded in his log] but there are certain things that have to be done. . . . It will be necessary for the 7th Division to take over its zone of action south of us. So far, Puller has been forced to protect his own south flank. . . . Then it is necessary for Puller to relieve the 5th Marines in the area facing Yongdungpo in order that the 5th Marines can assemble its battalions for the crossing. Then there is the question of bridging material. . . . General Almond promises bridge material. This is an empty promise, as the 1st Marine Division has the only bridging material available.

The problem of bridging the Han was certainly not unforeseen; it was, according to General Almond, one of the factors which influenced the decision to have an Army corps headquarters rather than a Marine headquarters, the Army being thought to be more qualified in such land operations. Why nothing seems to have been done about this problem is a real question.

On August 23, O. P. Smith had heard the X Corps engineer talk of plans for the crossing and then admit that he had no bridging capability yet. In the X Corps command post exercise of September 11, it was brought out that the corps still did not have the requisite bridging equipment. After the landing, on September 18 (D+3), the corps engineer assured General Craig that X Corps would get a bridge across the Han capable of taking heavy equipment (the tanks were what had to get over, to support the 5th Marines). Yet Smith and Craig knew that the only bridging or ferrying capability in X Corps resided in the 1st Marine Engineer Battalion, whose resourceful commander, Partridge, had foreseen this eventuality as far back as San Diego, and brought along 50-ton floating-bridge sections which would at least serve as pontoon ferries for the tanks if nothing else was handy. As of September 19, nothing else was.[2]

Selecting the exact crossing site over this mighty river was a process of elimination. There had to be access roads on the near shore and exits on the far; shoreline gradients had to permit launching and landing Partridge's heavy bridge sections; and the river itself must be free of mudbanks on which amphibian tractors might belly down and ground. Of three possible sites, one was too close to Yongdungpo and fully exposed to enemy interference. Another, the ferry crossing near Kumpo Town, was too far away. Midway between was an abandoned ferry site at Haengju which filled the bill. This crossing ran almost directly between the Hills 131 (on the near shore) and 125 (on the enemy side) which we have already noted. Taking one of VMO-6's helicopters on the 19th, General Craig looked over all three and verified that Haengju was the place.

Giving Murray the necessary means (the division recon company, amphibian tractors, shore party and engineer support), General Smith ordered that the 5th Marines cross the Han at Haengju on September 20, seize Hill 125, wheel sharp right (southeast) up the right bank, advance on Seoul and uncover other crossing sites for the 1st Marines. How Murray was to accomplish this was of course up to him.

Initial Failure

"Except for the press, Murray had the situation well in hand," General Smith noted in his *Aide-Mémoire* following a forenoon visit to the 5th Regiment CP after talking with Almond about the forthcoming crossing. Foreshadowing the Vietnamese war's overexposure to press and TV, the command post, wrote Smith, "was overrun with correspondents and kibitzers."[3]

> While the American people are entitled to know what is going on, this should not extend to the point where correspondents look over the shoulder of a commander while he is making his plans.

The plan for the crossing was simple enough. After dark, Captain Houghton would lead a team of swimmers from his recon company to the far shore. They would scout the riverbank and immediate slopes of Hill 125. All well, Houghton would then call over the remainder of the company in amtracs. The unit's mission would be to secure Hill 125 (a mile-long feature in itself) and two lesser neighbors—Hills 51 and 95 —which, with 125, comprise a triangle of eminences commanding the crossing site. An hour before dawn Taplett's 3d Battalion, 5th Marines, followed in column by the 2d and 1st Battalions, would cross in LVTs, pass through the reconnaissance company screen and wheel toward Seoul. Engineers and shore party would consolidate.

Superficially a "school solution" crossing by the book, this plan had weaknesses. There was little knowledge of enemy presence or dispositions on the north bank and particularly on Hill 125 (but surely Houghton's patrol would take care of this). Item, the main body of recon people crossing in amtracs, which are even noisier than tanks, would advertise the operation far and wide, and hours before Taplett's battalion was to cross (in other words, the plan had the disadvantages of crossing by stealth and crossing in assault, with the advantages of neither). Item, Houghton's company—127 strong—was to secure, occupy and defend three large hill masses, each at least a mile away from the others—a battalion-sized job under most circumstances. Finally, the 5th Marines had no alternate plan in case things failed to work out (but of course they were bound to work out).

It would not be quite true to say that there was no alternate plan at all. When Taplett returned to his command post after receiving his orders, he instructed his executive officer and S-3 to work up a private plan for an assault crossing. Then he took his company commanders onto Hill 131 for visual reconnaissance of Hill 125. As Taplett later said, he felt that the reconnaissance company operation was "doomed to fail."[4]

Confident and always eager to be in the forefront of things, General Lowe, President Truman's advance man, now announced to General Smith that he intended to accompany the first wave across the Han— omitting, however, to add that Captain Houghton had already said no. O. P. Smith replied that a sixty-five-year-old major general had no business crossing an estuary with the young men of the recon company. Lowe who, as Colonel Snedeker said, "was not a rear-area observer," produced his White House *laissez-passer*. For once it failed to work: General Smith said Lowe could cross with the reserve battalion of the 5th Regiment, card or no card. General Lowe huffed and puffed a bit, but lost some interest when he learned that the first wave was to swim the river rather than storm over in amtracs.[5]

For two hours, beside Lieutenant Colonel Lawrence C. Hays, Murray's executive officer, Houghton sat on Hill 131 and studied Hill 125 and the neighboring terrain; there was not a sign of the enemy. Then or perhaps earlier, Houghton suggested that he look over the far shore from an OY liaison plane or chopper (no need, was the answer); second, he asked Larry Hays if he could swim over immediately after dusk. Hays, coolheaded and given to thinking things through, said the plan should be carried out as ordered. (What would Hays have said had he known Houghton secretly hoped to sneak into Seoul before the night was out?)

The events of the next few hours are an example of what happens in war when one lowers his guard, even a little.

What the 5th Marines did not know was that an infantry battalion of the *In Min Gun* had that very afternoon cautiously entered the Haengju area and, as night fell, was in the act of occupying Hill 125, a natural redoubt.[6]

About eight that evening, after sunset, Houghton mustered his patrol and gave final orders (Major Brush, regimental operations officer and a soldier of experience, was concerned over lack of photo coverage and still grumbling because he felt the company commander shouldn't be in the first wave). There were 14 swimmers: Captain Houghton, Second Lieutenant Dana M. Cashion, Technical Sergeant E. L. deFazio, and nine other enlisted Marines; and two naval officers—one, Lieutenant Horace Underwood, whose Korean boyhood in a missionary family made him a skilled interpreter, the other, Ensign Judah L. Siegal, a Navy PIO with a tape recorder.[7]

All hands stripped. Clothes, weapons, radios, Siegal's tape recorder, went into two plastic assault boats. Then, squishing through the chilly mud, they entered chillier water, breast-stroking smoothly for silence and towing the assault boats as they went. Halfway over—bane of night attacks—an uncoordinated artillery concentration lit on the far shore in Haengju and set a house afire which, in Technical Sergeant deFazio's subsequent notes, "lit up the place like a Xmas tree."

A few yards offshore, still undetected, the lead swimmers saw two men moving along the bank. "Go get them, Gunny!" ordered Houghton. Accompanied by Corporal Anderson, deFazio grabbed his pistol from the assault boat, churned up from the knee-deep water and jumped the pair. When able to speak again, they told Lieutenant Underwood they were refugees and were placed under guard.

Crouching on the bank, Houghton whispered to Cashion to take a four-man patrol to Haengju on the left, along the saddle to their front, and up onto Hill 125, which was still silent. Then, elated at being the first U.N. troops back across the Han, Houghton radioed, "The Marines have landed and the situation is well in hand." Hunched over his tape recorder, Siegal thought this was great.

On the south bank, nine amtracs bearing the rest of the company, an engineer platoon, and artillery and 4.2-inch mortar forward-observer teams, were marshaled for crossing. Even though Cashion was still not back, Houghton was jubilant—not a sound to be heard, not a shot fired. To his exec across the river he sent word for the crossing to commence. Out of the black night came a series of tremendous blasting coughs, then a pounding chug that carried too clearly across the wide river. No doubt about it, the tractors had started.

Moments later, as Lieutenant Cashion brought in his patrol short one man who had seemingly disappeared, Hill 125 exploded. Automatic weapons raked the shore, mortar concentrations began falling. In the light of the burning houses the Marines could see bullets whipping the Han. Still confident that his company could land and carry Hill 125, Houghton plunged into the river to guide the tractors in. About this time, heavy mortars (some said our own four-deuces falling short) crashed down. One round exploded in the water within 20 feet of the captain, who was still in the shallows. The concussion nearly broke him in two and everything went blank.

Perhaps it was just as well. As he went out, for some unaccountable reason the leading tractors turned left, pointed downstream, and eventually grounded on the mud flats toward Kumpo. The rest turned back. Listening on the radio (he had had his staff monitor the nets for the crossing) Taplett knew the recon people were in trouble.

Obviously the swimmers had no future on the far shore. Corporal James Morgan took Houghton, still swimming on reflex, in tow. DeFazio had all hands cache their gear out of sight in the reeds. (When Ensign Siegal retrieved his tape recorder next day, his account had been effaced by "some enterprising young lieutenant who had put some choice remarks on the tape."[8])

Leading the swimmers back, deFazio took care that two wounded men were assisted and then set out to find Captain Houghton. Before dawn he located Houghton and Morgan in a grounded amtrac. Houghton had an injured back, was seeing double and was still in shock. With help from other recon officers and men, two of four LVTs were gotten off, and, making sure that his commanding officer was on his way to the clearing station, deFazio reported to Colonel Murray and Major Brush what had happened.

Over the Han

The Marines were on the spot and everyone realized it. General Craig said it in two sentences:[9]

The eyes of the world were upon us. It would have looked bad for the Marines, of all people, to reach a river and not be able to cross.

With little more than an hour before dawn, final plans were approved for a daylight assault crossing. Then it was up to energetic, pear-shaped Major Brush, stumping about on a cane with a badly torn cartilege in one knee, to get out the new order for H-hour at 0645. To give Murray and Brush a fillip, word came down from division that General Shepherd, Admiral Struble and General Almond were on their way up to Hill 131 to watch, while General MacArthur could be expected later.

Fire-support arrangements for the crossing were unsatisfactory. Many rounds fell short in the water. General Shepherd (who kept running notes that morning) recorded: "A very small and ineffectual preparation . . . took place. It ceased entirely at 0545 and for the next hour only intermittent firing took place."

As he had foreseen, Taplett, who had taken Wolmi Do so handily on D-day, was to cross in assault. Then he would seize the three hills which had been assigned to Recon Company, secure the bridgehead, and await passage of lines by Roise and the 2d Battalion. This sounds straightforward and simple, but put yourself in the place of Colonel Taplett—under orders for an unopposed crossing into a secure beachhead, he learns in the night that strong enemy units in unknown dispositions have thrown back the reconnaissance company; that, due to enemy resistance, the original crossing site is unsuitable; and (confirming his pessimistic prediction) his battalion must now cross in assault. Not quite so simple.

After some discussion (Murray was sleeping and Brush was reluctant to break him out), it was agreed that Taplett's battalion would cross by waves in column of companies. The leading company, Item, would wheel right and take Hill 125. George, the next, would plow ahead in its amtracs and seize 95, while How, the last company, would penetrate deepest, also in LVTs, and would secure Hill 51, beyond the Kaesong–Seoul railroad line. These assignments made, the available tractors had to be organized into waves, boat teams formed—in short, the preparations for any assault landing. Happily, Marines are not unfamiliar with such arrangements, whether for beach or riverbank. By dawn the battalion was ready. To cheer them up, someone had come on some North Korean surrender leaflets used on the Army during the attack south; young Marines passed them around, declaiming in the quaint English of the NKPA that their deaths "would wound their families with an arrow of keen pang."

At 0645 the first wave of tractors churned forward. Five minutes later, touching down on the muddy shore, they were met with arrows of keen pang—intense small arms and automatic-weapons fire, antitank rifles, and at least one antitank gun hammered at the amtracs. Afterward, over 200 hits were counted in the six LVTs of the leading wave. While Company I, under Captain McMullen, squared off to take Hill 125, the other two companies clattered through the enemy positions in Haengju and lurched ahead in the tractors toward Hills 51 and 95, neither held in any strength.

Captain McMullen's first task was to get his company on and over the lower ridge and saddle which extend northwest, parallel to the river, from Hill 125. Here, jumping off from Haengju village, still burning from the night before, he attacked up the long axis of the ridge with two platoons in assault, that on the left hooking around to flank the north (rear) face of the steep hill.

Aside from a forward air controller, all the support McMullen had came from the .50-caliber machine guns on the amtracs. Then came the morning strike group from VMF-214—four Corsairs which raked Hill 125 to cover the infantry advance. After that the strike leader detached a section of planes to fly the length of the highway leading into Seoul and knock out any reinforcements or other traffic heading for the bridgehead.

Hill 125's steep, bare slopes afforded the Communists fine observation and better fields of fire. Jockeying his platoons expertly, Captain Mc-Mullen, though wounded, kept the attack moving. Without cover, however, his mortarmen and machine gunners were hard hit. North Korean automatic weapons cut Item Company's 60mm mortar section to pieces before they could get a round off. When the attached machine gunners from Weapons Company tried to cover the mortars, they got more of the same. Sergeant James Guffey, the section leader, fell wounded. Corporal Marvin Prince and Private First Class Howard Chancey set up their gun and fired a series of bursts. When Prince slumped dead over the gun, Chancey heaved the body clear and resumed fire. Moments later, Chancey too was dead. The ammunition man, Private First Class Charles Fattaig, picked his way through the dead and wounded Marines about the gun, and once again resumed fire. Hit in a leg, Fattaig kept the gun in action. Hit again—an arm this time—he refused evacuation.

On the second machine gun of the section, the fight was almost as desperate. Privates First Class Donald R. Blanchard and Jack N. Coley got their gun in action. Blanchard, the gunner, was killed at his post. Coley hunched into position beside the dead man and squeezed off a long burst. By the time the rifle platoons were nearing the crest, Coley had been hit three times, but the blood-soaked gun never fell silent.

The 3d Platoon, under First Lieutenant William F. Sparks, had the hardest going. Their route took them up the spine and open slope toward the conical crest. Sparks was wounded and the platoon's casualties were heavy. McMullen sent his exec to take command, threw in his attached engineer squad and cooks, clerks and quartermasters from company headquarters, and sent them around the hill's left (north) face, while he pushed his support platoon straight through. Now, with all platoons committed—one around the enemy right, one around the left, and another going straight ahead—McMullen had his company-scale Cannae: the enveloped Communists suddenly fled headlong. As they stumbled down into the paddies north of the hill, it was Marine riflemen who had the observation and fields of fire. And where the rifleman left off, VMF-214's Corsairs took over with a vengeance.

In his notebook across the Han, General Shepherd wrote: "0845—Troops opposite our OP made a beautiful advance up Hill 125 and seized it." Nearby, General Smith's aide heard General Almond exclaim that Company I's attack was "one of the finest small-unit actions I have ever witnessed."[10]

More than 200 enemy dead were on the hill, and Item Company was short 43 dead and wounded Marines.[11]

The rest of the day went smoothly. At ten, Colonel Roise led the 2d Battalion across the river in amtracs to an assembly area near the railroad main line. Here, in Joseph Alsop's account, published four days later in the New York *Herald-Tribune*:

> The men shouldered their heavy packs, grasped their well-oiled weapons, and set off to do the day's work.

By midafternoon Roise, advancing with a tank platoon already ferried over, had the day's objectives, a pair of precipitous hills between which the Kaesong–Seoul highway and railroad passed. Four miles to the front, across a choppy sea of steepening ridges and cross compartments, lay the suburbs of Seoul.

While engineers and shore party launched pontoon ferries and regulated the endless chain of amphibian tractors and DUKWs from shore to shore on the Han, the rest of the 5th Regiment and its attached units passed over. In Roise's wake came the 2d Battalion, Korean Marines. These relieved the 3d Battalion, 5th Marines, on Hills 51 and 95, and Taplett hiked his people to an assembly area up a valley floored with paddies, to await orders as Murray's reserve. With his regiment over the Han, or nearly so, Murray in turn closed his command post at Kimpo and opened a new one at the hamlet of Sojong, north of the Han, behind one of the serrated ridges which still lay between him and Seoul.

As the sun set and the evening chill and mist began creeping over the paddies, General Smith had a firm bridgehead north of the Han, and the 5th Regiment was deployed for its attack on Seoul. And Colonel Rowny, the X Corps engineer, telephoned to tell the Marine division that equipment to bridge the Han had just reached Japan and would be flown to Korea in the near future.

". . . The Happiest Moment of My Life"

When the General came ashore on the 20th, he went straight to Hill 131 and arrived in time to observe the 1st Battalion, 5th Marines, cross the river. As reporters from the New York *Times* and Associated Press watched, he said to Colonel Murray, "You've done a perfect job." Murray thanked the supreme commander, then pointed upstream to the ominous hills girdling Seoul. "They'll all evaporate very shortly," was MacArthur's reply.

After that the party left for Yongdungpo, and thence, on Almond's breakneck drive, to visit General Barr. That night, satisfied that Seoul was within the U.N. grasp and knowing that Almond was preparing to open the X Corps CP ashore next day, MacArthur ordered his aides to pack for a return to Tokyo.

By chance next morning, one of Admiral Struble's staff learned that the General had never been back aboard *Missouri* (now lying at Inchon) since the day in 1945 when, with Admiral Nimitz, he received Japan's capitulation in Tokyo Bay. What could be more appropriate than a return visit? Admiral Struble extended the invitation.

Splendid, said MacArthur, and, after a farewell luncheon aboard *Mount McKinley,* went with Admiral Struble in his barge for an official call on *Missouri.* After full honors the General was conducted to the plaque on the battleship's quarterdeck where, almost five years earlier, the instrument of surrender was signed. For a moment, the General stood silent. Howard Handleman of INS (who had been there on September 2, 1945, too) could see that his eyes were filling. Then, unashamed of tears which rolled down his cheeks, he warmly thanked the admiral, held out his arms and exclaimed, "You have given me the happiest moment of my life."

At Kimpo, the *Scap,* MacArthur's command plane, was warmed up and waiting. So were General Shepherd (who had spent the day with the 1st Division), General Smith, and Generals Almond, Harris and Cushman. Accompanied in cavalcade by Whitney, Wright and Fox, the General drove up. With a heartfelt handclasp—warmed by memories of victory in Tokyo Bay and elated by impending victory in Seoul—he singled out O. P. Smith, pinned the Silver Star on his green utility jacket, and said: "To the gallant commander of a gallant division!"

As the *Scap* leveled off for Tokyo, General MacArthur unsnapped his seat belt, settled back and lit his private pipe (not the famous battered corncob but a long-stemmed, handsome, delicately shaped item). After a few moments he asked General Shepherd to come forward and brief him on what he had seen. His map posted to the time of departure, Shepherd gave the General his impressions: Resistance beginning to build up north of the Han . . . hard fighting in Yongdungpo . . . every indication the Communists would fight to the last in Seoul. . . .

The General listened, nodded, put his pipe aside and, with no warning, gave General Shepherd the Silver Star, which, he remarked, he himself had designed while Chief of Staff of the Army. When Shepherd demurred, MacArthur merely replied, "You have served your country with great distinction," which was undeniably true.

Night fell rapidly as the *Scap* droned southeastward toward Haneda. In his journal, General Shepherd somberly wrote: "I personally believe it will take a week of fighting before Seoul is secured."[12]

On to Seoul

In the newly taken towns [reported *Life*] the South Koreans poured out to welcome the Marines. . . . They pointed out enemy snipers, dug foxholes, brought out charcoal burners on which the Americans could heat their rations.

An ancient Hawaiian-Korean veteran of World War I even dug up his American Legion cap, carefully hidden from the Communists, and proudly put it on in honor of the 5th Regiment.

Although resistance was beginning to stiffen before the 1st and 3d Battalions, the 5th Marines were still making good progress and, between enthusiastic villagers and skirmish lines of correspondents, the day's advance on September 21 (D+6) had a gala tinge.

Not the least noticed ingredient in this atmosphere was one correspondent who had been faithful to the 5th Marines since the days of the perimeter. "Meeting Maggie Higgins at the front for the first time," wrote a colleague, "is like meeting Brenda Frazier in the gents' room at Grand Central Station. . . . Riding in a jeep with Maggie is like being a jockey on Lady Godiva's horse." Yet, besides being a brave and pretty blonde who, the troops said, wore mud the way most girls wear make-up, Miss Higgins was also a deadly competitor for the male reporters. One of the latter sourly remarked, "Maggie was never embarrassed at being one female among many males." Another—evidently beaten on at least one story during the campaign—snapped, "Higgins is about as winsome as a maddened adder." Determined and resolute she certainly was. Now with the 5th Marines, she was making good an earlier promise: "I walked out of Seoul, and I want to walk back in."[18]

The terrain which confronted Colonel Murray on the evening of the 21st—after a three-mile advance from the bridgehead—was hilly and ideal for defensive fighting. A Japanese army training area for many years (and in 1965 still an ROK training area), this approach to Seoul was well mapped, its fields of fire and observation were accurately charted, and Korean officers on either side knew the ground well. Unfortunately, most of its advantages accrued to the *In Min Gun*.

While the 5th Marines were forcing the Han, the Communist high command was throwing in its final reserves for the defense of Seoul. From Sariwon, near Pyongyang, arrived the 78th Independent Regiment, 2,000 infantry with reinforcing light artillery, engineers and heavy weapons, commanded by Colonel Pak Han Lin. Colonel Pak's first mission was to delay Colonel Murray.

Screened by the 78th Regiment were more formidable forces. The 25th Brigade, 5,000 strong, commanded by Major General Wol Ki Chan, trained in Russia, was composed of officers and noncommissioned officers who had served with the Chinese Communist armies. A solid agglomeration of little else but firepower, the 25th Brigade had only two infantry battalions, but four heavy machine-gun battalions, a 120mm mortar battalion, a 76mm gun battalion and an engineer battalion. The brigade had started from Chorwon the day the Marines landed; it closed in Seoul the 19th and 20th. General Wol was ordered to organize a decisive defense of the high ground northwest of Seoul. To give him even more strength, the Seoul City Regiment, which had formed a major part of the capital's garrison, was filled out from headquarters, service and supply troops, redesignated as 31st Rifle Division, and also moved to the northwest front. Commanded by Colonel Lee Kyong U, its strength was about 3,500.

In all, therefore, the Marine division (more exactly at this point, the 5th Regiment) faced a well-trained force of about 10,000 fresh troops generously equipped with combined arms, led by experienced officers, entrenching rapidly on strong terrain and preparing for a last-ditch defense.[14]

"There wasn't anything wrong with those North Koreans," General Shepherd later remarked, and this was what General Wol was about to prove.[15]

The ground General Wol had chosen to defend is now overgrown by the city. Slums blur terrain features which stood out only too nakedly in 1950. Basically, the Communist defensive position was the massif of Hill 296—An-San, the Koreans call it—a precipitous bare eminence with a series of radiating fingers and interlocking, mutually supporting ridges which extend southward almost to the Han and bar the way to Seoul. As an exercise in map reading, this ground is confusing and deceptive; for the tactician it is a nightmare.

On the morning of September 22 (D+7) Colonel Murray had three battalions in line. On the left, north flank, ready to jump off from Hill 216, was Taplett's 3d Battalion. Across the steep valley of the Sachon Creek loomed Hill 296, the battalion's objective. It was Murray's plan that this height would be taken and then, with Taplett holding position as a hinge, the center and right battalions would pivot in a leftward swing over their ridges into Seoul.

The center battalion, Major Ko's 1st KMCs (attached to the 5th Marines), held Hill 104, which the 3d Battalion, 5th Marines, had taken the day before. This ground is really a ridge which is the westernmost of the long fingers fanning south from Hill 296. The Korean Marines were to attack to the front across a low valley, seize a ridge (Hill 56) to their front, then continue forward to take two hills confusingly numbered 105 in each case. To compound the confusion of two Hills 105, the 1st Battalion, on the right, was to attack from Hill 68 and take still another Hill 105. (To keep up with the 105 situation, operations officers quickly designated them, respectively, as Hills 105 North, 105 Center, and 105 South.) All these enemy hills—56 and the 105 triplets, and adjacent pieces of terrain—are part of the complex system of radiating ridges south of Hill 296 which we have already described.

At 0700 the 5th Marines attacked. The battle for Seoul had commenced.

Thrusting southeast, Company H of Taplett's battalion made good progress up the north slope of Hill 296. Even so, their advance was impeded by heavy fire from Hill 338, a sharp, stony hill northwest of 296. Here the 25th Brigade had part of a machine-gun battalion. By midmorning, however, How Company was atop the hill. No sooner there, they received and, with tank support, beat off a company-strength counterattack from the jumble of ridges to the south. Before, during and after the attack, enemy small arms, automatic weapons, antitank guns and mortars played incessantly on the Marines and kept them in their foxholes.

On the far left (Taplett also had the mission of protecting the division's left flank), a platoon of I Company walked into unyielding resistance— at least a company—holding the village of Nokpon Ni. The fighting around Nokpon Ni went on all day, as did continuous Communist attempts to infiltrate the 3d Battalion's positions atop Hill 296.

In the center the Korean Marines made little headway. As they dropped into the valley from Hill 104, they were plastered with well-adjusted mortar and artillery fire, and with sheets of small-arms and automatic-weapons fire from Hill 56, the insignificant-appearing ridge to their front. Squads of the 25th Brigade counterattacked and infiltrated, some even getting all the way back to Hill 104 itself. Even with heavy air strikes from VMF-323, under control of Lieutenant Colonel Norman J. Anderson, the KMCs were forced back to their original positions. During the height of this brave attack by the inexperienced Koreans, Anderson led in a Corsair strike on Hill 72 (soon to be well known in the 5th Regiment as "Nellie's Tit"), blowing open a tank and felling accompanying infantry with rockets and 500-pound bombs. When the Corsairs landed, the plane captain found the Swiss-cheese holes of an automatic-weapons burst within three inches of the headrest on Major A. A. Lund's airplane; First Lieutenant J. L. McCollum had his map case pierced by flak which finally spent itself in his seat-pack parachute; and Second Lieutenant A. M. Blayden's engine section was shot through and through. Despite this reception, VMF-323 flew 42 sorties that day, all against the An-San massif. Except for D-day (when the squadron flew 43 sorties from *Badoeng Strait*) this was their highest daily record.[16]

On the ground, the day was trying, too. Colonel Murray had lost his exec, Lieutenant Colonel Hays, during the night, when a shell hit the regimental command post, seriously wounded Hays and wounded Murray less so. Despite his wound, Ray Murray kept on his feet. Hays was replaced by his old friend and Basic School classmate, Joe Stewart.

The KMCs were clearly stopped cold. Murray decided to outflank. Newton, he ordered, would swing the 1st Battalion far right and seize Hill 105 South from the west, thus supposedly bypassing the ridge which was holding up the Korean Marines.

The Communist mortars were deadly accurate ("They could really drop it in your lap," Captain Fenton recalled). Mortars or not, Newton swung A Company (Captain Stevens) down through the paddies almost to the Han, then back onto a knoll occupied by the government radio station. An antitank gun and machine guns (including one ex-U. S. Army .50-caliber gun) pinned the company to the deck. Here fell the 2d Platoon's leader, First Lieutenant Nathaniel F. Mann, Jr.; Mann was the platoon's fourth commander since the Marine brigade landed at Pusan on August 7. First Lieutenant Joseph A. Schimmenti, 3d Platoon, had his neck pierced by a bullet which passed exactly between esophagus and spinal column without grazing either. Later the regimental surgeon told Schimmenti, alive on borrowed time: "If I practiced ten years I couldn't incise your neck where that bullet did without killing you."[17] With Schimmenti's loss, every one of Stevens's platoon leaders was a noncommissioned officer.

Now Newton ordered Lieutenant Pederson and C Company to work past Stevens's right. More machine guns stopped Pederson, too. Meanwhile, the mortars found the 1st Battalion's aid station. The surgeon, Lieutenant (jg) Franc T. H'Doubler (whom the lieutenants all called "Hogan"), was wounded and knocked down. He picked himself up and went on caring for the wounded. Another concentration smothered the aid station; this time H'Doubler went down and couldn't get up. Neither could the chaplain. Wounded in the face and ankle, Chief Pharmacist's Mate Douglas Austin had the two remaining corpsmen get H'Doubler and the padre onto stretchers. Then, having patched himself up, the chief took charge. By the time another surgeon could get forward, Austin had handled more than 40 wounded. Only then did he let himself be properly tagged and evacuated to the clearing station.

Playing his final card late in the afternoon, Newton sent in B Company under Captain Fenton. Fenton attacked through Stevens's lines at the radio station behind an intense preparation by the 11th Marines and

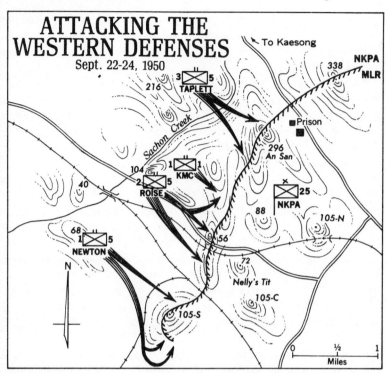

ATTACKING THE WESTERN DEFENSES
Sept. 22-24, 1950

VMF-323's last strike of the day. Within a quarter hour, so close behind the preparation that the riflemen were fairly leaning on it, Fenton and Pederson surged forward and took 105 South in a rush.

Colonel Murray's big problem was in the center. As night fell, his two flank battalions held hard-won positions on An-San and Hill 105 South. In between, the KMCs were back where they started, thus creating a half-mile re-entrant into the 5th Marines front. Next day, Newton and Taplett would have to hold while the Korean Marines (who had already taken heavy casualties) fought their way abreast.

But there were long hours until next day. To prevent a gap in the line—a gap that infiltrators would quickly discover under cover of darkness—Murray had Newton pull Able Company back onto Hill 68, leaving Baker and Charlie under Fenton, senior of the two company commanders, to hold 105 South. Barren, flat-topped like a truncated egg, commanded and observed by enemy-held ridges, 105 South was no vacation spot.

P

Before the sun set, enemy heavy machine guns began to scythe back and forth over the hilltop, while antitank guns, accurate as a sniper's rifle and a lot deadlier, flash-banged in with high-velocity rounds that left no time for a man to duck.

After dark, Communist infantry snaked up the east slope of the hill, surrounded and overran a platoon in C Company. Killing its crew to a man, they made off with a machine gun before being repulsed. Then commenced a deadly game of hide-and-seek. Creeping about the base of the hill with their prize, the North Koreans would fire a burst, then move to another position and do the same. To prevent disclosing his dispositions, Fenton forbade the Marines to reply. When no fire was returned, the Communists moved closer while the Marines waited. At last, when the silent riflemen could hear the scrape of enemy footfalls, the creak of web equipment and the squad leaders' hoarse whispers, the moment came. On command, every Marine on the line hurled a grenade in a fierce halo of flash and fragments. "That," laconically noted Ike Fenton, "discouraged the enemy and he withdrew."[18] Another discouraging factor to the defenders was a night fighter from newly arrived VMF (N)-542 that Max Volcansek kept on the prowl at low altitude over Seoul, the Han, and Yongdungpo. Few night sounds are more worrying than unidentified aircraft droning overhead.

At seven the next morning (September 23, D+8), Major Ko again launched his Korean Marines against Hill 56 and its connecting ridge. On each flank the U. S. Marine battalions held position but poured in all the fire they could. General Wol again gave as good as he got. The KMCs were drenched in artillery, mortar and automatic-weapons fire that made forward movement virtually impossible. North Korean prisoners later revealed that this day and the day before, the 25th Brigade took 40 per cent casualties. If so, there was no sign of it in the way they fought. Enemy fire was so intense that carrying parties with food and water couldn't make it to Hill 105 South until night fell.

One simple fact had not yet been realized by the attackers. This fact was that the Hill 56 system constituted General Wol's main line of resistance. To the rear, on higher ground, loomed more commanding ridges; logically, these should have been his main defenses, or so it looked. In trying to guess, like Wellington, what lay "around the other side of the hill," nobody had quite perceived what Major Ko was up against.

So at midday, charging off the morning's disappointment to KMC inexperience, Colonel Murray decided to commit his reserve. Roise was

directed to assemble the 2d Battalion behind the KMCs on Hill 104, pass
through them, and get on with the battle.

It was three in the afternoon when Roise jumped off. There was a brief
artillery preparation and a tank platoon in support. Divided by the railroad's main line, Company F on the right (Captain Peters) and Company D on the left (Lieutenant H. J. Smith) were to seize the troublesome ridge and continue the attack. Peters advanced first, across a long,
open thousand yards of paddy, toward the southern end of the ridge,
under fire all the way. The lead Pershing tank bogged down in a muddy
ditch, so the remaining four had to backtrack and get onto the railroad
tracks for firmer footing. Peters ordered Second Lieutenant S. E. Sansing's
60mm mortar section forward into supporting range to help the rifle
platoons, but, Sansing said, the radio message never got through. Peters
sent a runner to confirm the order, but, Sansing said, no runner ever
arrived (the runner was later wounded and evacuated, so nobody could
say positively whether he got through or not). Thus, while the rest of
Fox Company fought, its mortars remained well out of range.[19]

While Fox Company's unsupported rifle platoons clawed forward to
their objective, H. J. Smith was bringing his company along a so-called
sunken road which was in fact the cut of an incompleted railroad line
intended to straighten the existing section of tangent which served as a
boundary between the assault companies. Once Peters held the end of
the ridge, Smith was to advance on the left, supported by Peters, and
bite off Hill 56 proper. Then Smith would pivot left and move north,
clearing the ridge as he went.

No plan ever survives contact with the enemy, said Moltke, and
neither did this.

Fox Company made it to the tail of the ridge, a fanged razorback
with a railroad tunnel running through it. Once on the crest, they engaged
heavily with North Koreans dug in with numerous machine guns, while
at least four antitank guns sited to cover the tunnel against tanks, not
trains, hammered away. But the Marines' momentum was not to be
denied. Clearing their own hill, Peters's platoons hit Hill 56 so hard in
flank that the Communists withdrew. To the amazement of Smith, Dog
Company emerged from the sunken road and took possession of the hill
almost unopposed.

Now, D Company's 1st Platoon, under Second Lieutenant Ray Heck,
formed left into line and started up the saddle that connected Hill 56
with the long ridge going up toward the heights of An-San. The sketch

map prepared on the ground by battalion after the fight shows enemy positions and guns so dense along this ridge that you lose count.

Heck had his people in the open, halfway across the saddle, when the wooded knoll ahead opened up. The first blast of fire dropped Heck with a mortal wound. His platoon sergeant fell, one leg shattered by a machine-gun burst. Within five minutes, half the 1st Platoon were dead or wounded. Well forward, as was his habit, Lieutenant Smith, the company commander, rallied survivors and got them and the dead and wounded back to tenable ground on Hill 56, where the other two platoons were mopping up. Twilight was coming on, and Smith wisely decided this was no time to press his attack. Instead he took a tight defensive formation for the night ahead.

While Dog Company was losing the better part of a platoon, so was Fox. Although Peters's attack had jolted the NKPA off Hill 56, his own chunk of ridge was far from secure. Just beyond the tunnel, the greater part of a Communist company was still holding for dear life. With only 27 men left in his 2d Platoon, Lieutenant Anderson assailed the enemy at close quarters. In a melee of grenades, point-blank rifle fire and even bayonet thrusts (so often reported yet so rarely seen), the platoon killed most of their enemies and dislodged the rest. When Peters ordered them back (apparently taking the same conservative view of events as Smith), seven members of the 2d Platoon remained on their feet.

The situation of the 5th Marines when night fell on the 23d was roughly this. The 1st Battalion was pinned in its foxholes on 105 South. All day, Fenton's two companies had been beaten by plunging fire that picked off men in their holes. Movement was impossible. Rations and water came forward only after dark, when the wounded were gotten out.

The 3d Battalion, on Hill 296, continued to jockey with NKPA counterthrusts and support the attack in the center by fire. Taplett's most vivid memory of the day was of "Fireproof Phil," a six-foot, fair-skinned enemy officer who may well have been a Russian adviser. Exposing himself here, there, and everywhere, "Fireproof Phil" (the 3d Battalion's nickname) was invulnerable. Rifles, machine guns, mortars, even tank 90mm guns, all just missed him. Even the Weapons Company's special prize, a recaptured U. S. Army 105mm howitzer which they kept hot all day, was unable to do the job. He may be a Marshal of the Soviet Union today.

In the 2d Battalion, Roise had two companies barely holding perimeters along the ridge. Aside from their own weapons, all that stood between them and the 25th Brigade were the howitzers of the 11th Marines. "I cannot say enough about the artillery support we received that night," wrote Lieutenant Anderson. "It was magnificent." Most of it came from Battery B, commanded by Captain Arnold C. Hofstetter. For Baker Battery there was no sleep that night, but there was little for the enemy on the ridge, either. Baker Battery saw to that.[20]

X Corps Takes Charge

When General Almond assumed command of operations ashore before dinner on September 21 at Inchon, all objectives short of Seoul had been taken, the Han River had been crossed, unaided, by the Marine division, and the assault on Seoul itself was under way.

Looking next morning at the situation map kept so neatly by Lieutenant Colonel John H. Chiles, USA, corps operations officer and an insider on Almond's "team" from GHQ in Tokyo, where he had been staff secretary until mid-August, the general could see that the main elements of X Corps were disposed and functioning as follows:

The Marine division, with the mission of taking Seoul, was closing in on the city from the northwest with the 5th Marines and from the southwest, via Yongdungpo, with the 1st Marines. The newly arrived 7th Marines were being phased into operations to cover the corps left (north) flank, where the Korean Marine battalions not attached to Murray and the 5th Regiment were already providing some protection on Kumpo Peninsula and the Haengju bridgehead. Besides protecting the corps flank, the 7th Marines were being swung into positions northwest of Seoul, from which they could encircle the city and cut off enemy escape routes while the 5th Regiment fixed the North Koreans' main force. Such a maneuver, which would require a few days, might conceivably permit the capture of Seoul and most of its defenders with little damage to the city.

The 7th Infantry Division (less its 17th Infantry, still south as General Walker's reserve) had landed within the Marine beachhead and gone forward to take over its zone of action on the corps right flank. The 32d Infantry, though well wide, was abreast of the right flank of Puller's 1st Regiment in Yongdungpo. One of Colonel Beauchamp's battalions had cut and was blocking the Anyang corridor, a principal approach to Seoul from the south.

General Cushman, commanding the X Corps Tactical Air Command, had his headquarters ashore at Kimpo airfield and was controlling all air operations in the objective area. The MAG-33 squadrons were operating from Kimpo ashore. Those of MAG-12 were afloat in the two faithful jeep carriers.

A few lesser units had not yet arrived, but soon would. The 187th Airborne Regimental Combat Team (a Stateside unit which it had been hoped could seize the Han bridgehead by parachute) would reach Kimpo on the 25th. To confuse historians, both the 17th Infantry (a U. S. Army formation already mentioned) and the 17th ROK Army Regiment were to land on the 24th and 25th respectively. Both were headed for the 7th Division. One last Marine squadron, VMF-312, was not due at Kimpo until the 28th.

General Almond's original and current plan called for the Marine division to seize all of Seoul. The boundary between General Smith and General Barr ran along the south bank of the Han so as to give the city as a single objective to the Marines. By September 22—as either Puller in Yongdungpo or Murray on Hill 104 could have told anyone—it was clear that, regardless of the fact that American troops were within sight and a few thousand yards of Seoul's Duksoo Palace, the Korean capital was far from recaptured. Only the day before, as we have seen, General Shepherd privately foresaw another week of fighting for the city.

The liberation of Seoul and restoration of civil government to South Korea were psychological, political and symbolic objectives of great importance. General MacArthur had kept them high in mind from the earliest days of the war. With an eagerness which reflected his master's touch, General Almond (whose second hat was still as MacArthur's chief of staff) badly wanted to deliver Seoul by September 25, exactly 90 days after the North Korean attack, in June. His main problem was lack of cooperation on the part of the *In Min Gun.*

Unfortunately, Almond and some of his staff tended to see the problem not in terms of enemy resistance but in what they considered unduly slow progress by the Marine division. Colonel Chiles, the X Corps G-3, later remarked, "The Marines were exasperatingly deliberate at a time when rapid maneuver was imperative." Never a patient man, General Almond felt the same way and so expressed himself with increasing frequency.

Even though he could not yet know that Murray and the 5th Regiment were up against the better part of 10,000 North Koreans, General Smith could clearly see that General Wol's defense of northwest Seoul was too much for one regiment to handle. Thus, as soon as the 5th Marines had uncovered a suitable crossing site opposite Yongdungpo, O. P. Smith planned to send over Puller's regiment, swing it into line with Murray, and then wheel left up the main part of Seoul. After September 23's hard fighting, he felt that the moment had come.

Late that afternoon, General Almond called a conference at the corps command post back in Inchon. The subject, basically, was how to take Seoul by the 25th. Earlier, Almond had pressed O. P. Smith "to guarantee that the 1st Marine Division would capture the city by 25 September." The Marine general of course declined to make any guarantee.[21]

There is some difference as to what Almond said to Smith at this conference. The Army's carefully researched official history (here citing interviews with Almond himself and officers on his staff) says that Almond told Smith he would give the Marines 24 hours longer "to make headway." If not, Almond announced that he would alter division boundaries and bring in the 7th Division to do, he inferred, what the Marines could not. General Barr's division, he said, would cross the Han, seize Nam-San, and envelop General Wol out of Seoul.[22] ("If General Almond thought it was necessary to goad Marines into fighting," General Smith later wrote, "he displayed a complete ignorance of the fighting qualities of Marines.")

O. P. Smith's account of this meeting, recorded at the time in his log, makes no reference to what most Marines would have considered as a threat by Almond to take part of their battle away from them. Since then, General Smith has denied that any such threat was voiced. In his log he simply noted that Almond proposed, instead of sending the 1st Marines over to join Murray, that he swing them up the left (south) bank of the Han, cross the river near Nam-San, and attack Seoul from the southeast. Such a scheme would be the school solution of using the 5th Regiment as the holding element, while the 1st maneuvered. General Smith demurred on three counts: (1) Murray had more than he could handle and needed help; (2) any such maneuver would eventually have the two regiments firing into each other and would, at best, present hampering problems in fire-support coordination; (3) for logistic, tactical and administrative unity, he wanted to get all his regiments on the same side of the Han. And finally, the Marine general predicted, the North Koreans would defend Seoul street by street regardless of what flanking maneuvers were conducted; therefore, attempts to maneuver rather than fight the NKPA out of town would prove futile.[23]

"The Marine division was consistently suspicious of X Corps and other Army echelons. They also resisted any corps revision of their own plans," Colonel Chiles said afterward. No doubt this is the way General Smith's demur appeared to Almond. In any case—if we rely on Smith's contemporary record—the corps commander then flatly announced (no 24-hour grace period) that he would let Puller's regiment cross as Smith desired, but would change the division boundary and send the 32nd Infantry into Seoul, too. And, before he forgot, the 1st Marine Amphibian Tractor Battalion was to take them across. Colonel Chiles confirmed these instructions by message to Colonel Bowser at 0930 next morning.[24]

Regardless of which version you choose (very likely the varying accounts are complementary), General Almond had, effectively speaking, cast the die. The notion that greater "headway" was to be made on Hill 56 would, that afternoon, have seemed a bad joke to Captain Peters and Lieutenant H. J. Smith. Thus, the 24-hour stipulation, if actually made, would have produced the same end result: part of the 7th Infantry Division would soon be crossing the Han. "A political undertone," remarked O. P. Smith's aide, "underlay all the tactical planning."[25]

Next morning, while the 1st Marines were crossing over from Yongdungpo, Almond visited General Barr at the 7th Division command post and revealed his decision. Here the corps commander told Barr that he would attach the 17th ROK Regiment to the 32d Infantry, together with the Marine amtrac battalion (without which nobody could get across the Han), and that these units would attack into Seoul. Then he visited the command posts of the 1st and 5th Marines, personally instructed the two Marine regimental commanders as to what he wanted done, returned to his own CP and did the same with Colonel Paik, CO of the 17th ROKs. This done, there was lunch, and at 1400 a commanders' conference at Yongdungpo circle, scene of Barrow's recent exploit.

Generals Smith, Barr and Hodes were waiting when Almond arrived with Colonels Forney and Chiles. So was Colonel Beauchamp, on whom the crossing would actually devolve, and so was the usual cluster of correspondents.

Almond tersely announced the boundary change and his decision to send the 32d Infantry across the Han at 0600 next morning (the 25th). "Dave Barr," he said, "I want you to take the 32d Infantry across the river at six tomorrow morning; and Smith, you get your amtracs on the road right now." The abrupt change of plan came as a surprise to

Beauchamp. "The meeting was short," he later recounted, "and General Almond issued his orders quickly and emphatically and turned us loose."

Although the conference was short, Almond said one thing too many. At one point he assured General Smith that he (Almond) had already discussed the new plan with Puller and Murray, told them what he wanted done, and that they were ready to carry out the roles he had assigned them. General Smith was a forbearing man, but the stress of battle, combined with what he felt to be unrealistic pressure for "headway" and a scarcely concealed slap at the Marines' fighting ability, prompted certain feelings. "The time," he grimly noted, "had come for an understanding with General Almond."

> I had already had one instance [wrote General Smith in his log] where General Almond had given direct orders to Puller. I told General Almond that I would appreciate it if he would not give orders direct to my regimental commanders, that if he would issue his orders to me, I would see that they were carried out.

In General Barr's words, "Smith just hit the ceiling."

Face to face with the fury of a patient man and looking apprehensively at the ring of correspondents and startled staff officers, Almond tried to smooth things over and told the Marine general he would talk things over after the conference. As soon as the others left, O. P. Smith emphatically repeated his request, whereupon Almond said there must be some misunderstanding, as he had never given any orders to the Marine regimental commanders. Always careful to be informed at such moments, Smith replied that Puller and Murray certainly thought they had been given orders, whereupon Almond tried to mollify the Marine by saying he would correct that impression. "There," noted Smith, "the matter rested."[26]

The modified X Corps plan called, as we have seen, for the 32d Infantry to cross the Han and enter Seoul from the southeast. It was designed to edge the North Koreans out of the city by a short envelopment. How it would succeed remained to be seen. Meanwhile, no one doubted that General Almond had assumed full charge of operations ashore.

Breaking the Northwest Defenses

As these words are written [reported Joseph Alsop] the city of Seoul lies spread out beneath the Marine positions on the heights. The battle

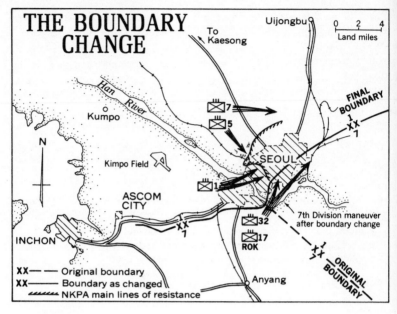

THE BOUNDARY CHANGE

for the Korean capital has begun with hard fighting against violent resistance.

Once again—it was September 24 (D+9)—Roise's 2d Battalion, 5th Marines, had the main effort. His two assault companies (D and F) had weathered the night on their ridge. Fox Company was down to 90 men, however, and Dog was only slightly better. It was Roise's plan to pass his reserve company, Jaskilka's Easy, between the other two and capture Hill 105 North while the depleted companies cleared Hill 56 and the ridge.

At the same time, Colonel Puller would bring over the 1st Regiment, relieve Newton's battalion on 105 South, and attack up the long axis of Seoul. With the 1st Battalion relieved by Puller, Newton would then displace left and relieve Taplett on Hills 216 and 296. The resulting compression of the 5th Regiment's frontage would enable Murray to apply more power and depth to the drive against General Wol's un-yielding defenses.

Soon after daybreak the 11th Marines thickened their fires into an attack preparation for Roise's two companies on the ridge. After 20 minutes' hammering, the howitzers checked fire and VMF-214 took over. *Sicily*'s first strike—five Corsairs—came in low despite morning haze and smudge pots which the defenders were burning all over Seoul. The usual Marine aviation safety limit in such strikes is "a yard a pound" (i.e., with 100-pound bombs, don't bomb closer to friendly troops than a hundred yards). This morning the 2d Battalion was more than willing to take its chances on VMF-214: the Corsairs slammed in 500-pound bombs less than a hundred yards from the men on Hill 56 and never scratched a Marine.

From here on the riflemen took over.

Captain Peters had reorganized into two jury-rigged rifle platoons, about 20 men apiece. The rest of the company, machine gunners, mortarmen, radiomen, runners and ammunition carriers, accounted for 50 more. All three platoon leaders —Lieutenants Anderson, Harry J. Nolan and Albert F. Belbusti— were wounded but carrying on. Nolan had to be evacuated, but Anderson and Belbusti stayed on their feet. In a sharp, brisk assault, Peters's platoons won ground that gave them a field of fire, and proceeded to beat down their opponents by aimed shots from M1s and BARs, laced by hornet-stings from VMF-214's Corsairs. While this was in progress, Corporal Welden D. Harris succumbed at the head of his squad to his third wound in 24 hours; ripped by a grenade while leading the way into a pillbox the afternoon before, Harris was hit again by small arms early on the 24th, and finally fell at midday in the forefront of battle.

No Navy corpsman was there to staunch Harris's mortal wound: every one of Fox Company's corpsmen had already been killed or seriously wounded.[27]

While Company F was clearing the lower part of the ridge and beating the NKPA back onto Hills 72 and 105 Center, Lieutenant H. J. Smith and Dog Company were locked in a furious struggle to clear the upper ridge. By now, nobody had any doubt that they had hit General Wol's main line of resistance.

In the haze of smudge pots and smoke from burning houses north of Hill 56, H. J. Smith launched his company northeast toward the wooded knoll and long ridge that had hit them so hard the previous afternoon. Lieutenant George C. McNaughton's platoon was in the lead. The mist was so thick that they were on top of the enemy before either knew what had happened. A close-in exchange of grenades and point-blank fire ensued. "You could practically hand the grenades to the enemy," McNaughton recalled. To break the frontal fight in which his platoon was locked, McNaughton, already wounded in the shoulder, sent a squad under Sergeant Robert Smith to flank the enemy's left and work up the east (reverse) slope of the ridge. Smith and his squad were literally blasted off the ridge. In less than ten minutes seven were killed and four wounded. Pharmacist's Mate James Egresitz, who charged forward to bring in the wounded, was killed before the end of his first trip. One man, a BAR-man, and two wounded were the only people who got back.

Quickly following up, the Communists counterattacked. Fortunately, the company's light machine guns were sited to cover the right flank. Corporal David Kiene, who commanded the gun section, was shot in his tracks but Corporal Kenneth Stewart, senior squad leader, took over. As gunners and crewmen went down under the intense, short-range enemy fire, ammunition carriers manned guns. Wounded gunners, like Private First Class James O'Toole, got themselves patched up in the aid station and crawled back to their guns. Some were lucky and some, like O'Toole, were killed at their posts. When there were no more ammunition carriers left, First Lieutenant Karle Seydel, the machine-gun officer, went back. In all, Seydel made five trips for ammunition across the fire-swept slopes.

Obviously stopped on the right, Smith committed his support platoon on the left under Second Lieutenant Lee R. Howard (hero of the tank ambush on September 17). Howard attacked valiantly and was stopped as short as McNaughton and, like McNaughton, wounded too.

By ten in the morning, H. J. Smith's situation was grave. His three rifle platoons, respectively, had nine, ten, and eleven men on their feet. Smith asked Roise to send in Easy Company to help them, but this could not be. It was up to Easy to take Hill 105 North, and the day—how long, oh Lord, how long?—was young. About this time, Smith's 60mm mortars burned up their last round, and Second Lieutenant George Grimes brought up the mortarmen to continue the fight with rifles.

Now the haze began to burn off and there was more trouble. The Communists could see even better what they were shooting at, and Dog Company was drenched with small-arms, machine-gun and mortar fire from north, south and southeast. The only directions from which fire wasn't pouring in were west (Hill 104) and southwest, where Fox Company was slowly winning its bitter fire fight.

But the sun shone on the unjust as well. First Lieutenant Karl Wirth, the 11th Marines' forward observer, began to see targets also. So could the battalion's 81mm mortar FO, Sergeant Roy Dunmire. As the Communists poured it on, so did the Marine howitzers and the heavy mortars with their ugly, king-sized shell.

Smith knew that the ridge had to be taken, and that Dog Company, that day at least, would never be a man stronger.

Grouping every surviving Marine of the company into an assault element—33 men, less than a normal-strength rifle platoon—and an 11-man support to bring up the machine guns and ammunition, Smith asked battalion for an air strike. Five of VMF-214's Corsairs carefully adjusted flight paths, then screeched in with 500-pound bombs, 20mm cannon hammering, and, up the ridge a little, flat runs to tumble down every napalm tank in the flight. The last F4U made two successive dummy runs almost into the foxholes. That was the prearranged signal to advance. No trumpets were sounding, but Dog Company's charge was as headlong and unflinching as the Light Brigade's.

It was no mob scene, either. Right and left guides kept direction and alignment, just as it says in the book, senior guide on the right (a staff sergeant), junior (a sergeant) on the left. The attack was that of an organized, living entity that refused to die.

What the enemy thought at this moment will never be known. What they did we do know. They broke and ran.

Those who remained will never run again. Enemy bodies, hurled and huddled atop each other in bunkers, foxholes, gun positions, in the open, lay shot and gutted and seared all over the ridge. (Roise's people stopped next day, in fatigue and disgust, when they had counted 1,500 stinking dead; division later set the score at 1,750.) Evidently the howitzers, the mortars and the Corsairs, and the M1 rifles, too, had slain beyond all comprehension.

Amid these horrors Smith reorganized to mop up the rest of the ridge. Striding out ahead of his men in the moment of victory, Lieutenant Smith was hit by a final shot and died on what the histories now call Smith's Ridge. McNaughton took command and finished the job.[28] At the far end of that ridge, Andrew Geer tells in *The New Breed* how the company reorganized:

> McNaughton asked for a show of hands on various grades because men from all the units of the company were on the hill.
> "How many staff sergeants?"
> Two hands rose.
> "How many sergeants?"

Four hands came to view.

"How many corporals?"

Four Marines raised their hands. Eighteen men indicated they were privates.

When McNaughton began to give instructions, Grimes interrupted, "Hey, George, aren't you interested in second lieutenants?"

Including second lieutenants, machine gunners, ammunition carriers and runners, there proved to be 56 men left to hold the ridge (as they subsequently did against one last counterattack). Twenty-six were wounded, including both McNaughton and Grimes, but refusing evacuation. Out of its strength of 206 officers and men, Company D, 5th Marines, had sustained 176 casualties: 36 dead, 116 wounded and evacuated, 26 wounded and present for duty. One other officer in Company D's battalion was likewise wounded and present for duty. Colonel Roise, hit at midday when enemy 120mm mortar shells pounded the battalion OP, stayed on his feet and fought his battle until nightfall.

After Dog Company's fight, anything else would have been anticlimax, but, as it happened, not much so. When Jaskilka brought E Company forward, he actually had to retake Hill 56, Smith's point of departure. By that time of day it was better not to plunge deeper into the fire-swept amphitheater which lay beyond Smith's Ridge, so Easy held Hill 56, mopped up, and made ready for next day.

On the morning of the 25th (D+10) the 3d Battalion was to keep grinding down the main southeast spur of An-San while the 2d was to hammer through toward Hill 105 North, which is the lower bastion of that spur. Taplett's job, however wearing, was straightforward. Roise's was still complicated. Two lesser hills—88 and 72, mutually supporting—barred the approaches to Hills 105 Center and 105 North. Hill 88 was another spur of An-San, more or less parallel to Smith's Ridge. Hill 72 not only directly flanked the way to 105 North, but enfiladed all three others in one direction or another.

Behind a crashing artillery preparation by the 11th Marines, Company E jumped off, with Dog Company, still in the assault, echeloned to the left rear, working around the contours to the left and back onto Hill 88. By midday, against moderate opposition, that job was done. But Hill 72 still prevented Jaskilka from getting at 105 Center. In reporting back to battalion how things stood, confusion arose as to just which hill 72 was. The operations officer asked first for map coordinates; then, to be sure,

for a description. Never at a loss, Jaskilka said, "It looks like Nellie's tit."
It did and does, and so was ever after named in the 5th Regiment.[29]

Leading his platoon in a sharp assault, Lieutenant Deptula seized
Nellie's Tit. With the way thus cleared, the rest of Easy Company forged
ahead and were on 105 Center by midafternoon. Soon afterward, the
3d Battalion's assault companies probed down their spur from An-San
under flanking fire from Hill 338, and George Company took 105 North
after heavy fighting. According to prisoners, three NKPA battalions had
defended the Hills 72, 88, 105s Center and North. Their losses that day
were said to have totaled 500.

Nobody can say what became of General Wol, but it is a matter of
record that, on the afternoon of September 25, the western defenses of
Seoul were cracked through and the general was finally, but certainly
not easily, beaten.[30]

Early on the 25th, Marines of the 2d and 3d Battalions could see a
pleasantly green southern spur of Nam-San with a large comfortable
western-style house and a group of school buildings nearby. This was
Chosen Christian College, first western missionary college in Korea, and
home to one officer in the ranks of the 5th Marines. Lieutenant Horace G.
("Hedge") Underwood, USNR, that same interpreter/intelligence officer
who had swum the Han with the reconnaissance company, had spent
his boyhood in that house and grown up on that hill. Chosen Christian
College had been founded in 1915 by his grandfather, had prospered
under his father, and he himself had carried on the family tradition
by teaching there after four years in the Navy during World War II.
Though longtime Presbyterian missionaries, the family were a branch of
the Underwoods of typewriter fame.

Interrogating a batch of 25th Brigade prisoners, Hedge Underwood
learned that the college was now a principal enemy headquarters, possibly the command post of General Wol. Without hesitating, Underwood
passed this information to the regimental intelligence section. Not long
afterward, the ordinarily encouraging sound of outgoing volleys from
the 11th Marines told him that, seconds later, as he watched, he would
see his family home of three generations, and the handiwork of those
generations, blown to rubble.[31]

The 32d Infantry Crosses the Han

Nobody except O. P. Smith went down to watch the 1st Marines cross the Han from Yongdungpo, but the 32d Infantry and 17th ROKs drew a capacity audience.[32]

Another ferry crossing—Sinsa-ri—across the Han from Nam-San (South Mountain) had been chosen on the 24th as the crossing site. As soon as the 1st Amphibian Tractor Battalion received word of their attachment to the 7th Division for this event, the CO, Lieutenant Colonel Erwin F. Wann, Jr., went with his staff to division headquarters and reconnoitered for the best place to cross. Sinsa-ri being selected, they then went to Colonel Beauchamp's headquarters, helped his staff with the amphibious aspects of the plan (organization into waves, boat teams, shore party functions, etc.) and, satisfied that things were in hand after a post-midnight conference with the regimental and battalion commanders, got ready for dawn.

Not long after the amtrac people got to sleep for an hour or so, Admiral Struble and General Almond, key staff officers and the press were being awakened. Energetic early riser that he was, Almond led the group to the crossing site at 0400. H-hour was to be 0630 but much activity was in progress. After dawn broke, General Barr came down. "Where have you been?" snapped Almond. In his direct, unruffled way, Barr replied, "Up on top of that bluff back there, where I can fight my division if I have to. I'm not going to stay down here and fight one battalion."

The 32d Infantry was to cross in column of battalions, Lieutenant Colonel Charles M. Mount's 2d Battalion in assault. Mount was to advance straight ahead and seize South Mountain. The 1st Battalion (Lieutenant Colonel Don C. Faith, Jr.) was to follow, wheel right, and advance northward around the east face of Nam-San. The 3d Battalion, under Lieutenant Colonel Heinrich G. Schumann, would also wheel right but would defile along the riverbank and secure Hill 120, a lesser eminence upstream. Within the 32d Infantry bridgehead thus established would follow the 17th ROKs who would advance past Hill 120 to secure Hill 348, a commanding feature in the eastern approaches to Seoul. General Hodes was charged with coordination of the crossing.

Soon after a foggy dawn, at 0545 the Marine tractors embarked Colonel Mount's people, started engines, and formed for crossing. At 0600 the 48th Field Artillery Battalion and 32d Infantry mortars commenced an attack preparation. Promptly at 0625 the first tractor wave waddled into the Han; on the dot at 0630 the first wave touched down. Resistance was negligible: one 76mm gun fired a few rounds of direct fire, and light small-arms fire pinged off the tractors' steel sides. After

0800, when all the battalion was across, the sun burned off the fog, and VMF-214—controlled by Marine tactical air control parties attached to the 7th Division—sent in five Corsairs for saturation strikes against Nam-San.

Stopping to assure New York *Times* correspondent W. H. Lawrence that "The 7th Division is doing a lot of good, very fast," General Almond rode over in midmorning to see how in fact the division really was doing. To his dismay, he found the 2d Battalion halted on the far shore rather than pressing forward to secure the height that lay ahead. As there seemed to be no enemy resistance holding up the battalion, the general spoke briefly but emphatically to the commanding officer and the advance resumed. By three that afternoon, Colonel Mount had over-run lightly manned defenses on Nam-San's peak and—without, however, clearing his zone to the boundary with the Marine division—began digging in a tight perimeter.

An hour after the 2d Battalion reached the top of Nam-San, the 32d Infantry was over the river and the amtracs began lifting the 17th ROKs. This unit, its title "the Seoul Regiment" (the same as the NKPA 31st Regiment on the other side of town), had been selected by the ROK Army to play a role in the reconquest of the capital city. The Seoul Regiment also crossed with scant opposition (a little mortar and small-arms), and struck out vigorously through gathering darkness toward Hill 348.

Thus, what General Almond later described as "the maneuvering element" of X Corps was across the Han. Whether, as the general hoped and expected, it would in fact envelop and expel the defenders of Seoul remained to be seen.[33]

". . . A Few Bombs Right on the Button"

"Several Corsairs placed a few bombs right on the button," was Lieutenant Tilton Anderson's dominant recollection of a particularly tight moment during the 2d Battalion, 5th Marines' fierce onslaught against Smith's Ridge. During these latter days of the battle for Seoul, as earlier, such were the recollections of many another Marine and soldier in X Corps.

It is easy, both in reading and writing the history of a campaign such as this, to look on the timely, precise, unfailing close air support as part of the routine—even the window dressing, if you will—of the battle. Yet this nonpareil air support (and few campaigns, before or since, have had

Q

better) didn't just happen. It resulted from sound doctrine, from superb training and airmanship, and from a tested control organization on the ground, spearheaded by young aviators as muddy and exposed and as far forward as any rifle platoon leader. And for its great successes—as for any success in war—the aviators paid their price.

The 19th Antiaircraft Artillery Regiment, NKPA, knew its job, which, at this juncture, was trying to shoot down Corsairs in and around Seoul. Seoul, says the Marines' official history, was "a flak trap." On September 24, during repeated sorties to support the assault on Smith's Ridge, five out of ten F4Us employed were ripped by flak. The aircraft got back, at least to Kimpo, in all five cases, but others were not so lucky.

Major Robert Floeck, a veteran of VMF-214 who had so deftly knocked out So Wolmi Do's defenses on D-day, was leading his flight on September 23 in search of an armored column south of Pyongyang. Near Kumchon, on the south bank of the Yosong River, antiaircraft guns found their mark and Floeck's Corsair caught fire. Whether he lived to bail out or was thrown clear with chute partly opened will never be known. The flames of his aircraft were his pyre. For what consolation it might be, his flight pinpointed the battery and gave it every bomb, rocket and bullet they had. They reported back "confident" it had been destroyed.

The next day was VMF-214's last day on the line. After recovering her last strike on the 25th, *Sicily* was to go into Inchon to rearm, refuel, conduct upkeep, and rest. As was proper, Lieutenant Colonel Walter E. Lischeid, the squadron commander, led the first strike that morning. At low altitude over Seoul, he entered the sights of an antiaircraft battery on Nam-San, soon to be in the hands of the 32d Infantry. As the pink-tracer stream ripped through his Corsair, he turned away, jettisoned his 500-pound bomb in the Han and headed for Kimpo. In the approach pattern, only two miles to go, there was a burst of bright flame under his fuselage, the airplane did a three-quarter roll and flamed in. Major Robert P. Keller assumed command of the squadron for the rest of the day's work, and that night VMF-214 ended its role in the campaign.

This day was hard on squadron commanders. Although he never bothered to note the fact in his squadron's action report, Lieutenant Colonel Richard W. Wyczawski, CO of VMF-212, was wounded and shot down on the 25th. Only the day before, Wyczawski's squadron, flying from Kimpo, had nailed up a record for the 1st Marine Air Wing: 12 flights, comprising 46 sorties, in one hot day's work.

But it was Maxie Volcansek, commanding VMF(N)-542, who survived September 25 on borrowed time. Leading a forenoon flight in the 7th Division's zone near Suwon, he was hit by flak and wounded, but returned for two more passes before deciding it was time to head for Kimpo. His F7F-3N was in rather shaky condition. Approaching Kimpo, his 150-gallon wing tank, so far unignited, tore loose and wedged, shuddering, between fuselage and one of the engine nacelles. Aside from lodging a tank of avgas a few feet from Volcansek, not to mention a hot engine, this mishap also affected the airplane's flight characteristics so that he had to increase speed to about 200 knots, more than twice landing speed, to keep from stalling out and dropping like a brick.

After carefully informing Kimpo of his problem, Volcansek decided to bail out. He had just 1,000 feet to go. When the canopy blew clear, he found himself pinned in the cockpit by the 200-knot slipstream with the airplane losing altitude even so. Kicking the aircraft into a straight nose-down attitude he tossed himself free, only to have the vertical stabilizer flash past his head centimeters distant. Praise be, his chute had been perfectly packed. It opened instants before the ground rushed up. Within an hour he was aboard a rescue helicopter.[34]

The Marine division, at least to an extent, tended to take its forward air controllers for granted as part of the scheme of things. This was anything but the case in the 7th Division. As Admiral Struble subsequently put the matter:[35]

> Neither the Air Force nor Army in the Far East Command area were ready for close air support of ground troops, as the Navy and Marine Corps commonly understood the problem.

However, since all tactical air support for X Corps in this campaign was being provided by General Harris's 1st Marine Aircraft Wing (albeit disguised as Tactical Air Command, X Corps), it was simple to fit out the Army division for the Marine system. To find the extra teams, the Marine Corps, as in getting the 1st Division to war strength, had to look afield—in this case by shifting people and equipment by air from Camp Lejeune on the East Coast. Once assigned to the Army, Captain Charles E. Crewe, believing in his product, proceeded to hold school with missionary zeal, and not only farmed out his own people, but trained additional teams from the 7th Division so that they could get just as much (and as good) tactical air support as the Marine division. Brigadier

General Homer W. Kiefer, USA, of the 7th Division, liked the Navy-Marine system so well that he recommended that the Army standardize on it.[36]

Despite the ever-present clouds of red dust and the battered makeshift look that every forward airdrome presents, Kimpo was getting organized. True, VMF-212 could find only one grease pencil in the squadron to keep their briefing boards up to date (and made the boards out of wallboard from shot-up quonset huts). True also that the A&R (repair) crews of MAG-33 still had to cannibalize wrecked planes for precious spares, true even that once they stripped the metal skin off a riddled Russian YAK to patch up an almost equally riddled 7F7-3N.

Yet the 5th Air Force—deficient in many important details (such as having no serviceable night-fighter interception gear)[37]—was running an eye-opening airlift into Kimpo and Suwon, with C-119s and C-54s coming in at ten-minute intervals under the experienced eye of Major General William H. Tunner, USAF, World War II commander of the Burma-China "Hump" airlift. Looking for ways to speed up the process, General Tunner growled, "The trouble with airplanes is that they spend altogether too much time on the ground."[38]

8 *SO TERRIBLE A LIBERATION*

The situation is very serious.

PRAVDA, September 23, 1950

"BY THE TIME we got to Seoul," General O. P. Smith reminisced, "the 1st Regiment was as good as the 5th."[1] Well that they were. When Puller's regiment crossed the Han on the morning of September 24 (D+9), the zone of action which stretched ahead went squarely up the long axis of Seoul, fifth city of the Orient. To the front lay crowded slums, railroad yards, factories, crooked streets, barricades, mines, roadblocks, and an enemy who desired that Seoul be consumed by its liberation.

Into Seoul

Although Murray's desperate fighting in the western outskirts had uncovered a crossing site opposite the Yongdungpo sandspit for the 1st Marines, neither O. P. Smith nor Puller was a man to take unnecessary chances. Covered by 5th Marines troops (Ike Fenton on his miserable Hill 105 South), C Company of the engineer battalion checked the riverbank. The precaution was well taken: the first thing they found was a large minefield. By eight in the morning—late in the day by Chesty Puller's clock—the mines were cleared. Then came a reconnaissance party in amtracs, followed in due course by Allan Sutter and the 2d Battalion. Sutter advanced inland a few hundred yards against light, scattering fire, and established touch with right-flank positions of the 5th Marines. Then he wheeled half-right to the east and commenced moving toward the day's objective, a hill (79) with a fine view of Yongsan railroad yards, the electric power plant and the gasworks. Still farther upstream were the ruined railroad and highway bridge abutments whose early capture was much desired in case X Corps engineers developed a bridging capacity. As there were neither bridges nor tank ferries here, B Company of the tank battalion (assigned to support Puller) was being sent around via Haengju ferry on what would prove to be an exciting trip.

Meanwhile the 1st Battalion crossed, and soon afterward so did Colonel Puller. Finding the battalion standing by in an assembly area, Puller greeted the commander bluntly: "What the hell are you doing, Hawkins?"

"I'm in reserve, sir."

"Well, you won't be in it long. Get in the attack."

"Sir, we can't pass Sutter. He's moving fast. Are you going to stop him so I can get out front?"

"Hell no. I had trouble enough getting 'em started."[2] Then, by way of clarification, Puller added, "You'll just have to advance a little faster."

A little faster at this point meant double time and high port for most of the 1st Battalion. The ordinarily minuetted passage of lines which is taught in the schools became, in Captain Wray's memory, ". . . just knots of men driving across the landscape so fast that the enemy didn't have a chance to get organized."

As Barrow's Able Company whipped through Carter's Easy, the latter called to his friend, "What the hell's going on?"

Imperturbable even at double time, Barrow replied, "Take it easy, Johnny. This constitutes a passage of lines—Puller style."[3]

Aside from the fact that celerity is practically always a military virtue, there was one good reason to move the battalions eastward without delay. Hill 105 South, regardless of the fact that Marines had been on top of it for two days, still had NKPA at the bottom. As each of the two battalions crossed its front, the malign hill spat at them with small-arms and automatic-weapons fire, inflicting a few casualties. Despite this and other desultory obstructions, including the usual crude minefields, Hawkins had his battalion on Hill 79 by 1500. Here—acting on Puller's instructions—Barrow outraged the 5th Marines by running up a set of colors on a schoolhouse (the first flag raising inside the city limits), where a *Life* photographer just happened to be around to snap the picture. Thereafter, as Andy Geer recounted, "Each unit obtained a supply of flags and the race was on."[4]

Next morning (September 25, D+10) Puller had two battalions in line: Sutter more or less in touch with the 5th Marines on the left,

Hawkins holding Hill 79. Ridge's 3d Battalion which, in division reserve, had covered the Yongdungpo end of the crossing, was now released and preparing to pass through Sutter. Thus Colonel Puller's attack up the center of town would have the 1st and 3d Battalions abreast. Behind—on Puller's sound judgment that "They're the only ones who can tell the cowboys from the Indians"[5]—was Major Kim's 2d Battalion, Korean Marines, mopping up as at Inchon.

The 1st Marines' jump-off on the 25th called for tactical finesse: Ridge had to displace eastward through Sutter's 2d Battalion, then wheel north. Meanwhile Hawkins, on Hill 79, would pull back a little, pivoting on its left, to align with the 3d Battalion.

Like most of Puller's attacks this jumped off on time, which was 0700. However, there were no tanks. Company B, the 1st Tank Battalion's usual direct-support unit for the regiment, was delayed by a private battle of its own.

Remember that the tanks had to go around by Haengju where the Marine engineers had their ferry, in order to rejoin Puller on the north shore. Captain Williams, in command of the tankers, had two platoons, two dozer tanks, and a section of flame tanks. Because of mines specifically, and the problems of tanks in this terrain generally, Williams also had Lieutenant Babe and a handful of engineers, as well as an infantry support—a rifle platoon commanded by Staff Sergeant Arthur Farrington.

The tanks were already running late. Trying to come in along the Kaesong–Seoul railroad line, whose bridges were the only reliable ones for the Pershing tanks, Williams had encountered minefields on the 24th. Despite Babe's usual energetic efforts, these took time, and Williams had to make his way back to Puller that night to tell him the armor might well be delayed.

The approach to the 1st Marines' new zone took Williams through a no-man's-land vacated by the 1st Battalion, 5th Marines, and left behind by Puller's advance. Cautiously approaching an egg-shaped hill on the right with a flat, truncated top, Farrington's fire team in the point saw arms stacked beside some huts to the front. Then one of the engineers, like Macbeth at Dunsinane, saw trees moving down the slope of the hill toward the right flank of the column. By the map, this was behind the 5th Marines' front lines; Captain Fenton, whose two companies had held the top without ever getting to the bottom of it, would have regarded this ambush, for such it was, as par for the course on Hill 105 South.

As the Marines deployed for action to the right front, grenades showered out of the cluster of huts, accompanied by a vicious, swelling burst of fire. Lieutenant Babe was in the act of forming his engineers as infantry when he pushed his luck once too often and dropped with a wounded arm (". . . and he a ball player, too," Farrington wrote afterward). As Babe fell, three of his men rushed a demolition charge against an offending hut and blew it to pieces. Meanwhile, Sergeant Farrington, a spunky, blue-eyed little NCO and a sharp tactician, advanced to the right and built up a firing line on a knoll facing 105 South across an intervening draw. Behind the infantry, the engineers guided a flame tank forward to where it could play on the slope of the draw. The enemy fire slackened.

The Korean interpreter with the Marines called to the Communists to surrender. Picking up the phrase, the Marines yelled it, too. In Farrington's words,

> Everything got quiet as we yelled. The "trees" on the hillside stopped moving. A Korean stood up halfway up the hill and held his rifle over his head. He started down the hill, steep, still holding his rifle. I just knew that he was going to be shot by his own or my men. For several minutes he was out of sight in the draw. Upon appearing on the knoll, we ordered him to strip in full view of his comrades. That did it. They started coming in in numbers, all carrying their burp guns. We stripped every one as he came in—pretty hard trying to get trousers off over leggings. . . .

As this was going on, the Marines covering the rear, back on the road, heard noises from a hut. Were these huts what they seemed? Banging on the hull of the command tank, Technical Sergeant Pasquale Paolino, the engineer gunnery sergeant, explained his suspicions over the external telephone that tanks carry aft for infantry use in such moments. With the gunnery sergeant coaching them on, the tank gunners rapped out five quick rounds that blew the huts into shards and kindling. Behind lay a large cave mouth.

As the flame tank moved grimly in, caves being its special prey, 15 North Korean soldiers straggled out, hands up, and surrendered. Moments later, seeing these unharmed, a swarm of Communists began pouring out of the cave while the Marines held fire. When the last Red was in the open, the 50 infantrymen and engineers had 131 stark-naked prisoners (including two female comrades, who were chivalrously provided with long johns from somebody's pack).

The enemy wounded were hoisted on board the tanks [Farrington recounted], 129 bare asses were lined up three abreast . . . when about 40–50 Koreans jumped up to the left of the railroad tracks. They had been lying there doggo behind us all this time. We killed them with rifle, machine-gun, and 90mm fire as they went across the paddies, into the villages, and across the far railway.

With 150 dead counted in the draw and on the hillside, Hill 105 South was at length liberated.[6]

Williams finally brought up his tanks and his catch to Puller's CP well after noon. Before he could tell his tale of victory, Puller rasped around the stem of his bulldog pipe, "I'm not interested in your sea-stories, young man. You're late. Get your unit into position. We've got fish to fry." As the crestfallen young officer withdrew, Puller's face softened and he said to Farrington, "Thanks, sergeant. I can sure use those tanks down there."[7]

Puller's fish to fry consisted of one alley fight after another. Every intersection was barricaded after the fashion of the Paris Commune: carts, earth-filled rice bags, poor people's furniture and rubble. Likening Seoul to Stalingrad, *Pravda* reported on September 23:

Cement, streetcar rails, beams and stones are being used to build barricades in the streets, and workers are joining soldiers in the defense. The situation is very serious. Pillboxes and tank points dot the scene. Every home must be defended as a fortress. There is firing from behind every stone. When a soldier is killed, his gun continues to fire. It is picked up by a worker, tradesman, or office-worker. . . . General MacArthur landed the most arrant criminals at Inchon, gathered from the ends of the earth. . . . He sends British and New Zealand adventure-seekers ahead of his own executioners, letting them drag Yankee chestnuts from the fire. American bandits are shooting every Seoul inhabitant taken prisoner.

The 1st Regiment's fire teams would have agreed at least with *Pravda*'s report of "firing behind every stone." To overcome this resistance, riflemen and tank machine guns scourged the barricades, doorways and rooftops. Remembering Marine tactics at Veracruz, Puller had his people advance from house to house, smashing through interior walls. Engineers crawled forward, probed, scooped, cried, "Fire in the hole!" and exploded the enemy mines. Behind the demolitions men the tanks clattered up and blew holes in the barricades with their guns or crunched them with tracks and dozer blades. Sufficiently obdurate resistance brought in four-deuces with earth-shaking crumps, or even the artillery or the Corsairs.

The 1st Battalion, it will be remembered, had launched northeast into the heart of Seoul. Hawkins had two companies, A and B, in assault, the former on the left. Opposition was at first light, tantalizingly so for Able Company, which in these hours formed the spearhead of the regiment. By midday Captain Barrow had his company on high ground overlooking the railroad yards and passenger station to his right front (northeast). For the officer who had thrust deep into Yongdungpo (and for his superiors) the temptation to advance reckless of flanks was great. Pressure descending from X Corps trumpeted, in Colonel Chiles's phrase, that "rapid maneuver was imperative."

Along with his forward observers, Barrow carefully checked the low ground ahead and the railroad embankment beyond. As he was preparing for the next bound forward, an observer lowered his binoculars and said, "Gooks." From behind the embankment there peered enemy heads. Barrow ordered all his machine guns forward. The FOs commenced transmitting fire missions to mortars and the 11th Marines.

As the first concentrations began to swish in, there was "a mass scurrying. Literally hundreds [Barrow later wrote] scampered from behind the railroad embankment . . . and we were killing them without any loss to ourselves." Amid all this, pressure mounted from battalion for A Company to advance. Barrow switched off his radio and, in the guise of a liaison officer bridging a radio failure, sent back Swords, his most persuasive lieutenant, to try to convey to Hawkins what was happening. Swords returned soon after with the battalion commander himself; what Hawkins saw convinced him, and Barrow turned on his SCR-300 again.

"Our advance this day was a foot-by-foot basis," said Ridge, whose 3d Battalion was on Hawkins's left. Ridge's advance took his battalion doggedly up Ma-Po Boulevard, once a busy, pleasant avenue lined with sycamores, groceries, wine and tea shops. At the day's end—while air strikes and artillery continued to hammer the enemy beyond the railroad station—Ridge held a built-up rise, Hill 97, to the right rear of which Hawkins was on Hill 82.[8]

Elsewhere in the X Corps zone about Seoul the Communists were being gnawed away. As we have seen, Murray had at long last cracked General Wol's line and established the 5th Marines, still somewhat precariously, on the long shoulder of An-San that drops southward along the edge of town. One battalion of the 32d Infantry, General Almond's "maneuver element," was standing pat atop Nam-San and had been digging itself in since three that afternoon.[9] Litzenberg's 7th Marines, well shaken down by patrolling and security missions on Kumpo Peninsula and north of the Haengju bridgehead, had been assigned a zone of action on the left of the corps, with the mission of wheeling right to cover the 5th Marines' flank and to cut the Seoul–Pyongyang highway. As night fell, Litzenberg's 2d Battalion was on high ground overlooking this major escape route. In all, about 40 per cent of the city was in U.N. hands.

"Enemy Fleeing . . ."

Night had fallen on Seoul in its agony. The darkness was broken only by the loom-up of flames from burning buildings or the chilly white light of an occasional star shell. Intense fighting had gone on at every barricade as long as there was light to line up sights, hold, and squeeze trigger.

O. P. Smith's driver had heated the general a can of C rations over the little Coleman stove General Shepherd had given him before landing, and the general, no more a gourmet than his driver a *cordon bleu,* was soberly spooning up supper. Down in the G-3 Section, by the light of hissing pressure lanterns, Colonel Bowser was getting out next day's order so it could reach the regiments in decent time. Just after eight, the EE-8 field telephone on the hot line from X Corps G-3 jingled insistently.

The incoming message which was quickly passed to Bowser read as follows:

> Info addressee [X Corps TacAir Commander] reports enemy fleeing city of Seoul on road north of [*sic*] Uijongbu 1003-1665, and he is conducting heavy air attack and will continue same. You will attack *now* to the limit of your objectives in order to insure maximum destruction of enemy forces. Signed. Almond.

The cause which prompted this startling order had been an air observer's report a half hour earlier of "what looks to be a mass evacuation of Seoul." On receiving this, General Almond, in his later words, arrived at "a command decision regardless of the recommendations of Staff or others." "Mass evacuation" quickly became "enemy fleeing," and so the order went out.[10]

Aside from its premise that the enemy who had fought so hard all day was fleeing by night, and aside from its alarming directive for an unplanned nocturnal plunge through the belly of an Oriental city, there are certain aspects of this order which should be noted.

1. By its own text it literally relates to movements *north* of Uijongbu, a town 16 miles from Seoul.

2. The map coordinates given in the message do not fall on the Seoul–Uijongbu road at all. One set (1003) bears no relation to any location in the vicinity of Seoul. The other (1665) falls on a highway leading north from Seoul, but it is not the Uijongbu road: the coordinates fall on the Seoul–Kaesong highway not far from the positions of the 2d Battalion, 7th Marines, who had blocked this road before nightfall and were certainly not reporting any exodus. While (as Bowser soon verified from Chiles) the Uijongbu road was, regardless of coordinates, the highway in question, it suggests much as to the functioning of X Corps headquarters that an attack order of this importance could have been sent out with so gross an error undetected.[11]

3. While this order for a general night action to destroy a supposedly fleeing enemy went to both the Marine division and the 7th Division, corps subsequently instructed the latter division to hold position and support the Marines' attack by fire. If we are to believe that the 32d Infantry was seriously considered as the "maneuver element" intended to maneuver the NKPA out of Seoul, here surely was the moment above all. Yet the 32d Infantry received no attack order that night, and of course did not attack.[12]

But the foregoing points are those of history, after the event. To Bowser, experienced operations officer that he was, the message seemed inconceivable. There was no evidence whatever of a fleeing enemy along the barricades and he doubted the ability of any aviator at night to distinguish herds of refugees from herds of soldiers. And that a night attack—most complex, delicate and difficult of all attacks, requiring the utmost in prior planning and coordination—should be ordered on the spur of the moment through the teeming warrens of an unfamiliar city was almost beyond comprehension.

Bowser promptly phoned Chiles to find out what was happening. The questions as to coordinates and the 7th Division were cleared up. But when Bowser questioned the order itself, Chiles, as completely Almond's man as Almond was MacArthur's, simply said the order was to be carried out and the Marines must attack. Bowser went outside, waited for a moment to get his eyes accustomed to the black night, then picked his way to General Smith. Captain Sexton, the aide, hesitated to disturb the general at supper, but the G-3 is no man to turn aside.

General Smith bolted the last of his C ration, shook his head, and ordered that a call be put through to General Ruffner, Almond's chief of staff.

When the call came through, General Smith asked that Ruffner reaffirm the order just received. He said (1) the Marine regiments had no indication whatever that the *In Min Gun* was fleeing, and (2) as an officer of Ruffner's experience hardly needed telling, it was, to say the least, inadvisable to stumble headlong into a night attack under existing conditions.

General Ruffner, tactful, sympathetic, professional cavalryman that he was, had no recourse but to tell the Marine general that the order had gone out exactly as Almond had dictated it himself, and was to be executed without delay.

General Smith has never disclosed his exact feelings when he put the phone down, and perhaps it is just as well. Feelings or not, he had no alternative. He immediately telephoned Murray and Puller, while Bowser called Litzenberg (7th Marines) and Brower (11th Marines). As soon as he got through to Murray and Puller, General Smith told them they must attack, but that the attack must be coordinated carefully, must follow main avenues, and that there should be no effort to score a hasty advance. As senior regimental commander, Puller was to effect coordination.[13]

As it happened, at the very moment General Smith conveyed these tidings to Ray Murray, the 3d Battalion, 5th Marines, which had been receiving tank and high-velocity fire throughout the early evening, was being hit by the enemy in force. When Murray turned to Colonel Stewart, Joe Stewart replied, "I'm afraid we'll have to delay pursuit of the fleeing enemy until we see if Tap [Taplett] can beat off this counterattack."[14]

Orders, however, are orders. Puller and Murray accordingly decided on a coordinated attack by both regiments, to jump off at 0145. Colonel Brower's howitzers would give them a 15-minute preparation. To effect coordination between the two infantry regiments, Taplett, besides beating off his attackers, was to send out a patrol toward the 1st Marines. Ridge, left-flank battalion commander of that regiment, was to do the same.

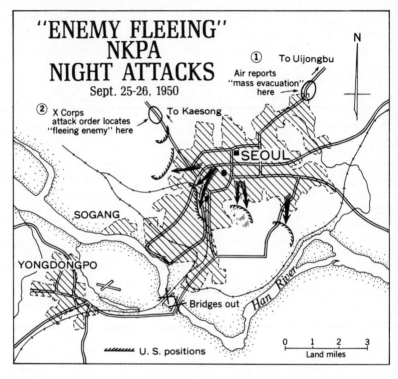

Ridge had had a hard day's advance up Ma-Po Boulevard, and his battalion held the shoulder of something of a salient. To his left, toward the 5th Marines, the North Koreans occupied a corresponding re-entrant along the boundary between the Marine regiments. Because of the heavy fighting encountered all day, because of the length of frontage involved and, above all, because Ridge was a canny, pessimistic, suspicious officer, he decided to hold his front in maximum strength that night. Company I, on the right, occupied Hill 97 (known to the troops as "Slaughterhouse Hill"). On the left, G Company held a knoll and a roadblock on Ma-Po Boulevard. How, Ridge's third company, filled the gap between the other two. To strengthen his defense ("For obvious reasons I never told Puller," said Ridge) he pulled back some 200 yards on Ma-Po to a dogleg which occurs where the road crosses the Kaesong–Seoul railroad tracks. Making textbook use of his weapons company commander, Ridge ordered Major Simmons, of far cheerier though equally probing mentality, to site and coordinate the crew-served weapons of the 3d Battalion so as to cover every chink and cranny of the front. This done, Simmons was to establish and occupy a battalion OP on a knoll commanding the Ma-Po dogleg, where George Company's CP was also located.

Simmons personally laid out the roadblock, which was commanded by First Lieutenant Harold Savage. In addition to riflemen and mines out front, the roadblock included a heavy machine-gun section, a 3.5 rocket squad and a 75mm recoilless gun section. Simmons also sited the battalion's 81mm mortars in "unconventional proximity to the front line," only 150 yards rearward.

At about midnight, Ridge was shaken to receive orders to prepare for a night attack. "I protested to such a degree," he recounted, "that I thought I would be relieved. Since this did not work, I then procrastinated by having problems with artillery registration." Ridge was of course not the only person in the Marine division who was protesting. When he in turn issued instructions to his companies and to Simmons, via conference call, Simmons pointed out that the planned artillery preparation would be bound to fall on the 1st and 5th Marine patrols. All Ridge could say was, "Well, that's the fortunes of war."

The patrol leader whom Simmons sent out to gain touch with the 5th Marines was Corporal Charles E. Collins. Collins had two fire teams and three Korean guides. Close to 0130, only 15 minutes until H-hour for the attack, Collins made contact. But his contact was not with the 5th Marines. Instead, his patrol virtually collided with a large body of enemy infantry, tanks and self-propelled guns. These troops were not fleeing; they were forming for an attack on the Ma-Po Boulevard roadblock of the 3d Battalion, 1st Marines.

There was a heavy burst of small-arms fire from both sides. Collins did exactly the right thing. Dropping into kneeling position with his M1, he ordered his people to get word back to the roadblock, no matter what the cost. As the rest of the patrol scampered rearward, Collins covered them with aimed rapid fire from his rifle.[15]

At 0130, minus Collins, the patrol returned and warned Simmons what was afoot. About this time, Ridge's stalling over the artillery preparation paid off: H-hour for the attack was delayed until 0200. Just then the defenders of the roadblock began to hear the clank of tanks.

"As I was verbally battling, via telephone and radio," Ridge related,

... Ed Simmons came up on the tactical radio with a voice at nearly the level of high C and said, "Enemy tanks are coming down the Boulevard—they're about to hit us!" My response was "Thank God!", whereupon Ed's voice dropped back to normal and he asked, "What did you say?" Almost immediately thereafter, battle was joined.

The first round fired by the enemy was an 85mm armor-piercing shell from a tank which killed Simmons's radioman by his side ("Overkill for him—but underkill for me," he said). Amid a storm of high-velocity shell and small-arms fire, two T-34 tanks and a mass of infantry bore down. At close range the Marines opened fire with all they had. One tank was hit and stopped; the other spun on its tracks and took cover behind a corner. Lieutenant Savage fell wounded; Sergeant Robert Caldwell, senior NCO on the block, took command, and reported back to Simmons that he had done so.

This was no mere probe. (In fact, the attackers were a reinforced battalion from the 25th Brigade.) Although the Marines, poised for an attack of their own, could hardly have been more ready to receive the enemy, the fierceness of the onslaught—like *banzai* charges in the Pacific —was unmatched. While General Smith was in the act of deferring the night attack, the 11th Marines' forward observers, encountering no further "difficulties" with registration, called in three battalions—everything not engaged in supporting Taplett's fight, which was still going on, too.

About 0230 [Simmons reported] enemy small-arms fire reached a crescendo and the distinctive sound of their submachine-guns indicated that the assault was about to begin. I ordered the artillery to shorten their range to the minimum that would clear the mask of the high ground we were occupying. The 81mm mortars continued to fire at minimum range.

Despite the fury of artillery and mortar fire crashing down, the Communist battalion, supported by 10 or 12 tanks or self-propelled guns, surged in. At 0315 the 11th Marines had to reduce their fires—virtually continuous for the past hour and a half—to keep from burning out the tubes of their howitzers. When the artillery slackened, the enemy tank attack renewed, silhouetted clear against the fires set by white-phosphorus mortar barrages. One self-propelled gun, evidently aware of the location of the battalion OP, fired round after round, just over the top of the building. Three more tanks or self-propelled guns concentrated their fire on the roadblock during the 11th Marines' enforced lull. Renewed artillery support was mandatory.

As it happened, the 31st Field Artillery Battalion, General Barr's medium howitzers, had previously been in general support of the 1st Marines, and one of their liaison officers was still with Puller's regiment. Seeing the desperate attack in progress, with numerous enemy tanks and self-propelled guns in action, this young officer called his fire-direction center and asked for heavy defensive concentrations, even though the 31st was actually no longer in support of the Marines. Lieutenant Colonel Patrick Welch, USA, the battalion's well-loved Bostonian commander, unhesitatingly broke the rules and accepted the mission, personally bringing in "Battalion, 20 rounds"—a sledgehammer barrage of 360 155mm shells— among the enemy tanks.

Moments later the voice-call "Blade" (1st Marines) came up on Welch's radio, and a deep voice with a tidewater Virginia accent said, "I don't know who in the hell you are, but *Thank God!* . . . Out." At least this night, Lewis Puller was well pleased to have the Army hard by.[16]

By now almost every building out front had been set afire by the rain of shells, giving George Company, as well as the others, light to shoot by. But ammunition began to run low, and Ridge had to get in more of everything by an improvised ammunition train made up of every jeep in sight. As for the artillery, the 11th Marines shot up all their on-position reserves before daybreak and cleaned out an entire Army dump as well. The regimental four-deuces shot 326 rounds, and the 3d Battalion's 81mm mortars, 650. Simmons's machine guns fired 120 boxes (30,000 rounds), topping a previous Marine Corps record from Guadalcanal, where machine gunners under Sergeant "Manila John" Basilone shot 26,000 rounds against a furious night attack by a Japanese regiment. Basilone's battalion commander that night was Lieutenant Colonel Lewis B. Puller.[17]

As daybreak neared, Simmons became increasingly concerned over the succession of very near misses (a mil or so in elevation, not more) which the Communist self-propelled gun was steadily firing over the OP. When darkness waned he judged that the enemy gunner would quickly adjust the error. Sending for one of the 75mm recoilless rifles, he placed it beside the house so as to command the full length of the Ma-Po dogleg and, in his words, "gave the gunner a project." In the first streak of dawn, the gunner discerned his quarry, closed the firing key, and blew the SP into a heap of junk. Only one thing had been overlooked: in siting the 75 reckless, nobody thought about the backblast. Even before the shell found its target, the whole side was blown off the flimsy house

R

that had sheltered the OP, and, said Simmons, "the battle ended on that note."[18]

By early daylight, Puller came up to the 3d Battalion's command post. "You had better show me some results of the alleged battle you had last night," was his greeting to Ridge. The immediately visible results included seven tanks, two self-propelled guns and eight 45mm antitank guns, all shattered in the night's action. More than four hundred North Korean soldiers lay dead, many more wounded had obviously been dragged away, and 83 shaken prisoners were in hand. "I believe Puller was satisfied," said Ridge.

As the correspondents flocked to the scene, one asked Colonel Puller about the reported enemy retreat of the night before. The reply was characteristic: "All I know about a fleeing enemy is that there's two or three hundred out there that won't be fleeing anywhere. They're dead."[19]

Besides the 25th Brigade's main effort down Ma-Po Boulevard, there were three other hard-fought Communist assaults during the night. One, as we have seen, was by a reinforced company against Taplett's battalion. The first probe came at 2230, and attacks continued almost all night, the last being fought off at 0445. Later, more than a hundred dead were counted outside Taplett's positions. After this attack subsided, he sent out his patrol toward the 1st Regiment. Since the planned rendezvous of the two patrols had been on Ma-Po about 500 yards forward of Simmons's roadblock, it is not surprising that the 5th Marines' patrol was turned back by strong enemy forces. There was one "casualty": the patrol leader, Second Lieutenant Lawrence O'Connell, fell through rotten planking in a dark courtyard—straight down into a cesspool eyeball-deep in fragrant night soil.[20]

About the time that the Marines realized the worst was past, the NKPA launched its third violent attack, this time against Lieutenant Colonel Mount's battalion of the 32d Infantry atop Nam-San. Hearing the din of fighting 900 feet below and seeing the rolling flames of midtown Seoul, the soldiers had expected trouble all night. At 0430 Mount's outposts heard the clatter of tanks downhill in the network of roadways with which Nam-San (the Rock Creek Park of Seoul) is reticulated. Shortly afterward a reinforced battalion surged against Mount's company perimeters.

George Company, on Nam-San's western high point, with its beautiful view and terraced shrine, held firm. Fox Company, to the east on a lower knob, was not so lucky. The Communist attack penetrated and finally overran the company. Mount threw in his reserve and by 0700 regained the original positions after a hard fight. One hundred ten dead enemy were counted inside the 2d Battalion's positions; 284 more strewed the mountain's dells and groves.

Colonel Mount's friend and fierce rival, Lieutenant Colonel Don Faith, whose 1st Battalion, 32d Infantry, was east of Nam-San and downhill from Mount, was also attacked in the gray dawn. This clash, which settled into a heavy fire fight, was apparently a secondary effort to the Nam-San assault.[21]

Commenting on the night's fighting to a New York *Times* correspondent, General Almond said:[22]

> Nothing could have been more fortunate than the tank-led enemy counter-attacks. It gave us a greater opportunity to kill more enemy soldiers and destroy his tanks more easily than if we had had to take the city house by house.

The suggestion that Seoul didn't have to be taken "house by house" would have come as a surprise to the riflemen of the 1st and 5th Marines and 32d Infantry, who had not yet learned that just before midnight on September 25—90 days to the minute since the Communist invasion— Seoul was liberated. General Almond released this fact to the press shortly before midnight and so reported to General MacArthur in Tokyo. Next day, he issued the following communiqué:[23]

> Three months to the day after the North Koreans launched their surprise attack south of the 38th Parallel the combat troops of X Corps recaptured the capital city of Seoul. . . . The liberation of Seoul was accomplished by a co-ordinated attack of X Corps troops. . . . By 1400 hours 25 September the military defenses of Seoul were broken. . . . The enemy is fleeing the city to the northeast.

That same day, as the attack ground slowly forward against unremitting enemy resistance at every house and street corner, the Associated Press rather conservatively reported, "If the city had been liberated, the remaining North Koreans did not know it."[24]

Obviously taking the X Corps commander's report at face value, General MacArthur personally drew up and released United Nations Command Communiqué 9 on the afternoon of the 26th:

> Seoul, the capital of the Republic of Korea, is again in friendly hands. United Nations forces, including the 17th Regiment of the ROK Army

and elements of the U. S. 7th and 1st Marine Divisions, have completed the envelopment and seizure of the city.

For once, Radio Pyongyang was more accurate. Its September 27 broadcast said, "The People's Forces in Seoul are desperately resisting . . . and will fight to the last man."[25]

General Almond made no further reports of continued fighting for Seoul and maintains to this day that the city fell before midnight on the 25th. Commenting on a subsequent statement in an official history that the Marines in particular felt his announcement "a bit premature," he wrote, "Soldiers always feel that way when mopping up the last defenses of a captured area. Military results and newspaper views often differ." Alluding to the point, Colonel Chiles echoed his commander: "History is replete with examples of mopping-up exercises following seizure of military objectives."[26]

To MacArthur's credit, his United Nations Command Sixth Report (October 21, 1950) straightforwardly recorded: "The liberation of Seoul . . . was completed on 28 September with only mop-up fighting continuing."

"Ma-Po Wore a Different Look . . ."

Walking warily up Ma-Po Boulevard behind the 2d Battalion, 1st Marines (whom Puller committed to spell Ridge's battalion after their night fight), *Time*'s Dwight Martin reported on the morning of the 26th:

> This morning Ma-Po wore a different look. The burned and blackened remains of the boulevard's shops and homes sent clouds of acrid smoke billowing over the city. Buildings still ablaze showered sparks and ashes high into the air to cascade down on red-eyed, soot-faced Marines.
>
> In the center of the street, six Pershing tanks wheeled into position to advance. Directly in front of the lead tank lay the body of a Red soldier who had been caught in the burst of a white phosphorus shell. The corpse was still burning as the tank's right tread passed over it, extinguishing the flame and grinding the body into a grisly compost. . . .
>
> A group of Marines waited behind a wall, tending three of their wounded and a wounded enemy soldier. The corpsmen shouted for an ambulance. A Marine from the other side of the street replied: "Bring 'em out on litters. The Major says we've lost four ambulances, seven corpsmen and four drivers since last night. We ain't got the ambulances to replace 'em.". . .
>
> Further along, behind a barricade just seized by the Marines, we saw another amazing sight. Less than 50 yards away, through dense smoke, came 40 to 50 North Korean soldiers. They dragged a light antitank

gun. Apparently they thought the barricade was held by their side. The Marines first stared in disbelief, then opened fire with every weapon available. The Reds screamed, buckled, pitched and died on Ma-Po's pavement.

General Almond visited the Marine division this morning. There is no record of what passed between him and General Smith. Then he went down to see Colonel Murray, whose regiment was still grinding slowly into bitter resistance in the western edge of town (and did in fact finally effect patrol contact with the 1st Regiment).

Intending to contrast the undiminished fighting ardor of the city's defenders to the report that they had been fleeing, Ray Murray quoted the old Marine saying, "There's always some son of a bitch that don't get the word."

Instants later, transfixed by an icy stare from Almond's blue eyes, Murray realized that the corps commander attributed the allusion to X Corps headquarters rather than the *In Min Gun*. "I looked around for a sword to fall on," Murray later said.[27]

The main job of the 5th Regiment on the 26th was finally to clean out the long lower spur of An-San (Hill 296), and this task remained in the hands of Taplett's battalion. Taplett launched a two-company sweep down the ridge.

Captain McMullen's Company I had the hardest going, on the left and on the bare, high ground. The intense enemy fire from 25th Brigade troops inflicted heavy casualties from the start. The two assault platoon leaders were wounded early. Undeterred, McMullen committed his reserve and pressed ahead into a heavily entrenched strong point, defended by over 200 Communists. The momentum of McMullen's advance pushed the enemy out of their positions. Then came a wild, swirling counterattack. Item Company held, but only just. And in the final moments of the free-for-all, McMullen fell wounded. He thereby qualified for his seventh Purple Heart in two wars.

Amid less spectacular but hard fighting on lower ground to the right of Company I, two members of George Company—Lieutenant Counselman and Sergeant Jack Macy—each received his fifth wound since the Marine brigade's arrival in Korea 53 days earlier.[28]

At long last, what remained of Seoul's western defense could be dealt with by mopping up.

Watching the relentless, heartbreakingly slow progress of the 1st

Marines through the holocaust of central Seoul, the London *Daily Telegraph*'s Reginald Thompson was moved to write, "Few people can have suffered so terrible a liberation." Later, in what otherwise must be one of the worst books written about the Korean War (*Cry Korea*), Thompson said:

> It is an appalling inferno of din and destruction with the tearing noise of Corsair dive bombers blasting right ahead, and the livid flashes of tank guns, the harsh, fierce crackle of blazing wooden buildings, telegraph and high-tension poles collapsing in utter chaos of wires. Great palls of smoke lie over us as massive buildings collapse in showers of sparks, puffing masses of smoke and rubble upon us in terrific heat.

Frontally assaulting eight-foot barricades every two or three hundred yards, mopping up every house, even flushing Communist defenders from the city's malodorous sewers, engineers, tankers and riflemen of Sutter's battalion hacked their way up Ma-Po's car tracks. It took, they figured, about 45 minutes per barricade. After each assault there followed a lull to reorganize, evacuate casualties, sometimes to refuel and rearm tanks. Then the platoon leaders wearily took on the next one. In a long day of this kind of thing, the 2d Battalion, 1st Marines—a hard-driving battalion of proven fighting qualities against sustained opposition—gained exactly 1,200 yards.

On the 1st Regiment's right, Hawkins worked forward from Hill 82, sending Wray's company through the passenger-car yards of the railroad station, a dowdy relic of Japanese times. Here there was a confusing game of hide-and-seek among cars, platforms, ash pits, water tanks and interlocking towers. After capturing the station in a brisk fight, Wray's people found warm bodies of South Korean women and children, hostages massacred by the Himmlers and Berias of North Korea.

The other two companies of the 1st Battalion hooked below and right of the railroad station. Besides securing Nam-San's long projection into the 1st Marines' zone, they had to establish contact with Mount's battalion of the 32d Infantry, which remained on its perch. One significant capture by Baker Company was the ridge where today stands the handsome headquarters of the Korean Marine Corps.[29]

At midday on the 26th General Smith realized that the 1st and 5th Marines needed help if the stubborn defense of Seoul were to be liquidated. Taking the 7th Regiment from its flanking role to the north, he directed that Litzenberg attack due east toward northern Seoul, pinch out Murray's tired regiment, and wheel north beside Puller. This envelopment of Seoul from the north was in reality O. P. Smith's commitment of his reserve.

Leaving one battalion, that of Lieutenant Colonel Raymond G. Davis, to protect the division and corps left rear above Haengju ferry, Colonel Litzenberg launched the 2d and 3d Battalions east. To gain contact with Murray, he ordered Major Webb D. Sawyer (2d Battalion) to send one company southward down the Kaesong–Seoul highway into town.

The two assault battalions of the 7th Regiment had to fight terrain as much as the enemy. Their advance, across compartments, was designed to secure the precipitous hills, small mountains really, that girdle Seoul on the north. Once at the Seoul–Uijongbu highway, the regiment would be in position to advance north on the latter place.

Although both battalions had scattered, troublesome fighting in the rocky hills and valleys, it was D Company, 7th Marines, sent south to make contact, which ran into trouble.

Captain Richard R. Breen led Dog Company down the highway which runs narrowly between Hills 296 (An-San) and 338, both well known to the 5th Marines. As the Marines advanced, they were welcomed and cheered by dense crowds of citizens who apparently preferred liberation, however traumatic, to life under a Communist regime. Advancing rapidly, the company apparently overshot the 5th Marines (who held high ground on either side). Passing the Sodaemun (North Gate) Prison, leading elements reached the Arch of Independence, a quarter mile below the prison.

Without warning, at 0830, a heavy blast of automatic-weapons and small-arms fire opened up, felling the advance guard commander, Lieutenant W. F. Goggin. This frontal attack then spread rearward. Soon the entire company was fighting, right, left and ahead. All through the forenoon, Captain Breen tried to subdue his opponents with no success. What he had walked into was a section of the 25th Brigade's final line of resistance.

By noon the company had made no progress. In fact, enemy units had closed the defile to its rear. Dog Company was surrounded. Breen, already wounded once, pulled his people rearward into better ground for a perimeter defense, carefully bringing in his dead and wounded in a deliberate withdrawal. When Colonel Litzenberg called by radio to see if the company needed help, Breen replied, "We're okay, Colonel." Two

Air Force C-47s dropped ammunition, rations and medical supplies, one aircraft being so badly shot up by Communist flak that it had to crash-land at Kimpo.

In the night, the regimental surgeon, Lieutenant (jg) Edward Burns, USN, led a convoy of jeep ambulances through the enemy lines and took out the worst of D Company's 40 wounded. Next morning, despite the last-stand implications of the situation, the enemy had wilted, and a relief column of tanks, infantry and engineers reopened the road out, and the company withdrew. Captain Breen, suffering from his second wound, then turned over to a successor.[30]

By the afternoon of the 26th, the 3d Battalion, 32d Infantry (Schumann's), had swung wide of town out toward Hill 348 in Seoul's eastern approaches. Now, they discovered, the enemy really did show signs of fleeing. On the main road leading east, one of Colonel Schumann's companies fell on a column of some 40 vehicles, several artillery pieces, and what obviously was part of a senior headquarters. Conceivably this may have been the remnants of the 18th Division. The soldiers attacked boldly, cut the column to pieces, and inflicted heavy casualties.[31]

"It Looks Like the 4th of July . . ."

There comes a time in every battle when men know they have won. This is what Foch meant when he said, *"La victoire, c'est la volonté"* ("Victory is a matter of willpower"). That time, and that conviction, became clear early on September 27 (D+12).

When the weary 3d Battalion, 5th Marines, moved out to clear the very last resistance from the lower end of their great spur of An-San, there were no more fierce tempests of fire. Instead, there was only the sound of "the distant and random gun, that the foe was sullenly firing." By midmorning George Company had solid contact with Sutter's battalion of the 1st Regiment, and Taplett had wheeled left (northeast) and taken the Middle School. Ahead, still decked with red banners and grinning portraits of Josef Stalin and Kim Il Sung, stood Government House and Changdok Palace.

Abreast of Taplett, the 2d Battalion, 1st Marines, pushed ahead. Here, too, though the *In Min Gun* had not collapsed, Sutter's people could smell victory. At 1057, guided by Richard J. H. Johnston, a New York *Times* man who knew Seoul from earlier times, Marines of the 2d Battalion raised the flag of her oldest ally over France's deserted Embassy

—an act of liberation as little remembered in the Elysée Palace today as those of 1918 and 1944.

Then there was a hot fight west of the Duksoo Palace where the two car lines cross. Self-propelled guns and towed artillery pieces covered minefields and barricades. Lieutenant Cummings, who had such a close shave in the defile between Mahang-ri and Sosa, knocked out both Communist SPs, but then ran his own tank onto a mine. Today, aside from a bad jolt, he was in no trouble; the riflemen were in close and already swarming at the barricades. Up the car track to the left (the line that takes families out to Sodaemun Prison on visiting days), George Newton had the 1st Battalion, 5th Marines, scrambling up the jagged rock pile of Hill 338, which had so venomously harried the flanks of the 5th Marines on An-San.

Just after three, with the final urging of a flame tank, the Communists caved in ahead of Taplett. Moving at the high port up Kwangwhamun Boulevard, Company G, 5th Marines, burst into the Court of the Lions at Government House, ripped down the red flag, and Gunnery Sergeant Harold Beaver ran up those same colors his forebears had hoisted 103 years earlier atop the Palace of the Montezumas.[32]

When Easy Company, 1st Marines, still guided by Dick Johnston, reached the Russian Embassy, it was abandoned. Measuring American behavior in such moments by their own standards, the Russian delegation had decamped. Conceivably they might have been influenced by *Pravda*'s dispatch of September 23 which purported to publish MacArthur's order of the day for the capture of Seoul:

> Before you is a rich city. In it are many sweets and wines. Take Seoul and all the girls will be yours. The property of the inhabitants belongs to the victors and you can send it home in packages.

After running up the Stars and Stripes in lieu of Hammer and Sickle, E Company pressed forward to the nearby American Embassy residence. Weeds were knee-high on what had been Ambassador Muccio's trim lawn; the house was stripped of all furnishings, which had been trucked away to Pyongyang some days after Communist occupation of Seoul. Seeing the Marines, a squad of NKPA machine gunners in the gateway threw down their arms. Recognizing Johnston as a friend from old days, Chon, Ambassador Muccio's chauffeur, materialized from some hidden place and rushed to make obeisance; the riflemen almost shot him before Johnston could explain. As the Marines broke out another set of colors and bent them on the halyards, there came the crack of a sniper's rifle and the whine of a ricochet. A dozen Marines raised their pieces toward the rooftop of the nearby Duksoo Palace. With one motion, the company commander, Captain Charles D. Frederick, stopped them. "One sniper," he said, "one Marine." Then he designated a rifleman, who slid his elbow into a hasty-sling, sighted in, squeezed off a round, and dropped the Communist from his perch. After that, at 1537, the colors went up without further interruption.[33]

Gunnery Sergeant Max Stein gazed about Seoul as American flags began to appear, and every young Marine just hoped that AP's Joe Rosenthal, who snapped the Iwo Jima flag raising, might be along for this war, too. "It looks," growled Stein, "like the Fourth of July around this burg."

And when Army people chaffed Colonel Puller about the Marines' flag-raising fixation, the reply spoke like a howitzer: "A man with a flag in his pack and the desire to run it up on an enemy strongpoint isn't likely to bug out."[34]

While Marines beat down the final resistance in Seoul, the 32d Infantry perforce remained static on Nam-San, since (as O. P. Smith predicted) its fires would rake the 1st and 5th Marines' advance. When Puller had his regiment abreast of South Mountain and wheeled eastward, Beauchamp then was able to advance and secure the southeast suburbs. Here, as elsewhere, the arrival of United States troops, even amid the wrack and havoc of the tormented city, was greeted with Korean enthusiasm. Across one freshly contested street, infantrymen of the 32d advanced past a banner: COMIES ARE RUNNING AWAY. CHASE EM. CHASE EM.

Linkup

Although only 70,000 North Korean soldiers ringed the Pusan perimeter, which by mid-September contained 140,000 Eighth Army and ROK troops, General Walker found it hard to overcome the inertia of defense grown habitual. Not until a week after Inchon did Eighth Army begin to make real headway toward the hammer-anvil linkup with X Corps which was an essential of MacArthur's strategy.

By September 23 (when the 5th Marines were hammering at the western gates of Seoul) the Communists were in evident retreat. Amid a multipronged breakout and pursuit, the 1st Cavalry Division, commanded by Major General Hobart R. Gay, received the mission of

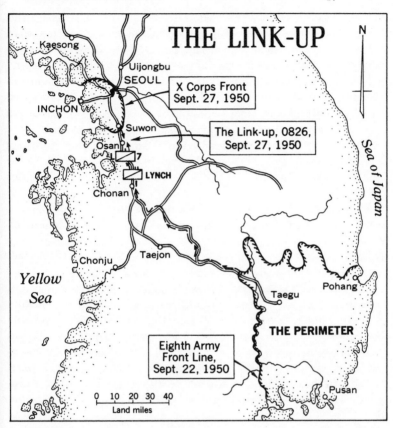

THE LINK-UP

N

Kaesong

Uijongbu
SEOUL

X Corps Front
Sept. 27, 1950

INCHON

Suwon

The Link-up, 0826,
Sept. 27, 1950

Osan

7

LYNCH

Chonan

Sea of Japan

Chonju

Taejon

Yellow
Sea

Pohang

Taegu

THE PERIMETER

Eighth Army
Front Line,
Sept. 22, 1950

Pusan

0 10 20 30 40
Land miles

pushing up the central corridor toward the X Corps beachhead. Gay in turn organized a task force numbered 777, built around Custer's old regiment, the 7th Cavalry, which was to drive north, disregarding flanks or lateral contact, avoid engagement with retreating enemy, and move night and day. The 3d Battalion, 7th Cavalry, under Lieutenant Colonel James H. Lynch, reinforced and designated "Task Force Lynch," was General Gay's spearhead.

At midmorning on September 26, with little more than a hundred miles to go, Lynch began his final thrust north, bypassing herds of disorganized, leaderless NKPA soldiers, cheered by villagers whose homes were still blazing in the track of retreating invaders. Carried away in the pursuit, Lynch's original point—a detachment of three Pershing tanks—

plowed ahead so fast and far that they even outran radio contact. By ten that night, amid a blaze of hair-trigger American antitank fire which killed one tank crewman but luckily did no major damage, the three tanks made it safely into the lines of the 31st Infantry, north of Osan.

Next morning, at a bridge above Osan, a 31st Infantry outpost momentarily blinked in the glare of history when, at 0826, L Troop, 7th Cavalry (that bay-horse troop wiped out to a man on the Little Bighorn in 1876), followed through and made solid contact from the south. Just 12 days since the Marines had landed at Wolmi Do, Eighth Army and X Corps had linked up. No doubt the ghost of George Armstrong Custer whistled "Garry Owen."

With the smash of hammer on anvil, the fate of the *In Min Gun* was sealed. Hard local fighting against die-hard pockets of resistance lay ahead, but, as an army, that of the North Korean Peoples Republic was finished.

Of the 70,000 invaders who had penned General Walker, it is estimated that only 25,000 made it back across the 38th parallel. Communist divisions were down to battalion or company strength: the 2d NKPA Division, for example, by September 30 numbered but 200 officers and men. Between September 16 and the end of the month, Eighth Army bagged 9,294 prisoners, destroyed or captured 239 T-34 tanks and 74 76mm self-propelled guns. How many enemy were killed and how many simply melted into the countryside will never be known, but the numbers were great. The invader had been repaid in full.[35]

Pursuit North

While all eyes watched the linkup and the apocalyptic liberation of Seoul, the 7th Marines were fighting a private campaign uphill and downdale among the crags north of the capital city.

On September 28, as preparations were in progress downtown for the official liberation ceremony, Colonel Litzenberg got his regiment astride the Seoul–Uijongbu highway. The next day was one of skirmishing and mopping up, and on the 30th (D+15) the 7th Marines got the orders they had been expecting.

Attaching tanks, engineers, Major Parry's artillery, and other supporting units, General Smith ordered the 7th Regiment as an independent combat team (a brigade, virtually) to attack rapidly to the north up the corridor through the mountains and seize Uijongbu, 16 miles above

Seoul. Uijongbu is an important road and rail junction at the upper end of a long defile running north from Seoul. From here also, a main highway angles northeast across the peninsula into Wonsan, Korea's major east coast port. Not only does this system of highways provide an important escape route north from Seoul but, as the Uijongbu–Wonsan road crosses Korea, it intersects the east coast roads which, after the U.N. linkup, afforded the *In Min Gun* its only avenue of retreat from the south. Colonel Lee Kyong U's NKPA Seoul City Regiment (31st Regiment or 31st Rifle Division, as it had been hastily cobbled together during the latter days) had the mission of blocking the road to Uijongbu.

At 0630 on Sunday morning, October 1, leaving the chaplains little time for their devotions, Litzenberg jumped off, possibly consoling himself that even so Christian a soldier as Stonewall Jackson always found dispensation if he had to fight on the Sabbath.

With strike and reconnaissance air cover from General Harris's 1st Wing at Kimpo, the 7th Marines struck out in column of battalions. The 3d Battalion, under Major M. E. ("Hal") Roach, had the van, but it was Litzenberg's plan—code-named "Blitz"—that Lieutenant Colonel Raymond G. Davis's 1st Battalion would execute a feint to enable rapid penetration by Roach. Trouble was expected at a place called Nuwon-Ni, about three miles short of Uijongbu. Here, between two mountains, Tobong-San and Surak-San, steep slopes shoulder down into the defile and provide ideal ground for an NKPA Thermopylae. Approaching this gorge, Roach was to hold the road with tank support while Davis (who in two months would win the Medal of Honor at Yudam-Ni, a place nobody yet knew) attacked the ridges on a broad front.

"Time spent on reconnaissance is rarely wasted," runs the soldiers' axiom. Here, at Nuwon-Ni, the combined aerial reconnaissance, map reconnaissance, and reconnaissance in force by Ray Davis produced exactly what Colonel Litzenberg needed to know. Davis's feint drew heavy enemy mortar, artillery and small-arms fire during the afternoon, while Roach's advance guard hit a dense minefield in the mouth of the Nuwon-Ni defile. By nightfall, the enemy had been found and fixed, and Davis held the first series of ridges confronting the advance.

At first light on the 2d, Lieutenant J. F. Cole, commanding VMF-312, led his squadron's initial flight out of Kimpo to support the 7th Marines. Like the Marines on the ground, those in the air were relatively newcomers: Cole's Corsairs had flown across from Itami, Japan, only on September 28. New or not, VMF-312 lashed the Seoul City Regiment's entrenchments with bombs, rockets and napalm. To make sure they laid no duds, the pilots executed a final pass with incendiary bullets to touch off an unignited napalm tank, a devotion to economy which would have wrung praise from Alain Enthoven himself.

But the NKPA antiaircraft gunners still knew their business. Before the day was out, VMF-312 had lost three airplanes. The least damaged of these made it safely to Kimpo but was so riddled that it never flew again.[36]

This second day's attack confronted unyielding resistance. Even with two battalions athwart the road (Roach on the left, Davis on the right), with steady hammering from Parry's howitzers, and with Cole's Corsairs swooping and shrieking, the Communists grudged every yard. It is indicative that half of the villages within two miles of Nuwon were reduced that day to mere locations and on the 1953 map of this area bear the notation "Destroyed." This was no easy day for the 7th Marines.

Save that he qualified for two Purple Hearts while a lieutenant in France, General Cates was by reputation a lucky officer. Thus the presence of the Commandant as a knowledgeable spectator on October 3 seemed a good omen to the 7th Regiment. Accompanied by O. P. Smith and observers from Marine Corps Headquarters, General Cates, true to form, arrived in time to see the defense of Nuwon swept aside. Major Webb D. ("Buzz") Sawyer's 2d Battalion shouldered into the valley, overran mortar and artillery positions, and was in the outskirts of Uijongbu (Destroyed) by five in the afternoon. Reaching for his radio transmitter, Sawyer got Colonel Litzenberg on the air and reported, "This is the Mayor of Blitz."[37]

Another senior officer running true to form that day was General Lowe who, as might have been expected, was well up front. Together with Colonel Litzenberg, he was driving up the highway in a jeep when a Communist 12.7mm machine gun let go a 20-round burst that riddled the vehicle and, as General Cates later remarked, "damn near killed both of them."

Thus, in a final assault and a final burst of fire, the Inchon-Seoul campaign drew to a close. When General Cates passed through Tokyo on his way back to Washington, certain planners at GHQ were already thinking ahead to imminent problems of peace and demobilization.[38]

"He Who Is Prudent and Lies in Wait ..."

In October 1950, as she always does, Nemesis, goddess of retribution, stood ready in the wings.

As early as September 8, amid the Delphic pronouncements emitting from the G-2 Division, Far East Command, was this:[39]

> If success of the North Korean Red Army doubtful, the Fourth Chinese Field Army (under General Lin Piao) will probably be committed.

Soon after Inchon, Peking began concentrating some of its best divisions along the Yalu. There were other signs of steadily increasing Chinese Communist interest in the fate of North Korea. On September 30, for example, Chou En-lai warned the world that China "will not supinely tolerate" the invasion of North Korea. All through the perilous weeks of fighting about Pusan, China had remained immobile. Now she was mobilizing. Would she march?

More than two thousand years before Clausewitz, Sun Tzu wrote, "Weapons are ominous tools to be used only when there is no alternative."

By the close of the Inchon-Seoul campaign, could China consider the alternatives exhausted, or was some final contingency still undisclosed which might determine Peking's next step?

"He who is prudent," Sun Tzu also said, "and lies in wait for an enemy who is not, will be victorious."[40]

9

HOME BY CHRISTMAS

~~~~~~

In the moment of victory, tighten your helmet-strap.
JAPANESE PROVERB

ON SEPTEMBER 28, the day Seoul finally fell, the thirteenth day since the landing at Inchon, the eighth since the crossing of the Han, X Corps finally received its bridging equipment, or most of it. By dint of Herculean labors the corps engineer got a pontoon bridge across the river about midnight, having had to borrow two of the Marines' floating-bridge sections in order to finish the job.[1]

Time was short: General MacArthur would arrive at Kimpo next morning, and so would President Syngman Rhee. For the triumphal entry into Seoul, a bridge was essential.

Other demands were essential, too. The Marine division was to provide two honor guards, one at Kimpo, the other at the fire-blackened National Capitol in Seoul. A cordon of Marines was to line the route from airfield to Capitol. The Marine band would play (a problem here: the bandsmen had brought weapons but left instruments at Kobe—Fifth Air Force was directed to airlift them to Kimpo, Priority I, by nightfall the 28th). To make sure every detail was nailed down, X Corps ordered all battalion commanders concerned to report to the corps CP at Ascom City for an after-dinner conference at eight on the evening of the 28th.[2]

This last struck O. P. Smith as supererogatory. Street fighting was still going on in much of Seoul. "I called up General Ruffner," he jotted in his log on the 27th,

> and pointed out to him that we still had a war on our hands and that we would not call in battalion commanders for night conferences. I told him we would have a representative of the G-3 Section present. . . .

General Smith was not alone in his reservations. When General Mac-

Arthur learned of the arrangements being made, he canceled them entirely. No band, no sheet-music airlift, no honor guards, no troop cordons, U. S. troops to be present in force but well out of sight, Korean Marines and soldiers in the limelight. "I will personally conduct the proceedings," the General stated.[3]

Aside from his unfailing sense of the appropriate, MacArthur's decision may have been prompted by a chilly admonition from Washington that any plans on his part for restoration of the Rhee government must have prior approval. MacArthur's reply accurately pointed out that no question of restoration existed since the Rhee government had never ceased to function, and that what he intended was simply to return "the existing government to its constitutional seat." By now the futility of such duellos with MacArthur should have been but evidently was not yet fully obvious to the Joint Chiefs of Staff.[4]

At ten in the morning on September 29, the *Scap* touched down at Kimpo. Accompanied by Mrs. MacArthur, the General stepped to the asphalt taxiway, wearing his beautifully creased field costume the informality of which was perfected by the lack of a necktie. Five Chevrolet staff cars that had come over the beach soon after Jim Crowe's porcelain toilets were arrayed in waiting, the lead one with a five-star plate, which proves that the major finally accomplished his mission. Behind the five staff cars were 40 jeeps, every one spic and span—an essential precaution since the X Corps MPs at the National Capitol had orders to exclude dusty jeeps. After the members of the entourage had filled the staff cars, the press and lesser persons climbed into the jeeps and the procession sped toward the Han, past Hill 131, and over Colonel Rowny's brand-new bridge.

Ever since daylight, Marine battalions had been combing the General's route of approach and the vicinity of the bullet-pocked, fire-blackened Capitol. The 3d Battalion, 5th Marines, was north of the Duksoo Palace. The 1st Battalion of the same regiment was on the high ground north and west. Ridge had his 3d Battalion, 1st Marines, out of sight but nonetheless lining the General's path. Puller's 1st and 2d Battalions and Litzenberg's 2d and 3d were still fighting in the northwestern outskirts of the city which had been liberated four days earlier. Around the interior and the compound of the Capitol was a detachment of Army military police in knife-pressed, tailor-made ODs with gleaming black airborne boots laced with white nylon parachute cords.

Syngman Rhee, flown up from Pusan in General MacArthur's old plane, the *Bataan,* arrived with Mrs. Rhee an hour after the General, and like him was conveyed to the Capitol.

The assemblage at the Capitol was imposing. Besides General Mac-Arthur and the entourage, there were Ambassador Muccio, Admirals Struble, Joy, Andrewes and Doyle, General Walker, Generals Stratemeyer and Kenney of the Air Force, General Almond, Generals Smith, Barr and Craig, and the two Marine regimental commanders who had borne the heat and burden of the day, Puller and Murray (the former almost excluded by the Army MPs because his driver chose an entrance restricted by the day's protocol to staff cars only). Admiral and Mrs. Sohn headed a large group of Korean officers and officials while more junior people— selected unit and ships' commanders, including several British officers in whites—filled the vaulted National Assembly chamber hung with heavy mulberry-color velvet drapes. In the nature of things, practically every man in the room carried side arms. Looking about, an irrepressible newsman with Korean experience muttered, "There haven't been so many gats in this place since the last time the Legislature sat."

At the stroke of high noon, President Rhee and Douglas MacArthur entered, arm in arm. Except for the photographers, capering and posturing like monkeys, the audience stood in respectful silence. Through the windows drifted the grisly smells of the charred and battered city, while the sound of distant small-arms fire rose and fell, and intermittent artillery concentrations, felt as much as heard, shook the building.

At the lectern, Douglas MacArthur spoke the opening lines:

> Mr. President: By the grace of a merciful Providence our forces fighting under the standard of that greatest hope and inspiration of mankind, the United Nations, have liberated this ancient capital city of Korea. It has been freed from the despotism of communist rule and its citizens once more have the opportunity for that immutable concept of life which holds invincibly to the primacy of individual liberty and personal dignity. . . .

As MacArthur spoke, some concussion, possibly the artillery, shook loose great panes (not mere tinkling slivers) of the heavy molded glass panels overhead. Those who had them hastily donned helmets lest they be felled in the moment of victory.

The General never flinched. Bareheaded, undismayed, unhurried, he concluded:

In behalf of the United Nations Command, I am happy to restore to you, Mr. President, the seat of your government that from it you may better fulfill your constitutional responsibilities.

In the utter silence, with sacerdotal mien and gesture, MacArthur thereupon sonorously intoned:

Our Father, who art in Heaven, hallowed be Thy name . . .

Tears coursed his cheeks but his voice was unfaltering. Then there was another pause, almost unbearable in emotional surcharge, and, turning to the undefeated old President, the General said:

Mr. President, my officers and I will now resume our military duties and leave you and your government to the discharge of civil responsibility.

Syngman Rhee had his prepared remarks, but those history remembers were extemporaneous:

We admire you. We love you as the savior of our race. How can I ever explain to you my own undying gratitude and that of the Korean people?

Leaving the Capitol soon afterward, Admiral Doyle most remembered MacArthur's rendition of the Lord's Prayer. "If there had been any chaplains around," he later said, "they would have had to have gone back to school again."[5]

According to Reginald Thompson, one British correspondent was so overcome that he cabled the entire text of the General's remarks, including the Lord's Prayer, at 15¢ a word.[6]

Two more ceremonies remained, one to honor the dead, the other the living.

On October 6 the 1st Marine Division Cemetery at Inchon, which had also served for the dead of other U. S. Services and the ROK forces, was redesignated the United Nations Cemetery, and so dedicated. The Marine division chaplain led the invocation. Then General Almond laid a wreath on the grave of an unknown soldier. O. P. Smith followed suit for a Marine, except that—as there were no unknown Marine dead— he chose the mound which covered the remains of Corporal Richard C. Matheney, late 5th Marines, who, before he fell, had successively won the Bronze Star, the Silver Star, and the Navy Cross. General Barr did the same for one of his people, and so did Colonel Lee, an ROK officer. Then the poignancy of the volleys and "Taps," followed by the national anthems of Korea and the United States, final guerdon for those who survived and those who had not.

Four days later, on the invitation of Colonel Shin, O. P. Smith and his principal staff reviewed the Korean Marine Regiment.

The four KMC battalions were paraded in line on the athletic field in battered Inchon. A Korean Marine band (a resource hitherto unknown to General Smith) played spiritedly as the U. S. Marine general trooped the line, then took post, tall and spare, at the saluting base.

"These Korean Marines were quite remarkable," General Smith noted in his log. They had been through a hard campaign, taken appreciable losses, and were barely six months old as a Service anyway. Yet they stepped out well, had complete, correct green uniforms, their packs and web equipment were uniform and properly worn, they were equipped with well-worn but spotless rifles, machine guns and mortars. That all hands were shod in tennis shoes did not detract. Many U. S. Marine observers could remember the tennis shoes worn by the flower of the Imperial Japanese Army, who were good soldiers, too, but mainly now dead.

Afterward, in the fashion of such occasions, the officers repaired to the upper floor of Inchon's fire headquarters, one of the few buildings to have survived. Here the wives of the KMC officers had laid on a sumptuous feast, washed down by Korea's premium OB beer and by whiskey for those who chose. There were mutual congratulations, speeches, exchange of presents. No one there could know that this regiment of Marines would become the 1st Marine Division's fourth infantry regiment and that, for more than three years of cruel war yet unforeseen, Korean and U. S. Marines would fight side by side, support each other, share each other's rations, mourn and avenge each other's dead.

Still less could any man have foreseen that, 15 years later to the day, in 1965, a keen-edged, tough Marine brigade, led by officers and NCOs seasoned in the fighting for Seoul and in many other battles afterward, would be mounting out from Pusan for Cam-Ranh Bay—spearhead of the Korean Expeditionary Force in a new war, a war to preserve the freedom of a small Asian country hard-pressed by Communist invaders from the north.[7]

The Reckoning

If ever a man lived up to a promise, Douglas MacArthur made good
on his "I shall crush them." In the words of his report to the United
Nations after the capture of Seoul, he truly stated:

> Events of the past two weeks have been decisive. . . . A successful
> frontal attack and envelopment has completely changed the tide of
> battle in South Korea. The backbone of the North Korean army has
> been broken and their scattered forces are being liquidated.

To say that Operation *Chromite* changed the entire course of the war
is understatement. In immediate results alone the fortnight's campaign
accomplished the following.

1. It caused the disintegration of the North Korean perimeter about
Pusan.

2. By liberating the national capital and dislocating the logistical
system of the Communists, it brought about the destruction of the *In
Min Gun*.

3. It returned the United Nations to the 38th parallel and thus pre-
served the Republic of Korea. In so doing—for the first and only time
since 1945—it restored to freedom a capital city conquered by Communists.

4. It retrieved the honor of American arms, so smirched in the
retreats, surrenders, bugouts and ineptness of the fighting in the south.[8]

More important than these military results, Inchon underscored what
America had nearly forgotten in the five years since her hour of greatest
victory—what, indeed, she often forgets, save when she needs a victory—
that America is a maritime power, that her weapon is the trident, and her
strategy that of the oceans. Only through the sure and practiced exercise
of sea power could this awkward war in a remote place have been turned
upside down in a matter of days.

Every great campaign spawns its statistics.

To defeat the thirty to forty thousand defenders which the *In Min Gun*
threw piecemeal against X Corps, 71,339 soldiers, sailors, Marines,
airmen, and ROK troops landed at Inchon and bore their part in the
battle.

The cost of this victory to the United States was 536 killed in action or
died of wounds, 2,550 wounded, and 65 missing in action. Among the
Services, Marines, on the ground and in the air, paid the highest price:[9]

SERVICE	KIA/DOW	WIA	MIA	TOTAL CASUALTIES
U. S. Marine Corps	422	2,031	6	2,459
U. S. Army	106	411	57	574
U. S. Navy	8	118	2	128

In balancing its books on September 30, the X Corps War Diary rounded out the number of enemy killed at 14,000, his prisoners in hand, 7,000. These figures are about as correct as any that will ever be arrived at. Some 50 Russian tanks were destroyed, 47 by Marine ground or air. In addition, the Marine division alone destroyed or took 23 120mm mortars, 2 76mm self-propelled guns, 8 76mm guns, 19 45mm antitank guns, 59 14.5mm antitank rifles, 56 heavy machine guns, and 7,543 rifles. How many former American weapons, from artillery pieces down, were retaken from the Communists will never be known, but the number is large.

The X Corps Tactical Air Command flew 2,533 close-support sorties during the campaign. VMF-212, based at Kimpo, led the list with 551 sorties. Eleven 1st Wing aircraft were shot down—none by enemy fighters, all by Communist flak. Expanding and continuing its pioneer employment of military helicopters, VMO-6 flew uncounted combat helicopter sorties.

To support the campaign, the Navy alone dropped 5,328 bombs and 50,420 pounds of napalm. Its guns and rocket launchers fired 5,269 6-inch shells or heavier (including British), 7,117 5-inch shells, 14,526 rockets (mostly 5-inch), 519 3-inch shells, and 860,047 40mm, 20mm, and .50-caliber projectiles, mostly from aircraft.[10]

Another quite different category of Navy support lay in the field of public relations. During the first nine days of the campaign, 367,714 words of copy were filed via the heavy-laden communications of *Rochester* and *Mount McKinley*. In barely restrained triumph, Admiral Struble's PIO reported afterward that the press coverage disclosed "not a single case of any correspondent criticizing any military phase of the operation"—in other words, that the PIOs won. This rosy view was not, however, entirely shared: Maggie Higgins savagely commented in her account of Inchon, "The main effect of military public-relations officers is to hamper correspondents."[11]

The military conduct of the campaign was, in general, of a high professional order. It was this professionalism which, time after time, accounted for the success of the thousand-and-one improvisations and jury-rigs which had to be made. Despite the crushing handicaps under which his division labored, for example, it was General Barr's professional character and leadership which carried the 7th Division through, "buddy system" and all.

Only one major improvisation in Operation *Chromite* failed to measure up. The role and functioning of headquarters, X Corps, are open to serious criticism. Broadly speaking, this criticism stems from two points: (1) in an amphibious assault of unparalleled difficulty and complexity, the senior military headquarters, X Corps, possessed no experience or competence in landing operations; and (2) because of its hasty and improvised character, X Corps headquarters repeatedly fell below the performance which could have been expected of a going concern, and must be expected of a high headquarters in combat, amphibious or inland.

Both criticisms gain added force because, among many necessary improvisations in this campaign, X Corps headquarters was an unnecessary improvisation. Without going into the motives which prompted the decision to activate X Corps rather than employ the existing Fleet Marine Force headquarters of General Shepherd, it is enough to point out (as did MacArthur's G-3, General Wright) that Shepherd's headquarters, besides being amphibiously trained, was a going concern and could be expected to function as such. Additionally, it was, of course, commanded by an officer whose three-star rank was appropriate to the command of a corps, rather than (as in the case of X Corps) by a major general.

Among the specific deficiencies which may be charged to X Corps are that it provided little if any direction in the planning of the campaign, and far too detailed direction in its conclusion. Its echelonment for embarkation violated every applicable principle—its commander separated from his own staff, that staff separated from the corresponding naval staff, and the commander in turn separated from his naval counterpart. The prolonged delay of the corps commander in landing his headquarters and assuming control of operations ashore is inexplicable. By comparison with four representative European and Pacific operations under U. S. Army command (Sicily, Normandy, Southern France, and Leyte) where no American corps headquarters landed later than D+1, General Almond's failure to assume control ashore until D+6, halfway through the battle, withstands explanation. We can only assume that, in his capacity as MacArthur's chief of staff, Almond felt he must defer assumption of X Corps responsibilities until after the General departed on D+5.

It is the assertion of some (General Almond in particular; see note 34, Chapter 6) that abstention from the amphibious phase of *Chromite* by X Corps headquarters was logical and appropriate—as General Almond put it, ". . . that, until the 1st Marine Division landed, X Corps had no function but to sit in observation." The assumption underlying this view is that a corps (i.e., expeditionary troops) headquarters has no amphibious functions—in fact, no military *raison d'être* until it takes charge of a ready-made land battle ashore.

Anyone familiar with amphibious warfare will recognize, however, that a multitude of operations and activities should be performed by the corps commander and staff while still afloat, before assuming control of operations ashore—and that discharge of these duties calls for the presence of the corps commander in the same ship with the overall naval commander, for close, continuing liaison between the corps and the naval staff, and adequate communications for the corps headquarters while afloat. None of these conditions existed at Inchon.

To cite only a few responsibilities in the amphibious phase (which X Corps discharged lamely or not at all), the corps shore party must be brought into being, beaches organized and consolidated so as to maintain the logistic thrust of the battle, and the flow of supply from afloat regulated to support the requirement of the corps as its units land. The decision to commence general unloading cannot be made by the naval commander without close consultation with the corps commander and staff. Corps air and naval gunfire officers must plan and obtain deep supporting fires. Flow of replacements must be controlled and casualties evacuated. In these and many other matters the corps staff must establish and maintain an initiative vis-à-vis the naval forces, and do so long before the corps commander girds himself to assume command of operations ashore. All this demands participation and involvement, not sitting in observation aboard an MSTS transport wholly unsuited for the purpose.

In matters of combat support which are the responsibility of a higher headquarters, X Corps made a poor record. We have examined the failure to bridge the Han during the battle (conceivably even a failure to inform the fighting units of the corps commander's real intentions). The inadequacy of motor transport arrangements to work the port of Inchon and keep supply flowing forward were obscured and to some

extent made good by Far East Air Forces' airlift into Kimpo of classes
of supply available at Inchon which should readily have been trucked
to users over road nets and terrain posing no serious problems. In both
instances, and in lesser ones, too, X Corps not only failed to carry out a
corps task but ended up by calling on the resources of subordinate units
to perform wholly or in part for X Corps what X Corps should have
performed for them.

In tactical operations X Corps provided dilatory and only partially
effective coordination for its two divisions during the advance on Yongdungpo and Anyang. Its promulgation of a night attack order with
totally faulty map coordinates was a novice's blunder that might have
cost human lives. Finally, while combat decisions can never be weighed
on the same scales as careless map reading, the two best-remembered
tactical interventions by X Corps—commitment of the 32d Infantry to
the battle for Seoul and the "fleeing enemy" order for an impromptu
night attack—remain matters for question and reservation.

The implications of the "enemy fleeing" order have already been
fully examined, but the question might still be raised: Did commitment
of the 32d Infantry into Seoul achieve General Almond's objective of
rapidly maneuvering the Communists out of the city? The answer, on
two counts, is no. First, after securing Nam-San, the 32d Infantry did
not maneuver, but stood fast atop the mountain and mopped up Seoul's
eastern suburbs. Second, during the period (September 25-28) when the
Communists were supposed to be fleeing the city as a result of pressure
from the X Corps "maneuver element," the defenders inflicted 708
battle casualties on the Marine division alone (appreciably more than
were sustained [574] by the 7th Division during the entire campaign)—
surely not the indication of a force being maneuvered out of town, or in
headlong flight.

While the failings of X Corps fully justified the apprehensions voiced
during planning by Generals Wright and Hickey, blame for these failings
cannot be entirely levied upon the corps commander or the staff. By his
act of military nepotism in permitting a trusted, loyal chief of staff to
act simultaneously as a corps commander, Douglas MacArthur erred
gravely. A commander of his experience must have realized (certainly
should have realized) the incompatibility of the two functions. It can be
surmised—in the nature of matters, there will be no evidence—that in

making his decision MacArthur never had an opportunity to examine
the full implications of jury-rigging X Corps and, to compound the
mistake, of subcontracting the command to his chief of staff. While this
may be so, MacArthur ought nevertheless to have recognized that no
man could command a corps in an invasion (unless the post were
accepted as ornamental) and at the same time function as Douglas Mac-
Arthur's chief of staff. Given the climate of MacArthur's headquarters,
it would be impossible to imagine an officer of General Almond's drive
and ambition failing to grasp such an opportunity; MacArthur should
have known better than to extend it.

But all decisions about the corps command, the command structure
and in fact virtually every significant aspect of *Chromite* must be viewed
in the context of inter-Service animosity and personal friction which
characterized the time and therefore the operation. These factors have
already been amply documented. That, after all, they were overcome and
that they did not bring about greater real harm reflects great credit on
the men of good will like Doyle, O. P. Smith and Barr, and upon all the
fighting men.

In an evaluation of the events leading up to Inchon-Seoul, a senior
officer of the Russian Navy, Captain G. Doidzhashvli, wrote in 1950:[12]

> When, in the summer of 1950, the American imperialist marauders,
> the newly appeared pretenders to world domination, provoked the
> bloody holocaust of Korea, the Wall Street house-dog, General Mac-
> Arthur, demanded that the American so-called "Marines" be immedi-
> ately placed at his disposal. This professional murderer and inveterate war
> criminal intended to inflict a final blow on the Korean people. . . . The
> events in Korea have shown graphically that the Marine Corps stal-
> warts did not turn a deaf ear to the appeal of their rapacious
> *ataman*. They have abundantly covered Korean soil with the blood and
> tears of hundreds and thousands of Korean women, old people, and
> children. . . .

Civil wars, Communist wars, and Asian wars are unhappily noted for
their ferocity. The Korean War was all three. It is characteristic of the
Communist double-think mentality as well as the Aesopian language of
Marxism that loud charges of atrocities, such as the above, should have
been leveled early at the liberators of Seoul. The defense of the Korean
capital in such a way as to compel its liberators to shatter it was a horrible
act of psychological warfare from which it could readily be concluded

that the cause was wanton extravagance of U.N. firepower rather than the wantonness of defenders who called forth such firepower. This distinction was clearly stated in October 1950 by an authentic voice of conscience, Eleanor Roosevelt, who, in deploring the need to wreck Seoul in order to free it, laid the blame squarely at the North Koreans' door.[13]

Not only did the NKPA cause the ruin of Seoul, but they stripped it systematically (as they did Inchon) of all usable industrial machinery and even office furniture, conducting such removals until the very last minute. While they carted away the assets of the city, the security police murdered prisoners and hostages in droves, actually stepping up operations after the Inchon landing. In Taejon alone, General Walker's advance came on mass graves of some 7,000 freshly slain South Korean civilians, as well as 40 American prisoners. It was a commonplace during the Inchon-Seoul campaign for troops to discover scenes of mass murder. As of October 31, 1950, the United Nations Command had compiled war-crimes statistics involving a total of some 26,000 murders by the Communists in South Korea.[14]

Cannae

Down at Green Beach, on Wolmi Do, today stands the only battle monument erected by Americans. Each year on September 15 (for the Koreans do not forget) delegations visit the impressive concrete cenotaph with its bronze plaque to lay wreaths in memory of those who landed at Inchon. The wording of the plaque is simple. It says that here the leading elements of the 7th U. S. Infantry Division landed at Inchon in September (no date) 1950. Inexplicably, the 3d Battalion, 5th Marines, whose leading elements landed in assault at this spot at 0633, September 15, 1950, are neither mentioned nor memorialized.

The revisionism implicit in this monument quite aptly bespeaks the larger camouflage of revisionism with which history has draped the conquest of Inchon and the liberation of Seoul. It is curious that so dazzling and decisive a victory—a master stroke, really—should be already near forgotten or, when remembered, remembered in a haze of inaccuracy.

Inchon, for example, has been touted as a triumph of Armed Forces unification. Even the official Marine Corps historians felt it necessary to conclude their work with these fulsome words:

The victory was not won by any one nation or any one branch of the military service. . . . The Inchon-Seoul operation was conducted jointly by the United States Army, Navy, Air Force, and Marine Corps.

President Truman—never mentioning the Marine Corps, let alone Generals Shepherd or Smith—attributed victory to "the splendid cooperation of our Army, Navy, and Air Force," specifically singling out General Walker, Admiral Joy and General Stratemeyer for Presidential "thanks and congratulations."[15] One can imagine the feelings of Struble, Doyle and Almond, to name but three, when this commendation was published by the White House.

The truth is, the fact of unification was virtually irrelevant at Inchon, and very nearly so for the rest of the campaign. As Admiral Doyle, supreme realist, pointed out in his action report, Inchon was only possible and was only accomplished because of the expertise, experience and knowledge acquired by the U. S. Navy and Marine Corps during the Pacific War. After summarizing the difficulties (and who could have known them better?), Doyle concluded: "The successful assault on Inchon could have been accomplished only by United States Marines."[16] MacArthur's equally realistic view is clearly recorded in his D-day signal, "Navy and Marines have never shone more brightly. . . ."

Another sort of revisionism which Inchon evokes is a tendency to downgrade this campaign as a kind of freak—an operation that shouldn't have succeeded but did. Was *Chromite* somehow unworthy because closely calculated long odds paid off? Taking MacArthur's hyperbole of August 23 that the odds against success were 5,000 to 1, writers who should know better have used this figure of speech as a serious basis for saying that Inchon was a mere gamble and next to foolhardy at that.[17] How much wiser, instead of meaningless quantifications like 5,000 to 1, to view the operation with Doyle's informed conservatism as "not impossible." Speaking to somewhat the same point, O. P. Smith later remarked: "We had a break at Inchon, all right—we had the know-how."[18]

An indication of the tendency to downgrade Inchon—and no doubt of the state of inter-Service relations at the time—is the fact that, despite generous awards of unit citations to comparable Army formations during the Korean War, the Department of the Army withheld its Distinguished Unit Citation from the 1st Marine Division for what history must record as one of the finest accomplishments in the annals of American arms. After it became clear that the failure of the Army to award its Distinguished Unit Citation to the Marine division was, in O. P. Smith's words, "not accidental," the Navy Department in 1951 issued the Navy's Presidential Unit Citation to the Marines for Inchon-Seoul, even though they had been under Army command. Ironically, the 32d Infantry, the 96th Field Artillery Battalion, and other Army units bear the streamer of the Navy's highest collective decoration on their colors because they were at one time or another attached to the Marines during a memorable campaign their own Service would not recognize.[19]

Other revisionists seem to feel that the Inchon-Seoul campaign just shouldn't have happened.

Voicing a dogmatic view no doubt akin to General Bradley's—that amphibious warfare was superannuated and passé—General O. P. Weyland of the Air Force said of Inchon, "Its actual effects were quite secondary to the air attacks in the destruction of the NKPA. . . . The new forces might have been introduced to better advantage at Pusan."[20]

While not, so far as is known, very much advanced in print, a some-what comparable, equally revisionistic thesis is often expressed (mainly by those with Eighth Army associations) that Inchon was simply a "grand-stand play." Like General Weyland's, this viewpoint says that the re-sources of X Corps, if given to General Walker in the perimeter, would have won as great a triumph. In all likelihood, this attitude draws sustenance from the rightful resentment of the Eighth Army (and of General Walker while he lived) over the staff manipulations which kept Almond and X Corps outside of Walker's command while under his second hat as CINCFE chief of staff, Almond (who had no love for Walker, or vice versa) never hesitated to impose his will on Eighth Army. Disregarding its undoubted underlying emotional bias, this contention, highly speculative and hypothetical, is, to say the least, not strongly sup-ported by the sluggish eventual transition to the offensive by Walker's 140,000 troops against an encircling army numbering but 70,000.

Finally, in a process of guilt by association, other revisionists have seen *Chromite,* for all its strategic éclat, effaced because it didn't win the Korean War after all; and somehow discredited in Douglas MacArthur's later, unrelated discredit over having misjudged the Chinese.

Inchon refuses to be brushed aside by history not merely because of its military brilliance, but also because it upset or reversed so much— the tide of the war, Communist hopes for smash-and-grab conquest, the drooping pennon of American arms. In smashing the North Korean

Peoples Army, Inchon achieved our original war aim, the defensive one of forestalling invasion. Moreover, it revindicated amphibious assault (and, more fundamentally, maritime strategy) as a modern technique of war. In so doing, it almost unquestionably averted abolition of the U. S. Marine Corps and naval aviation.

More broadly than any of the foregoing, this campaign had two ultimate effects.

First, from this moment forward, the Communist world—then still a menacing, monolithic bloc—never again initially resorted to naked invasion as a means of changing the world balance of power.

Second, by underscoring the need for effective capabilities in the real war of limited objectives ceaselessly in issue between the two systems, Inchon awakened the United States from illusory, almost hypnotic, pre-occupation with hypothetical nuclear holocaust—the so-called "Third World War" which today seems less likely than ever. In Inchon-Seoul may be seen the seeds of John F. Kennedy's insistence (shared by Robert S. McNamara) that American arms be prepared not merely to maintain the shield of nuclear deterrence but, protected by that shield, to wage limited war—the war which, as Liddell-Hart, George Kennan and Robert McClintock point out, is the only kind that makes sense today.

Inchon must be considered a masterpiece. Whether in superb virtuosity of execution or, at the chill altitude of high command, as a Napoleonic example of nerve and acceptance of calculated risk, it remains, in the words of David Rees, "a Twentieth-Century Cannae, ever to be studied."[21]

Of the general who at Inchon equaled Hannibal, Alfred Thayer Mahan might well have been thinking when he listed as the greatest attribute of high command:[22]

> That exclusiveness of purpose which is the essence of strategy, and which subordinates, adjusts, all other factors and considerations to the one exclusive aim.

Surely this passage characterizes Douglas MacArthur's unwavering sense of the objective (after all, the dominant principle of war), his unrelenting pressure in gathering the necessary forces, his unremitting insistence on speed in execution. But for all three, Operation *Chromite* could never have succeeded. But neither could it have succeeded without Doyle, O. P. Smith, and the forces and the expertise they made uniquely available. It is sometimes said that MacArthur "conceived, planned, and executed" the great stroke at Inchon. Certainly MacArthur conceived and planned Inchon, and resolutely defended it against all comers, and in this lies his glory; but Inchon could never have been anything but a concept without James H. Doyle and Oliver P. Smith. They executed it.

Did he but know it when he stepped down from the dais in Seoul's National Assembly, Douglas MacArthur's finest hour had run. Inchon-Seoul, MacArthur's greatest feat of generalship, was also his last victory. Yet in this mellow, clear victorious autumn sunset, history sees the flawless, untarnished MacArthur as he would wish to be remembered. At Inchon, MacArthur was bold, judicious, assured and unwavering. Those who doubted his judgment—the lesser men who wanted to play things safe—exemplified the reverse.

The irony of MacArthur's masterpiece was that it bore the seeds of his downfall. After he, alone, prevailed over doubters domestic among his own staff, doubters expert of the Navy and Marines, doubters exalted on the Joint Chiefs of Staff, he became untouchable. Swathed in the mantle of infallibility won at Inchon, MacArthur was foredoomed to fall with the rapidity and the magnificence and the finality of Lucifer.

On September 27, with the approval of President Truman, the Joint Chiefs of Staff authorized General MacArthur to pursue operations north of the 38th parallel. On October 1, ROK infantry, advancing up the east coast, crossed the line. Six days later patrols of the 1st Cavalry Division probed across in the west, approaching Kaesong in late afternoon.

No one yet knew that Red China had determined that the crossing of the 38th parallel by U. S. troops—made possible by Inchon—was the contingency which would precipitate Chinese intervention in Korea. On October 28, when Shepherd visited General MacArthur in Tokyo, the General said he expected the war to be over in a month and the troops would be home by Christmas.

NOTES

Chapter 1

1. White, William S., New York *Times,* October 20, 1949. The *Times* of that date gives the full text of General Bradley's statement. I was among those present on this occasion.
2. *Unification and Strategy,* report by the House Armed Services Committee, March 1, 1950, p. 6.
3. The quotations from Generals Marshall and Wedemeyer are from Morison, S. E., *History of the American People* (New York, Oxford University Press, 1965), pp. 1052 and 1061.
4. For a balanced general summary of the unification controversies, see Millis, Walter, *Arms and the State* (New York, Twentieth Century Fund, 1958), Chapters 4-6. As unification particularly affected the Navy and Marine Corps, see Heinl, R. D., Jr., *Soldiers of the Sea* (Annapolis, U. S. Naval Institute, 1962), Chapter 9. By the same author, see also "The Right to Fight," U. S. Naval Institute *Proceedings,* September 1962. The texts of official proposals by the Chiefs of Staff, U. S. Army, and U. S. Air Force, for abolition and crippling of naval aviation and the Marine Corps are given in House Report No. 961, Committee on Expenditures in the Executive Departments, on H.R. 4214, 1st Session, 80th Congress. The ". . . damned wardroom" quotation ascribed to President Truman was given me in March 1947 by Brigadier General M. A. Edson.
5. Information on the Truman/Johnson FY 50 budget and its implications may be found in Millis, *Arms and the State,* pp. 283ff., and in Heinl, *Soldiers of the Sea,* p. 526. Figures on amphibious shipping and craft are from the Basic Naval Establishment Plans (BNEP) of the Chief of Naval Operations, 1947–1951 inclusive (Office of Naval History, Washington). For details on the "Revolt of the Admirals," see *Unification and Strategy Hearings,* op. cit. The officially recorded details of Admiral Denfeld's dismissal as CNO are found in Navy Secretary Francis P. Matthews's letter to the President, October 27, 1949, and President Truman's memorandum of approval, same date (both in Office of Naval History, Washington). The Johnson-Conolly quotation comes to me from a primary source who cannot for the present be identified.
6. Statement by Douglas MacArthur to JCS representatives, Tokyo, August 23, 1950, quoted in Karig, Captain Walter; Cagle, Commander Malcolm W.; and Manson, Commander Frank A., *Battle Report: The War in Korea* (New York, Rinehart, 1952), p. 168. Also see notes 39–42, Chapter 2.
7. For details on deployment and operations of Mobile Training Team A and Amphibious Group 1 in the Far East, I have relied on my interviews with Vice-Admiral James H. Doyle, July 31–August 1, 1966; report by Commander Amphibious Group 1 (ComPhibGrp 1) to Commander-in-Chief Pacific Fleet (CinCPacFlt), February 9, 1951; and memorandum notes by Commander J. V. Noel, staff PhibGrp 1 (both documents in Office of Naval History, Washington). Admiral Doyle's account of his conversations with Bradley and Mac-Arthur is given in his comments on the initial draft of this history.

8. Truman, Harry S., *Years of Trial and Hope* (Garden City, N.Y., Doubleday, 1956), p. 330.
9. Far East Command (FECOM) *History of the North Korean Army,* 1952 (in Office of the Chief of Military History [OCMH]); *North Korea: A Case Study in the Techniques of Takeover,* State Department Publication 7118 (Washington, Government Printing Office, 1961), pp. 17, 85–86, and 117.

Chapter 2

1. *Military Situation in the Far East,* hearings, Joint Senate Committees on Armed Services and Foreign Relations, 1st Session, 82d Congress, p. 231 (hereinafter cited as *MacArthur Hearings*).
2. The time differential between Washington, D.C., and Korea is 14 hours. Sunday noon in Korea is 10 P.M. the previous date in Washington, as dates go forward one day when one crosses the international date line going westward. Dates and times given herein are those of local events described.
3. Cates, General Clifton B., unpublished *Record of Events, 25 June–17 August, 1950,* kindly furnished by General Cates for use in this work.
4. *Ibid.*
5. *Ibid.* "Joy" was MacArthur's naval component commander, Vice-Admiral C. Turner Joy. "Blue Flag" was the term for a type of private message transmitted between senior commanders in the Navy. Interview with General Cates, March 10, 1966.
6. Sherman's action on Cates's recommendation began on July 1 with a message to Admiral Radford, commanding the Pacific Fleet, in effect double-checking Cates's offer. When Radford confirmed that Fleet Marine Force units could indeed be provided, Sherman on July 2 finally communicated with Joy in the Far East. Messages cited are in the Office of Naval History, and the sequence of events is given and commented on in Cates, *Record of Events.*
7. Commander-in-Chief Far East (CINCFE) message to Chief of Naval Operations (CNO), July 2, 1950.
8. Historical report, Commander Amphibious Group 1 (ComPhibGrp 1) to Pacific Fleet Evaluation Group, January 17, 1951 (Annex AA to Volume XV, Interim Evaluation Report #1, on Korean War Operations), in Office of Naval History. The plans officer's remark is in Cagle, Commander Malcolm W.; and Manson, Commander Frank A., *The Sea War in Korea* (Annapolis, U. S. Naval Institute, 1957), p. 42.
9. Cates, *Record of Events* and interview, March 10, 1966. The approval of MacArthur's request is found in JCS message to CINCFE, July 3, 1950. Some accounts give this JCS meeting as July 2. In this, as in other discrepancies of dates, I rely on contemporary entries, such as the Cates *Record of Events* and the journals kept by other participants.
10. Shepherd, General Lemuel C., Jr., unpublished *Journal, 2 July–16 December, 1950,* kindly made available by General Shepherd.
11. Interview with Admiral Arthur D. Struble, March 17, 1966.
12. Truman, *Years of Trial and Hope,* p. 347.
13. This interview is reconstructed from Shepherd *Journal* and from my interviews with General Shepherd in 1958 and on July 27, 1966; also from interview with Lieutenant General V. H. Krulak, September 15, 1965, and from the latter's address to the Naval Historical Foundation, January 30, 1958.
14. Struble interview.

15. Willoughby, Major General Charles A., *MacArthur* (New York, McGraw-Hill, 1954), p. 367, attributes to General Almond a statement that MacArthur's request for Marines "met a cool reception" from General Collins (apparently inferring that the Army didn't want Marines committed), but General Collins, during my interview of March 30, 1966, said he had "utterly no recollection" of any such reaction. Collins's private assurance to MacArthur at the last is found in Schnable, Lieutenant Colonel James F., "The Inchon Landing," *Army,* May 1959, and confirmed in Marine Corps Board Study, *Evaluation of the Influence of Marine Corps Forces on the Course of the Korean War,* August 4, 1952, p. I-B-3 (in Marine Corps Historical Branch). Admiral Radford's account of the July 13 meeting and dialogue is derived from my interview of March 24, 1966.

16. Undated memorandum from General Shepherd to Admiral Radford, reporting on Tokyo trip.

17. Shepherd interview, July 27, 1966.

18. Interview with Lieutenant General Edward A. Craig, May 8, 1951 (in Marine Corps Historical Branch).

19. Cates, *Record of Events*. Also see articles by David Lawrence, New York *Herald-Tribune,* July 3, 7, 11, and 21, and August 15, 18, and 21, 1950.

20. CINCFE message to JCS, July 21, 1950. In a memorandum to the JCS, July 24, 1950, Admiral Sherman said that, if a two-RCT Marine division were formed for Korea, the only remaining Marine tactical units left would be one BLT (battalion landing team) in the 2d Marine Division, and one with the 6th Fleet. In his interview with me, Admiral Radford remarked, "Marine Corps Headquarters had to be given an awful shove to accept a readiness date earlier than November." But, he added, they did a fine job getting the division organized, and at great cost to the rest of the Corps.

21. CINCFE message to JCS, July 23, 1950.

22. Note that this decision meant that the Marine division would still have only two, rather than the normal three, infantry regiments and their supporting troops (i.e., the 5th Marines, already in Korea, and one regimental combat team to be mobilized, the 1st Marines). On August 1, 1950, the JCS gave still further ground and allowed a third regimental combat team, the 7th Marines, to be formed to sail for the Far East not later than September 1, 1950. Cates, *Record of Events*. See p. 37 and note 33, below.

23. The Capps remark is in Karig et al., *The War in Korea,* p. 161. That by Commander Kelly is in Manson and Cagle, *Sea War in Korea,* p. 81.

24. This description of Inchon is based on the intelligence annexes and action reports by Commander, Joint Task Force 7 (CJTF-7) and ComPhibGrp 1, for the Inchon operation (in Office of Naval History); on H.O. 97, *Sailing Directions, Southeast Coast of Siberia and Korea,* 2d edition, 1951; and on my own reconnaissance ashore and afloat in September and October, 1965.

25. Karig et al., *War in Korea,* p. 193. The correct name of the channel above Palmi Do is the Salee River, well known to those who have studied our 1871 landings in Korea.

26. Struble interview. A "ground," as distinct from a moored, mine is one which rests on the bottom of a shallow channel or harbor. Almond's remark is quoted in Karig et al., *War in Korea,* p. 165.

27. The North Korean order of battle is taken from the intelligence annex, special action report (SAR), 1st Marine Division, May 2, 1951. Information on status of enemy defenses and preparations from the same source and from action report (AR), ComPhibGrp 1, October 22, 1950, both documents in Office of Naval History.

28. CJTF-7 Operation Plan 9-50 (Intelligence Annex), September 3, 1950 (in Office of Naval History).
29. Schnable, *The Inchon Landing* (interview Schnable/Major General Wright, December 1951). Collins interview. Comments by Major General Edwin K. Wright on draft of this history, April 7, 1967. Of the Kunsan version General O. P. Smith later commented: "This alternate plan was really a cover plan. I don't think there ever was any intention to land there. Possibly the intention was to leak information about the Kunsan landing in the hope of deceiving the enemy." Memorandum, May 16, 1951, in Marine Corps Historical Branch.
30. Struble interview.
31. The best and most concise analysis of the tidal problem and its military implications is in 1stMarDiv SAR, p. 12. The quotation by Colonel Bowser is from his comments on the draft of this history, January 12, 1967.
32. Pacific Fleet Interim Evaluation Report #1, Annex Z to Volume XV, in Office of Naval History.
33. Shepherd *Journal,* quoting General Cates, August 14, 1950. Giving support and impetus to the efforts of the two Marine generals to get the Marine division its third infantry regiment, MacArthur, in a teleconic conference with the JCS on July 24, 1950, said, "I regard the third RCT as essential."
34. Remark given me in August 1950 by Colonel Harry N. Shea, then on duty in the Office of the Chief of Naval Operations. The "Schools Troops" were (and are) a training and demonstration unit maintained at Marine Corps Schools, Quantico. An alternate function for such schools units is to provide a reserve for extreme contingencies.
35. A forward echelon of the division staff, including the operations and intelligence officers, had flown to Tokyo on August 16. The complete echelonment of General Smith's headquarters for movement to Japan is given in Smith, Oliver P., unpublished *Aide-Mémoire, Korea,* 1950–51, p. 38 (in Marine Corps Historical Branch).
36. *MacArthur Hearings,* p. 1295.
37. Radford interview.
38. Collins interview.
39. Struble interview. Some question has been raised as to whether Sherman saw Struble before or after the August 23 conference, or both. Careful reconciliation of Sherman's and Struble's movements from the log, USS *Rochester,* August, 1950; from 7th Fleet War Diary (WD), August, 1950; and from Shepherd *Journal* makes it clear that the only personal meeting which could have taken place between the two was aboard *Rochester,* in Sasebo Wan, on August 22, a conclusion which Admiral Struble accepts. The further question may be raised as to how—before MacArthur unveiled the Inchon concept (subsequently on August 23)—Sherman could have known enough about the operation, even after Doyle's briefing, to make up his mind. My conjecture, which cannot be satisfied until the Navy opens its "Blue Flag" files to historians, is that, using this highly private channel, Admiral Joy kept Sherman in the picture, as he did in other instances.
40. When queried on this point, General Almond wrote, "If General Shepherd was not present at the strategic conference on 23 August it was not through any design on the part of General MacArthur or anybody else. . . . As far as General Smith's being present is concerned, General Smith had many duties. . . . The fact that he was not at the conference on 23 August may have been a matter of his availability. After all, General Smith was not required at this conference . . . General Smith's function as landing force commander was that of carrying

out the decision of the overall commander." Letter to author, August 31, 1966. The quotation from General Shepherd is from Shepherd interview, July 27, 1966.'

41. Considerable historical conflict exists as to exactly what took place at this conference and who attended. The usually meticulous official history of the Army—Appleman, Lieutenant Colonel Roy E., *South to the Naktong, North to the Yalu* (Washington, Government Printing Office, 1960)—consistently misdates it by a month, as having taken place on July 23. My account of the conference and preliminaries is synthesized from interviews with Admirals Radford and Doyle and General Collins (all participants), from Admiral Doyle's comments on initial draft of this history, from his letter to me of October 26, 1966. My list of participants is a composite based on the primary sources mentioned, together with the logs annd war diaries, USS *Rochester,* and Commander 7th Fleet, and General Shepherd's *Journal* (not a participant, he was nonetheless in Tokyo and, like O. P. Smith, conferred intimately and almost continuously with the naval participants in the MacArthur conference). In addition, varying lists of participants appear in MacArthur, General of the Army Douglas, *Reminiscences* (New York, McGraw-Hill, 1964); Montress, Lynn, and Canzona, Captain Nicholas A., *The Inchon-Seoul Operation* (Washington, Government Printing Office, 1955); Karig et al., *War in Korea;* and the various MacArthur books. Montross and Canzona are most nearly correct. Although most accounts say Struble and Shepherd attended, the former was in Sasebo and the latter was not invited. Sherman as "lukewarm" is found in Willoughby, *MacArthur,* p. 372. The Collins quotation is from my interview, *op. cit.* "Spoken like a Farragut" is from Admiral Doyle's letter of October 26, 1966. In his comments on the draft of this history, General Wright says, "I do not remember and I cannot imagine" (any remark by MacArthur about withdrawal). On the other hand, Admiral Doyle, a principal in the exchange, recalls the words and circumstances clearly.

42. My summary of MacArthur's speech is based in part on his own version *(Reminiscences,* pp. 349-50), where Sherman's "Thank you . . ." appears; and on all sources given in note 41 above. The final ". . . that man's optimism" was attributed to Sherman by Admiral Joy in correspondence cited in Cagle and Manson, *Sea War in Korea,* p. 76.

43. Smith, Major General Oliver P., unpublished *Log, Korea 1950–51* (in Marine Corps Historical Branch and, together with General Smith's *Aide-Mémoire,* kindly made available for use in this history). Also Shepherd *Journal* and Wright comments, *op. cit.*

44. Shepherd's conferences with Almond and MacArthur are covered in detail in Shepherd *Journal.* Further information has been provided in Lieutenant General V. H. Krulak's letter to author, February 14, 1967.

45. JCS message to CINCFE, August 28, 1952. My account of the Sherman-Collins homecoming is based on a revealing series of official photographs taken at National Airport, now in the Army Photographic Center, Washington. "Nothing extraordinary" from "Pentagon spokesmen" first appears in the New York *Times,* August 19, 1950.

46. Smith's initial meetings with Doyle, Almond, and MacArthur are fully described in Smith *Log* for this date. (In future citations of this source, entries will be assumed to be for the date of related-events unless otherwise stated.)

47. Smith *Log.* Admiral Doyle's judgment of the X Corps staff is in letter ComPhibGrp 1 to Commander-in-Chief Pacific Fleet (CinCPacFlt), February 9, 1951, in Office of Naval History. With regard to the problem of bridging the Han, General Almond states (letter to General C. L. Ruffner, January 13, 1967)

that, during the planning, he instructed the Corps Engineer to take steps to bridge the Han into Seoul "at the earliest practical moment *after its capture*" and to have the requisite bridging material "available for his purpose within a period of *ten days after the landing*" (italics supplied). This statement suggests that the Corps Commander never intended to have the Han bridged until Seoul was taken, and in any case not earlier than D+10 (September 25). If these were in fact General Almond's intentions, they were not clear to General Smith and his staff, who recorded assurances from Almond and his engineer that the Han would be bridged in time to support the assault units attacking north of the river. See Chapter 7, p. 191.

48. Smith *Aide-Mémoire*, p. 52.

49. Not least among Inchon's complications and handicaps was the three-way split of General Smith's staff. At no time until battle did he have the 1st Marine Division headquarters in one place. When the brigade left for Korea in July, it took a generous share (too generous, some felt) of the existing division staff at Camp Pendleton; these could not rejoin division headquarters until Inchon itself and, having their own war to fight in the Pusan perimeter, were of limited use in the Inchon planning. As we have seen (note 35, above) the staff was divided for movement to Japan; even when these echelons reunited, another split became necessary. The tight mounting-out schedule of the division's units at Kobe demanded a staff group at the port, remote from Tokyo. *Ibid.*, pp. 54–55.

50. In his comments on the initial draft of this history, Admiral Doyle attributes the radical scheme of bringing in the LSTs during the assault to Lieutenant Colonel William E. Benedict, USMC, of his staff. He says his first thoughts were of the hazards if the assault should be thrown back, but he quickly approved because, in his words, "I had the utmost confidence in the Marines. In my book, they could not fail." Information on the ex-USN Japanese LSTs is from General Wright's comments on the draft of this history.

51. Smith *Aide-Mémoire*, pp. 98–100. The quotation about the regimental commanders' reactions is from comments by Lieutenant General A. L. Bowser on the draft of this history, January 12, 1967.

52. Although the title "Joint Task Force 7" first appears in Admiral Joy's (ComNavFE) Operation Plan 108-50, August 20, 1950 (in Office of Naval History)—a date which antedates Admiral Struble's assignment to command, or even knowledge of, the *Chromite* operation—Admiral Struble asserts flatly that he originated the "Joint Task Force 7" designation. He writes:

> The ComNavFE order establishing JTF-7 was *not* issued on August 20 or anywhere near that date. As I previously stated, I decided on the term, "Joint Task Force Seven," and communicated it to Joy orally and he accepted it. The date would have been about 27 August.

53. General Smith commented (*Aide-Mémoire*, pp. 46–47):

> Although the relationship between the 1st Marine Division, as Landing Force, and PhibGruOne, as Attack Force, was clear from the outset and in accordance with USF [i.e., standard Navy/Marine] doctrine, the command status and command responsibilities of the assault landing phase of the CG X Corps, CJTF-7, and ComNavFE were vague and confusing. None of the latter commands ever appeared under well-defined titles, and none of the accepted titles which would have been appropriate to these echelons were used.

In comments on the draft of this history, Admiral Struble justified the departures from naval terminology and doctrine complained of by General Smith on the grounds that the Army and Air Force had not in 1950 officially accepted or recognized "the so-called Navy/Marine doctrines, terminology and command echelons." Curiously, however, Admiral Struble's Inchon plan (CJTF-7 Operation Plan 9-50, in Office of Naval History) expressly prescribes (paragraph 3.(x)(3)): "The doctrine contained in USF 6, USF 63, and USF 66 will govern . . . the amphibious operations." This portion of the order obviously was never enforced, and, from Admiral Struble's comment about throwing the book away, would not seem to have been intended to be.

54. Struble interview.
55. Appleman, *South to the Naktong*, p. 503n, gives the X Corps troop list an aggregate strength of 69,450 officers and men but omits the Tactical Air Command (1st Marine Aircraft Wing) whose strength ashore was 1,889 (SAR, Tactical Air Command, Annex A, November 10, 1950). By adding the aviators I arrive at 71,339.
56. Schnable, *The Inchon Landing;* Appleman, *South to the Naktong*, p. 490, citing interview with Almond, December 13, 1951; Montross and Canzona, *The Inchon-Seoul Operation*, p. 43; and Almond letter to author, August 31, 1966. To compensate, at least in part, for X Corps's obvious lack of amphibious background, Colonel Forney was designated Deputy Chief of Staff, and 12 Marine officers plus a number of enlisted Marines were assigned to the key staff sections of G-2, G-3, G-4, Communications, and Fire Support Coordination. Although unvoiced in official records of the transaction, there can be little doubt that an important—possibly decisive—factor in the decision to improvise X Corps rather than rely on FMFPac was the Army's standing policy (dating from the Saipan controversy of 1944) never to permit Army divisions to serve under Marine command. Still in force as of 1967, this policy has fortunately never been reciprocated by the Marine Corps, whose divisions have frequently served in Army corps.
57. Interview with Major General David G. Barr, USA (ret), October 12, 1966; Appleman, *South to the Naktong*, p. 492.
58. Smith interview.
59. Wright comments, *op. cit.* In this account General Wright says, "One evening in mid-August, while working on a new draft of the basic plan . . . I took a compass and, placing the point in the center of the landing area, described an arc. . . . I labeled the area inside this arc 'Objective Area' and made a map note that the area was excluded to all but naval and Marine aircraft. This map was presented to the Chief of Staff and C-in-C (MacArthur) and was approved."
60. Struble interview; letters to me from Admiral Struble, September 3 and October 28, 1966. Bowser comments, January 12, 1967.
61. This is my own target count and target analysis based on overlay of enemy installations as of August 30, 1950, given in the intelligence annexes of 1st Marine Division and Amphibious Group 1 operation plans for Inchon.
62. Smith interview; Smith *Aide-Mémoire*, pp. 72–74; Struble interview and letters of September 3 and October 28, 1966; Bowser comments, January 12, 1967.
63. Smith interview and *Aide-Mémoire*, pp. 89–94; Montross and Canzona, *The Inchon-Seoul Operation*, pp. 77–78.
64. Smith *Aide-Mémoire*, p. 76.
65. Smith *Log*, September 3, 1950; Struble interview and letter of September 3, 1966.
66. Texts of the exchange of messages between MacArthur and the JCS (differing in detail, no doubt due to paraphrase) appear in MacArthur, *Reminiscences*, pp.

351–352, and Appleman, *South to the Naktong,* p. 495. General Collins told me that "the President was very much interested in the operation" and had General Bradley keep him up to date on all developments. General Collins dismissed Louis Johnson's assertions (during the MacArthur hearings) to the effect that he, Johnson, had played a leading role in "carrying, along with General Mac-Arthur, the responsibility for Inchon."

Chapter 3

1. War Diary (WD), FNS *La Grandière,* July 29–November 24, 1950, as translated by French Naval Attaché, Washington (in Office of Naval History).
2. Report of Proceedings (ROP) Flag Officer Second-in-Command, Far East, No. 1, June 25–July 9, 1950.
3. Log and WD, USS *Hanson,* September 9, 1950. When *Hanson* came to their rescue, Clark and his Army officer companion declined to give their names or any identifying information, even to *Hanson's* captain, except to state that they were on a mission with South Korean nationals ashore. The quotation given here (and other quotations attributed to Clark) is from Karig et al., *War in Korea,* pp. 176–189, a source which should be accepted with reservation on this operation.
4. This account of the Clark expedition, which differs in many particulars from those so far published, has been reconstructed from the log and WD, USS *Hanson;* from Field, James A., Jr., *History of U. S. Naval Operations, Korea* (Washington, Government Printing Office, 1962), pp. 183–185; Willoughby, *MacArthur,* p. 372, which discloses both the code name and the fact of CIA involvement; and from Karig et al., *The War in Korea.* The somewhat fanciful accounts given in the last source and in the Marine Corps official history can doubtless be attributed to security considerations, as can the unavailability to date of the identity of Clark's Army teammate. Conceivably this "officer" may even have been an intelligence agent operating under cover of fictitious military status. My attempts to obtain further or firsthand information from Commander Clark in 1966 proved unavailing.
5. Sources for this section, unless otherwise noted, are AR, ComPhibGrp 1, and Smith. *Log* and *Aide-Mémoire.*
6. Interview with Commander C. E. Breen, September 15, 1965 (Breen was assistant communications officer, USS *Boxer,* in 1950).
7. CJTF-7 AR, Annex M, supplemented by interview with Commander Merle MacBain, who was CJTF-7 Information Officer. Because of her sex it was originally intended that Miss Higgins would cover Inchon from the hospital ship which, with its complement of Navy nurses, had "facilities" for the one lady correspondent. This arrangement was in no way to Miss Higgins's liking and, when protest proved unavailing, she hitchhiked from Japan to Pusan and talked her way on board one of the 5th Marines' attack transports, thus insuring that she would cover the initial assault (while many competitors, assigned by Army PIOs to X Corps and 7th Division ships, chafed afloat). Higgins, Marguerite, *War in Korea* (New York, Doubleday, 1951), pp. 136–139.
8. Interview with Brigadier General Joseph L. Stewart, February 1966. Craig interview (in Marine Corps Historical Branch). Comments by Major General R. L. Murray on draft of this history. In addition to absorbing replacements, each battalion got a third rifle company, thus bringing the regiment to war strength.

9. Smith *Log,* September 9, 1960.
10. Sources for the trip from Tokyo to Sasebo are Shepherd *Journal,* interview with Howard Handleman, September 28, 1966, Wright comments, and Carl Mydans's account in *Time* magazine, September 25, 1950.
11. Doyle interview and comments on the draft of this history; Smith *Log* and *Aide-Mémoire,* pp. 128–129; Krulak to Naval Historical Foundation, *op. cit.* In his comments, General Bowser says, "As G-3 of the landing force, I was required to move from a stateroom, which included an office and good communications, to a single bunk two decks below, with absolutely no facilities in which to carry out my duties."
12. Smith *Log,* and interview with Howard Handleman, September 28, 1966.
13. Although similar remarks are attributed to Colonel Puller on D-day in his biography (Davis, Burke, *Marine!* Boston, Little, Brown, & Co., 1962, p. 252), Brigadier General Edwin H. Simmons (interview with author, January 14, 1967) vividly recalls the episode, circumstances, and wording given here.
14. SAR, Tactical Air Command, X Corps; and SAR, VMF-214 and 323 (all in Marine Corps Historical Branch).
15. Report by Commander Task Force 77 (CTF 77), "TF 77 Operations During the Korean Campaign," Volume 1, March 19, 1951 (in Office of Naval History).
16. Field, *Naval Operations, Korea,* pp. 183–189.
17. *Ibid.,* p. 190; WD, USS *McKean,* September 1950; Commander Mine Squadron 3 letter to CNO, March 10, 1951 (in Office of Naval History).
18. AR, Commander Cruiser Division 5, November 5, 1950.
19. Interview with Captain Oscar B. Lundgren, USN, November 11, 1965.
20. Quoted in Karig et al., *The Korean War,* p. 202.
21. Lundgren interview. In comments on the draft of this history, July 7, 1966, Captain Lundgren recalls the gun on which *DeHaven* opened fire as being on the northwest side of Wolmi Do, but the coordinates given in the ship's action report place the gun as stated in the text.
22. Sources for my account of the D−2/D−1 bombardment are the ARs, ComCruDiv 5, USS *Toledo, Rochester, Mansfield, DeHaven, Lyman K. Swenson, Collett,* and *Gurke;* the dispatch operational summary of CJTF-7, and Lundgren interview (all in Office of Naval History). In addition, the Los Angeles *Times,* September 17, 1950, has a vivid account by Relman Morin of the D−1 action as observed from *Rochester.*
23. Struble interview.
24. Karig et al., *The Korean War,* p. 210.
25. *Ibid.*

Chapter 4

1. Doyle interview; Smith *Log;* Shepherd *Journal.*
2. AR, Commander Rocket Division 11, September 27, 1950 (in Office of Naval History).
3. Although I have found no official record of this, Lieutenant Colonel Park Bong-Son, KMC, told me in 1965 that Captain Kim, the senior harbor pilot of Inchon, was smuggled out and helped to pilot the attack force up to Inchon.
4. This account of the Advance Attack Group's movement up to Inchon is derived from the AR, Commander Transport Division 111, September 29, 1950; of Commander Rocket Division 11; Lundgren interview; ARs of the individual ships; and H.O. 97, *Sailing Directions.*
5. Ibid., as well as ComPhibGrp 1 Operation Order 15-50, September 3, 1950; AR,

ComPhibGrp 1 (CTF 90); and NWIP 22-6, *Ship to Shore Movement,* USN (all in Office of Naval History).

6. SAR, 3d Battalion, 5th Marines, August 30–October 6, 1950; Montross and Canzona, *The Inchon-Seoul Operation,* pp. 87–92; Geer, Andrew C., *The New Breed* (New York, Harpers, 1952), pp. 123–125. In this, as in all subsequent accounts of ground action, I have based my description on reconnaissance of the ground in 1965.

7. Doyle interview, Shepherd *Journal,* and Montross and Canzona, *The Inchon-Seoul Operation,* p. 90. Some accounts say that MacArthur's message was written after going below, but Admiral Doyle vividly recalls taking it down while the General was still on the bridge. After some delay Admiral Struble answered MacArthur's compliment to the Navy and Marines by a message attributing the success of the landing to "the combined efforts of the Army, the Air Force, and the Navy" (CITF-7 message, September 16, 1950). Among those who up to this time had done all fighting ashore and contributed a major share of the air effort, Struble's failure even to mention the Marine Corps seemed either puzzling or pointed and gave rise to comment even at senior levels.

8. SAR, 3d Battalion, 5th Marines; Shepherd *Journal.*

9. Sources for the capture of So Wolmi Do are the same as those given in note 6, *supra.*

10. MacArthur's trip in Admiral Struble's barge is described in Shepherd *Journal;* in Struble, Shepherd, Lundgren, and Handleman interviews (Mr. Handleman was one of the correspondents on the barge); and in Struble letter, October 27, 1966. An unfortunate and unfair side effect of General Shepherd's advice that it was not MacArthur's business to expose himself off Red Beach was a snide newspaper account suggesting that Shepherd—like MacArthur a lionhearted combat soldier—was worried over his own safety.

11. The butcheries perpetrated by the North Korean Security Police have been voluminously documented both in U. S. military archives and in the files of the United Nations, whose General Assembly passed a resolution of condemnation. The United Nations Command's Eighth Report (November 6, 1950) records war crimes resulting in the killing of some 26,000 South Korean civilians during the Communist occupation of the country.

12. Enemy surprise and reactions in Seoul were described to me in September 1965 by Lieutenant Colonel Park, KMC, who at this time was cut off and in hiding in the city.

13. AR, USS *Boxer,* September 14–October 5, 1950 (in Office of Naval History). Comments on draft of this history by Major General N. J. Anderson, July 25, 1966.

14. Marine Corps Historical Branch interview with Major M. J. Sexton, May 16, 1951.

15. Marine Corps Historical Branch interview with Captain F. I. Fenton, November 6, 1950.

16. In addition to the journalistic accounts by James Bell (*Time,* September 25, 1950) and Miss Higgins (*War in Korea,* Doubleday, New York, 1951, pp. 143–145), my sources for the Red Beach assault are: SAR, 1st Marine Division; action reports of all ships and units specifically mentioned; Montross and Canzona, *The Inchon-Seoul Operation,* pp. 102–108; Andrew Geer, *The New Breed,* Harper & Row, Publishers, Incorporated, pp. 125–126; NWIP 22-6, *op. cit.*; and letter, Captain F. F. Eubanks to Commandant of the Marine Corps (CMC), June 2, 1955, in Marine Corps Historical Branch.

17. A carefully compiled account of this episode is in Montross and Canzona, *The Inchon-Seoul Operation,* pp. 110–111. As seen through naval eyes, the LSTs' landing is vividly described in Karig et al., *The Korean War,* pp. 236–240. Individual reports from the respective LST (in Office of Naval History) are laconic on this phase of the operation.
18. New York *Herald Tribune,* September 17, 1950.
19. Fenton Historical Branch interview.
20. My sources for the capture of Observatory Hill are: SAR, 1st Marine Division; action reports of units specifically mentioned; Montross and Canzona, *The Inchon-Seoul Operation,* pp. 111–113; Geer, *The New Breed,* p. 127; and Fenton Historical Branch interview, and letter, March 21, 1951 (in Historical Branch).
21. Davis, Burke, *Marine!* (Boston, Little, Brown, & Co., 1962), p. 247; interview with Lieutenant General Lewis B. Puller, November 3, 1966.
22. As in all other cases where a terrain feature is hereinafter referred to by number, the number is its elevation in meters.
23. Smith *Log.*
24. Letter, Lieutenant Theodore B. Clark, USN, to CMC, March 11, 1955.
25. SAR, 1st Marines, January 6, 1951 (in Marine Corps Historical Branch).
26. *Ibid.;* Davis, *Marine!* p. 257.
27. Letter, Major Edwin H. Simmons to CMC, March 28, 1955 (in Marine Corps Historical Branch). The text given here differs, for reasons not clear, in material respects from that ascribed to Major Simmons in the official Marine Corps narrative (p. 116) citing the same source.
28. Letter, Lieutenant Colonel Jack Hawkins to CMC, March 8, 1955. Commenting afterward on this miscarriage, Commander C. E. Allmon, Blue Beach primary control officer, philosophically wrote (letter to CMC, March 9, 1955): "When the ramps went down, the Marines, being Marines, debarked in a hurry. The sailors, seeing their boats empty, and being sailors, retracted and headed seaward in a hurry."
29. This account of the Blue Beach ship-to-shore movement is based on SAR, 1st Marines; on letter, Major Robert P. Wray to CMC, April 23, 1955; letter, Lieutenant Colonel Jack Hawkins to CMC, March 8, 1955; holographic note by Colonel R. W. Rickert to CMC, April 15, 1955; letter, Major General L. B. Puller to Captain N. A. Canzona, May 11, 1955; letter, Admiral A. D. Struble to CMC, April 20, 1955—all the foregoing being in Marine Corps Historical Branch—on Montross and Canzona, *The Inchon-Seoul Operation,* pp. 113–122; Davis, *Marine!,* p. 257; and Puller interview.
30. AR, Rocket Division 11.
31. This account of Admiral Struble's trip to Blue Beach is based on Shepherd *Journal;* Struble interview and letter, October 27, 1966. The exact dialogue (of which differing versions are in print) was given me by an officer who was in the barge but asks to remain anonymous. Admiral Struble now recalls only that the NCO's admonition was "very forcibly put."
32. SAR, 11th Marines, November 26, 1950 (in Marine Corps Historical Branch).
33. Smith interview.
34. *Ibid.*
35. Shepherd *Journal.* In comments on the draft of this history, General Wright says of Doyle: ". . . A great commander, with somewhat of a genius for diplomacy. I spent a long time in the amphibious details of Operation *Torch* and *Overlord* without seeing his equal as an amphibious naval officer."

Chapter 5

1. SAR, Tactical Air Command (TAC) X Corps, notes that virtually all Marine aircraft shot down in this campaign fell victim to hits on oil coolers whose armor had been stripped for peacetime operations by order of Bureau of Aeronautics directives.

2. This account of the morning air operations is derived from SAR, 1st Marine Air Wing (MAW), Annex J, February 20, 1951 (in Marine Corps Historical Branch); and WD, USS *Sicily,* September, 1950 (in Office of Naval History).

3. Marine Corps Historical Branch interview with Lieutenant Colonel Charles H. Brush, April 19, 1951.

4. SAR, 1st Marines; Davis, *Marine!* p. 258.

5. Sleger, Second Lieutenant J., undated memorandum in Marine Corps Historical Branch. Montross and Canzona, *op. cit.,* say this action took place at 1335 but SAR, 1st Tank Battalion, November 20, 1950 (in Marine Corps Historical Branch), as well as Lieutenant Sleger, say 1000.

6. SARs of units mentioned; Montross and Canzona, *The Inchon-Seoul Operation,* pp. 136ff.; and Marine Corps Historical Branch interview with Major Kenneth Houghton, August 3, 1954.

7. Shepherd *Journal;* Smith *Log.*

8. SAR, 5th Marines; SAR, 1st Tank Battalion; Montross and Canzona, *The Inchon-Seoul Operation,* pp. 147ff.; comments on draft of this history by Brigadier General J. L. Stewart and by Colonel H. S. Roise.

9. Cates interview.

10. This account of MacArthur's inspection has mainly been synthesized from eyewitnesses: Smith *Log;* Shepherd *Journal;* Carl Mydans article in *Life,* October 2, 1950; and Krulak to Naval Historical Foundation. Except as otherwise indicated, dialogue from and concerning Colonel Puller is from Davis, *Marine!* p. 262, while the story of McNaughton's flushing out enemy troops from underneath MacArthur's parking place is in Marine Corps Historical Branch interview, January 7, 1955.

11. The issue of the relative merit (as seen through customers' eyes) of Navy-Marine vs. Air Force tactical air support systems and performance in Korea became so acute that, in order to avoid embarrassment, the Defense Department, never at a loss in suppressing or withholding information, sent strict instructions to Korea that the comparison was not to be discussed, or facts furnished even to Congressional inquiries if made in the theater. For facts on Louis Johnson's attempt to abolish Marine aviation, see Heinl, *Soldiers of the Sea,* p. 527.

12. Smith *Aide-Mémoire,* p. 202.

13. Cates interview.

14. This account of the advance on Kimpo is derived from SAR, 5th Marines; SAR, 1st Battalion, 5th Marines, and SAR, 2d Battalion, 5th Marines; and *Life* magazine, October 2, 1950, p. 32.

15. SAR, 3d Battalion, 5th Marines.

16. Montross and Canzona, *The Inchon-Seoul Operation,* pp. 158–159.

17. Pomeroy, Captain William D., memorandum, April 19, 1955, in Marine Corps Historical Division.

18. *Ibid.*

19. Shepherd *Journal* and interview, July 27, 1966.

20. This account of the night's action is reconstructed from SARs, 1st and 2d Battalions, 5th Marines; Pomeroy memorandum, *op. cit.;* undated memorandum

from Major Samuel Jaskilka in "Comments File, Korea, Vol. II," Marine Corps Historical Branch; and *Life,* October 2, 1950.

21. AR, USS *Rochester;* ROP, Flag Officer Second-in-Command, Far East, No. 6, March 20, 1951.

22. All information on helicopter operations and reactivation of Kimpo comes from SAR, TAC X Corps.

23. Geer, *The New Breed,* p. 134; Pomeroy memorandum, *op. cit.*

24. For information on X Corps' pre-emption of the 7th Motor Transport Battalion, see Smith *Aide-Mémoire,* pp. 191ff., and SAR 1st MarDiv, Annex D. For Kimpo supply problems see SAR, TAC X Corps, p. 5, and SAR, MAG-33, Annex D.

25. SAR, TAC X Corps; SARs, VMF-212, WMF-312, and VMF(N)-542 (all in Marine Corps Historical Branch).

26. Details of the Special Operations Company's plan to capture Kimpo are given in Smith *Aide-Mémoire,* p. 92; in unpublished ms., *Evaluation of the Influence of Marine Corps Forces on the Course of the Korean War,* Marine Corps Board, Quantico, Virginia, pp. II-B-21 and II-B-29 (in Marine Corps Historical Branch). General Smith's remark about "headlines" is in his comment on Historical Branch interview with Major Sexton, *op. cit.* The quotation about the tide is from Geer, *The New Breed,* p. 123. Apparently, General Almond was unaware that Ely actually made this attempt since, in his letter to me of August 31, 1966, he says, "My recollection is that the operation was canceled... and if there was any continuation of Ely's efforts after that it was done without my knowledge."

27. The September 18 North Korean communiqué appears in the New York *Times,* September 19, 1950, together with the quotations from *Jen Min Jih Pao.*

28. This reconstruction of enemy action is based on intelligence annex, SAR, 1st Marine Division, *op. cit.*

29. Shepherd *Journal;* Doyle interview. The Wright/Hickey message is CINCUNC/CINCFE of September 19, 1950 (in OCMH). In his comments, General Wright dissents as follows:

> General MacArthur did not question the ability of Eighth Army to break out of the perimeter.... Timing was his concern.... He discussed (and it was just a discussion) the desirability ... of a landing at Kunsan. General MacArthur did *not* indicate that "a new army commander might well be needed." He had the highest faith in General Walker.

30. One proposal to get Eighth Army moving was that O. P. Smith's third regimental combat team, 7th Marines, then en route to Korea, should be diverted from X Corps to Eighth Army as a spearhead. Smith interview.

31. Field, *Naval Operations, Korea,* p. 205; SAR 1st MarDiv; Condit, Kenneth W., "Marine Supply in Korea," Marine Corps *Gazette,* January, 1953. Jim Crowe's "porcelain crappers" remark comes from my friend Colonel Angus M. Fraser.

32. Smith *Aide-Mémoire,* p. 102; *mansae* is the Korean translation of *banzai* and is used as a cheer in the same way.

Chapter 6

1. SAR, 1st Marines.

2. Carter, Captain Johnny L., letter to CMC, April 19, 1955 (in Marine Corps Historical Branch).

3. Westover, Major George C., undated comments of draft ms., *The Inchon-Seoul Operation* (in Marine Corps Historical Branch).

4. This account of the 1st Marines' advance is based on SARs of units mentioned; letters by Lieutenant Colonel T. L. Ridge, Lieutenant Colonel Edwin H. Simmons, and Captain Johnny L. Carter (all in "Comments File, Korea, Vol. II," *op. cit.*); and on Smith *Log* and *Aide-Mémoire*, pp. 194ff.

5. Ridge, Colonel Thomas L., letter to CMC, May 13, 1955 (in Marine Corps Historical Branch).

6. Smith, General Oliver P., letter to Lynn Montross, June 28, 1955 (in Marine Corps Historical Branch). In his interview with me (November 3, 1966) General Puller said he was visited by Generals Almond and Barr on the afternoon of September 18 to discuss arrangements for commitment of the 32d Infantry on Puller's right. Puller urged that the regiment be brought directly up the Inchon–Seoul highway through the Marine division zone and then moved, right front into line, beside the 1st Regiment. If the 32d advanced from Inchon in the yet unsecured 7th Division zone (with its diverging main supply route, the Inchon–Anyang road), Puller said, "They won't catch up with us until we're in Seoul." According to General Puller, however, General Almond vetoed the suggestion.

7. Fenton interview, *op. cit.*

8. Sources for the action by the 1st Battalion, 5th Marines, action on Hills 118, 80, and 85 are that unit's SAR; Newton, Lieutenant Colonel George R., letter to CMC, June 2, 1955; Fenton interview; and undated memorandum comments by Captain Poul F. Pederson in "Comments File, Korea, Vol. II." All the foregoing are in Marine Corps Historical Branch.

9. Fenton, Captain Francis I., letter to Captain N. A. Canzona, June 1, 1955, in Marine Corps Historical Branch.

10. Hawkins, Lieutenant Colonel Jack, letter to CMC, May 21, 1955; SARs of units mentioned; Fenton letter, *op. cit.* WD, USS *Sicily,* September 20, 1950, confirms that this strike was by VMF-214, not VMF-323, as stated in the Marines' official history.

11. This account is based on SAR, 1st Marines; SAR, 1st Tank Battalion; and Puller interview.

12. 7th Infantry Division Field Order No. 2, September 19, 1950.

13. The account of this night action along the highway is synthesized from SARs of units mentioned; from Carter, Captain Johnny L., letter to CMC, May 31, 1955; Geer, *The New Breed,* pp. 138–140.

14. On September 27, 1965, I was present at the moving ceremony wherein Seoul's distinguished Mayor Tchi-Yung Yun proclaimed Private First Class Monegan posthumous honorary citizen of the national capital whose liberation he so bravely aided.

15. Interview with Colonel Robert P. Wray, August 15, 1966, and his letter to CMC of May 30, 1955 (in Marine Corps Historical Branch).

16. Interview with Major Henry A. Commiskey, August 17, 1966, and Wray interview.

17. The fact that the 32d Infantry was far right and south of the Inchon–Seoul highway (and that the 31st Infantry was fanning ever farther south and away from Seoul) is explained by the original X Corps scheme of maneuver, which called for the 7th Division to wheel right from Inchon, passing clear of Yongdungpo and taking position as "anvil" for the Eighth Army. Thus the 7th Division units had to fan southeast. In fact the Army division's main supply route (MSR) was the Inchon–Anyang highway.

18. Shepherd *Journal.*

19. Showing the pitfalls which eager PIOs sometimes fall into, *Time* magazine's October 23, 1950, cover story on General Almond contains the following statement: "Ned Almond . . . has also chased and reprimanded recklessly speeding military truck drivers."

20. The attack on the ridge is described in Captain Carter's letter of May 31, 1955, *op. cit.;* in SAR, 1st Tank Battalion; and SAR, 1st Marines. WD, USS *Badoeng Strait,* confirms that this air strike was by VMF-323.

21. By far the best and most vivid account of the 3d Battalion's action here is Simmons, Lieutenant Colonel Edwin H., letter to CMC, May 19, 1955 (in Marine Corps Historical Branch).

22. Geer, *The New Breed,* pp. 147–148.

23. In mid-1966, Commiskey denies that he did this and says he simply lifted the mines out of the treadway and put them to one side for the engineers to dispose of. But Colonel Wray, then his CO, who was with him at the time, so reported then, repeated the story in his letter to CMC, *op. cit.,* and positively affirms today that he saw the entire thing. It should be borne in mind, however, that these were antitank mines and therefore less sensitive to pressure than antipersonnel mines; on the other hand, they carried 15-pound charges as opposed to a pound or two in an antipersonnel mine.

24. In his interview, *op. cit.,* General Puller told me he had never received any report of the A Company penetration of Yongdungpo. As for committing his reserve battalion, he correctly pointed out that the 3d Battalion, though in regimental reserve, could not, at this time, be committed without division approval because of the scarcity of reserves available to General Smith in the two-regiment Marine division.

25. Geer, *The New Breed,* p. 150.

26. *Ibid.,* p. 153.

27. Besides SARs of units mentioned, my sources for Barrow's action are: Simmons letter, May 19, 1955; Hawkins letter, May 21, 1955; Puller interview; letter to me from Colonel Robert H. Barrow, 31 January, 1967; Montross and Canzona, *The Inchon-Seoul Operation,* pp. 225–232; and Geer, *The New Breed,* pp. 149–152.

28. My sources regarding this boundary dispute are Barr and Puller interviews; interview by Colonel Appleman with General Barr, February 1, 1954 (in OCMH); and Geer, *The New Breed,* p. 148.

29. This account of 7th Division operations is largely based on Colonel Appleman's fine history, *South to the Naktong,* pp. 520–523, supplemented by Barr interview.

30. Smith interview.

31. Smith *Aide-Mémoire,* pp. 242–246; Montross and Canzona, *The Inchon-Seoul Operation,* pp. 201–202 here, as elsewhere in Korean Marine matters, I have also had help from my friend Lieutenant Colonel Park Bong-Son, KMC.

32. Smith *Aide-Mémoire,* p. 250; Montross and Canzona, *The Inchon-Seoul Operation,* p. 201; comments by Major General Raymond G. Davis on draft of this history.

33. SAR, 1st Marine Division, Annex DD, p. 7.

34. General Almond dissents strongly from this conclusion. He writes (letter to author, August 31, 1966):

> General MacArthur desired my presence on the *Mt. McKinley* which he considered the command ship of the force. Aboard that ship was the amphibious force commander, Admiral Doyle, the landing force commander, General Smith, and if Admiral Struble, the overall commander of all forces afloat did not have a

bunk assignment on the *Mt. McKinley* he lost a lot of sleep because he was on the *Mt. McKinley* to my knowledge most of the time. X Corps headquarters and staff could not possibly have been accommodated aboard the *Rochester*. . . . General Ruffner, a Major General, was in charge of my staff aboard the *Buckner*. He knew as I did, and as did every other person, that until the 1st Marine Division landed, X Corps had no function but to sit in observation. . . . I cannot think of a more satisfactory command arrangement . . . than for me to be aboard the *Mt. McKinley*.

In connection with the above it should be noted that, while *Mount McKinley* may have been the best vantage point for MacArthur and entourage to watch the landing, she was certainly not "command ship of the force." *Rochester*, flagship of CJTF-7, performed that function, while Struble was much more than "overall commander of the forces afloat." As Commander Joint Task Force 7, Admiral Struble commanded the entire operation and all its forces, Almond's included.

35. Doyle interview and comments on the draft of this history. General Almond's personal van is described in *Time* magazine, October 23, 1950.

36. Diary of CG, X Corps, September 21, 1950 (in OCMH). Almond letter, August 31, 1966.

Chapter 7

1. Interview with Colonel Robert M. Calland, July 27, 1965.

2. Craig, Lieutenant General Edward A., letter to General O. P. Smith, January 14, 1952 (in Marine Corps Historical Branch). As stated in note 47, Chapter 2, General Almond now indicates he never planned to bridge the Han until after the capture of Seoul and in any case not before D+10. In the same source (letter to General C. L. Ruffner, January 13, 1967) General Almond goes on to say:

Unfortunately, part of [the bridging] equipment was blown into the sea by the tempestuous weather which struck a part of our convoy enroute to the landing operations. This Colonel Rowny conveyed to me within the first few days after the landing at Inchon. . . . I told Colonel Rowny that the bridge material and the construction of the bridge was essential to General MacArthur's desires to the reestablishment of the Rhee government in Seoul at the earliest possible time . . . that as soon as Seoul was secure that I expected to notify General MacArthur and have use for the bridge.

Major General E. L. Rowny, USA, who was Almond's engineer, in letter to me of February 15, 1967, generally confirms the foregoing assertions by General Almond. He says that "ten or 15 percent of the total" bridging equipment was lost "because of a storm off the south shore of Japan." He also says that replacement material airlifted from Hawaii did not mate up with gear on hand, and, further, that "a freak storm with winds up to 80 miles an hour blew up" on the night of September 25–26 and undid much of the work to modify the mismated equipment. But, he says:

The main value of the bridge was psychological. General MacArthur stated he would reenter Seoul on the 29th—an important anniversary date—the bridge was to be a symbol that firm communications had been reestablished. He rode in as scheduled; the bridge having been completed only hours before.

On the other hand, neither the X Corps War Diary (G-4 Section, Technical Narrative, Engineer, in Marine Corps Historical Branch), the report of Amphibious Group 1, nor any ship's report records the loss overboard of any equipment during movement to the objective. USS *Oglethorpe,* which apparently lifted the bulk of the engineer material, specifically records after Typhoon Kezia: "No loss or damage to cargo or material" (WD, USS *Oglethorpe,* September 1950, in Office of Naval History). When queried on the point, Admiral Doyle wrote me on January 19, 1967: "I have absolutely no knowledge of the 'blown overboard' bridge equipment and I am certain that I would have been informed if any such loss had occurred." With regard to the "freak storm" and 80-knot winds on the night of September 25–26, I have checked the log, USS *Rochester,* September 1950 (in National Archives) and find no record at Inchon, only a few miles from Kimpo, of any wind force either day above 11 knots, or over 22 knots during the entire operation. The barometer was steady throughout September 25–26. The only contemporary statement on the problem by the corps engineer (then Colonel Rowny) is in WD, X Corps, Engineer, *op. cit.:* "The rapid advance of X Corps troops toward Seoul advanced the anticipated date for construction of a floating bridge over the Han. Sufficient bridging material was not on hand."

3. Smith *Log.*
4. For careful analysis of the plan and its defects, see Montross and Canzona, *The Inchon-Seoul Operation,* pp. 187–190 and 194. For information regarding the 3d Battalion, 5th Marines, in this phase of the operation, I have relied on comments by Colonel R. D. Taplett on the draft of this history.
5. General Lowe's vain attempt to go with Houghton is described in Smith *Log,* and in Captain Canzona's notes in Marine Corps Historical Branch.
6. Marine Corps Historical Branch interview with Lieutenant Colonel Charles H. Brush, April 19, 1951, and comments by Colonel Brush on draft of this history.
7. My account of the crossing and its repulse—still the subject of many conflicting versions—is based on Marine Corps Historical Branch interview with Major Kenneth J. Houghton, August 3, 1954; correspondence between Captain Canzona and First Lieutenant E. L. deFazio (in Marine Corps Historical Branch); Taplett and Brush comments, *op. cit.,* and Historical Branch interviews; Geer, *The New Breed,* pp. 142–145; and Karig et al., *The Korean War,* pp. 262ff.
8. Sexton Historical Branch interview; Geer, *The New Breed,* p. 145, says the tape contained "several choice stories that had nothing to do with crossing the Han." In his comments, Colonel Taplett says, "They were pretty good!"
9. Craig, Lieutenant General Edward A., letter to CMC, August 25, 1954 (in Marine Corps Historical Branch).
10. Sexton Historical Branch interview.
11. My account of the river crossing by 3d Battalion, 5th Marines, is based on SARs of units mentioned; Taplett comments; Shepherd *Journal;* Montross and Canzona, *The Inchon-Seoul Operation,* pp. 194–197; and Geer, *The New Breed,* pp. 145–146.
12. General MacArthur's trip ashore and departure are covered in Smith *Aide-Mémoire,* p. 249; Shepherd *Journal;* WD, USS *Missouri,* September 21, 1950; Handleman interview; and New York *Times,* September 21, 1950.
13. *Life* magazine, October 9, 1950, pp. 51–60.
14. SAR, 1st Marine Division, Annexes B and C; SAR, 5th Marines.
15. Shepherd interview, July 27, 1966.
16. WD, USS *Badoeng Strait,* September 1950.
17. Geer, *The New Breed,* p. 156.
18. Fenton Historical Branch interview.

U

19. Anderson, Captain Tilton A., letter to Captain Canzona, August 26, 1954, in Marine Corps Historical Branch.

20. Besides sources given in notes 16–19 *supra,* my sources for the fighting on September 22–23 are SARs of units mentioned; Brush Historical Branch interview and comments on draft of this history; Smith *Aide-Mémoire,* pp. 253–262; comments by General Murray on draft of this history; Montross and Canzona, *The Inchon-Seoul Operation,* pp. 233–243.

21. Smith *Aide-Mémoire,* p. 263. Chiles's "The Marines were . . . deliberate" is in his comments on ms. of *South to the Naktong* in OCMH.

22. Appleman, *South to the Naktong,* p. 527; General O. P. Smith letter to Chief of Military History, November 15, 1957 (in OCMH). In his letter to me of November 10, 1966, General Almond repudiates the assertion that he gave General Smith any 24-hour ultimatum. He also emphatically denies a report which has circulated to the effect that he threatened to relieve General Smith if the Marine attack failed to make satisfactory progress. "I never made such a threat in my life in any command I exercised," he wrote.

23. Smith *Log* and *Aide-Mémoire,* pp. 263–264; Smith letters to Chief of Military History, November 15, 1957, and February 25, 1957 (both in OCMH); Smith letter to Lieutenant Colonel H. W. Edwards, May 19, 1955 (in Marine Corps Historical Branch); and General Smith's letter to me of October 7, 1966.

24. *Ibid.* G-3 Journal, X Corps WD, September 24, 1950 (in Marine Corps Historical Branch).

25. Sexton Historical Branch interview.

26. My account of this conference is based on Smith *Log* and *Aide-Mémoire,* p. 266; on Barr interview; on Colonel Charles E. Beauchamp, letter to Colonel Appleman, July 15, 1953 (in OCMH); and on Appleman, *South to the Naktong,* p. 528. General Murray (interview with me, September 30, 1966) does not, however, recall that Almond ever countermanded the direct orders that caused this debate.

27. SAR, 2d Battalion, 5th Marines; comments by Colonel H. S. Roise on draft of this history; Anderson/Canzona letter, *op. cit.;* Montross and Canzona, *The Inchon-Seoul Operation,* pp. 245ff.; Canzona, Nicholas A., "Dog Company's Charge," Naval Institute *Proceedings,* November 1956.

28. Sources for Dog Company's capture of Smith's Ridge are: Canzona, "Dog Company's Charge," *op. cit.;* SARs of units mentioned; Roise comments; Fenton Historical Branch interview; Montross and Canzona, *The Inchon-Seoul Operation,* pp. 247–249; and Geer, *The New Breed,* pp. 157–161.

29. Jaskilka notes, "Comments File, Korea, Vol. II," *op. cit.;* In a holographic, undated memo in the Marine Corps Historical Branch, Jaskilka credits Captain E. A. Deptula with the "Nelly's Tit" appellation.

30. Sources for the action on September 25 are SARs of units mentioned; Brush Historical Branch interview; Montross and Canzona, *The Inchon-Seoul Operation,* pp. 257–258; and Geer, *The New Breed,* pp. 162–163.

31. *Time* magazine, October 2, 1950. For further background on the Underwood family in Korea, see also *Time,* March 28, 1949. Despite heavy damage sustained during the attack on western Seoul, the college has been rebuilt and reopened. Its title today is Yon-Sei University, and it is the principal private university of Korea. Commander Underwood, now retired, is back in Seoul.

32. This account of the 7th Division crossing the Han is based on SARs of units mentioned (especially that of 1st Amphibian Tractor Battalion); on Appleman, *South to the Naktong,* pp. 528–530; and on Barr interview.

33. Almond letter, August 31, 1966.
34. SARs of squadrons and other units mentioned; WD, USS *Sicily;* Marine Corps Historical Branch interview with Colonel Max J. Volcansek, March 15, 1955.
35. Struble, Admiral Arthur D., letter to CMC, April 25, 1955.
36. Kiefer, Brigadier General Homer W., USA, letter to CMC, January 10, 1951.
37. SAR, VMF(N)-542.
38. *Time* magazine, October 2, 1950.

Chapter 8

1. Smith Interview.
2. Davis, *Marine!* p. 270.
3. Geer, *The New Breed,* p. 164.
4. *Ibid.,* p. 165; SARs of units mentioned; Puller, Brigadier General Lewis B., letter to General O. P. Smith, January 28, 1952 (in Marine Corps Historical Branch); *Life* magazine, October 9, 1950.
5. Davis, *Marine!* p. 277.
6. SARs of units mentioned; Farrington, Chief Marine Gunner Arthur, comments on draft of this history, November 2, 1966. Also see "Find My Tanks," Bruce Jacobs, *Male* magazine, March 1953.
7. Davis, *Marine!* p. 272.
8. SARs of units mentioned; Chiles's *South to the Naktong* comments, *op. cit.;* Barrow comments, *op. cit.;* Ridge comments, *op. cit.;* for a vivid description and view of the railroad embankment and vicinity under heavy air and artillery attack, see *Life,* October 9, 1950.
9. Appleman, *South to the Naktong,* p. 530. Smith, *Aide-Mémoire,* p. 288, says: "The inactivity of the Battalion Commander did not escape the critical notice of General Almond."
10. Texts of this order, substantially identical, are found in WD, X Corps (G-3 Journal, September 25, 1950), in SAR, 1stMarDiv, and in General Smith's papers. It was sent at 1945 and receipted for by G-3, 1st Marine Division, at 2009. The air observer's report appears as entry J-43 in X Corps G-3 Journal, *op. cit.* General Almond's characterization of the order as "a command decision" is in his letter to General Ruffner, *op. cit.*
11. In his letter to General Ruffner, General Almond comments: "If there was any confusion on blurred or erroneous coordinates on the map referred to, this was no doubt cleared up at the time by responsible commanders without its having to be done 16 years later by one who wasn't there."
12. When Bowser asked X Corps G-3 what the role of the 7th Division (i.e., 32d Infantry) was to be, he ". . . was told that the 7th Division would hold its positions, support the attack by fire, and be prepared to attack on order." (Comments on draft of this history.)
13. Smith *Log, Aide-Mémoire,* pp. 288–292, and interview. The Bowser quotation is from his letter to me, January 24, 1967. The X Corps G-3 Journal, generally kept in minute detail, omitted to record the Marine division's reclama to Colonel Chiles on this order.
14. Geer, *The New Breed,* p. 167.
15. SAR, 3d Battalion, 1st Marines; Ridge comments; report by Supporting Arms Coordinator to CO, 3d Battalion, 1st Marines, September 27, 1950 (kindly provided by General Simmons); Simmons interview, January 14, 1967. Collins survived. After covering his people's withdrawal he dived into a cellar while the

battle raged all around. Before dawn, disguised in a white Korean gown, he made his way back from no man's land and reported in.

16. Interview with Colonel Patrick Welch, USA, September 25, 1966.
17. Ammunition expenditures are taken from Supporting Arms Coordinator memo, *op cit.* The Basilone episode is found in Heinl, *Soldiers of the Sea,* p. 369.
18. Simmons interview.
19. This account of the NKPA attack against the 1st Marines is synthesized from SARs of units concerned; Smith *Aide-Mémoire,* pp. 288–291; comments by Colonels Ridge and Simmons on draft of this history; Montross and Canzona, *The Inchon-Seoul Operation,* pp. 261–263; Geer, *The New Breed,* pp. 168–170.
20. Geer, *The New Breed,* p. 170.
21. Appleman, *South to the Naktong,* pp. 530–531.
22. New York *Times,* September 27, 1950.
23. X Corps Communiqué 5, issued 1445, September 26, 1950 (in New York *Times,* September 27, 1950).
24. Associated Press dispatch, datelined Seoul, September 26, in New York *Times,* September 27, 1950. X Corps Command Report, *Chromite,* October 2, 1950, concedes: "[on the 26th] the advance through Seoul was painstakingly slow."
25. Quoted in New York *Times,* September 29, 1950.
26. "A bit premature" is the verdict of the Marine Corps official history (Montross and Canzona, *The Inchon-Seoul Operation,* p. 264). The remarks by General Almond and Colonel Chiles are from their comments on *South to the Naktong* (in OCMH).
27. Interview with Major General Raymond L. Murray, September 30, 1966.
28. SAR, 3d Battalion, 5th Marines; Geer, *The New Breed,* p. 171.
29. SAR, 1st Marines.
30. SAR, 7th Marines; comments by Major General Davis; Marine Corps Historical Branch interview with Major J. D. Hammond, August 17, 1954; and Montross and Canzona, *The Inchon-Seoul Operation,* pp. 264–270.
31. Appleman, *South to the Naktong,* p. 531.
32. SARs of units mentioned; Geer, *The New Breed,* pp. 174–175.
33. New York *Times,* September 28, 1950.
34. Geer, *The New Breed,* p. 175
35. The account of Walker's breakout and linkup is generally based on Appleman, *South to the Naktong,* Chapter XXVIII. Comparative strengths of Eighth Army and the NKPA invading force around the perimeter are given in the same source, p. 547; Lynch's dash north, pp. 593–597. The ultimate state of the *In Min Gun* is described in Appleman, pp. 602–604.
36. SAR, VMF-312.
37. Geer, *The New Breed,* p. .ͻl; SAR, 7th Marines; comments by Major General Davis.
38. Cates interview.
39. FECOM "Daily Intelligence Summary," September 8, 1950 (in OCMH).
40. The Sun Tzu quotations are from Griffith, Brigadier General S. B., *Sun Tzu: The Art of War* (London, Oxford University Press, 1963). For a carefully documented study of Chinese moves and intentions before intervening in Korea, see Whiting, Allen S., *China Crosses the Yalu* (New York, Macmillan, 1960), a RAND Corporation study.

Chapter 9

1. Smith *Aide-Mémoire,* pp. 314–315; letter to me from General Smith, Septem-

ber 19, 1966. In his letter to General Ruffner, *op. cit.*, General Almond dismisses as "a quibble" whether the bridging material was provided by X Corps or had, in part, to be borrowed from the Marine division. Here again, the point is that, instead of receiving support from X Corps resources, a subordinate unit had to support the corps.

2. *Ibid.* New York *Times,* September 28, 1950.
3. CINCFE message to CG, X Corps, September 28, 1950.
4. CINCFE message to JCS, September 23, 1950; MacArthur, *Reminiscences,* p. 355.
5. Doyle interview.
6. My description of this ceremony is based on Doyle interview; Handleman interview; Smith *Log* and *Aide-Mémoire,* pp. 315–317; New York *Times,* September 30, 1950; *Time* magazine, October 9, 1950; Thompson, *Cry Korea,* p. 86. The full text of MacArthur's remarks is given in *MacArthur Hearings,* p. 3481.
7. Accounts of the cemetery dedication and the KMC review are found in Smith *Log* and *Aide-Mémoire,* pp. 342–345.
8. For an unvarnished study of these disgraces see Kinkead, Eugene, *In Every War But One* (New York, Norton, 1959).
9. Casualties for the Inchon-Seoul campaign have been difficult to arrive at and will probably never be known with certitude. U. S. Navy casualties during the Korean War, for example, were never compiled by battle but simply by month, and are not known, except on that basis, by the Office of Naval History, Bureau of Naval Personnel, or Bureau of Medicine and Surgery, all of which have been consulted. The Navy figures given here were reconstructed from individual action reports of ships, air groups, and other units containing Navy personnel. My Army figures are the 7th Division casualties given in *South to the Naktong,* augmented by those sustained by nondivisional Army units attached to the Marine division. The Marine figures are the total of casualties reported by the 1st Marine Division and 1st Marine Aircraft Wing (therefore differing from casualties in *The Inchon-Seoul Operation,* which summarizes only Marine division casualties). Besides the U. S. casualties given, the Royal Navy sustained 1 killed and 2 wounded; and the Korean Marines reported 29 killed and 96 wounded. ROK Army figures are unavailable.
10. AR, CJTF-7.
11. AR, CJTF-7, Annex M; Higgins, *War in Korea,* p. 151.
12. Captain Doidzhashvli's book, *The Bloody Path,* is quoted in Leckie, Robert, *Conflict* (New York, Putnam, 1962), pp. 209–210.
13. "My Day" column, October 1950. Curiously, a rumor has long circulated that Mrs. Roosevelt bitterly criticized the U. S. forces for having wantonly destroyed Seoul. Actually her one published reference to the subject did just the reverse.
14. Eighth United Nations Command Report, November 6, 1950 (in *MacArthur Hearings,* vol. II).
15. Message from President Truman to General MacArthur, quoted in Montross and Canzona, *The Inchon-Seoul Operation,* App. I. MacArthur's purportedly complete text (*Reminiscences,* p. 356) omits the names and mention of the three officers in question.
16. ComPhibGrp 1 AR, p. 21A.
17. For an example of this view, see "Inchon–Analysis of a Gamble," Commander Malcolm W. Cagle, in U. S. Naval Institute *Proceedings,* January 1954.
18. Smith interview.
19. General Almond states (letter to author, August 31, 1966) that he recommended

the 1st Marine Division for the Army's Distinguished Unit Citation, but there is no record of any such recommendation in the files of Marine Corps Headquarters or of Department of the Army (OCMH and AGO). In his letter of August 27, 1951, to General Smith, General Shepherd commented on "the apparent reluctance of CINCFE to recommend Marine units for the Distinguished Unit Citation." General Smith's "not accidental" quotation is from his letter of August 20, 1951, to General Shepherd. As of that time (1951) Distinguished Unit Citations had been awarded by the Army to the 2d and 24th Infantry Divisions and two brigades taking part in the Pusan perimeter operations.

20. Weyland, General Otto P., USAF, "The Air Campaign in Korea," in Stewart, Colonel James T., *Airpower* (Van Nostrand, New York, 1957), p. 18.
21. Rees, David, *Korea: The Limited War* (New York, St. Martin's Press, 1964), p. 96.
22. Mahan, Rear Admiral Alfred Thayer, *Naval Strategy*, 1911.

THE SINEWS OF BATTLE

The professional reader (and the professional writer) will take for granted a general knowledge of the organizations, the weapons, the ships and aircraft which fought at Inchon and Seoul, but no history of such a campaign would be complete without a summary of the way in which forces were organized and the tools they used.

With few exceptions, the fighting organizations and their tools—the sinews of battle—were those of the USSR (as described in Chapter 1) and the United States in World War II.

Ground Forces

Although the *Chromite* operation was conducted, at least nominally, under a corps headquarters, it was nonetheless a campaign in which the division, either Marine or infantry, was the dominant fighting organization. In modern warfare, the division is said to be the smallest unit (comparatively speaking) which embodies all the combined arms and services required for sustained combat. In 1950 the Marine division at war strength (22,343) was a heavier, stronger division than the infantry division (18,804).

The teeth of a division, as distinct from its administrative and logistic tail, are its three infantry regiments (each of three battalions), its artillery, and its armor. To support these fighting units, the division includes engineers, medical, signal, military police, motor transport, and supply and maintenance units. As distinct from the infantry division of the Army, the Marine division of course includes units, equipment and skills of primary importance in amphibious operations. In 1950 the Marine infantry regiment had a strength of 3,902; the Army regiment numbered 3,774. The Marine infantry battalion (1,123) outnumbered the Army battalion (917) by about 20 per cent.

In artillery the two divisions were exactly comparable: each had one battalion of 18 medium (155mm) howitzers, and three battalions, each equipped with 18 105mm light howitzers. In infantry firepower, however, as shown by the following table, considerable disparity existed between the Marine division and the infantry division.

Weapon	Quantity USMC	Army
Carbine, caliber .30	9,740	7,474
Rifle, M-1, caliber .30	8,748	6,913
Pistol, automatic, caliber .45	3,196	2,769
Browning automatic rifle (BAR), caliber .30	903	412
Shotgun, riot, 12 gauge	6	—
Thompson submachine gun, caliber .45	99	—
Machine gun, heavy, water-cooled, caliber .30	54	40
Machine gun, light, air-cooled, caliber .30	575	160
Machine gun, caliber .50	187	354
Rocket launcher, 3.5" (bazooka)	376	546
Recoilless rifle, 75mm	12	39

Weapon	Quantity USMC	Army
60mm mortar	81	84
81mm mortar	54	40
4.2″ mortar	24	36
Flame thrower	111	—

Epitomizing the comparison between the two divisions is the fact that, in 1950, the Marine division, 18 per cent stronger, had 27 per cent more men armed with the basic weapon of infantry combat, the M-1 rifle.

In armor the two divisions were nearly equal, though not numerically so. The Army division had 144 tanks of all types; the Marines had but 100. However, the Army figure included light tanks, whereas the Marine tanks were all medium, except for 9 flame-thrower tanks, of which the Army division had none. Being shaped for sustained land operations, the Army unit's motor transportation (3,800 vehicles) far exceeded that of the Marine division (2,409).

Broadly speaking, all the weapons used in battle may be classed as either direct fire (flat trajectory) or indirect fire (curved trajectory). The flat-trajectory weapons —rifle, carbine, pistol, machine gun, bazooka, recoilless rifle, the high-velocity 90mm guns on the tanks—engage targets which can be seen. The high-trajectory weapons —grenade launchers, mortars and howitzers—are used against targets "on the other side of the hill," which are physically masked by intervening terrain from the firing weapon.

Ships and Aircraft

As *Chromite* was an amphibious operation, we are interested only in the ship and aircraft characteristics which directly influenced the landings.

The naval forces at Inchon included a battleship (armed with 16-inch guns), cruisers (8-inch and 6-inch), destroyers (5-inch), and rocket ships (1 5-inch gun, multiple automatic 5-inch rocket launchers). These ships provided the naval gunfire support required to sustain the landing until artillery could play its normal role ashore. In addition, one heavy cruiser, *Rochester,* configured with communications and accommodations as a fleet flagship, performed that function for CJTF-7.

Besides the widely varying assortment of improvised merchant and MSTS shipping used to land follow-up forces and echelons, the amphibious assault shipping consisted of attack transports (APAs) which carry the bulk of the personnel of assault battalion landing teams; attack cargo ships (AKAs) carrying the cargo and much of the equipment of assault units; landing ships, dock (LSDs) which themselves carry and launch large landing craft (LCUs) carrying tanks and heavy vehicles; so-called tank landing ships (LSTs) capable of making ramped beach landings for vehicles and top-priority supplies or of launching amphibian tractors (LVTs) offshore; fast transports (APDs), converted destroyer escorts used to land company or smaller-sized units for raiding, reconnaissance, or other special work. The two workhorse landing craft are the LCVP (a ramped craft used to land assault infantry, light vehicles and weapons) and the LCM, a heavier ramped landing craft with correspondingly heavier capabilities. In addition, the amphibian truck (or DUKW) is a wheeled amphibian vehicle (as distinct from the tracked LVT) which is primarily used to land artillery. The amphibious command ship (AGC), such as *Mount McKinley,* is fully described in Chapter 3 as to purpose and characteristics, which we need not repeat here.

Since the combatant air effort for *Chromite* was entirely by naval and Marine aviation, the aircraft involved were all naval. The AD (Skyraider) was the principal heavy attack aircraft and was based on the fast carriers of Task Force 77, which also provided fighter cover for the operation using F4U (Corsairs) and early-model F9F (Panther) jets. Although nominally a fighter, the Corsair was a powerful attack aircraft in its own right, when so armed, and was mainly so employed in this campaign by both Navy and Marine squadrons. Besides the major types of aircraft just mentioned, the amphibious force included more specialized types for night work, light fixed-wing OY (Grasshopper) planes for artillery spotting and liaison work, and the very novel HO3S-1 Sikorsky helicopters.

The carriers from which air operations were initially conducted were either the fast attack carriers (CV) such as *Philippine Sea* or *Boxer,* or the escort ("jeep") carriers (CVE) such as *Sicily.*

Officers' ranks and enlisted ranks and ratings are those contemporaneous with the event. Personnel are identified by Service only when the context would permit confusion. Service abbreviations, when used, are: USA, U. S. Army; USN, U. S. Navy; USMC, U. S. Marine Corps; USAF, U. S. Air Force; RN, Royal Navy; RM, Royal Marines; KMC, Republic of Korea Marine Corps; ROK, Republic of Korea Army; ROKN, Republic of Korea Navy; NKPA, North Korean Peoples Army.

AGC–Amphibious force flagship

AKA–Attack cargo ship

AP–Armor-piercing

APA–Attack transport

APC–Tablet of aspirin, phenacetin and caffeine, a standby of naval medicine

APD–High-speed transport

BAR–Browning automatic rifle

CAP–Combat air patrol

CG–Commanding general

CINCFE–Commander in Chief, Far East

CINCPACFLT–Commander in Chief, Pacific Fleet

CJTF-7–Commander Joint Task Force 7

CMC–Commandant of the Marine Corps

CO–Commanding officer

CP–Command post

CPX–Command-post exercise

CTF–Commander task force

CVE–Escort carrier

D-day–The unnamed day on which a particular operation is to commence. When used with plus (+) symbol means days after D-day, with a minus (−) symbol, days before D-day.

DOW–Died of wounds

DUKW–Amphibian truck

FBHL–Force beachhead line

FEAF–Far East Air Forces

FECOM–Far East Command

G- –As prefix followed by numbers 1 (Personnel), 2 (Intelligence), 3 (Operations and Training), and 4 (Supply), either the general staff section concerned with the function in question or, colloquially, the assistant chief of staff for that function.

GHQ–General headquarters

GP-bombs–General-purpose bombs

H-hour–The specific hour on D-day on which hostilities commence.

H-table–A table shaped like an H at which air-control personnel operate aboard an AGC

HMS–His (Her) Majesty's Ship

JCS–Joint Chiefs of Staff

JTF-7–Joint Task Force 7

KIA–Killed in action

LCM–Landing craft, mechanized

LCVP–Landing craft, vehicle and personnel

LSD–Landing ship, dock

LSMR–Landing ship, medium (rocket)

LST–Landing ship, tank

LSU–Landing ship, utility (now designated LCU)

LVT–Amphibian tractor

M-26–M-26 medium tank (Pershing)

MAAG–Military assistance advisory group

MAG–Marine aircraft group

MATS–Military Air Transport Service

MAW–Marine aircraft wing

MIA–Missing in action

MP–Military police

MSR–Main supply route

MSTS–Military Sea Transport Service

NC–"No change," naval gunfire spot

NCO–Noncommissioned officer

OP–Observation post

PC–Patrol ship

PIO–Public information officer

PPI-scope–The glass viewing screen on which radar images are projected

RCT–Regimental combat team

SCR–followed by numerals, designation of types of military radio sets

T-34–USSR model medium tank

TF–Task force

USS–United States Ship

VMF–Followed by numeral, Marine Fighting Squadron

VMO-6–Marine Observation Squadron 6

WIA–Wounded in action

Aircraft Designations

Unless otherwise designated, aircraft are U. S. Navy types. Numeral in parentheses indicates number of engines.

AD–Skyraider, Douglas (1)

C-47–DC-3, Douglas, USAF (2)

C-54–Skymaster, Douglas, USAF (4)

C-119–Packet, Fairchild, USAF (2)

F4U–Corsair, Vought (1)

F7F–Tigercat, Grumman (2)

HO3S-1–Helicopter, Sikorsky

IL-10–USSR attack aircraft (1)

OY–Cub, Piper (1)

YAK-3–USSR fighter-attack (1)

MILITARY SYMBOLS

The military symbols used in the maps and diagrams of this book are in general those used by the U. S. Armed Forces in the 1950s. Where these have been departed from, or in the case of matters peculiar to amphibious warfare, I have tried to clarify the sketch or legend in question.

Symbols on maps appearing within a rectangle indicate a military unit, within a triangle, an observation post. When the rectangular block rises from a vertical line so as to have the appearance of a flag, the symbol represents the command post or headquarters of the unit in question.

Types of Units

Antiaircraft artillery ....

Armor or mechanized ....

Aviation ....

Cavalry ....

Engineer ....

Field artillery ....

Infantry (Marine or Army) ....

Reconnaissance ....

Tank (as distinct from armored or mechanized) ....

Unit Size and Identity

Unit symbols, as given above, are presumed to be U. S. Marine Corps or U. S. Army *unless* underneath the symbol appears "KMC" (Korean Marine Corps), "ROK" (Republic of Korea Army), or "NKPA" (North Korean Peoples Army). An arabic numeral on the right side of a unit symbol is the number of the division or regiment depicted (or, if the unit is smaller than the regiment, the number of the parent regiment). On the left of the unit block, an arabic numeral signifies which battalion of the given regiment is indicated; a letter, which company (or, for headquarters and service company, "H&S"; for weapons company, "Wpns"). Unit sizes are indicated herein as follows:

Platoon .... ● ● ●

Company, troop, battery I

Battalion, squadron II

Regiment III

Brigade, Marine Air Group X

Division, Marine Aircraft Wing XX

Corps XXX

Field Army XXXX

Examples

Company A, 1st Marines ....

2d Battalion, 32d Infantry ....

5th Marines ....

11th Marines (field artillery) ....

25th Brigade, NKPA ....

18th Division, NKPA ....

X Corps ....

3d Battalion, 1st Korean Marine Regiment ....

Note that the symbols given here are not all-inclusive for all types of units, or echelons. This appendix is intentionally confined to symbols and units appearing on the maps and charts of this work.

BIBLIOGRAPHY

The literature of the Korean War is still meager, and that bearing directly on Inchon-Seoul even more so. Therefore, the bibliography which follows is mainly a listing of general sources on the war, in which, to varying degree, material relating to Operation *Chromite* appears.

Appleman, Roy E., Lt. Col., USAR, *South to the Naktong, North to the Yalu* (Washington: Government Printing Office, 1961).

Cagle, Malcolm W., Cdr., USN; Manson, Frank A., Cdr., USN, *The Sea War in Korea* (Annapolis: U. S. Naval Institute, 1957).

————, "Inchon—Analysis of a Gamble," U. S. Naval Institute *Proceedings,* January 1954.

Davis, Burke, *Marine! The Life of Chesty Puller* (Boston: Little, Brown, 1962).

Fehrenbach, T. R., *This Kind of War* (New York: Macmillan, 1963).

Field, James A., Jr., *History of U. S. Naval Operations: Korea* (Washington: Government Printing Office, 1962).

Geer, Andrew C., Maj., USMCR, *The New Breed* (New York: Harpers, 1952).

Heinl, Robert D., Jr., Col., USMC, *Soldiers of the Sea* (Annapolis: U. S. Naval Institute, 1962).

Higgins, Marguerite, *War in Korea* (New York: Doubleday, 1951).

Karig, Walter, Capt., USNR; Cagle, Malcolm W., Cdr., USN; Manson, Frank A., Cdr., USN, *Battle Report: The War in Korea* (New York: Rinehart, 1952).

Leckie, Robert, *Conflict: The History of the Korean War, 1950–1953* (New York: Putnam, 1962).

MacArthur, Douglas, General of the Army, *Reminiscences* (New York: McGraw-Hill, 1964).

Montross, Lynn; Canzona, Nicholas A., Capt., USMC, *The Inchon-Seoul Operation* (Vol. II, *U. S. Marine Operations in Korea*) (Washington: Government Printing Office, 1955).

Rees, David, *Korea: The Limited War* (New York: St. Martin's Press, 1964).

Schnable, James F., Lt. Col., USA, "The Inchon Landing," *Army* Magazine, May 1959.

Senate Committees on Armed Services and Foreign Relations, *Hearings on the Military Situation in the Far East* ("MacArthur Hearings"), 1st Session, 82d Congress (Washington: Government Printing Office, 1951).

Truman, Harry S., *Years of Trial and Hope* (New York: Doubleday, 1956).

Whitney, Courtney, Maj. Gen., USA, *MacArthur: His Rendezvous with Destiny* (New York: A. A. Knopf, 1956).

Willoughby, Charles A., Maj. Gen., USA; Chamberlain, John, *MacArthur, 1941–1951* (New York: McGraw-Hill, 1954).

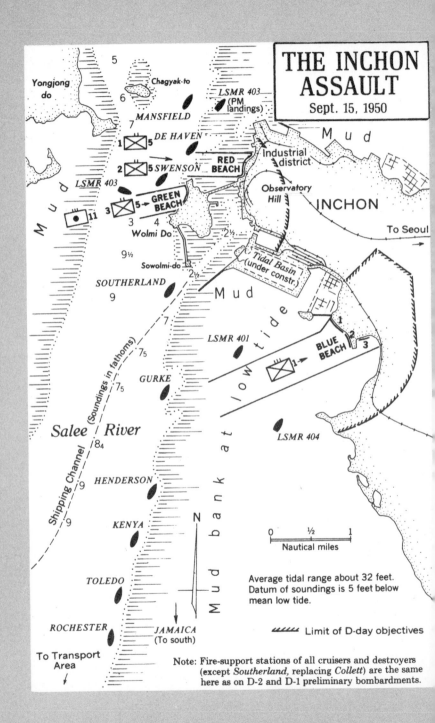

THE INCHON
ASSAULT
Sept. 15, 1950